Motherhood

Motherhood

How should we care
for our children?

Anne Manne

A Sue Hines Book

ALLEN & UNWIN

First published in 2005

A Sue Hines Book
Allen & Unwin
83 Alexander Street
Crows Nest NSW 2065
Australia
Phone: (61 2) 8425 0100
Fax: (61 2) 9906 2218
Email: info@allenandunwin.com
Web: www.allenandunwin.com

National Library of Australia
Cataloguing-in-Publication entry:

Manne, Anne.
   Motherhood.

   Bibliography.
   Includes index.
   ISBN 1 74114 379 9.

   1. Motherhood. 2. Motherhood – Social aspects.
   3. Work and family – Social aspects. 4. Feminism. I. Title.

306.8743

Edited by Caroline Williamson
Cover and text design by Sandra Nobes
Typesetting by Midland Typesetting
Printed in Australia by Griffin

10 9 8 7 6 5 4 3 2 1

To Rob, Kate and Lucy

Contents

Prologue

Down among the children

'One's life is not a case
Except of course it is.'
Les Murray

My generation breathed in the assumptions of feminism as naturally as air. Our participation as equals in the traditional male worlds of work and achievement came more easily to us than perhaps to any previous generation of young women. It never occurred to me that Freud's aphorism characterising maturity as 'Lieben und arbeiten' (loving and working) ought to apply only to men, although by work I did not envisage necessarily paid work, but work in the sense of a central meaningful purpose in life. This would have been dependent upon the sense I felt of the importance—which I still hold to—of women being able to draw into their lives the capacity for economic independence, the possibility of making a contribution to the public realm, and the kind of human flourishing that may come with the use of one's talents.

Yet when I became a mother in the 1980s, I found it very difficult to integrate my deepest feelings with what feminism had taught me. The vocabulary of feminism and that of motherhood seemed not to join up. I came to a dead halt before the power of this new experience, as if those old signposts, for the moment, could illuminate no more. I found myself making the decision to go 'down among the children' for the early years of their life. That decision was for me quite unexpected, stepping 'out of the world', or the public realm, the world of work, and moving to what Hannah Arendt calls the world of labour in order to raise my children.

This book should not be regarded as a manifesto for what all women feel on the birth of their children. Quite the contrary. But I do know that some aspects of my experience are shared by many other women. During the period I was at home, the majority of families, in Australia and overseas, made the same choice. It remains, in the twenty-first century, most parents' preference for the first few years of their children's lives.

I will begin by way of a memoir for two reasons. First, I believe, like the Danish writer Isak Dinesen, in the power and truth of a human story, and what can be learnt from that. The second is that this book is directed at the common reader, and the language in which the childcare debate is often couched—anxious-avoidance syndromes, separation distress, quotients and correlations, non-compliance and transient distress syndromes—can obscure more than illuminate what is central: lived human experience.

Transformation

Before I became pregnant with my first child I thought about childcare as a kind of abstraction. I had not the slightest understanding of how it would affect a child, but I did have a strong sense of what it might mean for women in realising their legitimate aspirations in the wider world.

During my pregnancy, there were some tiny incidents, those unexpected moments that lifted themselves out of the ordinary, casting a sudden light upon what had until the instant before been in shadow. They did not necessarily mean much at the time, but settled like a kind of sediment, to rise again for contemplation when the time was right. One such moment was when I heard a mother describe a city childcare centre. You could just 'hand them over', she said, with all the nappies and bottles and baby paraphernalia, and go shopping, undisturbed by whining demands. 'It's just the best place!' she enthused. But her son, then aged eight, told a different story. 'I hated it,' he said, '*I just hated it.*' He said it in a quiet, flat tone but with real intensity, almost to himself, as if expecting no one to listen to him. I did listen, however, and my first collision with those different versions—one from the adult and the other from the child—of the childcare experience had a profound effect on me.

Another such moment was when a scientist I knew, near the end of his life, had fathered a child, and spent much of his time looking after her. I remember being startled when this scientist, whose career had been a distinguished one, said that his most important contribution to the world was to have reared a member of the next generation. It was startling, of course, because such sentiments from men were still uncommon, and because it came from someone whose career and life had all the external signposts of success. He found no activity more rewarding than looking after his young daughter.

On the other hand, there were some women I knew who ignored my pregnancy as if it were an unpleasant secret, a failure or a lapse.

By accident, on the same day three acquaintances learned of my pregnancy. The first was a social worker whose eyes narrowed and whose first question was an incredulous 'Will you have it?' She thoughtfully pointed to the benefits to her own health of sterilisation, and suggested one could always adopt a child from a Third World country at a later date. The second was a well-meaning friend who instantly outlined all the 'options' of available childcare, and who looked more than a little scandalised when I suggested I might want to do the looking-after myself. The third was a Polish working-class woman who had, alone in her family, survived the Holocaust. She was overjoyed for me, and bubbled with enthusiasm. She listened, puzzled, to my ambitious plans for the following year, and then said firmly: 'Anne, you will have no time or love but for the baby.' Of the three it was the third who came closest to the truth.

For many men as well as women, the experience of becoming a parent is a revelation of what is deepest in us, of our humanness and our mortality. Many women, distinguished, homely, exceptional or ordinary, have described the process of bonding as a kind of 'falling in love'. There is of course the other aspect, more spoken about these days than the lyrical meaning of the event—the mundane aspect of the care of one who, as Virginia Woolf put it, 'leaks from every orifice', and who refuses to sleep. (The first law of parenthood it seems is the renunciation of sleep!) It is time we restated a truth, acknowledged by maternal feminists like Sara Ruddick, that the full-time care of a baby is not, as one early women's liberation pamphlet put it, 'Like spending all day, every day in the exclusive company of an incontinent mental defective.'

When I considered going back to work, it was not only that my children, having not read the equal opportunity handbook in the womb, had other ideas. It was also that my priorities, for a time, changed radically. What had seemed a reasonable course of action before birth— using daycare in those weeks and months after birth—now seemed unthinkable in relation to this tiny vulnerable human being that both of us as parents spent so long, and with such intensity, trying to 'read', to understand the language of gesture, to find what things or actions soothed her or made her happy.

That shift in perspective revealed something else. Our contemporary emphasis on work and public achievement obscures a central human reality: one cannot live by a curriculum vitae alone. The philosopher Michael Oakeshott speaks of the moral narrative that is someone's life. In this moral narrative, but not in one's curriculum vitae, what ultimately matters is not just the things of ambition, but more deeply the question of how one is to live. And especially, how one is to live in relation to those one loves. A curriculum vitae is something that always looks forward, to the next public achievement, to the next career move. But there is another perspective that sees life lived instinctively, if not explicitly, from the point of view of death. That is to say, one thinks about things, after a certain age, in terms of how one might see one's life when facing death. Did I do what should have been done? Did I give love as it should have been given? For women who are mothers and for men who are fathers, there come other questions as to how one has lived. In some deep sense, the feeling that one has done wrong in relation to someone you love is a feeling for which there can be no consolation.

I did work part-time after the first few months, leaving our baby in the care of her father. Although I found the morning in my favourite haven—a well-equipped university library—a welcome break, by the afternoon I experienced an overwhelming desire to be with my baby. There was a kind of bodily anguish to it. It felt right when we were together and wrong when we were separate. If my children's instinct was to keep me close, mine was to keep them close.

I remember feeling estranged from the prevailing public conversations about children; the tone was resentful, emphasising only the burdens, the obstacles that children presented to the realisation of public achievement. One day—deep in that 'in love' stage of the nursing mother—I was sitting on our verandah with my baby blissfully asleep after breastfeeding. A French painter was talking on the radio about her life, her painting and motherhood. I was not in the mood to listen to resentment; I just wanted to glory in the very being of this child. To turn off the radio, however, I would have had to move and disturb her. Unexpectedly, what the painter said gave me heart. She was not dishonest about the fatigue or the lack of time when her children were small. But she gave us another way of seeing it. Being a mother had opened her to a kind of love so deep, made her confront her own vulnerability so profoundly, that this love worked not against but with her creativity.

I also recall, just in the first few months, being intensely preoccupied. An old friend came to visit. He had always relied upon me as a kind of touchstone on whom he could sound out his opinions, and normally we spent many hours pleasurably arguing over what might be true. On this occasion he wanted to discuss US foreign policy. I found myself unusually remote from his intensity, and felt relieved when he finally drove away. How irritating, I felt, to be forced to discourse on such matters when one has something as important as a newborn baby to think about! And I caught myself in the thought, and laughed aloud to think of the distance I had travelled.

Many women have written truthfully about the dividedness they feel between the fulfilment of their talents and the power of their love for the child they have brought into the world. Even working part-time, I sensed what this division could mean. There was not only the painful sense of not really answering the demands of either as well as I wished. Suddenly all time spent at one task was simultaneously time spent away from the other. Time with my child, particularly, was no longer uncomplicated. I felt ambivalence in everything I did. I admired those women I knew who managed that dividing better than I did, though none found it easy. I did not feel, just for the moment, that I had room in my heart for both. My way of resolving this dividedness was to choose, for a time, one part of life over another. I never considered this as a renunciation, but as a postponement.

Being plunged into parenthood can be a central transforming event in someone's life, for men as well as women. One becomes someone else. Often we feel, on bringing a child into the world, as if a great question has been asked of us, and we feel unsure how to respond. Some feel it to be more a burden than an honour. Parents of a newborn baby can find themselves overwhelmed by its fragility, by the importance of the task that confronts them. Yet their effect upon us goes even deeper than this to something Simone Weil called attention to:

> At the bottom of the heart of every human being, from earliest infancy until the tomb, there is something that goes on indomitably expecting, in the teeth of all experience of the crimes committed, suffered, and witnessed, that good and not evil will be done to him. It is this above all that is sacred in every human being.

Deeper even than the 'social construction of motherhood' or patriarchy, are children's faces, full of hope and expectation that you will treat them well. Some feminists have written of the false and oppressive ideal of the 'good mother' as socially imposed, or something dreamt up by men; yet in wishing to be a good mother or a good father, we are also responding to children themselves. It is not just the 'social construction' of motherhood that makes us feel guilty. It is the expression on the face of a child.

The first parent

Tim Winton in *The Riders* writes lyrically of a man's experience of being the 'first parent'. Through the character of Scully he describes what it is to feel the raw helpless gratitude for a child's very being, the deep pleasure of being the first parent a child will run to, the one who has 'most of their days'.

The matter goes even deeper than that. For a mother or a father, being the 'first parent' can be felt just as deeply, as a kind of 'work', and at the centre of life's meaning. This is no less true of at-home fathers than it is of the many women who have taken on that role. Taking on the role of 'the first parent', however, should not make others invisible.

From the first moments of our children's births their father was there. My mother found him in the hospital nursery walking up and down hugging his baby daughter close, her flat little nose pressed into his neck. He was no stranger to caring for bodies not quite in control of themselves. As a teenager he had looked after his mother, who was crippled with multiple sclerosis; he'd get up several times a night to give her painkillers, or to bathe her ulcerated legs. He already knew what it was to sleep lightly, to live in that state of half-alertness to another human being whose body has betrayed them. The broken sleep of these small human beings was not an alien experience to him.

He carried them in his arms or on his back, their small fists twisted around his black curls. And because he was so intimately involved in their physical care I never feared leaving them with him. He invented different stories, ones that went on for years, ever more elaborate, for each child. For our eldest he created a little girl called Isobel with bright red shoes who lived in the moon and had wild adventures. For our second it was an ancestor fairy called Princess Pearl, who lived in the bush gully below our house, who watched over her, gave her little presents and wrote her messages of love from the past.

Children can have their own preferences, however, as to who should be the first parent. When our younger daughter was born, my husband had a year of leave. I felt at its end very strongly that we were the twin pillars of her life, almost interchangeable, although she still turned to me when upset. As a newborn baby she had a 'reverse cycle'. She slept all day and was awake all night. She woke up at 10 or 11 p.m., and stayed wide awake until falling into a deep sleep at 6 a.m., just as my older daughter got up. She did not cry; she just looked with a calm interest at the world. I was so tired I began to hallucinate. We took shifts.

On the first night I left instructions. Her blankets were to be just so, the baby was to lie this way, and so on. When I awoke for my shift at 2 a.m., none of my instructions had been obeyed. Our little daughter was lying on her back, her legs crossed, arms flung back as if she was sunning herself on the beach in the Riviera. Her blankets were humped up in a kind of messy, improper tent, but she was sleeping blissfully. When I gingerly tried to move her into the right position I was rewarded with an ear-splitting shriek.

I decided he understood this baby at least as well as I did, and from then on I left his methods well alone. Whether it was because of that early time they spent together, or because she had a temperament very like his own, I sometimes felt her father was ahead of me in understanding her. If ever I suggested something was not quite from motherlore, he would reply, with finality, 'But she likes it.' And so she did. He found out her rhythms and ways just as I did, and understood her calm quietness where I was sometimes temporarily puzzled. Her first words were together, on the same night, Mama *and* Papa. We have photos taken by a friend at the beach when she was about two, which capture the exceptional closeness of father and daughter.

For our elder daughter, however, it was a different story. On the days I spent at the library, by afternoon she became increasingly unsettled, fussing, restless, and finally crying, refusing comfort. According to the childcare manuals, she was too young to be upset by who was caring for her. Was it possible she was missing me? One afternoon I came home a little early and heard her crying. I rushed in to find my husband cradling her, trying to soothe her. When I picked her up she turned her head towards my shoulder. She took a long, deep, suspicious sniff, turned her head to one side, smiled and fell asleep. She smelt her mother.

The rhythms of childhood

The choice that I made for us to be together, rather than separate, was dependent on the new understanding I came to of the importance, the centrality to human existence, of children. I certainly knew that no one I could hire would love my children as I would. I had always felt at home in the world of achievement and work. When my first child was born, I had the sense of stepping from that world into another, as if into a different culture, where the values and priorities were quite different. It was an egalitarian world in which few bothered to ask the question, 'What do you do?' It was in general an unapologetically female world, although many of the women in it would have welcomed more contributions from the men in their lives.

Even the sense of time was different. Child time is outside what the sociologist Jules Henry calls 'the austerity of time,' but inside Slowness. It was not routine or regular, moving sometimes chaotically, with astonishing speed, sometimes as if in a slow-motion film. It can be frustrating and difficult, particularly for those parents trying to keep a foot in both worlds. I was reminded of the mental adjustment I once made when travelling by Indian railway, where the trains never arrived on time.

It is certainly possible to do other things within this period. Many women I knew were very enterprising. They worked *alongside* their babies, in small business, farming or from home, or reorganised shiftwork so that their child would never be without one parent. Others were lucky enough to have a devoted grandmother close by and willing to help out. Women who are able to keep one foot in the door of work— lest that door slam completely shut—are better placed when this period of early childhood comes to an end than many women who opt out completely.

The issue for me, then, and for these women, was not work as such, but the kind of work that separates children for really long hours from those who love them most.

Watching children, I came to feel that childhood itself has its own rhythms. The most powerful limit comes from separation anxiety, that aching desire to keep one's parents close, which is at its peak from the age of seven months to around two years. In terms of an adult lifespan, it is very short-lived. It generally resolves itself quite naturally after the age of two or so—sometimes earlier, sometimes later. Children's capacity to do without their parents grows steadily as they get older. The temporary limits imposed by separation distress can be borne more easily by being shared between two parents. It might mean as little as a few years of cutting back a little out of a working life of forty-five years.

Observing children, I noticed that often those who were not pushed into early 'independence' go on to become the most independent children later. It was certainly true of my children. For children allowed to move through this period at their own pace, that primeval anxiety seemed to lessen more easily and with less difficulty, and was perhaps more permanently resolved, than if they were hurried.

Children move through distinct stages in early childhood, at different speeds. The balance between their deep need for their parents and their need for their peers changes, so that the group care in which preschoolers can flourish may well be an alien and distressing experience for a nine-month-old baby.

The term 'separation anxiety' does not really give a powerful sense of what is experienced by a baby or a toddler when parted for long hours from the people it loves most. It is an emotion closest to grief. Children have a different sense of time to adults, and may experience a period of time as forever that we, as adults, consider quite short. Not all children experience separation in the same way; some respond more intensely than others. As with all things there is the imponderable of temperament. Certain things may mitigate the distress felt, such as the attentiveness of the caregiver, their loving kindness or lack of it, and what degree of attachment the child has to the substitute. But not always. One friend put her baby into full-time care when the baby was nine months old. Meeting me in the street, she anxiously assured me that the baby was 'quite happy' in care. But the baby told a different story. When the caregiver's name was mentioned, she put her arms around her mother's neck, and with a look of indescribable sadness, laid her head down on her mother's shoulder.

What must be understood here is that childcare for a baby intrudes into the midst of an intense love affair. Adults may think that because little is said, little is felt. But there is both force and delicacy in what babies and young children feel. Their emotions are complex and deep long before language. They grow into an ability to express what is already felt, more than in the ability to feel. Sometimes no one will do except the loved one, and the only remedy is restoration to the company of the person they love. We do not expect an adult to easily replace a beloved person with another. It violates our sense of the preciousness of individual people, and even our sense of what love is. Yet we expect this of a baby.

In my own life I came up against separation distress in my children as if before an invisible barrier. It did not last for long. Somewhere during their third year, my sense of that invisible barrier lessened, and over time finally dissolved. But before that time, there was no mistaking its power.

Crying on the inside

I also observed it in other children and found myself profoundly moved by it. Although my mother quite often came down from the country to stay, we needed some kind of supplementary childcare. I decided that a regular part-time arrangement would be better than an infrequent and maybe traumatic experience with a near stranger. I did my homework, talking to other parents, local infant welfare nurses and caregivers about what was available, but above all spent quite a lot of time observing different childcare settings.

The local daycare centres were quickly ruled out. They described themselves, naturally, as 'quality' care, whatever that might be. In one, all babies who were mobile were usually confined to their cot or playpens, and the ratio of caregivers to children was poor; in another the caregivers were insensitive, with crying children left unconsoled.

I then explored family daycare, and spent considerable time watching the children with different caregivers. The usual advice was to select a caregiver, visit once or twice and then to leave your baby without a backward glance so as not to encourage protest. This extensive time I spent with different caregivers contributed to changing my views on my pre-motherhood, rather thoughtless embrace of the childcare solution for the youngest age groups. There was a general rule of thumb: the older the child, the better they coped.

Some people told me that their particular caregiver 'loved their children as their own'. Sometimes they would shake their heads reverently, as if disbelieving their luck in finding someone whose mothering skills, they felt, far exceeded their own. There was the occasional truly exceptional individual, perhaps an older woman who had finished raising her own children, who became a cherished person in the child's world. But in other cases I was puzzled by the idealising process that had gone on, since the carers seemed to me adequate, perhaps, but very far from wonderful.

So I rather naively asked the caregivers the obvious question: 'Did they love these children they cared for as their own?' Not one said yes. Rather, they pointed to the benefits they felt in the 'management' of the children that came from what they felt was their 'professionalism', or skill, or experience. They even felt they were more 'objective' because they were less 'involved'. They did become fond of the children, and of some more than others, though they tried hard to be fair. They found the idea that they loved the children in their care as their own rather startling, and quite false. Many of them were kind and warm, and often very experienced and skilled with young children. Despite that, I observed a natural coolness, with fewer interactions between caregiver and child than when children were with their mothers. There was an absence of the relaxed expressiveness that you see in relations between parents and children. This expressiveness ranged from passionate love and embraces, to irritability and anger, with frustration and rage being expressed just as freely with parents as love and tenderness.

One woman was a gentle, placid and kindly person with three children under four in her care. The children were generally cared for in a small family room, close to the front door. Every time the doorbell rang there was a tumble of excited children to the door. 'Mummy, Mummy!' they all shouted, their voices raised in unison. It was, quite simply, pitiful.

My next move was to look for a caregiver to work in my home. I had friends who had used this form of care. Some found exceptionally good people, a nanny or perhaps a retired grandmother who enjoyed the company of a young child. I remember seeing the child of a friend greet his carer, an older woman whose children had grown, with a cheeky grin and the open affection normally reserved for grandma. In such circumstances the children, too, seemed genuinely attached to these caregivers, though not in the same way as to their mothers. Such observations made me feel that childcare could be a very different experience for different children. These mothers were at the top of the occupational elite, however, and could afford the expense of this kind of care, as well as enjoying generous maternity leave and flexible working hours, not to mention supportive partners.

While this was eventually the long-term arrangement I came to, it was not without its problems. One former childcare worker, an impressive and dedicated young woman, spoke of her frustration over the number of children she was expected to care for; she felt she rarely got beyond the most mundane physical care to the emotional relatedness she felt the babies needed. She told stories of pathetic notes from parents in lunchboxes, asking for a little extra attention, of poor hygiene, and of children looking vigilantly out the window during the long afternoons while waiting for the arrival of their mother's car. Sometimes *both* mother *and* child reacted to separation with profound sadness.

In the very early years, my own children often reacted to separation painfully, unless they were left with their father or grandmother, other relatives or friends—in other words, people who were deep and familiar parts of their world. Once, my normal caregiver was ill. I was dealing with a serious back injury at the time and needed to swim regularly. I finally took the advice of friends to use the creche at the pool. Leaving my daughter with all her coloured crayons neatly lined up on a table in front of her and plenty of paper, I ignored her pleas for me to stay, and limped off. Something in her face as I walked away prompted me to go back after a few minutes to the railing where one could look down on the creche. Quietly sitting at her table in the corner, ignored by everyone, was my daughter, quite motionless, staring straight ahead with an expression of desolation, her pencils untouched. I went back in, to the horror of the caregivers, who said, 'She's been absolutely fine!' She was transformed instantly with relief and joy.

Of course, often children do not exhibit such visible manifestations of distress, and leaving them is unavoidable. One day, after attending a medical appointment, I arrived to collect my daughter from her minder, who reassured me that all had gone well. I asked my daughter on the way home, 'How was it?' When she responded that she had been unhappy, I asked, 'Did you cry?' 'No,' came the reply, 'but I was crying on the inside.'

A love of the world

After giving birth I felt alive to the world in a way and with a heightened intensity I had not felt since childhood—alive to its vividness and beauty, responsive to its colours and textures, to the raw pleasure of existence on my own skin. How could I not want to share that with my children? Such a way of seeing can only be offered; and just as a well-meaning gift may lie idle and unused, so too might this one. But perhaps, if it is not at first received gratefully, there might come a time when, like the unnoticed gift, its qualities might suddenly, quite unexpectedly, be valued.

Raimond Gaita has reminded us that we become like what we love, so that what children are given the opportunity of loving matters deeply. In some of the family daycare homes it occurred to me that what they might come to love would be television, since it was the main distraction offered.

What I gave my children the opportunity of loving could be something as simple as a whole day spent in the garden, or a trip to a nearby river, where I could stand my daughter near the rapids in the gentle eddies where the current was not strong, asking her to close her eyes and listen. Or she could learn to love music for the way that it expresses what cannot be otherwise expressed, to have the time to paint and draw for as long as she pleased rather than be hurried off to some new activity. Was it possible, growing up in a beautiful part of the Australian countryside, to make her spend most of her days confined to one yard, even with its expensive plastic play equipment and its supposedly stimulating 'developmental' activities? I wanted my children to feel in their bones the power of the landscape in which we live, and to experience the bush as their playground. They could grow up with, and not just experience on weekends, animals they loved. (And some that I did not love, including one guinea pig who was a serial killer, dispatching all of his fellow rodents to the land of never-never.) I was able, in the freedom of time we had together, to read to them, sometimes for hours. Books are not essential in everyone's life, but they are in mine.

I loved teaching my children new skills, but I certainly did not envisage my time at home as an endless parade of educational games. I expected them to amuse themselves too, and as they grew older we often enjoyed being busy with our own activities alongside one another, or in separate parts of the house.

Mothers at home are often depicted as isolated and depressed. This was not the case in the convivial community of other mothers in my neighbourhood. My children's first experience of a supportive, connected community was when I was at home. I decided very early on that parenting was like travelling in an unknown country: it is best and most safely done in the company of others. For that reason, I organised, with the help of the local infant health nurse, the first baby playgroup in the area. Playgroups and preschools followed. I often had reason to feel grateful to those women, not least the former nurses who on occasion late at night helped out with advice when my children were sick! It was often among that local community that one would see babies having their first separation experiences—I would arrive at someone's house to find one mother with two babies, the other being only a telephone call away when the minded baby had had enough. Interestingly, in this type of shared care I rarely saw the kind of distress that was so visible with the longer hours of formal childcare.

My children benefited too. Children from the earliest age are fascinated by each other; they learn from and model themselves on older children's behaviour. Other children were for mine a continual source of play, enjoyment and fascinated interest. Yet there were limits: usually a morning or an afternoon was enough.

One of my central objections to long daycare was the lack of privacy: spending one's entire day in the company of others whom one could not choose, in enforced sociability, without the possibility of withdrawing quietly when needed to one's own space. Or the thought of them waking up disoriented, as toddlers often do after their nap, to find a different caregiver to the one who put them down to sleep. Or for that matter, the way that even as babies they already had their biological rhythms dominated by the workplace clock, so that they could not sleep as long as they wished if they had had a bad night.

Most importantly, my decision to look after my children myself reflected the difference that I felt lay between love and care. Part of my Toddlers Bill of Rights would include the possibility of climbing into the lap of someone who truly, deeply, loves them, whenever they wish. There is in the emphasis that some feminists place on the word *care* instead of *love* a shift that is one of the linguistic emblems of our time. *Care* is a very different word from *love*. Care is cool and careful, reasoned, a word that implies distance and limits. Love is not. Love is passionate, implacable, intense, unreasoned. Children need most not trained, expert, professional care, but the passionate partiality of parental love. That love is not reproducible, just as to be a mother is not reproducible. Caring is. Mothering cannot be bought or sold, or reproduced by the marketplace. But caring can.

It is possible to obscure, for example with tales of the cognitive advantages of creche, or vivid accounts of child abuse by unhappy mothers, the sheer physical love that can exist between children and their parents. In the last year spent at home before school, my younger daughter went through a process akin to sailboat tacking, with apparent reversals in direction between dependence and independence, yet with the movement always heading inexorably towards independence. She loved her kindergarten, and sometimes I would be banished from the trip to the zoo or suchlike, because she was 'too big' to need me. But on other days she would spend the whole afternoon on my lap, being read to, or embracing me, her face buried in my hair, just breathing me in. We both knew that next year all this would change. And it did. The new experience of independence at school for her; the freedom to pick up the threads of work begun in the past for me. But I cannot pretend that within these gains there was not also, for both of us, a profound sense of loss.

My experience is not universal. I do not claim to speak on behalf of all women. And my point is emphatically not that women should restrict their lives to motherhood. I feel the importance of drawing men, too, into the task of rearing the next generation. But *how far* we move away from the traditional perception of what the word *mother* means, matters. Should we pretend that hired caregivers can give what mothers give to their children? Should we expect women to live like men when a child is just born? Must the old patterns be replaced by new patterns even more constricting—the imposition on all women of that male life pattern? Do we have to pretend that, at least for a time after having children, for at least some women, priorities don't change?

My journey into motherland was rather like the depiction of illness in Kafka's wonderful story *Metamorphosis*—an inexorable descent into social invisibility. So many friends and relations simply gave up expecting that I would do anything of 'interest' in the 'real world'. I was aware that for many around me the period spent undividedly in motherland meant I was forever destined for the 'Mummy track'. What I knew, however, was that the time would come when I would move back into my own life.

Gingerly, I dusted off my curriculum vitae with the gaping hole. I discovered that two of my referees were dead. I had married the third. It was not a promising beginning. Tentatively, I rang a fourth, a male feminist, who I had not seen in all the time I had spent in motherland. Would he even remember me, I wondered. Remember me he did. Yes, he was more than happy to be my referee, but why, what for, what had I been doing all this time? I told him I had been looking after children. There was an appalled silence.

'Good heavens. You have been . . . *what!*'

'What did you think I would be doing?' I asked curiously.

'I've often wondered what happened to you,' he said wanly. 'But I thought . . . you know . . . New York . . . London . . .'

I knew what he meant. A brilliant career. But here I was, down among the children. He sounded terribly disappointed, more embarrassed for me than if I had told him I had been imprisoned for embezzling university funds. I tried to explain but the words melted away and my voice trailed off hopelessly. We rang off and I sat for a few moments by the telephone, reflecting on how hard it is to explain—it is as if one steps back across a threshold into a different world with different values, a different universe. Everything that is a priority in the other, parallel universe is reversed, turned upside down. The centre of life in one world—children—is invisible to the other. There is no shared language. The most important, meaningful 'work' I had ever done counted for nothing. I felt like a bewildered migrant confronted by a culture that turns upside down the values of the world from which I had come.

Then the telephone sprang into life again. It was my friend.

'You know, I almost fell off my chair to hear what had happened to you. But listen,' he said. 'There is some teaching coming up in a course I'm running.' Then his voice became grim and determined. 'We've got to get you back, Anne. Into the *real* world.'

I appreciated his generosity. But in what sense had the world I had inhabited—growing up children—not been 'real?'

In the judgement of the 'real world', I suppose I stood still, or was 'doing nothing' for all that time, during which I did not 'progress'. Yet for all that, everything that came after was deeply shaped by my time in motherland. Though I was sometimes impatient to be where I am now, looking back I find I cannot but feel the leaving as a loss.

Part One

Feminism and the 'problem' of motherhood

1 Two paths to women's equality

Why we need feminism

I sometimes imagine that one can observe a precise moment and place when one age gives way to another. It often occurs in an out-of-the-way place, and often among quite ordinary people. I remember just such a moment in the feminist revolution. The place was a prosperous and respectable town nestled between the ancient hills that had given so generously of their gold in the previous century, a town with streets so quiet that one could hear the wisteria rustle, and where the bark of a dog might be an event. The time was early afternoon; the year 1970. There was nothing remarkable about the afternoon, just the quiet flow of ordinary moments as the people endured a great drift of heat that had sunk upon the town. In the local high school, drowsy from the heat, and, it must be conceded, the dreariness of the teaching, the students stared dreamily out of the windows at the darting movements of skinks among the peppercorns dotting the asphalt.

And then it happened. Suddenly, puncturing their reverie, came the headmaster's voice on the public address system. If voices have colours, his was blood red. He was angry about the untidiness of the yard, and reserved particular venom for the girls. 'What kind of *housewives* will you make, if you cannot even keep the schoolyard clean?' The girls, but not the boys, would remain behind to clean up the rubbish.

He was, I suppose, expressing an assumption of his own time—an ideal of womanhood as a cross between an angel and a housewife, as Isak Dinesen put it.

But the headmaster's time had come and gone. There was a moment of silence, and then a subterranean rumble, mounting to a roar, as a wave of female anger swept through the school. No girl stayed behind. What was once conventional thinking had become unthinkable. What was once an *ideal* had become an *insult*. The hour had struck.

We are in the midst of a social revolution: in women's roles, and in the relations between the sexes. This revolution has had many consequences. My book is primarily concerned with one of them. In 2002, the majority—55 per cent—of American mothers with babies under the age of one were working. Similar trends can be observed in the increased employment of mothers of preschool children in many wealthy societies all over the world.

Social theorist Agnes Heller has described it as a break with all preceding societies, in so far as the subordination of women has been embedded in all previous social relations. These relations had other components, of course—a sense of complementarity and difference, and, from Christianity, a sense of the sacredness of the mother. Women in earlier times could have the emotional upper hand, of course, since those formal relations could be, and were, disobeyed—subverted by the wild card of sex, or softened by the power of love. But that complexity need not obscure the central truth: that in the great antinomies—light and dark, white and black, male and female—it is men who have always been more valued. And being valued less refracts powerfully still through women's lives.

The new order ushered in by this revolution is a movement away from a society in which a great part of one's fate was determined according to gender (what the dour English historian of the family, Lawrence Stone, has called a system of sexual caste), to a world in which freedom's many forms—contingency, possibility, opportunity, but also uncertainty, even chaos—all play their part. One of the most powerful emancipation movements of our time and of the future will not be socialism, but feminism. How we respond to these changes will shape how we live, and particularly how children will live.

The emergence of a radical second wave of the women's movement was, in some sense, inevitable. Why so? Second-wave feminism erupted from several cultural fault lines, from deeply embedded conflicts or cultural contradictions.

The first contradiction emerges from what de Tocqueville foretold as the central and remorseless movement of Western societies away from the old regime of heritage and hierarchy, towards democracy. If in democratic societies the legitimacy of hereditary privilege is shaken, the legitimacy of the age-old dominance of men over women will, over time, also crumble. If the deepest value of the democratic age is equality, how can one accept inequality between men and women?

The second cultural contradiction is thrown up by equal education. There was a painful contradiction between women's traditional role, which had at its centre the ideal of renunciation of self (Kierkegaard defined a woman's being as 'existence for something else'), and the central impulse behind equal education—that human flourishing comes from the discovery and development of one's talents. It is this exceptionally deep conflict—that women might spend the first part of their life discovering their talents, and then be expected after marriage and children to spend the next part renouncing them—which created the kind of bitterness and explosive anger so visible in books like Betty Friedan's *The Feminine Mystique*, Germaine Greer's *The Female Eunuch*, or Pat Grimshaw and Lyn Strahan's *The Half-Open Door*.

The third conflict concerns the social contract, which in liberal democracies derives its legitimacy from the understanding that opportunities, rights, the possibility of public office, the operation of the law, will fall equally to all citizens. Once women had the vote, they were admitted to the social contract. Here again over time another contradiction appeared. The common understanding of traditional roles was that a woman's domain was the private one, the man's the public realm. Was it ever possible, once women were admitted as equal participants to the social contract between the state and citizenry, to sustain the belief that one group of citizens—women—could only contribute to or participate in the private, while another group of citizens—men—could move freely in both?

Lastly, there was a change in the ground rules of marriage. Longevity and smaller families meant that much less of a woman's lifespan was spent on childrearing; in Alan Bloom's words, 'At forty-five they [women] were finding themselves with nothing to do, and forty more years to do it. Their formative career years had been lost, and they were, hence, unable to compete with men.' Most painfully, there was the liberalisation of divorce law. The old marriage contract—that a woman give up work to concentrate on her family, supporting her husband in his career—left many bereft, when in middle age they found themselves alone with children to support. Even finding work, let alone a brilliant career, was difficult. No-fault divorce laws have resulted in what has been described as the pauperisation of motherhood. As divorce specialist Leonore Weitzman has argued:

> . . . the new laws confer economic advantages on spouses who invest in themselves at the expense of the marital partnership . . . Implicit in the new laws are incentives for investing in oneself, maintaining one's separate identity, and being self-sufficient. The new stress is on individual

responsibility for one's future, rather than the partnership assumption of joint or reciprocal responsibilities.

★   ★   ★

Alongside the struggle against racism, the movement for women's emancipation was one of the most powerful and important achievements of the twentieth century. At the heart of both liberation movements was a morally profound idea of justice. Liberation theory, as Jean Curthoys suggests, identified as 'the psychological key to power our ordinary and very pervasive assumptions of human inferiority—the simple idea that some people are more "important" than others.' Curthoys shows the kinship of that idea to the philosopher Simone Weil's insight that 'respect is due to the human being as such and is not a matter of degree'. This sense of the irreducible value of human beings was the key to the rebellion against the valuing of white over black, male over female.

Understanding the violation to human dignity involved when one person is considered less valuable than another, accorded less respect and therefore excluded from the constituency of equal rights and opportunities, is at the core of what is irreducibly valuable in feminism. In both pre- and post-feminist worlds there are graphic, shocking confrontations with the consequences of lower status as a 'less valuable human being'. It can be a matter of life and death. In contemporary Jordan, men who murder women in their family who have eloped or committed adultery or are even simply suspected of doing so—these are dubbed 'honour killings'—risk only a derisory six-month sentence, while the penalty for murder of other human beings is fifteen years. In China, the One Child Policy has caused not only a huge rise in abortions of female foetuses, but rampant female infanticide. So many female infants have been aborted or killed that according to Chinese government figures in 2005, 119 boys are born in China for every 100 girls. In some rural areas where boy preference is strongest, the ratio is close to 150 boys to every 100 girls. Within the next few decades it is estimated that there will be a shortage of female partners for as many as 50 million men.

Although Western women may not encounter female infanticide and honour killings in their own lives, their devaluation as the second sex is still deeply present alongside new forms of equality. As the social theorist Zygmunt Bauman reminds us, life in post-modernity exists in fragments. We have come very recently from a different world. In that world, women had no capacity to control their fertility. They had no rights against their body being used for sex against their will by their husband—for no law protected against rape in marriage. The old regime was a coercive one; motherhood was a kind of compulsory identity. A domestic life for married women was not a matter of choice but enforced by law: for example by compulsory resignation from work on marriage.

It was taken for granted that a woman's time and energy was at a male's disposal and that only time left over from tending to a family could be claimed as one's own. Lorraine Rose, one of the psychotherapists interviewed for this book and an early member of the Women's Electoral Lobby, grew up in a large Catholic family and remembers having to perform all her brothers' housework. If they slept in after a late night out, she had to cancel all her plans for the day and wait patiently for them to get up, in order to make all their beds. She was not allowed out until she did. It was unthinkable that her brothers—being male—should smooth out their own rumpled sheets.

My husband was shocked in the late 1960s to hear his English professor express the view that it was easy to improve the critical study of English literature—just get less women and more men to study it. So deep was the belief at that time—a mere few decades ago—in the intellectual inferiority of women that not even one of the young women present protested. Nor have such assumptions disappeared; they are often merely better masked. The British psychologist Oliver James cites recent studies which have shown that the same work is judged to be superior when participants believe a man, rather than a woman, has done it.

I remember as a child experiencing this belief in female inferiority as a primeval blow, like an axe struck into the very centre of my soul. Later, while some teachers acted as encouragers and mentors, others saw my intellectual precocity as problematic—properly belonging to the higher caste of males. A girl 'growing up clever' was sometimes made to feel like a small wrinkle in the universe in need of smoothing out.

Weil describes the idea of justice as 'so beautiful a thing.' It is only in confronting this powerful antinomy—male superior, female inferior—that one can begin to grasp why for many women, whether they pay lip-service to feminism or not, the ideal of equality of respect between men and women is an idea of radical beauty. Remarks like Weil's get us close to what, at its deepest, is at stake for women in the talk of equality. The idea of respect, that profound desire for recognition or being seen truly by others, centres on the existential cry from the heart of every human being: see me, value me, respect me, for who I really am, and not for my sex or colour, what I do, or who knows me, or the size of my house or bank balance. Equality of course also means the many practical forms of fairness like equality of opportunity. Yet those things are means by which justice is achieved, and not ends in themselves. That is why we may say of feminism what Raimond Gaita says of the anti-racist movement:

> It can hardly be doubted that the world is a better place for it even though foolish things have been said and done in its name ... Like feminism, to which it has been aligned and compared, it has expressed a concern for equality, which cannot adequately be captured in talk of equal access to goods and opportunities. Treat me as a person; see me fully as a human being, as fully your equal, without condescension—these are not demands for things whose value lies in the degree to which they enable one to get other things. These are calls to justice conceived as an equality of respect, calls to become part of a constituency within which claims for equity of access to goods and opportunities may appropriately be pressed. It is justice of the kind often called social justice because of its insistence that our state and civic institutions should, to the degree that is humanly possible, reveal rather than obscure the full humanity of our fellow citizens.

On love, ideology and the unbearable lightness of being

If in important ways feminism is aligned with anti-racism, as my earlier example of female infanticide shows, that way of seeing also misses something important. Relations between men and women are also reciprocal relations based on love and sexual desire, albeit ones historically distorted in men's favour, all of which makes Lawrence Stone's rendition of the 'system of sexual caste' too crude. If love between a man and a woman can be based on power and not love, it can also be based on love more than power. Love can make the lover more attentive to the ways that inequality has denied not just women in general, but this particular, beloved woman, the equality of respect that recognition of her humanity requires.

There are further difficulties. All these changes touch most deeply not merely on the private realm, but on what Vaclav Havel described as our 'lyrical relation to life'. There is nothing within racism that means there is something of value lost if we overturn it. In relations between men and women, the matter is a little different. The feminist revolution concerns all those areas of deepest meaning to us, the most intimate aspects of identity and human life. Our sense of ourselves as male and female shapes and is shaped by what we feel constitutes love and sexual desire, of what it means to be a good mother or a good father, and the nature and mode of generosity and reciprocity within a family.

After the revolution, what will remain of our conception of what it means to be a mother? Will we settle for the notion that the mother can be replaced by professional caregivers providing a commodity service known as childcare? Will it become permissible for women to glory in a lover, but not in a child? What sense of mystery, complementarity, or otherness between the sexes will remain?

A male feminist friend who believed in the androgynous ideal once patiently explained to me that in future nothing would flow from being male or female: we would all just be *persons.* He paused, displaying with a gesture of the hand his imaginary Utopia. 'So you mean', I replied, 'that for all important intents and purposes, we would all be the *same?*' He beamed approval at my ready grasp of his vision. But as he said 'Yes!' a feeling flashed through me. I inspected it. That feeling was *boredom!*

There is another problem. The vices of the traditional world, of sharply delineated roles and the consequent limitations on women's lives, are inextricably tied up with its virtues—family stability, security, a sense of community, a system of care for vulnerable children, the sick and the elderly—via traditional female roles. The virtues of our own age—greater freedom, including sexual freedom, and a greater emphasis on the rights of the individual—are also tied intimately to its vices: a tendency for the deepest human relationships to be commodified and have meaning emptied from them, where people seek fleeting connection in a society of strangers, where the heart becomes a lonely hunter. As Eric Hobsbawm observes in *Age of Extremes*, the weight of the old rules, even unjust ones which bore down heavily on the human spirit and caused suffering, may be replaced not by something better but by no rules at all.

These thoughts take us to the heart of the human condition under postmodernity, to a certain loss of meaning. The shadowland of con-tingency is chaos. We float, rudderless and alone, upon a grey sea of endless possibility. The loss of meaning can be a form of suffering as severe as that which comes from injustice: the anxiety and anguish that comes with postmodernity's unbearable lightness of being. This lightness is not so much to do with the politics of the dishcloth, for women's continued responsibility for the household humdrum is one reflection of relation-ships still distorted in men's favour—especially at a time when so many women work.

There are other parts of our identity as male and female, however, where the bossy confidence of those who wish to transform sex roles is severely strained. No program for transformation can be truthful if it is not, for example, sensitive to the extraordinary love a mother may feel for her child. One young career woman rang me to talk about the difficulty she had in leaving her child in childcare. She was a feminist and a sole parent—but she had, as she put it, fallen in love with her child. She spoke of how she had to reassure herself that if anything ever happened to this beloved child, she would not die too. Her voice became very thin and stretched, trailing away uncertainly: 'I would survive, I would . . .'. But it was not me she needed to convince; it was herself.

The depth of such responses call attention to, as Gaita puts it:

> the way in which human beings limit our will as does nothing else in nature . . . the power of human beings to affect one another in ways beyond merit has offended rationalists and moralists since the dawn of thought, but it is partly what yields to us that sense of human individuality which we express when we say human beings are unique and irreplaceable. Such attachments, and the joy and grief they may cause, condition our sense of the preciousness of human beings. Love is the most important of them.

The sex-role sociologist's grid, in contrast, descends upon reality in a way that makes even the language with which we might express an imaginative conception of life, or give any depth to our conceptions of what it is to be a mother or a father, disappear into dust. Some speak as if we are all just *role players*, as if to change roles is as simple as putting on a different coloured overcoat, when in truth there are areas of our lives—in sexuality, in our sense of what it means to be a mother or a father for example—that go much deeper. Our sense of what those things mean very probably begins long ago, in that part of our story that is childhood, in the formation of our identity. Such things may be central to who we think we are. To use a marvellous term of Gaita's, they are part of our creatureliness. They include aspects of female experience such as the visceral bodily experience of maternity and birth. Susan Johnson's superb memoir, *A Better Woman*, tells how her body was unexpectedly damaged by a fistula after giving birth. She writes, as Foucault might have put it, of the 'never saids' of modern birth:

> in wrenching back childbirth from the hands of the (mostly) male doctors . . . we forgot that birth involves danger, the loud hot breath of the wolf . . .

We turned the experience of birth into our own private movie, casting ourselves in the starring role. In truth we have turned our faces away from the fact that at each and every birth death hovers about the room, the silent presence. We do not wish to remember that babies die, strangled in their own cords only minutes from light, nor do we wish to dwell on the fact that women still bleed to death in distant rooms . . . even in your clean laundered bed you will still feel the rush of air against your skin as he passes.

Motherlove, too, has its own kind of Eros. Women the world over go into the nursery, tiptoe to the crib and put a finger under their newborn's nose. They are feeling for breath, for life. Having given life, women feel a special kind of vigilance in keeping the baby alive. Mothers often fear that no one else will have quite the same focus on the task of nurturing as they do. Stalwart feminists have described to me, shamefaced, the 'invisible skeins' that bound them to the baby, and even whispered about the maternal instinct. Women may find it more burden than honour, although most answer it with generosity. Some crumple under the weight of responsibility; a rare few flee it altogether. Women grieve over lost children as if over a terrible betrayal; they mourn children they give up for adoption, grieve after miscarriages, stillbirths and abortions all their lives.

Like all passions, motherlove may not speak at all to some, or wildly and destructively to others. But a tepid, tameable thing it is not. The psychoanalyst D. W. Winnicott likened the primary preoccupation with an infant's wellbeing to a temporary psychosis. With older children a mother's feelings may be no less raw. One friend packed herself off to grief counselling, so profound was the shock of a rebellious teenager slamming the door shut on her life. Another, a mother of a drug addict, stretched her arms out, supplicating, begging understanding from her family in her inability to cut off from him: 'It would be like an amputation.' Some feminists too, like Daphne de Marneffe and Sarah Hrdy, admit to feeling not some neat and manageable emotion, but the surprising strength of their desire to be with their children.

Is motherlove not rife with ambivalence, including moments of great darkness and wild anger? Like all passions, including sexual love, it will have all of these. But no more than the existence of those elements within love and sexual desire convinces us that those passions do not exist, should such negative elements convince us that motherlove is a 'myth'. And we can no more snare it in the ideologist's net than we can snare sexual love. Love at its deepest makes us utterly vulnerable. The temptation to put ideology in the place of intensity, pain and the fear of loss, trying to make a grid of ideas control and contain the power of those feelings, is great. Helen Garner wrote brilliantly in defence of Eros—by which she means not just sex but a kind of life force: 'the quick spirit that moves between people' which keeps 'cracking open what is becoming rigid and closed off . . . explodes the forbidden . . . mocks our fantasy that we can nail life down and control it . . . as far beyond our attempts to regulate it as sunshine is, or a cyclone.'

Solzhenitsyn in his book *Lenin in Zurich* gives a mocking description of the great ideologist and architect of the Russian revolution arguing with his lover Inessa about free love. Lenin confronts her with Marxist theory, with 'an unbreakable net of logic'. In the next sentence Solzhenitsyn captures perfectly the relation of ideology to life; just as 'the dark water from the depths of the lake runs unhindered through the fisherman's net . . . Inessa with her concept of free love was not to be caught in the net of class analysis.' The depth, complexity, passion or ambivalence of sex, or the love of a mother or father for a child, can never be truly caught in the ideologist's net. Love does not make for the ease or arrogance of those who march with the regiment. Ideology erases doubt. Love creates it. Love, as Freud once put it, makes us humble.

What kind of feminism?

All this means that there could hardly be a more important project than to get feminism right. Women's emancipation, and how we go about achieving it, matters profoundly. I say women's emancipation, rather than feminism, for we should at the outset distinguish between that ideal of justice, 'so beautiful a thing', and the social movement—feminism—that sprang up to achieve it.

What feminist Sandra Farganis calls 'the social reconstruction of the feminine character'—whether in relation to women's greater public role, women's sexuality or, the focus of this book, redefining motherhood—is a central social phenomenon of our time. The whole culture is seething with questions about motherhood. Reproductive technology, contraception and widely available abortion mean sex has largely been severed from reproduction. Motherhood as a monolithic experience is breaking up. The consequence is fierce community division. A single newspaper article—whether on in vitro fertilisation for single or gay women, on abortion and adoption, on childlessness or childcare, working mothers versus stay-at-home mothers—is able to trigger a furious reaction.

Motherhood is one of the most potent battlegrounds. Visit any book-shop and you will find the shelves creaking under the weight of the motherwars.

Feminism is furiously, notoriously ambivalent on the question of motherhood. It is also extraordinarily diverse. No one can claim to represent '*the* feminist position on motherhood'. There are lively debates *within* feminism over motherhood. Nor is that diversity an esoteric or academic matter. Different stances within the movement refract powerfully on the themes of this book, for the women's movement has thrown up radically different paths for transforming motherhood and the landscape of childhood. It is necessary to make judgements about better and worse paths through this transformation.

Like the many varieties of socialism in the late nineteenth century which tried to bring greater justice for the working class, there are now many voices trying to achieve greater equality for women. While deeply embedded and longstanding injustices to women mean that the future must be feminist, feminism itself has, as Beatrice Faust once put it, 'as many positions as there are names in a telephone book'. That raises the question—what kind of feminism?

Among those feminist voices trying to make sense of what it means to be a modern woman, there are significant differences of emphasis. Each position leads to markedly contrasting public policies.

The first fault line centres on sameness and difference. Does equality mean sameness with men: the same rights, the same opportunities for paid work and public roles, but also the same life shape—full-time work from adulthood to old age? If so, what is the place of motherhood?

If one central part of the liberation project is to overturn women's special responsibility for children, is that aim best achieved by the separation of children into institutional care—the transformation of childcare into a commodified service provided by the state or market —or by parental leave policies encouraging the sharing of that labour with men?

Were traditionally feminine activities, like caring for young children, simply imposed by patriarchy in the interests of men? Or are they one part of female desire? Is there a 'higher' male standard of life to which women should be assimilated? Or is there something particular, different and valuable in female culture, particularly the ethic of care emerging from the life practices of mothering? Is there not something to celebrate in the experience of being a mother? How do we create a society in which caregiving is not penalised?

Other disagreements centre on the question of diversity among women. How can the feminist movement, with its predominantly white, middle-class leadership and constituency, speak on behalf of women from different social classes, from different religious and ethnic backgrounds? The academic concern over diversity began by centring on the fashionable areas of 'difference', such as respect for ethnic or working-class women's experiences, but it could not long be contained by it.

By the beginning of the twenty-first century there were deep, longstanding, obvious and seemingly intractable divisions among the female populations of all rich modern societies over the meaning of motherhood. The dilemma of whether to work or stay home with young children, the debates on the best ways to raise children, had exploded into a bitter, apparently irresolvable conflict that came to be called the motherwars. Can women legitimately choose, after the revolution, traditionally female activities such as mothering? If a central value of the liberation movement in overthrowing the constricted female role under patriarchy was freedom, how could one group of women dictate to any other group how they should live?

Recognition of the ways women's emancipation has transformed the world for the better, then, does not preclude us from interrogating feminism. Rather, its very importance demands that interrogation. It *does not* mean, *must not* mean, the suspension of all critical faculties, or the substitution of the obedience to the old regime with unthinking obedience to a new ideology. It needs independent thinking, which looks with an unblinking eye at problems as well possibilities, losses as well as gains. A feminism worth something will be supple and flexible, able to respond to new circumstances, new problems. We need critical thinking, not the blind obedience of those foot soldiers who cannot, as Tolstoy put it, give up the pleasure of marching with the regiment.

2 Equality as sameness: the loneliness of the postmodern cowgirl

'The equality we fought for isn't liveable, isn't workable, isn't comfortable in the terms that structured our battle.' Germaine Greer, *The Whole Woman*

'Feminism has not always helped me. How many times I have encountered a feminist book filled with innovative ideas for changed gender relations, the acceptance of whose argument requires just one small price: that I relinquish my attachment to spending time caring for my children.' Daphne de Marneffe, *Maternal Desire: On Love, Children and the Inner Life*

I must have been in early adolescence when I first read Simone de Beauvoir. It was a long, hot country summer. The only entertainment was to listen to the rise and fall of men's voices on the radio as they commented on the cricket. Bored, I perused my mother's bookshelves, running my finger along the dusty spines. At that age I was interested in anything with sex in the title, so I stopped at *The Second Sex* and plucked it out.

I did not yet know the shape of my future. I had already begun to recognise the contradictions and tensions between the exhortations to use my talents and the message that womanhood meant renunciation. I had observed the constrained lives of many women around me, although none of that had led me to despise them. Instead, alongside the injustice of their situations, I saw something else as well: their generosity that helped us, as children, to flourish; they were most often our allies.

As I opened the yellowed pages of the book, I dimly perceived that here was an attempt by a woman at answering my half-formed question: what might embodiment as a female, as a woman, mean? My adolescent self recoiled from de Beauvoir's answer. I could not believe it had come from a woman.

As part of the feminist canon, *The Second Sex* is perhaps one of those books more celebrated than actually read. For what is so striking in de Beauvoir's work is how much free expression is given to female self-hatred, how deeply she internalised a sense of male superiority, how uncritically she imbibed the masculine principle as the higher standard to which women must aspire. Such psychological responses to ingrained inequality are not unusual; some examples of Jewish and black self-hatred comes to mind. Moreover, her analysis is utterly dependent on a version of radical individualism. The ideal human type for de Beauvoir seems to be not a father but a free male individual, a lone cowboy unfettered by family responsibilities of any kind.

Reflecting the patriarchal thinkers of old, she identifies women with nature, whose mundane household activities exist outside the civilisation men inhabit, engaging in their 'transcendent projects'. The 'data of biology' of women's bodies make them the 'victim of the species.' In sex 'it is unquestionably the male who *takes* the female—she is *taken*'. Sexual development in the male is 'comparatively' beautifully 'simple', their sex organs are 'better developed', male animals have brilliant plumage, horns or voice, and a wonderful propensity for individuality, especially displayed in indifference to offspring.

Sexual development in females, in contrast, is one crisis after another. Girls are lucky to survive the 'dangerous and weakening' struggle of puberty which is obscurely, darkly linked in de Beauvoir's mind with the onset of mysterious diseases: osteomyelitis, tuberculosis, and curvature of the spine—from age fourteen to eighteen, '128 girls die to 100 boys'. Like a nineteenth-century male doctor horrified by the murky depths of the female body, de Beauvoir sees the 'curse' of menstruation as a ghastly physical process, associated with 'nervous instability', which means a woman loses 'unconscious control', 'freeing convulsive reflexes and complexes and leading to a marked capriciousness of disposition' and, ominously, 'serious psychic disturbance'. All once a month!

Men's 'sexual life is not in opposition to his existence as a person . . . runs an even course, without crises and mishap'. Women are 'more often ailing, and there are many times when they are not in command of themselves'. (I stole a careful glance at my mother at this point. She was a lone parent and sole breadwinner. She had a book in one hand and her ear on the cricket. Her nose was in the air. She looked very much in command of herself!)

De Beauvoir's assumption that male behaviour is the standard to emulate is also evident when (well before *Sex and the City*) she urges women, like 'busy men' . . . 'to satisfy her physical desires but also to enjoy the relaxation and diversion provided by agreeable sexual adventures'. She then discusses the barriers (like venereal disease or beatings) to one 'possible solution' which 'is to pick up in the street a partner for a night or an hour'.

Motherhood is no less grim, 'demanding heavy sacrifices'. A mother, once a 'conscious and free individual . . . has become *life's passive instrument*'. The unborn baby is a parasite, and morning sickness signals 'the revolt of the organism against the invading species'. Repeated child-bearing makes mothers 'prematurely old and misshapen', childbirth itself is painful and dangerous, breastfeeding a 'tiresome' servitude sapping her vitality. Women who are 'free from maternal servitude' 'can now and then equal the male' but generally they renounce individuality, for the 'benefit of the species'. Only the menopause (another crisis!) saves a woman from 'the servitude imposed by her female nature'; now infertile, women can finally acquire the 'vigour they lacked before'.

No woman who respects other women could write like this. No woman who loves her daughters, glorying in their femaleness, their capacity to bear children as well as their talents, could write like this. No woman who respects herself could write like this. In so far as de Beauvoir has a jaundiced view of the female and an over investment in the glories of the male, there is little doubt that she imbibed or internalised an extreme version of male narcissism.

To be saved from the unhappy condition of womanhood, it is unsurprising that equality for de Beauvoir will mean that women will have to get rid of their female identities and assimilate to the higher male standard. Her distaste for the female leads her inexorably towards the great anti-democratic danger of any social and political movement— vanguardism—where a small elite claims to know best the interests of the oppressed group and act on their behalf. De Beauvoir's answer to women's emancipation is a coercive one: women in general will only become free with the help of a vanguard of enlightened women who know their interests better than they do.

In a conversation with de Beauvoir, Betty Friedan said she 'believed women should have the choice to stay home to raise their children if that is what they wish to do'. De Beauvoir answered

> No, we don't believe that any woman should have this choice. No woman should be authorised to stay home to raise her children. Society should be totally different. Women should not have that choice, precisely because if there is such a choice, too many women will make that one.

My early, intuitive response to de Beauvoir later became for me a theoretical and ethical problem at the centre of the idea of 'equality as sameness'. At its best, equality as sameness alerts us to the radically different life chances women are offered compared with men. It promises and bestows practical, essential social tools to change all that. At its worst, however, such thinking can shade, just like the assimilationist thinking in black–white relations, into a peculiar triumph of masculinist thinking, in which anything distinctively female, like motherhood, is devalued. Thus, just as the old biological assimilationists wanted to breed out the colour from aborigines—to expunge signs of aboriginality—such a feminist project works on assimilating women to a superior male standard, expunging signs of anything distinctively female. In such a view, in so far as women live a traditional male life pattern dominated by paid work and career, they have succeeded. If they continue to value aspects of traditional female culture like motherhood, they have failed. Such an impulse is a perpetual refrain through *The Second Sex*, and through much other sameness feminism, eternally echoing Henry Higgins's famous complaint from *My Fair Lady*: 'Why can't a woman be more like a man?'

Angry daughters: The repudiation of motherhood

The hostility to motherhood implicit in de Beauvoir also can be found in many of the first writings of 1960s and 1970s feminism, sometimes called 'the repudiation of motherhood' by feminist historians. This period saw an explosion of new writing by 'angry daughters' in the heady, rebellious days of second-wave feminism.

I became a mother just after that time, in the 1980s. Much of what I read about motherhood in the quality press was written by women about my age or older, who had been deeply shaped by the feminism of this period. Home with small children, I hardly saw one affirmation of the experience of mothering in ten years. Indeed, I *still* read contributions that appear drawn from the spirit of that time. Feminism within the academy had already moved on, exploring difference and even celebrating aspects of mothering, but in the public sphere the 'repudiation' continued, as if frozen in a time/space capsule of its own.

Many of those 'repudiating motherhood' were and are truly the intellectual and political descendants of the position outlined in *The Second Sex*; they really are Simone de Beauvoir's babies. Raimond Gaita speaks of the foolish things said and done by the movement against racism that, nevertheless, still made the world a vastly better place. The same may be said of those early women's liberation statements on motherhood.

To read widely in this period—and to continue to take feminism as having moral claims of the utmost seriousness—one needs a certain poise. One must remember the backdrop of injustice that gave rise to feminism, and keep in mind the fact that in moments of intense cultural rebellion, balance and nuance fly out the window. Foolish things were said and done, but the essential work of dismantling the old coercive regime and the establishment of the practical and legislative framework of equality of opportunity was achieved. There was so much to be done (and much still remains to be done): tackling wage inequality; abolishing the marriage bar on employment; confronting social prejudice, discrimination and sexual harassment; setting up refuges for battered women, and so on. It was a time of intense cultural creativity for many talented women. New forms of art and women's writing emerged. Publishing houses like Virago in Britain and McPhee Gribble in Australia, run entirely by women, were established. Such achievements, in a very short time, were remarkable.

The strength, then, of sameness feminism is its emphasis on men's and women's common humanity, in opening up that framework of equal opportunities historically denied to women. Given the historic injustice suffered by women on the grounds of sexual differences, which were inflated and extended to justify oppression and inequality, no movement for women's emancipation can be taken seriously unless it has benchmarks and a minimal terrain of 'sameness'. And one can admire and appreciate the able, exceptional women in the vanguard of social change who broke the mould, confronted male dominance of the public and private spheres, and focussed our attention on the fate of 'the second sex'. In all this I am a supporter of sameness feminism.

At the same time, however, in early women's liberation, motherhood was often simply repudiated as oppression. The maternal feminist historian Kerreen Reiger, looking back through the debates of the 1960s and 1970s, found 'intense, unrelieved hostility toward the idea of motherhood'. Even to mention the word motherhood at a feminist conference was enough for the atmosphere to crackle with existential panic. Rhonda Galbally, long-time feminist and activist, launching one of Reiger's books, spoke of how during the 'repudiation of motherhood' period she had felt like a 'closet mother'.

Much of the writing, as later feminists acknowledged, has the tone of an angry adolescent daughter against a constraining mother. Like de Beauvoir, motherhood is conceived as being in opposition to 'selfhood'. The Mother in these early narratives is constructed as a dark and dangerous figure. Her children struggle from her neurotic and possessive grasp like little moths towards the light of freedom. (This is reminiscent of R.D. Laing, for whom the 'mother's first kiss is the first act of brutality!') Germaine Greer's early work *The Female Eunuch* gave a contemptuous depiction of the suburban mother, and contained an airy proposal for communes in Italy to do the work of childrearing. Shulamith Firestone likened giving birth to 'shitting a pumpkin' and suggested the need to embrace a technological solution: breeding babies in test tubes. For her, the 'problem' of motherhood could be eliminated by making the mother–child attachment taboo, and evenly distributing children among household members!

Juliet Mitchell described women with families as characterised by 'small mindedness, petty jealousy, irrational emotionality and random violence, dependency, competitive selfishness and possessiveness, passivity', while the family 'by its very nature . . . [is] there to prevent the future'. Betty Friedan thought the suburban home a concentration camp and accused mothers of having a 'sick, sad relationship with their children'. Friedan spends more time on the question of who will do the dusting than she does on who, in the liberated world, should take responsibility for children. One advocate of communal living suggested that 'we will be able to assume parental roles *when and for as long as we want* . . . Our children will have an advantage [in that] from the adults they can select their own parents, brothers sisters, friends . . .' [emphasis added].

That astonishing, vague blitheness on the question of responsibility for children is repeated in countless other examples from mainstream feminism which either marginalised motherhood or treated it as a state to be pitied, despised or ignored.

As the numbers of women in high-status jobs slowly grew, the status of mothers plummeted. An essential tension between the impulse to develop one's talents and the egalitarian respect for all women implicit in feminism was exposed. A new, sharp-edged contempt, a little like that felt by the newly urbanised peasantry for the 'rural idiocy' they had just escaped, was expressed in particular towards women who were full-time mothers. Friends of mine with young children who joined the Women's Electoral Lobby soon trailed away, feeling unwelcome.

If the core of the rebellion against male domination was Weil's ideal that 'respect was due to the human person as such and was not a matter of degree', there emerged an impulse antithetical to, even corrupting that notion. Realistically, the impulse to develop one's talents need not be, but often is, in tension with Weil's idea. Whatever the case, a new hierarchy among educated women began to develop. Some women (those with careers) were more equal than others. Only if you were developing your talents, or succeeding in the public realm or in paid work, were you worthy of respect. Mothers began dismissing themselves as being 'just a mother'. Working was sexy. Staying at home had all the Eros of a baby's posset. Soon a joke caught it: 'Before feminism housewives were second-class citizens. After feminism they were subhuman!'

As Bruno Bettelheim observed in relation to the kibbutz experiments, no new way of life can only be based on something negative, on rejection. A new movement must have ideals and affirmations too. In 1970s feminism there arose two important, new companion ideas to the radical rejection of mothering. As surely as the 1950s stay-at-home, suburban, 'exclusive' mother was stigmatised and depicted as a dangerous and toxic creature—a new bad mother—another ideal of what was a 'good' mother emerged: the 'working' mother. As British feminist Melissa Benn expressed it, 'the burden of proof shifted from the working to the non-working mother'. Mothers at home now had to justify themselves.

As the numbers of working mothers rose sharply in the US, Australia and Britain, books and articles extolled working motherhood. Supermums enhanced family life, made everybody richer, and raised smarter, more creative, independent kids, who flourished by being given better role models. (It went without saying that if a mother did not work she was a bad role model, a bad mother, and enhanced nobody's life.) Anita Shreve, in her book *Remaking Motherhood: How Working Mothers are Shaping Our Children's Future*, divined an invisible link between a paycheque and a child's IQ. One only had to slip behind the check-out counter at K-Mart and put the kids into daycare, a breathless Shreve assured her readers, to guarantee lifting a kid's IQ by twenty to thirty points! In *When Mothers Work: Loving Our Children Without Sacrificing Ourselves*, Joan K. Peters described how 'working moms make better moms . . . a mother-at-home, alone with her children, may be the worst child-rearing arrangement of any culture . . .' A new Reassurance Industry continues to fill whole shelves in bookstores with titles sternly exhorting women to banish guilt: for example, Eileen Gillibrand and Jenny Mosley's *When I Go to Work I Feel Guilty*, and Susan Chira's *A Mother's Place: Taking the Debate about Working Mothers Beyond Guilt and Blame*.

The opening of the public world of work, political power and careers, of course, did offer a tremendous advance over the old regime. Working *can* enhance not just a woman's life but family income and wellbeing (no small matter at a time of mounting income inequality). Some women at home *are* depressed or are less adequate mothers by virtue of giving up important sources of fulfilment. It *is* important for boys and girls to see women engaging in all facets of public and community life as equal citizens. And so on.

On the other hand, books of this genre airbrush out the tough realities of the Supermum version of working motherhood, in a way that's reminiscent of those propagandist paintings of the former Soviet Union. Such visual advertisements depicted the revolution in glowing terms; men and women arm in arm, smiling radiantly as they leant on pitchforks or gathered around the tractor for a sing-a-long while harvesting the bumper crop that only a socialist nation could achieve!

Thinkers such as Nancy Chodorow and Dorothy Dinnerstein came close to the utopian socialist hope that a new human being would be created by the abolition of 'exclusive' motherhood. Dinnerstein is particularly apocalyptic. If some 1950s male psychologists waved the big stick of delinquency as the imagined result of mothers working, Dinnerstein waved the big stick of environmental Armageddon as a result of them *not* working. In her vision women's exclusive care of infancy is the source of male anger at female dominance and behind mankind's exploitation of the planet. Children raised by mothers, her argument went, having experienced their own vulnerability by being totally dependent on one female caretaker, come to fear and loathe women's authority and power. As adults, men especially fear women's power, yet seek emotional dependence upon women—hence the barriers to women's taking public or powerful roles. Exclusive mothering produces men cut off from their own feelings of vulnerability and dependency, hell-bent on domination, including the domination of nature. Linking the male will to power over 'mother nature' to environmental catastrophe and threat of a nuclear holocaust, Dinnerstein warned her readers that if something is not done soon to 'break the female monopoly over early childcare', we can expect the imminent end of civilisation!

As an alternative to mothercare, Dinnerstein and Chodorow seesawed between the ideal of shared parental care between men and women, and institutional daycare. The emphasis they put on drawing men into childrearing was undoubtedly a new contribution to the issue of responsibility for children. Most sociologists, including conservatives like David

Popenoe, would agree that men's involvement in childrearing is usually greater in societies where women's status is higher (though which is cause and which is effect is not clear). On the simplest grounds of equity, men should pull their weight as parents, sharing not just the joys but also the burdens (especially in relation to mopping up vomit—I am an absolute stickler on this point!).

A father, like a mother, can love a child beyond reason. That love—to be 'crazy about the kid' as Uri Bronfenbrenner once put it—is so utterly important to children that one central thesis of this book is that shared parenting is an important alternative to mothercare. In my own life I felt the importance, and saw the happy results of close, involved fatherhood. Dismantling the idea of the father as the 'inessential parent' and affirming his capacity as a caregiver, then, is an enduring and important achievement, one that has made the world a better place. Chodorow and later commentators have contributed something of real value.

That said, Chodorow's *The Reproduction of Motherhood*, like other such accounts, has all kinds of flaws. In the 1970s it was necessary to dismantle the rigid, authoritarian interpretations of 'biology as destiny'; however, the emphasis on the 'social construction of motherhood' was something of an overcorrection. In *Maternal Desire: On Children, Love and the Inner Life*, the most important contemporary answer to Chodorow, Daphne de Marneffe argues that such psychoanalytic arguments, while more sophisticated than earlier depictions of mothering as 'false consciousness', nonetheless still position the desire to care for one's kids as a 'correctable condition'. A former student of Chodorow's, de Marneffe points out that many younger women like her are struggling with different issues:

> Daughters of 1940s and 1950s mothers, like Chodorow and Benjamin, were understandably motivated to analyse the problem of women trapped in a narrow domestic sphere . . . But daughters of 1960s and 1970s mothers, like me, needed to solve something different: namely, how to take advantage of the access women had gained in the workplace while not short-changing their desire to mother.

Unlike de Marneffe, many feminist psychological interpretations of the 'social construction of motherhood' look very dated in the light of some brilliant new work in attachment theory, psychoanalysis and neurobiology. This means all their accounts of early childhood are limited. Unlike developmental psychology, or the maternal feminists who based their 'ethic of care' on the real-life practices of 'good enough' mothers,

Chodorow relies on evidence taken from clinical cases—where mothering has gone badly. There are methodological problems with using clinical case material on which to build a universal theory, and limits in making inferences about 'normal' development from pathological development. That is not to say such clinical material has no place in the portrait we build of family life and its pathologies, but it is not the whole. I think what Chodorow captures rather well is not a universal pattern of development at all, but one particular Western family pathology—the implosion of children onto unsupported mothers by absent fathers. What I shall give in the second part of this book, 'Taking Children Seriously', is an alternative outline of children's development in the light of more contemporary theory and evidence.

It was, however, institutional childcare provided by the market, not shared parental care, that emerged in the 1980s as the most common alternative to mothercare. Responsibility for children was to be resolved by embracing a new ideal of collective childrearing. While the women's movement in its attitude to sexuality and careers was strongly individualist, collectivism was the solution for children. Children were not 'left' but 'shared', or 'returned to the community' via 'group care'.

Like all ideologies, the emphasis on community caught something real. Suburban mothers could be isolated; the mother–child relationship can be distorted when women are left too much alone with their task. Too often children have been, and often still are, left in the care of unsupported mothers. As a solution, however, the early liberationists' demand for twenty-four hour free daycare is another matter.

However, institutional childcare was not simply a practical idea; economic 'necessity' means parents need it, so society has an obligation to make it as 'high quality' as possible, for example. Nor was it thought to be just a new childrearing niche, neither better nor worse but different. The belief in The Group, in institutional care, was, and sometimes still is, held every bit as passionately, fervently and inflexibly as the communist's belief in the Collective Farm or The Plan, or an economic rationalist's belief in the free market. It is not possible to understand the childcare debates—the tenacity with which the uncritical belief in group care was held—without also grasping the passion of the utopian vision of which group daycare was a part.

The counterpoint, then, to the negative vision of mothercare was an idealised portrait of childcare. From daycare would emerge a new caring, sharing human being to begin the new world, free of sexism and all neuroses, eliminating both poverty and poor parenting in one fell swoop. Creches would replace the vagaries and imperfections of parental love with trained, 'professional' care. From institutional childcare, in short, would emerge a 'new child.' The enthusiasm of advocates like Alison Clarke-Stewart for daycare was so total that one American commentator wondered if perhaps daycare should be made mandatory for all children.

Nor was such a trend restricted to the US. In Australia the fervent ideological belief in the glories of The Group emerged at this time and has been maintained and sustained ever since by some activists. As one academic textbook on Australian childcare said, 'Feminists insisted that the idealisation of intense and exclusive mother–child relationships oppressed not only women but children'. Social commentator Eva Cox claimed in her Boyer Lectures that at-home mothers who did not use group child-care raised narcissistic monsters incapable of sharing. The radical claim from these writers is that creche was better than home, that children were better off without full-time mothercare. All of them. *Always*.

Mothers without a culture: the clash between work and family

The profound ambivalence towards motherhood expressed by these early feminists, the proscribing of at-home motherhood and the prescribing of paid work, is, of course, simply a neat inversion of the old regime's coercive insistence on 'biology is destiny', on motherhood and domesticity as a kind of compulsory life course for all women. However, one unintended consequence of equality as sameness, strictly interpreted, emerged in the egalitarian Mundugumour tribe which Margaret Mead studied. Boys and girls were raised to be the same, to be 'independent, hostile, vigorous'. Far from a truly egalitarian outcome however, one part of the traditional female condition—reproduction and childrearing—thus became a marked dis-advantage where 'any aspect of their personality that might hold an echo of the feminine or maternal is a vulnerability and a liability'.

Germaine Greer, moving on from her airy dismissal of motherhood in *The Female Eunuch*, intimated in *Sex and Destiny* that the West was beginning to approximate to just such a state. Prefiguring in her critique the dramatic fall in fertility among highly educated Western women, Greer argues:

the closer women draw in social and economic status to the male level, the more disruptive childbirth becomes. In order to compete with men Western woman has joined the masculine hierarchy and cultivated a masculine sense of self . . . she must step down from all that and enter the psychological equivalent of the birth hut . . . The woman who becomes a mother suffers a crushing loss of status.

One vivid example of how a strict interpretation of 'equality as sameness' can paradoxically disadvantage women comes from the experience of Sylvia Ann Hewlett, an American writer on work and family matters, who worked during the 1980s at the impeccably feminist Barnard College at Harvard. Boasting 'a Women's Centre, an abortion counselling service, a rape crisis centre, an annual feminist conference, and an undergraduate major in women's studies', astonishingly, however, this flagship of feminism had no family-friendly policies. Hewlett had no maternity leave.

Pregnant with twins, she found herself in danger of miscarriage. Despite reassurances from her obstetrician, she felt a deep foreboding that 'this pregnancy was in trouble' and 'longed . . . to take time off and concentrate my energies on growing those babies'. Not yet tenured, and feeling unable to risk losing her foothold in academia after years of unremitting effort, she kept working. At six months her waters broke, and after a fourteen-hour labour she gave birth to two dead babies.

She was allowed just two weeks off for the 'procedure', as it was termed, and was then expected to be back at full-time work. Colleagues found it 'embarrassing and a little messy, hard to mix with professional small talk'. She met other women who had suffered miscarriages, who kept their grief secret at work as if they had committed a crime, whose workplaces would not give leave of absences. 'They were afraid of professional repercussions and ashamed of showing their maternal vulnerabilities in the workplace . . . they would have received considerably more sympathy from their colleagues and support from the college, if, instead of losing a child, they had broken a leg on a skiing holiday.'

When Hewlett called for maternity policies, she was stunned to be told by some childless feminist colleagues who were 'less than enthusiastic about families' that she was 'trying to get a free ride' by wanting a maternity policy. 'Didn't I understand if women wanted equality with men, they could not ask for special privileges?'

She was turned down for tenure at Barnard anyhow. According to one tenure committee member, Hewlett wrote: 'I had "allowed childbearing to dilute my focus".' On her two dead babies Hewlett is blunt. 'The death of those twins put me in touch with the far-reaching importance of policies that support working parents . . . If I had been able to take some "parenting leave" those babies might well have survived.'

Other cracks in the edifice of equality as sameness began to appear: in the devaluation of motherhood and childrearing; in the explosive strains on working mothers that no airbrushing could disguise, as they attempted to work often as long and as hard as men, but without any of the home support; and in the crisis of quality in childcare. By the time Australian Prime Minister John Howard declared the clash between work and family the great 'barbecue stopper', the triumphalist tone of earlier celebrations of the Supermother period began to give way to titles like *The Second Shift, The Time Bind, The Overworked American, Crowded Lives, Having None of It, The Work/Life Collision*, as well as a world-weary chick-lit genre which was to the working mother what *Bridget Jones's Diary* was to single childless thirty-somethings. Allison Pearson's bestselling novel *I Don't Know How She Does It!* described fervently by Oprah Winfrey as the 'working mother's bible' about a woman lurching from one transatlantic domestic/work/love crisis to another, has a pace of life so frenetic that I had motion sickness just reading it, which is maybe why I keep getting the title muddled, calling it by mistake, *I Don't Know WHY She Does It!*

As de Marneffe argues: 'Most women today are not struggling to break out of the ideal that instructed them to sacrifice everything for their children. They are more likely to be beset with the quandary of the "do everything" model so they will have more relaxed time for their relationships.'

Baby hunger and the sovereign self

The Australian writer Joanna Murray-Smith gave birth to her first child

at the beginning of my thirties . . . around this neighbourhood and . . . the Upper West Side of Manhattan, that made me a 'young' mother. Women of my generation have been schooled in the advantages of delayed reproduction . . . what a lie all that turned out to be. Every time I hear a woman in her late 20s talk about there being 'plenty of time' I want to shake her. . . . women who want 'one day' to have children need to know that the longer they wait the less likely they are to conceive . . .

One of the most painful outcomes of 'equality as sameness' has been for women who discovered, in middle age, that the price of their careers was not having children. It was this phenomenon that saw Sylvia Ann Hewlett return, in 2002, to her theme of work versus family life. *Baby Hunger: The New Battle for Motherhood* centres on involuntary childlessness among high-achieving women. Sparking a furious debate in Australia and overseas, it showed the perils for women who had been encouraged to postpone children in favour of careers.

Only 16 per cent of the high-achieving women Hewlett surveyed thought it possible for women to 'have it all'. Women's 'new status and power', writes Hewlett, 'has not translated into better choices on the family front . . . Women can be playwrights, presidential candidates, and CEOs, but increasingly, they cannot be mothers.' Among those breathing the rarefied air at the top, the men are still far more likely than the women to have it all: a career, a relationship and children.

Hewlett's work showed the anguish of involuntary childlessness. In her nationwide survey of high-achieving American women, one third were childless at age forty. This figure rose to 42 per cent in corporate America. Yet only 14 per cent of these women voluntarily chose childlessness. For the rest, it was a 'creeping non-choice'—the deadly result of post-ponements due to careers, inability to find a partner, and the onset of age-related infertility. For high-achieving men, by contrast, there was very little disparity between their dreams and the reality. Seventy-nine per cent of high-achieving men said they wanted children, and 75 per cent had them.

Managing like a Man, a 1998 study of high-achieving corporate women by Judy Wajcman of the Australian National University, gave results strikingly similar to Hewlett's research. The lives of the male and female managers she studied revealed a marked disparity between men and women in their capacity to combine a career with family life. While over two-thirds of male managers do have children, two-thirds of their female counterparts do not. 'Childlessness,' Wajcman said, was for many women 'a precondition for a successful career'.

Although I am placing my account of 'baby hunger' within this critique of 'equality as sameness', let me make it plain that the rising level of childlessness should not solely be laid at feminism's door. It is connected to two interrelated social developments. The first is the rise in the numbers of unmarried or unpartnered women. The second is that delayed childrearing has resulted in a sharp increase in age-related infertility. Both factors are a consequence of one of the seismic cultural shifts that occurred simultaneously with feminism: the rise of radical individualism.

In Eric Hobsbawm's dour account of the cultural revolution we call 'the Sixties', he speaks of the emergence of a new expressive, radical individualism that owes more to Kropotkin's anarchism than to the neo-Marxism fashionable at that time. It was, Hobsbawm argues, 'a triumph of the individual over society'. . . 'a new libertarianism' 'in the name of the unlimited autonomy of unlimited desire . . . a self-regarding individualism pushed to its limits . . . The world was now tacitly assumed to consist of several billion human beings defined by their pursuit of individual desire.'

'Families Matter But Individuals Matter More' ran one newspaper headline. Such a radically new way of seeing, where self-fulfilment is an almost unopposed ideal for both sexes, gives a welcome legitimacy for women to be in the world in entirely new ways. No longer is, in an unproblematic way, women's individuality seen to be 'at odds with the family', as historian Carl Degler once put it so nicely, such that any hint of family responsibilities foreclose any further argument about emancipation. Yet the ideal of self-fulfilment can also be a radically destabilising one, especially in long-term relationships.

In this atmosphere, as Zygmunt Bauman puts it, there is a sense of the 'permanent temporariness of a relationship and its readiness for cancellation at short notice'. Unsurprisingly, men's and women's desires may pull in opposite directions. Sex has been severed from marriage and reproduction. In matters of the heart, there are no longer clear rules. And that, for women, is a decidedly mixed blessing.

Commitment phobia among the 'singleton generation' became a worldwide concern in 2002. Male 'commitment phobia' became a matter of intense interest within popular culture, and was expressed in international bestsellers like Ellen Fein's and Shernie Schneider's *The Rules* and Helen Fielding's *Bridget Jones's Diary.* More solid evidence, from social science, confirms the picture. Just after Hewlett's *Baby Hunger* was published, a study from America's National Marriage Project, based at Rutgers University, suggested that male commitment phobia is a genuine phenomenon. Men could now get sex outside marriage easily. Co-habitation offers men the benefits of marriage without its obligations.

The new 'rules' of the mating culture are 'oriented to men's appetites and interests', according to the young women in this study, who observed that their sex lives are following a male script. 'I'm turning into a man in some respects,' one woman says. 'I can go out there and dog them the way they do to me.' More commonly women complain about a harsh new double standard: men expect them to be submissive *and* strong, faithful *and* independent, while 'He's doing what he wants to do.' Casual sex was now an unquestioned part of singles culture, and the word love was rare.

The capacity for economic independence, which feminists have always maintained is the essential basis of equality, is certainly not enough on its own. Men now expected women to be employed and independent and to 'look after themselves'. 'She definitely has to work . . . or in the evenings it will be a one-sided conversation.' Some women commented that the new approval for women's economic activity was a mixed blessing: 'Women fought for the right to work, so now men expect you to work'.

The dismantling of the old patriarchal script may have freed women from age-old assumptions of compulsory motherhood. It has also freed men from their traditional obligations to be fathers. The hope of obligation-free sex is nothing new. As early as the 1950s, as Barbara Ehrenreich shows in *The Hearts of Men*, the magazine *Playboy* and other exemplars of masculine culture were singing the praises of the sexually available girlfriend and decrying parasitic and economically dependent wives.

Although the young men of the Rutgers study were enthusiastic about women's economic independence, they clearly also expected the continuation of traditional male domestic privileges. One man commented 'how helpful it was to have a girlfriend who could look after the house, pay all the bills and take care of the dogs when his work took him away from home for extended periods of time.'

The Rutgers study found that 'none of the men expressed a burning desire to have children', a view the researchers noted was 'likely to have been different if the study participants had been childless, unmarried women of similar age and background'. Many expressed an almost leisurely attitude: 'whatever happens, happens,' and 'I'll know when I'm ready,' and 'you can get married and have kids at any age.' They were unsympathetic to women's brief window on fertility: 'The men realise that women face time pressures to marry and bear children. At the same time, however, they express little sympathy for women's circumstances.'

Over the last decade other researchers have noticed increased delays in partnering, greater fragility of relationships, and more people living in non-family situations. For example in 2000, among Swedish women still childless at thirty, four in ten had no permanent partner. Likewise, Australian research by Monash University's Bob Birrell, Virginia Rapson and Claire Hourigan also showed steep rises in the numbers of men and women living outside relationships during the peak childbearing years, and longer delays in marriage. Carefully evaluating different census results from 1986 to 2001, they found a dramatic decline in partnering and marriage rates. Birrell and Rapson pull no punches about the significance of all this. It is 'a social revolution in the making. It implies an increasing unwillingness or incapacity to make a binding family commitment on the part of men, perhaps of women.'

While 72 per cent of women aged thirty to thirty-four in 1986 were married, by 2001 the number of married women in this age group had dropped to just over half. *Sex and the City* notwithstanding, the numbers of married women also declined from the late 1990s onward more sharply among less educated and affluent women and men without degrees—those hardest hit by economic restructuring. Only 41 per cent of low-income men earning $16,000 a year or less were partnered, compared with over 70 per cent of those earning more than $50,000. Birrell and Rapson discovered that falling marriage rates hold a central clue to falling fertility; once women marry, the overwhelming majority do have children. Eighty-five per cent of married women aged thirty-five to thirty-nine have at least one child. However, for 'an increasing proportion of women', they write, 'the establishment of a partnered relationship is being delayed, never occurs at all, or if it does occur, breaks down.'

And for them the biological clock ticks remorselessly.

Wendy Wasserstein, a Pulitzer-prize-winning playwright in her late forties interviewed in *Baby Hunger*, said:

> For me the reproductive thing has been huge. If I were a man I would decide at this point to marry some attractive accomplished 34-year-old woman who wanted children and was willing to put her career on hold to raise the kids. Instead of this standard male scenario I have just spent seven years trying to have a child [with IVF] on my own.

Wasserstein says of struggling with age-related infertility: 'It can be frightening, this yearning for a child—it's hard to fathom the desperate urgency.'

The writer Sophie Cunningham, a former publisher, spoke very movingly of her sense of loss over not having a child:

> The most depressed I have ever been is when I longed for a child in my early thirties . . . the experience was intense beyond imagining and I would

gasp in pain, or cry whenever I saw a baby. The prosaic term biological clock was totally inadequate to describe what I was going through. I wanted a child so much, and felt such anger that I did not have one that I was, in some ways, quite mad.

'Mother nature', remarked a feminist long ago, 'is a reactionary old bag.' And indeed she is. No equal opportunity initiative has changed the brutal facts of women's fertility. Female fertility drops sharply in the mid-thirties, and again at forty. Unassisted pregnancies after forty are uncommon.

Baby Hunger depicts high-powered older women in fertility clinics, staring at wallpaper plastered with lovable babies. In fact, IVF hype exceeds reality. The American Society for Reproductive Medicine tracked IVF success rates in 1999. Women aged thirty-five or younger have a 28 per cent chance of a live birth as a result of a single IVF cycle. By thirty-nine it falls to 8 per cent per cycle. By forty-four it falls to a mere 3 per cent.

For men the matter is different. They replenish their sperm every three months. Rupert Murdoch is an old man, albeit a rich and powerful one. Yet he has recently fathered a child with a woman decades younger. The male capacity to reproduce into old age is one of the great and enduring gender asymmetries, a kind of primeval injustice done to women. Men have time. Women don't.

Australian newspapers in 2002 exploded with the anger and anguish of women told they could 'have it all', who had been career-driven but wound up in their late thirties or early forties infertile, childless and sometimes partnerless. Virginia Hausegger, a television journalist for the ABC, wrote an impassioned and moving article about her own childlessness.

> I am childless and I am angry. Angry that I was so foolish to take the word of my feminist mothers as gospel. Angry that I was daft enough to believe female fulfilment came with a leather briefcase. It was wrong. It was crap . . . The truth is—for me at least—the career is no longer a challenge, the lifestyle trappings are joyless (the latest Collette Dinnigan frock looks pretty silly on a near forty-year-old), and the point of it all seems, well, pointless.

It was not only the emphasis on careers, however, which saw women in mid-life stricken with regret over lost children. The very individualism and belief in self-fulfilment that freed high-achieving women from the old notion of women's roles also increased freedom from tradition and responsibility for men. It is this conundrum that was responsible for the growing commitment phobia, and intensified what Ulrich Beck has described as the 'normal chaos of love'.

In this context, having children—that quintessential project of long-term commitment for both sexes—is much more difficult. Just underneath the surface of *Baby Hunger* lurks the shadow of enduring—perhaps indissoluble—gender asymmetries. In an important sense, they go to the core of our different bodily experience as male and female.

The loneliness of the post-modern cowgirl

The feminist Arlie Hochschild has described how commitment phobia has given rise to the emergence among women's advice books of a 'post-modern cowgirl' ideal—the counterpoint to the old male fantasy of the American cowboy, who lives 'alone, detached, roaming free with his horse', free of any permanent ties or responsibilities, unattached to any other human being. Hochschild notes how the ideal of the childless de Beauvoir —prefiguring the post-modern cowgirl—depending on no one, is cited admiringly, in Colette Dowling's *The Cinderella Complex*. Dowling speaks approvingly of Simone's isolated hikes panting up and down the French countryside as 'the method and the metaphor of her rebirth *as an individual*'.

Struggling with her reliance on and emotional attachment to Jean-Paul Sartre, rather than seeking to change the terms of endearment, de Beauvoir resorted to trying to eradicate her own needs. She embarked on punishing hiking expeditions,

> climbing every peak, clambering down every gully . . . exploring every valley . . . around Marseilles, through challenging solitary ten-hour hikes, 25 miles each day . . . Alone I walked the mists that hung over the summit of Sainte Victoire, and trod along the ridge of the Pilon de Roi, bracing myself against a violent wind which sent my beret spinning down to the valley below . . . I knew that *I could now rely on myself.*

For Dowling, it is frightening to encounter within oneself any emotional needs—for example, the desire, when ill, to be taken care of. Advice books like *The Cinderella Complex*, Hochschild argues, act as emotional investment counsellors, advising against getting involved with needy people, cautioning against reliance on others. Rather, they encourage women to 'rely on emotional asceticism', and to 'expect to give and receive surprisingly little love from other human beings'. Yet 'this does not mean individuals need each other less, only that they are invited *to manage their needs more*'.

Women are urged to invest in their female sexual—but never maternal—self, as a commodity, a ware for sale in a new free market of bodies. Thus in Helen Gurley Brown's *Having it All*, women are counselled to dye their hair, submit to cosmetic surgery, get botox injections to smooth out wrinkles and go on diets. They are also advised to 'control and tame' their needs, hoarding scarce emotional capital, and investing it wisely in the 'self as a solo enterprise', not in others.

Hochschild pinpoints how the exhortations to emotional control sit easily within assimilationism. They

> recycle the feeling rules applied to middle-class men in the 1950s. In doing so they illustrate a pattern common to many stratification systems—of the bottom emulating the 'top' in order to gain greater respect, authority and power. In so far as imitation represents in part a magical solution to redistribution of respect and power, female emulation of male emotional folkways is useless . . . women are encouraged to be 'cooler' while men are not in equal measure urged to be warmer.

What such fantasies cannot encompass is motherhood. More than perhaps any other human project it requires interdependence and reliance on others, the capacity to decentre from self and the surmounting of narcissism. The 'self as a solo enterprise'—indeed the whole project that resorts to individualism as the chief means of defeating patriarchy—is useless if at the end of it all is only the loneliness of a post-modern cowgirl confronting involuntary childlessness.

The examples I have selected in this chapter reveal the limitations of the model of equality as sameness when it comes to motherhood. The problem is we are *not* all the same. Sexual freedom, in the new world of 'permanent temporariness' of relationships, affects men and women differently. Urging young people to 'establish careers first' favours men's life cycle, not women's. Thus 'equality as sameness', precisely because it makes no acknowledgement of the truth—that for all our common humanity there remain enduring differences—can combine with the new sexual freedom and individualism in ways that are lethal to women's flourishing.

'We've gone down the path of "equal treatment" and it's gotten us so far. But not far enough,' says economist Jane Waldfogel. Yet none of that is cause to revert to age-old conservative and hierarchical assumptions about the 'nature of women', which explain in different guises the 'inevitability of patriarchy'. Instead, we need to be attentive to alternative voices *within feminism*, which go beyond the vision of 'equality as sameness'.

3 Meeting General Custer: maternal feminism and the ethic of care

When I was about eight months pregnant with my first child I asked a question of a perceptive friend who had a two-year-old child. 'What happens', I asked, 'after birth to the "I", to who you feel you are? Is it different?' I had lived an independent and autonomous life, living and travelling alone for long stretches. In common with many contemporary women I feared losing identity, selfhood, the clarity of separateness. Talk of 'merging' and 'psychological fusion' with infants left me feeling distinctly queasy. I did not yet know the love that was to make it all possible. I remember the carefully managed tone of my voice, of calm interest, beneath which panic bubbled, leaping through the cracks between words.

She said yes and then no and fell silent, frowning. Then she said she was more interested in her new self than her old self, although sometimes she felt deep resentment. The new self centred on a protective, preservative love—a kind of space beyond the self. I was to discover, rather dramatically, what she might mean.

The best way I can convey the pre- and post-motherhood self and body is to tell two stories. Two stories about falling. Falling from horses.

The first fall is a pre-motherhood fall. I was in my early twenties. I was out riding across country, galloping towards a fence. We had met the fence perfectly, when, inexplicably, the horse faltered. Half crumpling, he hit his knees hard on the top rail and began cartwheeling over the top of me. I remember this fall as clearly as I feel this moment. I see the blue sky wheeling away sideways, while at the same instant I was registering where my body was, where the horse's was, whether this was an easy fall or a bad one.

In horse sports there is a hierarchy of falls. On your feet is easy; the worst, rare kind, when you might die, is when a horse lands on top of you. As we parted company I was running, in a flash, this hierarchy of falls through my head, and I knew that for the first time in a lifetime of riding I was about to have a very bad fall. In the corner of my eye I could see his hindquarters were flipping up, and I was going down under his shoulder. Then adrenaline surged, slowing everything, expanding time, and I went into the fast spin I had perfected in the back blocks of a country childhood, out from under to hit the hard earth hip and shoulder, still spinning. My feelings afterwards were not of fear but exhilaration and a serene kind of power at having extricated myself so well. Parachutists, mountain climbers, those doing any sport of high risk, will all know the moment I am speaking of. Psychologically it was a good fall.

That brings me to my next, post-motherhood fall. Just before having children we had moved to a ramshackle farmhouse on the rural fringe. I had taken up riding again when my first baby was about five months old. Technically it was an easy fall; I landed on my feet. But the psychological repercussions were those of a very bad fall. I lost my nerve. I had to admit, for the first time since I was tiny, that I was feeling a terrible animal fear on the back of a horse. It was bewildering and humiliating. Everyone knows the old adage about climbing back on after a fall; it holds the essential wisdom that sooner or later the imagination full of near-catastrophe will fade, the pleasure take over, hope will triumph over experience. Participation in such sports is often contingent on an inner self-discipline. If catastrophic fantasies take hold—a body breaking open like an egg after falling from the sky, a body crushed by a horse—then the nerve is gone.

This time, however, none of that old self-discipline worked. I kept riding, but moved as if through treacle towards my horse, a kind of primeval dread slowing my every movement. Breaking the inner discipline against worst thinking, I gave fantasy full freedom, to see where my catastrophic thinking led. When I looked inward, past the humiliation, I discovered a new, strange, disembodied kind of fear, not for myself. I no longer felt afraid of my own death, for there was a life more important than mine. All the thoughts were of my beloved baby daughter, motherless, facing the world.

The fear *was for the body and soul that my child depended on*. It was a survival instinct with a twist, on behalf of another. One day I was sitting at a table with other women who had kept riding at a competitive level after having children. Looking carefully at each other before risking saying too much, one by one we all admitted how, for the first time since childhood, we now felt fear. Although the women were ambivalent, forming different responses to it, *every* woman said, 'What would happen to the baby?' if they were hurt.

That transformation, which in a rather narcissistic age is a transgression, was *not for ourselves*. It was self-protectiveness in the interests of the child. That transformation of the way we felt about what our bodies would risk was temporary—as time went on some did go back to top-level competition.

Not long ago I had a conversation with a friend with much older children, who was in the 'letting go' phase. She told me how anguished she was, following her teenage son through his adventures in South America, and also that she was thinking of taking up parachuting. These two parts of the conversation occurred simultaneously. The anguish and the freedom, the destabilising loss of the close attachment which exists alongside the gain of separateness, the escape from the limits to the self imposed by the responsibility for someone else—these belong very deeply together.

The ethic of care

My story above is about responsibility, about feelings of obligation to another, which transcend the claims of the self. Those feelings derived partly from pregnancy, lactation, and their emotional companion, the passionate attachment we call love. Sometimes I felt there was free will involved and a powerful sense of a moral decision, that I could have decided not to honour such feelings, but to deny them. At other times I had an equally powerful sense, of a bodily tie to my child so overwhelming that I could have as easily not answered those feelings as refuse to push in the last phase of labour. I decided to go with it, to not resist it but see where it led.

Whether such feelings—an aspect of what de Marneffe calls 'maternal desire'—are universal hardly matters, because so many women have spoken to me or have written of sharing such feelings as to render them commonplace. There are now many highly educated women writing about leaving or cutting back on high-profile careers, who all use the same expression: 'I fell in love with my baby.' For example, writer Ann Crittenden left a job as a journalist with the *New York Times* on the basis of such feelings:

> I was stricken with baby hunger: a passionate, almost physical longing for a
> child. I was determined not to become the woman on the T-shirt who looks

at her watch and says 'Oh, I forgot to have a baby!'. . . I fell hopelessly in love with this tiny new creature, with an intensity that many mothers describe as besotted . . .

In contrast to her position in *The Female Eunuch*, more recently Germaine Greer acknowledged in *The Whole Woman*:

The experience of falling desperately in love with one's baby is by no means universal but it is an occupational hazard for any woman giving birth. Most of the women who find themselves engulfed in the emotional tumult of motherhood are astonished by the intensity of the bliss that suddenly invades them and the keenness of the anguish they feel when their child is in pain or in trouble.

Simone de Beauvoir might frown upon such feelings severely. But if we are searching for an ethical feminism that goes beyond the limits of the sovereign self, and does not flatten life out by bleaching meaning and power from women's experience, then we need to find feminist thinking that can *both* open the realm of the public but also be nuanced enough to accommodate such feelings. No feminism is worth thinking about, it seems to me, unless it is capable of honouring those feelings of preservative love and maternal desire.

In the 1980s, maternal and difference feminists began, in relation to the 'problem' of motherhood, to put the questions differently. Recognising the ways femaleness could be internalised as inferiority, some feminists began reflecting on the implications of female embodiment. They sought to open new ways of being in the world, to explore and even celebrate what being a woman might mean. Many of the contributions concerned a distinctive female sexuality.

In France, the sense of femaleness as subversive, unique and valuable, what being a mother or what embodiment as a woman might mean, was explored by writers such as Luce Irigaray, Hélène Cixous and Julia Kristeva. In their often rather lush prose, the rejection of 'equality as sameness' had a distinctly erotic element. Taking fright at the rather 'masculinised' appearance that briefly symbolised the repudiation of traditional femininity within the women's movement, the new feminists of difference swanned about in defiantly feminine garb. They embraced sexual, physical difference, flaunting femininity and marking their physical differences visually from men. (In contrast, the understated, even dour sartorial ethos of Anglo and American feminists—jeans, no make up, little adornment, cropped hair and so on—reduced visual symbols of male and female difference as an opposite political tactic.) Hélène Cixous flounced into run-down classrooms at the University of Paris VIIIième 'dressed to the nines, complete with ermine coat'. Jane Gallop, an American interpreter of French feminism, vamped it up in lectures on the circuit where academic treatises gave way to a kind of performance art à la Camille Paglia, tottering to the rostrum in 'stilettos, sexy dresses and fishnet stockings'.

The ways that difference feminists thought about the implications of womanly embodiment present a highly interesting—and necessary—contrast with de Beauvoir. Consider for example Irigaray's critique of Freud's misogyny and phallocentrism—the way he adopted the notion of male development as the 'norm' by which female development is judged (and found wanting).

Irigaray argues that Freud did not really allow for two sexes. The phallus, for Freud, is the only organ of significance; a clitoris is an 'atrophied penis', a little girl's masturbation 'phallic'. It is scarcely surprising, therefore, that he makes the astonishing but revealing remark that for a woman, a baby is a 'substitute penis!' All this, Irigaray suggests, comes from the 'problematic of sameness':

> So we must admit that THE LITTLE GIRL IS THEREFORE A LITTLE MAN. A little man who will suffer a more painful and complicated evolution than the little boy in order to become a normal woman! A little man with a smaller penis. A disadvantaged little man. A little man whose libido will suffer a greater repression, and yet whose faculty for sublimating instincts will remain weaker. Whose needs are less catered to by nature and who will have a lesser share of culture. A more narcissistic little man because of the mediocrity of her genital organs. More modest because ashamed of that unfavourable comparison. More envious and jealous because less well endowed . . . A little man who would have no other desire to be, or remain, a man. [Emphasis in the original]

Irigaray, like Cixous, reverses the traditional devaluation of female anatomy. In her often lyrical but diffuse prose poems, the particular qualities of the female body are a metaphor but also lead to a certain mode of being in the world. The 'feminine', for Irigaray, becomes a quite different and subversive kind of consciousness. Cixous goes further. Rather than de Beauvoir's depiction of pregnancy as the mother's bodily ruination and defeat by 'the invading parasite of the foetus', pregnancy is symbolic of the way a female body can hold 'otherness', difference, within itself, without violence.

In Anglo-American societies, too, writers began exploring the moral terrain of the connected self. They moved beyond the celebration of the untrammelled sovereign self by thinkers like de Beauvoir, and began questioning the repudiation of motherhood in feminism. Sometimes described as a period of 'recuperation' within feminist theory, the repudiation changed dramatically to celebration, as 'angry daughters' became mothers themselves.

Central to the new direction was a re-evaluation of the ways in which, traditionally, female culture has carried the value of *caritas*—the Latin word meaning 'loving-kindness'. This 'ethic of care' is, as 'Rabbit' of John Updike's novels puts it, 'that strange way [women] have . . . of really caring about somebody beyond themselves'. Feminist and sociobiologist Alice Rossi, in an essay, 'Eros and Caritas', argues that changing fertility patterns have reshaped sexuality and our sense of our bodies. From a pro-natalist society, where fertility and children were valued, by the last quarter of the twentieth century, Western societies were either neutral or anti-natalist. That meant a dramatic shrinkage of the period of the life cycle involved with reproduction and childrearing, in which attachment, generativity and loving-kindness— 'caritas'—are valued. Instead, the youthful empire of Eros, of sex, passion and infatuation, has vastly expanded. Eros, that quintessential value of the world of the post-modern cowgirl—represented by *Sex and the City*—has triumphed.

Yet it is caritas, Rossi points out, with its values of loving-kindness and attachment, that is the quality needed through the long period of youthful human dependency. Rossi draws attention to the value of caritas: 'charity in the sense of altruistic concern for others on a par with—if not above—concern for self'. Yet the value of caritas is under threat.

As fertility falls and adult lives are less and less tied up with children, the centrality of children to human life diminishes. This, Rossi suggests, is why in the West we have experienced in the last generation a supplanting of fertility images by sexual ones—the replacement of the womb with the vagina as a symbol of feminine sexuality. Likewise, the breast is not the symbol of fertility, like the ancient earth-mother goddesses of old, but of Eros. By implication, women as mothers, and children, face a much more hostile environment, a world impatient with the values of caritas, and infatuated with the power of Eros.

Maternal thinking

Sara Ruddick's *Maternal Thinking* is a philosophical reflection on mothering that goes in a very different moral direction from the celebration of the sovereign self. Ruddick writes very well about not only the ethic of care but also the moral, philosophical and political dimensions of 'maternal thinking'.

Ruddick draws out the dimensions of thought, the moral grammar and the habits of mind emerging from the life practices of mothering. Many mothers, Ruddick suggests, have a special appreciation of the overwhelming responsibility that preservative love presumes. Ann Crittenden wrote:

> Being a good enough mother, I found, took more patience and inner strength—not to mention intelligence, skill, wisdom and love—than my previous life had ever demanded . . . As Ralph Waldo Emerson put it, 'In dealing with my child, my Latin and Greek, my accomplishments and my money stead me nothing; but as much soul as I have avails.'

Joanna Murray-Smith expressed this beautifully; the kind of selfhood we imagine work bestows can also come from the 'voluptuous, ramshackle life' of a mother. Julie Olsen Edwards puts the transformation of self dramatically: 'Pregnancy takes away one's right to suicide. You must take care of a life you birth.'

A world in love with freedom, individualism and achievement is often uneasy with any decentring from self, such as those daily efforts that constitute motherhood, from one often-mundane moment to the next. The ethic of care has always in theory been honoured in motherhood, but such honouring can take a counterfeit, even corrupt form, by sentimentalising it. Worse still is the condescension of a conservative who declares caring to be 'natural' to women, for that suggests effortlessness, not the truth of daily struggle. It is a moral achievement, appearing and vanishing in tiny lived moments, failing as well as succeeding. It is not birth that makes one a mother, for being a mother is not bestowed but earned; one must become one, learning on the job through trial and error, inventing afresh or 'making it up', as Ruddick puts it so well, as one goes along.

In some contemporary feminist writing, there is a powerful impulse to get rid of any obligation or notion of a good or even good enough mother, in order to better compete with men. Maternal feminists like Ruddick, while facing honestly the ambivalence that is often a part of such a powerful attachment, do not flinch from the idea of a good mother. Mothers accept a kind of discipline. We know from the sombre statistics on child abuse that babies can arouse a powerful ambivalence. Shocked by their own capacity for anger or aggression, by their failure to live up to the sentimentalised, greeting-card image of the Good Mother, some women take refuge in arguments that good mothering does not matter.

In contrast, Ruddick does something interesting with writer Julie Olsen Edwards' story. Edwards was shut up in a flat with a baby who never slept and cried constantly. She was driven to the brink of madness, of murderous anger, by sleep deprivation. But Edwards did not succumb. Instead, she boarded a bus, riding around the city all night, fearing to be alone with her baby. Telling the story years later, paralysed by shame, she was freed by the friend who asked the question, 'But what did you *do*?' Ruddick thus distinguishes between what women might *feel* in moments of desperation, and what most *do*, held back by the discipline, their commitment to preservative love. Ruddick says: 'Preservative love cannot alternate evenly with violence or negligence without ceasing to be itself. Although imbued with intense, ambivalent, thought-provoking feelings, mothering is an activity governed by a *commitment* that perseveres through feeling and structures the activity.'

Maternal thinking is the opposite of 'affectless' or emotionless thought. The very closeness and intensity of feelings in the work mothers do, make for the necessity of reflecting on them. The reflective nature of thinking about being a mother, what is required to honour the task, leads in an opposite direction to the image of drowsy sentimentality—the 'becoming a vegetable' which some imperceptive souls warned me would be the ineluctable outcome of motherhood. The fluidity and imperfection of our efforts to realise and grant to the vulnerable what they truly need means an unexamined life is impossible. Someone remarked to me in relation to this book that it was important for mothers to recognise and give weight to what mothering might teach us—and that the daily, visceral, often mundane activity of caring for others could lead to a reflective and intellectual enterprise like writing.

At the centre of preservative love is what Iris Murdoch called 'attentive love'. Yet that scrutiny of a child must not be so close as to prevent them exploring or feeling at home in the world. It must also be tempered by a sense of the limits of one's power, or—Murdoch again—

humility. 'Every natural thing, including one's own mind, [including one's own children], is subject to chance ... One might say that chance is a subdivision of death ... We cannot dominate the world.'

Ruddick often places 'maternal thinking' in a space between two flawed possibilities, showing the suppleness and flexibility of mind necessitated by the care of children. She contrasts the helplessness women can feel in trying to keep children safe in a world beyond their control, with their knowledge that small children must not feel their mother's surrender to a frightening world. Like Spinoza, 'mothers identify cheerfulness as a virtue'. To identify 'cheerfulness as a virtue', however, is not to claim it as an achievement, not to possess it but to strive for it; it comes, like most other maternal virtues, out of struggle, out of a recognition in themselves, often enough, of what is lacking. Maternal cheerfulness is required because with children, no matter what the circumstances, despair is forbidden. It is not a 'cheery denial'—a false degenerative sort that for reasons of self-pride refuses to tell the truth, mystifies reality, forces cheerfulness from children when they feel anguish and sadness. For a single mother who has left a violent relationship to raise her children alone and in poverty, such maternal cheerfulness in the face of life is a kind of courage; the 'matter of fact willingness' 'to start and start over again, to welcome a future despite conditions of one's self, one's children, one's society, and nature that may be reasons for despair ... In circumstances of personal or social disaster that warrant despair, maternal cheerfulness is an extraordinary feat.'

All of us struggle against the flaws in our nature. Almost everyone has encountered mothers who are possessive or over-controlling, demanding more than giving, neglectful more than attentive. And all of us will experience moments where we might display one (or all!) of these unhappy qualities. Yet it is not what we are striving for. So many mothers I have spoken to, or read memoirs by, clearly identify with Ruddick's sense that 'maternal thinking' is, at its deepest, the attempt to be truly attentive to another. It is a 'kind of knowing that takes truthfulness as its aim but makes truth serve lovingly the person known' or 'lets difference emerge without searching for comforting commonalities, dwells upon the *other*, and lets otherness be'. Ruddick draws on Simone Weil: 'The name of this intense, pure, disinterested, gratuitous, generous attention is love', and speaks of Iris Murdoch's sense of the necessity of 'seeing' the narrative, the story, the truth of a child's life, the 'objective reality' 'revealed [only] to the patient eye of love'. It is children seen by that 'patient eye of love' which, in Murdoch's words, 'teaches us how real things [real children] can be looked at and loved without being seized and used, without being appropriated into the greedy organism of the self'. Such 'attentiveness' is the opposite of 'fantasy', the 'proliferation of blinding self-centred aims and images'—for example, basking in the reflected glory of one's children's talents, or pushing them to be what they are not. It is about accepting their difference from oneself, their failures as well as successes. It involves an openness towards another person's reality: 'those little peering efforts of imagination which have such important cumulative results'. In a chapter called 'Fostering Growth', Ruddick comes close to describing what poet Judith Wright called 'enabling love'. Such a love has as its aim the person's eventual independence. It is altruistic because it is a love which, if all goes well, has a kind of ending written into it, a letting go.

Ruddick's 'maternal thinking' exposes a common fallacy: that feminism speaks with one unitary voice denouncing motherhood as servitude. It is important to recognise that one of the deeper reflections in modern times on the nature of mothering comes from a feminist. Motherhood is *not* simply oppression. Ruddick writes of the pleasure children bring:

> To suggest that mothers, by virtue of their mothering, are principally victims is an egregiously inaccurate account of many women's experience and is itself oppressive to mothers. For many women, mothering begins in a fiercely passionate love that is not destroyed by the ambivalence and anger it includes. Many women develop an early sense of maternal competence—a sense they can and will care for their children . . . Many mothers frequently have more control over the details of their work than many other workers do . . . feel a part of a community of mothers whose warmth and support is hard to match in other working relationships. When their children flourish, almost all mothers have a sense of wellbeing.

Meeting General Custer

Watching an interview with Sara Ruddick, I was intrigued to learn that she had an unusually good relationship with her own mother. Deep in the maternal feminist tradition is a very different 'internal working model', as the psychologists call it, of *what a mother is like*.

In much of sameness feminism, psychoanalytically inclined or not, of the 'repudiation of motherhood' ilk, I have to look hard to find women

I recognise. A mother (unless she works) is usually something of a psychological basket case: depressed, passive, helpless, incapable of action, flapping, vague, submissive, a dependent creature, so amorphous that she needs outside forces like the structure of work, or a feminist theorist, to stiffen her spine and pull her into shape. (Thumbnail sketches may be found in de Beauvoir's depiction of a mother as 'more or less infantile herself'.) There is an obsession with individuation and idealisation of separation, and a lot of nervous anxiety that she does not keep her 'boundaries' intact. A clinging vine, the parasitic fig that quietly strangles its host plant. Above all, a mother is a woman in need of fixing.

It is not that I have never met such women, or not known families trapped in the spider's web of guilt she usually weaves around them. But they do not add up to a true portrait of the capable, resourceful, unsentimental mothers (often spouting gallows humour about children and family life) who make up most of the invisible community of parents.

Even in the breadwinner era, when many women were less educated and commanded far less in the labour market, when one consults the work of memoirists and historians one is hard pressed to find these creatures. In an interview with the writer Tim Winton, Andrew Denton asked, '. . . you described the women in your family as fierce. In what way fierce?' Winton replied:

> In my family, the women were the tough ones. They were the organisers. They were the leaders. They were the strategists. They were the pushers, in the sense of the urgers . . . They were like generals and we were just foot soldiers . . . My dad's mum was a wonderful woman. She just organised the family. She organised the suburb. She lived in a tent in the backyard in the inner city in Perth for thirty years. It was a sort of Boer War-era tent under a mulberry tree. And the mulberries used to drop on it and it looked like it had bloodstains—like one of those Civil War medical tents where they used to saw people's legs off—'Oh, stop crying, you sissy!'. . . My father introduced Mum to his mother at the flap of the tent, you know? It was like going to meet Custer. And she was a little like that, you know?

The journalist Rachel Buchanan, writing about the contemporary obsession with the perfect bodies of sports stars, spoke of a body the nation would never celebrate:

> When I think of strength, endurance and beauty, there is one particular body which comes to mind. It is a body as familiar to me as my own breath. My

mother Mary has had eight children, starting way back in 1968. She has been pregnant for a total of five years of her life and has breastfed for at least that much time again. That's twelve years of training, twenty-four hours a day, with little support. For years she walked up the steep hill on top of which we lived, with a child on one hip and another in the pram. She lifted groceries, chopped wood, made furniture and jam, cooked meals, hung out countless nappies and netball socks, pushed cars that wouldn't start, carried sleeping children up the stairs to bed. No woman can do this without being fit and strong, which she is.

Some of our finest and most nuanced historians, like Janet McCalman, Elizabeth Roberts, Kerreen Reiger and Mark Peel, allow their subjects to speak for themselves. The mother who emerges is an altogether sturdier beast than the type of girlish *femininity*—helpless and hopeless—so often depicted during the repudiation of motherhood period.

In McCalman's *Struggletown*, the working-class mothers are the organising authority within the household, with men submissively handing over their wages. Roberts's oral history of Victorian working-class women in Britain gives a nuanced account of their strengths, their ethic of care and the solidarity among them essential to their very survival. In Reiger's sensitive account of the 'forgotten women's movement', the activist mothers fighting for female control over birthing practices and infant feeding impress with their energy, tenacity, capacity for leadership and organisation—thus unexpectedly transcending any stereotype one might have of such 'motherly' concerns. Again and again such accounts show women to be movers and shakers, doers, organisers, ones you could count on when one must pick oneself up off the floor of life and start all over again. This last is especially important, for it is sometimes suggested that mothering and the ethic of care is only a middle-class concern. This is intended as a sneer—luxuries poorer women cannot afford. In fact, it is among the poorer working-class suburbs that 'maternal thinking' and the values embedded in the ethic of care are most valued, needed and put into practice. They are often the difference between surviving or going under.

Strength is also the theme of Mark Peel's delicately judged portrait of 'activist mothers' combating the despair and unemployment in poor Australian suburbs hit by economic liberalisation. 'Activist mothering' is a term coined by a US sociologist, Nancy Naples, meaning 'links they forge between taking care of children and taking care of their communities'. Peel's mothers use the same vocabulary. 'They . . . emphasised mothers' work on behalf of strangers and neighbours, and treasured the arts of mothering. There was a universal regard—among women and men—for the competence of mothers, and great pride in being seen as a "good mum".'

Such women did not share in any desire to dismantle 'oppressive' ideas of good mothering; they were tough on 'bad' mothers. A 'shared pride' in mothering, however, dismantled conservative traditions that tend to stigmatise anyone outside the hallowed circle of virtuous, middle-class, married motherhood. They embraced and supported single mothers, new immigrants, foster carers across different generations. 'Their regard for strong, capable mothers focused less on how you became a mother and more on what you did once you were one.' They built links across ethnicity too—Spanish, Vietnamese, Aboriginal and Anglo—'shared mothering is a powerful bond, and it is no exaggeration to suggest that mothers built the strongest foundations of multiculturalism'.

On one occasion, when I was giving a talk, the discussion afterward sailed remorselessly onward to the usual baby-versus-briefcase dilemmas, with mothering positioned, yet again, as an impediment to the main game of paid employment, when an Aboriginal woman suddenly spoke up. She was bewildered by the implicit disparagement of mothering. 'Our men can't get jobs,' she said, 'and then'—she paused sadly—'*they have absolutely nothing.*' But mothers could still take pride in their work of care for families and community, job or no job. 'Mothering for us,' she said, shaking her head, puzzled at us, 'It's a part of our *strength.*'

Peel records a mother as saying laughingly that 'serious "caretaking" was our feminism'. Again, paid work is neither the centre nor the opponent; sometimes the ethic of care exemplified in their community building is via voluntary work, sometimes paid employment. Sometimes one evolves naturally into the other; work on behalf of communities begins in the home and the neighbourhood network, and becomes paid employment.

Even in very individualist societies it is women who often still give voice and practical expressions to the values of collectivism. We may see here too that what Ruddick's more philosophical investigation calls 'maternal thinking' can be extrapolated and carried over to other mothers, children and their care in very concrete ways. These women focused on collective rather than individual gains and began to think about justice:

the needs of your own children might have been activism's beginning but it spread beyond that to other people's children and then to all the others who were suffering . . . extended forward in time to the mothers who would follow you into the street or neighbourhood and who would be grateful that they didn't have to fight for the things mothers needed to do their job.

Activist mothering 'was strongly reciprocal. They lived in a world of implied and real obligations' which came out of gratitude for the ways such robust social networks had helped them. A widow with six kids after being helped goes on to help other widows; a daughter of alcoholics assists other families in the same boat; deserted wives, single mothers—all had been helped in some way in the past.

One of the social workers commented: 'It's women who have the energy to make a lot of these things happen . . . [and] it's groups of women who really get things going. They're the ones who steer and struggle. Who go on.' Their men spoke of them with profound respect as 'the rocks of this place' and 'the strong ones' and 'the foundations'.

The care penalty

In articulating the value of the 'ethic of care', maternal feminist voices have a different emphasis to conservatism. Conservatives often articulate a nostalgia for the order and grace of a private realm sustained by women's attentiveness, hankering after women's reassumption of complete responsibility for the redeeming joys and tragedies of the private realm—but they do not ever consider ways in which such a world depended on women's inequality and exclusion from the public realm, or the kinds of personal and public costs to women of that work. A traditionalist would see those qualities as particular to women only, as women's distinctive contribution to family and the private realm, bestowed by biology and thus carrying no obligation on men to share them. In a winner-take-all society, where material success, paid work and individual achievement are valued more than anything else, such costs are likely to be felt more sharply than ever.

For that reason it is understandable that some sameness feminists consider that difference and maternal feminists have entered and inhabited a dangerous country. Myra Strober of Stanford University says: 'I just don't see any good evidence for the difference perspective. It glorifies existing stereotypes of female behaviour.' Indeed, if sameness feminism is vulnerable to 'assimilationism', difference feminism is vulnerable to separatism, or relegating women to a separate (and powerless) sphere.

Mothering, as well as other forms of caregiving, does give rise to distinctive kinds of thinking. But like Iris Murdoch, I am dubious about extending such arguments to the special 'gynocentric' knowledge emerging in the wackier reaches of academic feminism. Ideas of a special 'female' physics, 'female' epistemology and so on, Murdoch absolutely rejected:

> Men 'created culture' because they were free to do so, and women were treated as inferior and made to believe that they were. Now free women must join in the human world of work and creation on an equal footing and be everywhere in art, science, business, politics etc . . . To lay claim to a *female* ethics, *female* criticism, *female* knowledge . . . is to set up a new female ghetto . . . It is a dead end, in danger of simply separating women from mainstream thinking of the human race.

Moreover, although difference feminists claim to reject 'essentialism'—they argue that the qualities associated with the ethic of care come from women's *position* as mothers and nurturers of families, not from any *natural* quality of womanliness—there is undoubtedly an uncomfortable proximity of some writers to the nineteenth-century idealisation of 'The Angel in the House'—Coventry Patmore's poem extolling women's 'higher, nobler, gentler nature'. At the very least we should temper such accounts of the female ethic of care with an awareness of recent work on the role of female aggression and capacity for envy within social hierarchies and peer groups. Anyone who has survived high school remembers the distinctive and cruel kinds of bullying and ostracism that girls can deploy.

At its most extreme, the celebration of femaleness can become a morbid kind of reverse sexism. It can carry within it a denigration of all things male: calling fathers 'co-mothers' (as Ruddick does) is a linguistic example of the repudiation of the masculine. In this it hardly differs from sexism, or the sexism implicit in the more strident forms of the repudiation of the feminine in sameness feminism. Even a cursory glance around families, friends and society would convince any fair-minded person that women do not have a monopoly on unselfish behaviour or the ethic of care.

There is a further problem. If women's ethic of care is not part of an 'essential' female nature, but rather evolved from their restriction to an oppressed realm, then women are likely to lose those distinctive and valuable qualities once they are liberated. They may become assertive—and selfish—

individualists of the 'lone cowboy' ethos. Jean Elshtain puts it sharply: 'it is impossible to have it both ways: to condemn women's second-class status and the damaging effects of her privatisation and, simultaneously to extol or celebrate the qualities that have emerged from the sphere women are to be "freed from".'

Mark Peel, more gently, also points to the fact that broader economic changes mean that the ethic of care embedded in the traditions of activist mothering he describes were 'at the crossroads', since 'more and more women needed to or wanted to work for wages, and some had paid work that did not mesh easily with their unpaid responsibilities'.

It is in fact a delicate balance between recognising what has been, and often still is, women's distinctive contribution to community, to family life, and acknowledging its worth, resisting its devaluation, while not forever consigning women to being solely responsible for caring. There is undoubtedly a danger that any assertion of 'difference' can be paraded as justification for entrenched sex roles and women's continued disadvantage as mothers. Men may easily seize upon the idea of 'equality as difference', as something which simply allows lip service to be paid towards equality, while continuing with the privileged position granted by the traditional domestic division of labour.

The writers of *Habits of the Heart* concede claims from maternal or difference feminism that women may have developed, from their work in caring for others, ways of seeing and moral sensitivities that have much to contribute. But they also acknowledge its downside:

> on top of demeaning work and low pay, working wives and mothers come home to families where the men still expect them to do the preponderance of housework and childcare . . . When women are more disgruntled with marriage . . . there is good reason. If women do more of their share of caring for others, it may not be because they enjoy it, but because custom and power within the family make them have to . . . women today have begun to question whether altruism should be their exclusive domain.

To do something about those issues we are going to need something altogether grittier than philosophical investigations into maternal thinking.

Retrieving the value of motherhood and the ethic of care would not get us very far if we only extolled the virtues of what so many mothers, working or not, do. If maternal feminism did not deal with the economic vulnerability of caregivers, or develop a cogent, realisable social policy dimension in response to that vulnerability, it would justly be aligned with conservatism and effortlessly incorporated into the status quo.

Just such a gritty dimension—which spells out an alternative vision of transformation—is supplied by a striking new genre of 'maternal' feminism. In the USA, Caitlin Flanagan remarked in 2004 that maternal feminism was 'hot'. Sometimes called 'social feminism', it *both* revalues the contribution, public and private, that women as mothers and caregivers make, but avoids the high-minded indifference of traditionalists to the injustice which may flow from that contribution being so undervalued in an individualist, market society. More practical and political than difference feminism, it also takes up where sameness feminism leaves off, pondering how to transform the 'overwhelming and systematic evidence' that it is mothers, rather than women in general, who are most penalised economically. Building on earlier maternal feminist arguments, it goes beyond them to make some coherent, cogent policy directions to both record the importance of what mothers do, but diminish, if not remove, the 'care penalty'. And importantly, given Ruddick's arguments about the wider implications of 'maternal thinking', it is developing a new political movement attempting to translate into practical politics the values of 'caritas': the care for others on a par with—if not above—concern for 'oneself', including the care for other people's children, not just one's own, as well as other vulnerable citizens.

4 The invisible heart: the shadow economy of care

'Today patriarchal coercion is unacceptable. On the other hand, pure selfish individualism is both ugly and unviable. Without at least some altruism, we cannot reproduce ourselves. If we believe we have obligations to care for one another, we should decide what these are and how they should be enforced.'
Nancy Folbre

Nancy Folbre begins *The Invisible Heart: Economics and Family Values* with an arresting parable. Some goddesses devise a competition among nations, a kind of Olympics with a twist. 'Health and prosperity for all' will be the prize granted to the nation 'who could collectively run the greatest distance in the shortest time'. But only the goddesses know how long the race will last.

The first nation assumes the race will not last long and sets its members to compete, 'every person for themselves'. Some citizens at first speed away, but as the race goes on, many fall by the wayside. There is no non-competitor off field to care for the sick and the injured. No women have time to give birth, or care for children to replace ageing runners. Before long it becomes clear that this nation will lose the race.

The second nation has divided caring and running according to gender. Men, in exchange for being in charge, run on ahead fast and hard, while women come along behind them, looking after children, the sick and the elderly, as well as those injured in the race. They give birth to new runners to replace those who are exhausted. At first all goes well. Over time, however, women begin to see that the rewards given to the men for running far outweigh those bestowed on caring. They know that many among them could run just as fast and hard as some of the men, and demand equal rights. When the men resist, the women go out on strike, causing chaos. This nation, too, is about to lose.

All eyes turn to the third nation. Like the canny tortoise against the hare, it is making slow but persistent progress. Everyone is required both to run and to take care of those who cannot run. It is less efficient short-term, but as the long race wears on, the strategy is revealed to contain great strengths. While the first two nations have collapsed, the citizens from the third nation grow strong as well as fast, while 'their freedom and equality fostered their solidarity'. Folbre ends mischievously: 'Of course they won the race. What did you expect? It was a race that goddesses designed.'

The shadow economy of care

It is always a sign of the dominance of one sphere of life that we pay homage to the 'higher' by exonerating the 'lower' by pointing to its contribution to the truly valued realm. For that reason I agree with Clive Hamilton's view in *Growth Fetish* that we lose something profound if our various labours of love in the private realm are merely redescribed as a form of 'work'. I am suspicious when discussions of children, who are precious in and of themselves, deteriorate into a depiction of them as 'society's greatest resource' as if they were the equivalent of a dusty pile of coal. Children do not have a 'use value'. The same moral ambiguity may apply to efforts to 'price' motherhood in terms of foregone earnings and missed opportunities. When Ann Crittenden's publisher suggested the title *The Price of Motherhood*, she thought, 'What a terrible title! I love being a mother!' That said, both Crittenden and Folbre's books tell something truthful about going 'down among the children'—the unjust social and economic disadvantages that may flow from that decision, as society is presently structured.

The Invisible Heart has in its title a nice play on the famous book by the classical economist Adam Smith, whose work on the 'invisible hand' of the market has been so influential in our own time. Folbre's focus is all aspects of social reproduction and caregiving—the terrain of the maternal feminists—without which no market work could occur. Folbre is searching for an alternative both to the unfairness of traditional patriarchal society, which assigned women to caregiving whatever their talents and preferences, but also to the individualist 'dog eat dog' ethos that increasingly characterises modern society.

The Invisible Heart builds on an earlier, radical, brilliant book, *Counting for Nothing*, by New Zealand economist and feminist iconoclast Marilyn

Waring. It is human capital, Folbre argues, as does Crittenden—an educated, skilled, disciplined and motivated workforce—which is one of the most important components of national wealth. In 1995, for example, the World Bank estimated that 59 per cent of the wealth of developed countries is embodied in human and social capital. Although many people contribute—grandparents, teachers, fathers and childcare workers—nonetheless mothers usually remain the primary caregivers and the most important influence in the development of children. Folbre examines the public and social goods for the whole community that women's distinctive work brings.

The impulse of mainstream economics has often been to trivialise non-market household production. When Gary Becker, who won the Nobel Prize for economics, first developed the 'Chicago Home Economics School', the professorship was described mockingly as the 'potty' chair. This was the untold story of the dependence of the market realm on the non-market realm that maternal feminists insisted on telling.

Women's unpaid work—Ann Crittenden calls it the 'dark matter in the universe of labour'—makes a huge, unrecognised contribution to economic life. Crittenden cites some examples from the research into non-market productive activity. Duncan Ironmonger's investigation in 1992 showed that at least half of all economic production came from unpaid work within households. The Australian Bureau of Statistics calculated that the value of unpaid work was between 48 and 64 per cent of GDP; while German studies show that up to 55 per cent of GDP occurs within this sector. Maternal feminists like Crittenden emphasise that it is especially important to 'value' such work, for while women are not the only providers of non-market labour, they do more of it than anyone else. Roughly two-thirds of their time is spent on non-market work, and one-third on market work. For men the proportions are reversed.

The devaluing of the 'unproductive' housewife did not come out of thin air. Rather, it emerged from a specific historical moment when men were vacating the household to take up wage labour, which, it was thought, meant that they required the services of a full-time wife and mother. Previously a good wife was considered an economic asset, for the household was once a site of production as well as consumption. Women produced many things we purchase today at supermarkets, pay for through wages, and consume at home. They made soap, candles, clothes and medicines; they grew and preserved vegetables and fruit; they kept hens, cows and goats. They dealt with the vicissitudes of everyday life, caring for young children, the sick and the elderly.

Men, however, had traditionally been responsible for the education and moral training of children. (Men were, even, modern mothers will be amused to know, 'blamed' when a child turned out badly!) As men vacated the private realm to take up often arduous wage labour, women took on the work of educating children to become the well-socialised citizens on whom the modern economy depended. Such an important task could hardly be carried out by the ignorant—hence the schools for girls that sprang up during the nineteenth century, the improvements in women's status and the gradual emergence of equal education. Central was the ideology of separate spheres; men's participation in the brutish world of commerce and industry was to be softened by the 'angel in the house', presiding over the haven in the heartless world.

The first important point to be grasped—and one with implications that reverberate painfully through the tension between work and family to this day—was that the separation of the spheres allowed specialisation and a much more efficient wage labourer. The second is that as men began to work for wages it was that work which was elevated and valued as 'productive'. Women's family labour became 'unproductive'. As Nancy Folbre puts it, 'The moral elevation of the home was accompanied by the economic devaluation of the work performed there.' This was not just a matter of cultural devaluation. The devaluation of the 'unproductive', 'idle' and 'dependent' housewife was written into national accounting systems.

All over the Western world, when the systems of national economic accounts came into being, homemaking, housework and the work of raising children became officially invisible. 'We may assume', asserted the nineteenth-century economist Francis Walker confidently, 'that speaking broadly [a wife] does not produce as much as she consumes.' As Crittenden remarks, 'Even as accomplished and astute a woman as Harriet Beecher Stowe couldn't see through the ideological veil.' In the year in which Stowe moved the household to Maine, she had 'made two sofas, a chair, diverse bedspreads, pillowcases, bolsters, and mattresses; painted rooms, revarnished furniture, given birth to her eighth child, run a huge household . . .' And yet, Stowe confided in a letter to her sister, 'I am constantly pursued and haunted by the idea that I don't do anything.' In Britain, housewives and mothers were classified as part of the 'unoccupied' class, in America as 'dependents'. In Australia the 1890 census also depicted them as 'dependants', along with children and 'all persons depending on private charity, or whose support is a burden on the public revenue'.

As women joined the workforce, the full 'worth of a wife' became more evident. Women with family responsibilities (but without wives!)

often achieve less in the workplace than men with wives. Many more career women than career men are childless. Yet as women's capacity for earning income and their investment in marketable skills increased, so too has the perception that time out from the labour force to raise children is merely 'wasted'. Here is an example:

> As a woman does not work during certain periods, less working experience is accumulated. Moreover, during periods of non-participation, the human capital stock suffers from additional depreciation due to a lack of maintenance. This effect is known as atrophy.

Needless to say, the investment these women make in their children does not count as the development of 'human capital stock'. The devaluing of unpaid work also means that if a mother breastfeeds her baby and cares for it herself it does not add to GDP, but if a mother works and gets a daycare worker to feed the baby it does. Or, as the old economics joke goes, when a man marries his housekeeper the GDP goes down!

Economists' discussions of human capital, maternal feminists point out, do not only emphasise investment in *ones own skills* at the expense of investing in one's children's. They also ignore what we now know about the exceptional importance of good nurturing in the early years before school. Instead, in another nice example of how a mother's work is 'disappeared', many speak as if the only important investment comes from outside institutions, like daycare or school. One Harvard economist cited by Crittenden defined human capital as 'the knowledge and skills that workers acquire through education, from early childhood programs such as Head Start to on-the-job training for adults'. As Crittenden puts it, 'In one stroke, he deletes thirty years of infant research, which shows that beginning education at age five is too late.' Emotional security, the confidence to explore one's world, facility with language and concepts, the fostering of curiosity and desire to learn, the capacity to concentrate and so on, all occur with the help of loving caretakers (especially mothers!) well before formal learning begins. Yet according to the economist, a mother's role in all this is nonexistent.

Two paths to women's equality

Feminists themselves have always been divided on the matter of women's unpaid labour. Some, like Charlotte Perkins Gilman in the early twentieth century and modern contemporaries like Barbara Bergman, have viewed housewives as unproductive and parasitic. Gilman argued that housewifery is 'not productive industry' while an 'unpaid wife' was a 'domestic servant in the extremely wasteful and expensive class of one servant to one man'. 'There is no equality in class', she opined severely, 'between those who do their share in the world's work in the largest, newest, highest ways and those who do theirs in the smallest, oldest, lowest ways.' Gilman favoured the abolition of the patriarchal family and residence in apartment blocks where there could be collectivisation of childrearing and domestic labour. Bergman, a modern feminist, opposes the counting of unpaid work in national accounts. When interviewed by Folbre she snapped: 'Anything which romanticises housework and childcare is bad for women.'

Maternal feminists, by contrast, feel Gilman & co. are guilty of 'throwing the baby out with the bathwater' and feeling a 'profound distaste for family life'. Gilman, suggests Crittenden, erred when she 'lumped the care of the children with all the other menial labor women were assigned, as if childcare were equivalent to dishwashing, and as if women could flee their children as easily as they could run away from dirty laundry'.

For social or maternal feminists like Folbre and Crittenden, this tendency is a kind of thinking 'strangely congruent with that of male-dominated legislatures and courts'. Crittenden points out that there have always been two feminist paths to women's equality:

> The first argued that only one road could lead to female emancipation, and it pointed straight out of the house toward the world of paid work. The second [path] sought equality for women within the family as well, and challenged the idea that a wife and mother was inevitably an economic 'dependent' of her husband. For the rest of the twentieth century the women's movement followed the first path, and it led to innumerable great victories. But in choosing that path, many women's advocates accepted the continued devaluation of motherhood, thereby guaranteeing that feminism would not resonate with millions of wives and mothers.

The marginalisation of mothers in the workplace, Crittenden writes, is usually shrugged off as one of life's inevitable compromises. It is mothers rather than childless women who remain unequal in the labour market. 'We should pay attention to the overwhelming and systemic evidence that mothers can never achieve economic equality in the labour market as things now stand . . . whoever cares for the kids will always get the short end under current arrangements.'

The care penalty in a market society

When everything is for sale, the person who volunteers time, who helps a stranger, who agrees to work for a modest wage out of commitment to the public good . . . who forgoes the opportunity to free-ride, begins to feel like a sucker. Robert Kuttner

When everything is for sale, Nancy Folbre remarks, 'women in particular begin to wonder why so much of the work they do goes unrewarded'. Folbre openly and honestly acknowledges that patriarchy was a reasonably effective means of ensuring, however unfairly, a system of caring for dependents. When we transform patriarchy, then, we must take care how we do it. Feminists, she says, have often fought patriarchy with individualism. The danger is that we will all become too selfish, unleashing the 'war of all against all'.

Individualism as a value system gives men no real incentives to change. Instead, the incentive is to remain competitive in the workplace and in life, by devolving care responsibilities onto others. Yet the needs of the sick, the young and the elderly remain, as well as the ever more demanding workplace, which requires the presence of a player 'off field' looking after the needs of every player 'on field' at work. Women are thus presented with a kind of Faustian bargain: sell your soul to the work ethic and succeed, or continue to honour the ethic of care but at increasing personal cost. The 'care penalty' for doing the right thing by others—the earnings forgone, the opportunities lost, the poverty in old age or in the event of divorce and so on, even the loss of esteem in the eyes of the world—is harsher than ever. A well-educated American woman with a college degree who stays home to look after the kids, Crittenden estimates, can expect to forgo up to one million dollars of potential earnings. And the rewards for behaving selfishly have also escalated.

Reciprocity and altruism, Folbre points out, have always been a part of the care system, between husbands and wives, between the generations—from parent to child and later from adult child to an elderly parent—and also collectively, as in the social provision for childhood, ill health and old age. All care work is based on an implicit 'contract' susceptible to default.

Selfish offspring neglect an elderly parent, children are forgotten by careerist parents, a wife's devotion to family is rewarded in middle age by abandonment and poverty. The caregiving of children can also, writ large, be subject to a kind of societal default. In our market society, Folbre says, children are increasingly treated as 'pets': expensive, time-consuming hobbies of a selfishly individualistic kind, with no larger social purpose. That new thinking has translated into a new, aggressive 'child-free ethos'—the claim that parents and children are parasitic drains on resources provided by those who are childless.

Under threat is the sense of 'generativity', as Erik Erikson called it: that sense of the older generation's gift of time, wisdom and resources to the new. The work of the 'invisible heart' must be enforced by social norms. Such norms have always been hard to enforce. Charles Dickens's novels are full of deathbed scenes where greedy relatives hover and harass the dying. Contemporary economic conditions, however, along with moral individualism, undermine rather than support the norms of care.

Folbre is tough-minded in her exploration of care systems. Built into societies, and individuals, she argues, is not only the capacity for altruism but also the capacity for assessing its cost. Historically, families with large numbers of children have been connected to religious values, affection for children and female inequality, but also to the understanding that adult children, not the state, would support their parents in old age. Virtue is not always its own reward, and those piously recommending that idea are often not those who make the sacrifices! One American survey showed that about two-thirds of carers of the elderly (three-quarters of whom are women) were depressed.

Over 25 per cent of all American workers had responsibility for some kind of elder care in 1996. Those pressures are certain to rise. Folbre points out:

> the supply of unpaid labour for home elder care will soon shrink. Unlike most of the women of my mother's generation, my peers are heavily invested in jobs and careers from which they cannot easily excuse themselves. And many of them live a long distance from their parents. The price of providing care has gone up for them.

That assessment of the cost of caring is contributing to the ever-increasing transfer of family caring functions to the marketplace—the commodification of care. There is, however, a moral limit to this. Commercialising care cannot ensure the loving attentiveness that is embedded in the particularity of love and a shared history. Both Folbre and Crittenden, like many other maternal feminists, emphasise the gift of family time to children, and point to European schemes of parental leave, as well as quality childcare. Such schemes allow for the expression of a mother's intense 'besottedness' with an infant and allow a flexible time for mother and baby to move through that love affair and out into the world. Yet even they tend to sidestep the question of what happens when the impulse and imperatives of the ethic of care collide with the work ethic, or with children's wellbeing. Although Crittenden admitted in an interview to being worried about young infants in daycare, she stoutly maintains throughout her book that high quality care is good for children.

Folbre, however, acknowledges that turning care over to the market—commodifying care—has inherent problems. To begin with, all the assumptions about the well-informed purchaser who can withdraw patronage from inadequate services fall down in the case of caregiving services. If people don't thrive in care, it can be difficult to find an alternative. Care services may be in such short supply, or so expensive, that the purchaser settles out of panic on the first, rather poor option they can find. Then there's what one might call the 'moral hazard' of the commodification solution.

> Even if the actual decision makers have the most exalted motives and want nothing but the best for those dependent on their choices (a dubious assumption in many cases) it is difficult for them to judge the quality of the ensuing care. After all, they are not the ones receiving it . . . in the face-to-face provision of care services with an emotional content, the quality of interaction can vary enormously. And this quality is difficult to assess.

Any attempt to lift the quality of care dramatically lifts the cost of care, since such services are always labour intensive. There are limits to efficiency; care services cannot be standardised or depersonalised without great harm to the person cared for.

More deeply, of course, it goes to the heart of how far any care 'service' can replace the particularity of love. The mother–child relationship is an anti-commodity relationship. Jayne Buxton, author of *Ending the Mother War*, discovered that even with an excellent nanny, her children cared not just for the 'quality of care' but who gave it.

> It was the most enormous shock to me that despite not having been my children's sole carer—which [feminists like] Ann Oakley saw as the root of

children's apparent need for their mothers—and regardless of the fact that my children were cared for from birth by a wonderful nanny whom they adored, it still mattered greatly to them that I was around. It still upset them when I worked too much, and saw them too little. And they regularly expressed their preference that I stay home with them.

Under patriarchy, not just social norms but laws enforced women's dependency. Legislation such as the marriage bar, which banned female employment after marriage, ensured that women were available to care for others. Because women had no other choice, we became accustomed, Folbre argues, to 'free riding' on women's caring labour. We are used to having things done for us, in close to a non-reciprocal manner, for free. We expect this to continue even when women work full-time. Both men and society as a whole, Folbre suggests, have come to like it that way. The problem, however, as the example of elder care shows, is that once women invest large amounts of time, energy and effort into training and investment in skills, we can no longer assume a universal supply of free, caring labour. Too many women find themselves in the grip of the 'nice person's dilemma'. Their sacrifices on behalf of others go unrequited, make them vulnerable to exploitation, and in the event of divorce lead to poverty. Opportunists in an individualist paradise can take advantage of those who are generous and cooperative. In the 'war of all against all,' Folbre sums up, 'nice gals and guys finish last'.

In the short-term, such a society can survive quite nicely. In the long-term many potential caregivers will begin to recognise what is valued, where benefits are directed, and wherein lies the 'care penalty'. There is a real question as to how much of modern society's 'crisis of reproduction', the dramatic decline in fertility, is related to the care penalty. The problem, according to Folbre, is that we are increasingly creating a world not just with a new 'economic environment' but also a 'new social ecology', one where 'individualistic competition for wealth offers no rewards for the work of care'. We must 'distribute responsibilities for care more equally and reward caring more generously . . . [and] show how we might do this—in practice as well as theory.'

Strong mothers equal strong children

A wonderful piano teacher who had taught my girls and already worked full-time one day took me aside and quietly inquired if there was extra work at my daughters' school. She explained: her second child, having just put the family through considerable expense while training as an architect, had decided her passion was natural therapy. The father, who had loyally provided for her through college, now resisted the new demands for continued support. But the mother felt daughter number two had found her true vocation, and on that basis was prepared to take on a third job (on top of catering to family and working full-time) to help her find her way. That mother was prepared to 'go the extra mile' for her daughter to fulfil her talents. It was her skills as a piano teacher, her capacity as a working mother, which enabled her to do so.

Women's tenacity, hard work and drive, and their capacity to put themselves out on behalf of others, may be expressed through resources put at children's disposal via paid work. Maternal feminists like Crittenden nudge the debates beyond the societal contribution of women's unpaid work, to make a very persuasive case that women's paid work can enhance the ethic of care, not diminish it. 'Strong mothers' with a capacity for contributing and controlling some of the economic resources within a family can and do help children.

For this reason, working motherhood and women's economic independence can work on behalf of children within the ethic of care, and need not be lined up against it. Of course resources are shared within families, and many devoted fathers put all their hard-earned money at the family's disposal. However, Lawrence Summers, former chief economist with the World Bank and former US Treasury secretary, has found 'overwhelming evidence that mothers channel much more of their income to expenditures on children than husbands do'.

Those struggling to alleviate poverty in the third world are increasingly taking heed of this divide in male/female behaviour. In Kenya and Malawi, researchers found that the higher the proportion of a household's income controlled by women, the higher the calorie intake of the household and the less spent on alcohol. In Brazil $1 in the hands of a woman has the same effect on child survival as $18 in the hands of a man. In southern India, men retained four to six times as much money for their own personal use as women did.

Crittenden argues that society should ensure that women are not deprived of economic opportunities, and she gives many examples that counter the stereotypes of 'selfish' working mothers and their neglect of their offspring. All this suggests there are great social advantages in protecting women's links to the labour force.

That said, there are clearly situations where work or the work ethic can compete with and win against the ethic of care. Women too can be open to the seductions of putting work first, exhibiting the 'most confirmed habits of cold and revolting selfishness' that Harriet Beecher Stowe thought beset a man 'drawn from the social ties at home and [who] has spent his life in the collisions of the world'.

Maternal feminists also—in a nice but overstated corrective to the 'angry daughters' for whom a mother appears the embodiment of evil— emphasise women's autonomy in making decisions about what a child needs. It is as if mothers will simply know, as oppose to being exhorted and urged by culture and society, how to 'do the right thing'. Many mothers *will and do* make the right decision about children's capacity for independence, and the pace at which it may be pushed. But it is also true that the ethic of care expressed in maternal practices is increasingly contested by the values of a corporate world, which demands that work comes first. In such a world the 'personhood' or development of a child may be contested by, and in competition with, women's 'personhood' and self-development. Children are seen as 'beloved impediments' at best, and at worst, as the Labor politician Wayne Swan once put it, as merely 'lead weights in the worker's saddle bags'.

Arlie Hochschild, undoubtedly one of the most perceptive observers of the feminist revolution, writes in *The Time Bind* of how the emotional magnets of work and home have, for some families, swapped places. Such a transformation has a profound effect on honouring the ethic of care. Although written by a staunch feminist, *The Time Bind* has an underlying theme of growing child neglect. Work, not home, is the dominant culture. Very young children are clocking up extremely long hours from early infancy in daycare, while practices like leaving children 'home alone' are rife. To match such disinvestment of parental time come new ideologies; an emotional asceticism is valued as producing 'independence' and children with few needs of their own.

In one chilling case, Hochschild drives home her point about what happens when both parents put work first. One couple have a child who is an epileptic in delicate health. He wakes up seriously ill, having lost all feeling down one side of his body. Nonetheless, in order to maintain their competitive position at work, they proceed with giving scheduled 'presentations'. The mother leaves him with the babysitter for the husband to take to the hospital after he has finished his presentation. She gives her speech and only then goes to the hospital. By now it is afternoon. So deeply has she internalised the value that work is everything that her deepest concern at first seems more for her 'office persona'—how she will be regarded by letting her personal problem intrude on work—than for her son.

> It upset me that I had to tell my boss my personal problem. Now I know that in his mind I'm a MOM, not an engineer. I dashed to the hospital. Danny was screaming. He'd pulled all the tubing and wires out of his hair. Then they gave him so much medication he fell asleep . . . One of us could have gone back to the office at that point, but neither of us did. Though we felt we should. I hate it that we felt that way when our baby was lying in a hospital bed with something so wrong.

Hochschild reports: 'but the next week Eileen was back at her desk at Amerco.'

Sarah Hrdy puts her finger on the necessary point: the 'problem for mothers (and children) today . . . is that a woman's ambition has to be played out in male-designed realms that have no tolerance for children, putting her toughness, aggression, and zeal to succeed in direct conflict with the young child's need for constant care and attention'.

In public policy terms we need to move to provide the kind of policies as well as workplaces that militate against that trend.

Implementing the ethic of care

> Today patriarchal coercion is unacceptable. On the other hand, pure selfish individualism is both ugly and unviable. Without at least some altruism, we cannot reproduce ourselves. If we believe we have obligations to care for one another, we should decide what these are and how they should be enforced.
> Nancy Folbre

A *Good Weekend* story on motherhood in 2003 told of an Australian lawyer giving birth on all fours while participating by phone in a business meeting, hiding her groans behind the cool composure of econospeak, as if in comparison bringing forth new life 'counts for nothing'. Compare that ethos with maternal feminist Kerreen Reiger's proposal:

> A conception of the 'equivalence' of all citizens is needed, one which does not privilege masculine ideas, but stresses 'equality of capability' and of well-being. Following this, women as mothers, as birth givers, would no longer be second-class citizens judged by masculine norms of workforce and public performance. Equivalence or fairness requires spelling out the particular

needs which arise from lived situations, such as the bearing of children, and thus some special/specific or differentiated treatment. With such a notion of citizenship, though, what is now called difference, whether of pregnant women, the aged ... would not be stigmatised. In effect all citizens have 'specific needs which they are entitled to give voice as part of a genuinely democratic community'.

There are gains for women as maternal citizens when the demands of social feminism are integrated into state policy. What is often not understood is the ways in which clear alternative directions—a social democratic and an individualist one, or one embracing the maternalist ethic of care and the other the hard-nosed ethic of individualism— emerged from the feminist revolution. European 'social feminism' has achieved much more along the lines of respecting women as maternal citizens, with distinctive needs as well as rights in the workplace, than the Anglo-American individualist ethic. It is now very clear that under the prevailing economic and social arrangements, 'equality as sameness' will grant only limited benefits, usually for the privileged few.

As Sylvia Ann Hewlett's *Baby Hunger* revealed, in the USA all too many women face a 'creeping non-choice' between a childless career and a careerless motherhood. They have minimal, unpaid leave. Work and family policies are underdeveloped. Poor women do it tough. Welfare mothers are forced back to work, in some states only twelve weeks after giving birth. With the least generous leave policies in the West, America unsurprisingly has resorted to commodifying childrearing through mostly for-profit daycare centres. Too many infants spend too long in poor quality centres. The marketplace has *not*, except for the wealthy, delivered affordable, high quality care.

The European model is more promising, if not quite the Promised Land. Earlier models of short, paid maternity leave and universal daycare have been replaced by a more progressive and popular alternative: extended parental leave. Mothers or fathers can take up to three years leave but have the right to return to their previous job. Increasingly, in France and Scandinavia, income replacement is offered. Swedish parents have the right to work six-hour days until a child is eight, on reduced salary, which further supports close relationships between parents and children. Such policies bestow the gift of parental time *at the same time* as preserving, via the right to return to one's previous job, labour force participation. This arrangement is most likely to truly accommodate most women's needs during the peak reproductive years.

The achievements are considerable. While no society has been able to resolve the clash between the competing priorities of work and children, in many European nations the bleak choice between career and motherhood is softened. Maternal and child poverty is less of a problem in Europe. In France, apart from free health care, and a year of paid maternity leave, every mother, no matter what her marital status or income, receives an allowance to be spent either on childcare or to replace income while at home with children under three. The earnings differential between childless women and working mothers in France is about 8 to 10 per cent, compared with 20 per cent in the USA, and up to 50 per cent in Great Britain. The child poverty rate in France is 6 per cent, compared with 17 per cent in the USA.

Essentially, European 'social feminism' has created a much more hospitable framework. Caregiving work is better respected and modestly compensated, while the right to paid work, when the most labour-intensive period of early childrearing is over, is held open. Policies such as parental rather than maternity leave allow for caring responsibilities to be shared more equally between men and women. Women's greater labour force participation gives men benefits too; men are much less likely to work punishingly long hours in Sweden or France. Parental leave policies give parents the opportunity to minimise the 'commodifying solution' of early infant daycare or avoid it altogether—but without severing their links with the labour market.

Here, now, is an example of a different pathway towards greater opportunities and justice for women. Here is a possible pathway—a humane maternal, social feminist alternative that offers greater opportunities for women but also supports the values of 'caritas'. It offers the possibility of honouring the ethic of care, rather than arranging our economic life in such a way that the interests of women and children persistently collide; and it goes beyond the moral impoverishment of the sovereign self.

The rise of maternal feminism

Sylvia Ann Hewlett suffered a miscarriage under a harsh 'equality as sameness' regime at Barnard College in the USA. In a striking development, a watershed seminar on maternal feminism was held at that same Barnard College in October 2003. It signalled, at the beginning of the twenty-first century, the emergence of a distinctive maternal feminism from the political shadowlands. It pulled together an unusual group: feminists, child advocates, mothers at home and work/family advocates. Calling for an end to the 'mummy wars' between women at home and women at work, the new maternal feminist movement is trying to achieve better conditions and recognition for mothers both in paid work and as at-home mothers. To create such a rejuvenated feminism, said one of the speakers, this is the 'perfect storm moment'.

That 'perfect storm moment' derives from the stark realisation that 'equality as sameness' has 'got women so far, but not far enough'. It draws into the political mainstream the road as yet not taken within the two paths to women's equality. It represents the desire of many mothers to see the maternal ethic translated into political action. The intention is an alliance—rather than internecine warfare—of mothers at home or at work, in a broad-based coalition, recognising the needs of both groups. Both groups struggle with the devaluation of non-market family labour. We all need greater recognition of the importance and 'worth' of the shadow economy that keeps family and community in good shape, and removal of the care penalty. And we need family and work policies such as parental leave and better childcare that make family life flourish.

It is an attempt to draw together the 'femmes and the tomboys', as Joan Williams calls them, or stay-at-home and working mothers, around areas of common concern over mothers' and children's wellbeing. Already many different national organisations have sprung up across the USA. Each group has a slightly different emotional and moral texture to their pronouncements on motherhood, and different positions along the continuum of androgyny (getting men to share parenting) and matern- alism (arguing for mothers' distinctive contribution to child wellbeing). There is less of a battle over which choice is right and more real bitterness about the hard choices mothers face:

> We like to think that all women have choices today. But what kinds of choices do mothers really have? The choice to work our rear ends off in corporate jobs that refuse viable part-time positions or quit and stay home? The choice to go on welfare after a divorce and then be forced to work at Wal-Mart? The choice to never see our kids during daytime hours or never put our college degrees to work?

Maternal feminists are studiously neutral on the question of work versus home. Enola Aird, one of the new-style maternal activists, was asked in an interview whether she was calling for women to return home:

No. I have been in the paid work force, I have worked at home full-time with my children, I have worked in the paid work force from home. I believe that mothers should be free to make their own decisions about whether to stay at home to care for their children or enter or stay in the paid work force. We must, however, find concrete ways to honour and support mothers and enable mothers—as well as fathers—to spend more time on the vital work of caring for and nurturing children.

Maternal feminists usually argue for a new policy framework that is neutral in terms of the particular choices women make, and allows for and is inclusive of the diverse paths women take on motherhood. That means 'maternal equity' policies—equality of treatment in or out of the labour force. For example, in Scandinavia, policies slanted towards working mothers have given way to fiercely neutral ones—parents may take a period of job-protected leave and an allowance to the equivalent value of a government-funded childcare place.

Although it has an essential economic and practical component to its thinking, ultimately this new maternal feminism does not rely on the unacknowledged contributions of women's caregiving work. It is a far more radical challenge. As Aird puts it:

> We will work to create a movement that goes beyond the current 'work and family' debate to a larger, more searching, 'culture and family' debate. We want to transform our culture so that the values that so dominate our lives, the values of the money world—radical individualism, relentless work, the quest for material success, and speed—yield ample room for the values of the mother world—care, connectedness, interdependence, and the other values necessary for nurturing human beings and building human relationships.

In some ways maternal feminism is more radical, seeking more profound structural change, than 'equality as sameness' feminism, which seeks to accommodate women to the rat race by minimising their family baggage. It is also easy to see why, during the resurgent period of free market ideals, the feminism which attempted to assimilate to the male life pattern as the norm, and which emphasised material success, paid work and a place in the marketplace, was the voice selected as representative of all women's interests. This voice was most compatible with the New Capitalism. Why else, when so much of feminist thought has moved on so decisively, does the accepted voice of women's rights still reflect a feminism frozen in time, somewhere circa 1970, from the 'repudiation of motherhood' period?

Only by understanding the values of the new capitalism can we begin to grasp why one strand of feminism, which was in touch with only a minority of women's preferences, came to dominate.

The maternal feminists' renewed emphasis on improving the conditions of motherhood, whether at work or at home, is supported by empirical evidence on women's behaviour and preferences after the equal opportunity revolution. Post-feminism, women's lives have not converged. Instead, women have continued to make different choices—sometimes radically different—about how one should live.

5 What do women want?

'Difference and diversity are now the key features of the female population . . .
And in a civilised society difference and diversity are positively valued.'
Catherine Hakim

Let the question rest with women themselves

John Stuart Mill, in his classic nineteenth-century statement of liberal feminism *On the Subjection of Women*, points out that what society, or men, traditionally interpreted as the 'nature of women' was an 'eminently artificial thing':

> the result of forced repression in some directions, unnatural stimulation in others. It may be asserted without scruple, that no other class of dependents have had their character so entirely distorted from its natural proportions by their relations with their masters.

To symbolise what patriarchal society does to women, Mill uses the evocative metaphor of a tree, of which one part is placed in a vapour bath, in the hothouse of intensive cultivation, while the rest languishes in the snow, any new delicate shoots burnt off by frost. Mill says parts of women's nature appear better developed, like their capacity for domestic life, because they are the only capacities so cultivated, while possibilities of achievement and education lie untended and unnourished in the wintry air. Yet 'with that inability to recognise their own work . . . [men] indolently believe the tree grows of itself in the way they have made it grow . . .'

The general opinion of men of that time was that a woman's natural vocation was that of wife and mother. Yet, since so many of society's laws were directed at preventing alternatives, patriarchal society was really acting as if motherhood were *not* their nature. Thus Mill wants someone to put the doctrine plainly. 'It is necessary to society that women should marry and produce children. They will not do so unless they are compelled. Therefore it is necessary to compel them.'

Mill puts forward his perception of how, under conditions of freedom, the matter of the way women live should be settled:

> For according to the principles of modern society, *the question rests with women themselves—to be decided by their own experience, and by the use of their faculties* . . . if women have a greater inclination for some things than others, there is no need of laws or social inculcation to make the majority of them do the former in preference to the latter.

How women are to live *rests with women themselves*. We should certainly be aware of those barriers created by traditionalist expectations, and be attentive to the ways that women, as they attempt to forge new life paths in the workplace and public realm, continue to 'sail into the headwinds of culture,' as American feminist Joan Williams puts it so nicely. But traditional norms are by no means the only force buffeting women. There is also a powerful tailwind emerging from the new economy. It requires a radically different family constellation to the old—two incomes to buffer against risk and maximise consumption—and shares an emphasis with equality feminism on paid work as the chief locus of fulfilment and meaning—the new 'natural' preference.

I can say with certainty after reading hundreds upon hundreds of articles and books by middle-class sociologists, writers, journalists, economists, politicians and bureaucrats, that the bulk of educated opinion no longer stands behind women's domestic or childrearing activities. Rather, that domain more likely brings disdain, denigration, even contempt. As one American commentator, David Gelertna put it, modern society has lined up in 'overwhelming force behind working motherhood'. Our devaluation of motherhood is now so deep that women for whom mothering is a central life goal have to keep alive the importance of what they are doing, as a desert dweller keeps alive a conception of a lake.

In such a society what is considered 'natural' to women may be just as distorted as in John Stuart Mill's time, opening some doors while closing off others. We can, for example, come to believe that a simple reversal of the old values and priorities will represent what women want, rather than listen respectfully to women's own voices. It is possible to arrive at a society where the 'hothouse vapours' are applied to the fanning of one kind of development, letting only those shoots bearing the titles of paid work, monetary success or public, competitive achievement, grow to flourish. Meanwhile, those tendrils marked motherhood and children wither on the vine, to fall on parched and dusty earth, receiving no sustenance, no nourishment, no answering, commending echo in the society around them.

We can develop a society that still does not *let the question rest with women themselves*, but continues to distort women's sense of themselves and what is valuable or desirable about them for its own ends. Like the tree in the Millsian metaphor, women's lives are still twisted into a shape not of their own making.

Forgotten women

After becoming mothers, many of my university-educated peer group returned relatively early to well-paid, high-status jobs. Work was central to their identity. Childlessness or one child were common, the use of child-care both the norm and, publicly at least, unquestioned. Emotional static clung to the question 'What do you do?' the way synthetic clothing sticks to skin in a thunderstorm.

Many books, articles and newspaper columns of the 1980s and 1990s were written for this group, highlighting real and often painful dilemmas: baby versus briefcase, work versus family. Often the impression given in such writing, however, was that few of us existed outside the fast lane of the freeway of modern life represented by the dual career couple. One such article in 2002, entitled 'Mum, Dad, and nanny makes three', claimed that 'nannies are increasingly being seen as the best child-care option for the modern Australian family'. In reality, a tiny 0.24 per cent of families used nannies. The assumption of equality feminism that women want to work, preferably full-time, and therefore will need childcare from their babies' earliest infancy, represents the preferences of a small minority of women *in any society, even when state polices have explicitly attempted to enforce working motherhood.*

Settling in the outer suburban rural fringe, I discovered that outside the fast lane was a whole countryside, separated from my peer group in temper, priorities and values. Observing and coming to profoundly respect those I came to call 'forgotten women', sometimes I felt as if I was in a different universe.

If for the first group the word 'work' had a hallowed, sacred ring to it, for the second it was the words 'mother' and 'family' that carried more emotional weight. These women were impressive in quite different ways from my peer group. They were the lynchpins of volunteer labour. They raised funds and worked for preschool committees, playgroups, school canteens, and local sporting and community projects. If they were employed it was for short hours, often at low-paid and low-status jobs. Others, wives of electricians or plumbers for example, would be registered in the statistics as 'working' because they did the 'books', managing the accounts for their partner's trade or business. Yet others were enterprising small businesswomen running operations from home. Primarily, however, they were mothers. Most importantly, it was usually the nonmarket family work that provided the centre and meaning of their lives. Many had at least two or three children, and some many more. The question 'What do you do?' was irrelevant. It took me several years of participation in community groups before anyone asked me what I 'did'. They knew what you did. You were part of the invisible community, putting your shoulder to the wheel of parenthood.

Given the contemporary emphasis on the benefits of paid work, as well as my own preconceptions, I often tried a simple thought experiment. If these women changed their lives to be more work-centred—using childcare and working full-time—would it make their lives better?

It would be false to say that work meant nothing to them. Work bestowed adult status, contributed some income over which they had autonomy, and gave a welcome break from the kids. It boosted household income and helped to fulfil some specific family goals. However, for most, to work full-time, uninterrupted, would have diminished their wellbeing. Their chief pleasure in life was their children.

There was another group of 'forgotten' women. When I published my first essay on motherhood in *Quadrant* magazine, it aroused a passionate, intense, private correspondence. Many letters, from across the political spectrum, came from women as if from a post-feminist samizdat. These were women who wanted to 'have it all', as the saying went—simply not all at once. Many were relieved that I was speaking of feelings that were outside the orthodoxy. Especially if they were feminists they felt troubled, confused, admitting in what sounded like subversive whispers to feelings about motherhood that could not be contained within the iron grid of ideology. One letter writer shared the care of her young daughter with the father:

People often say to me that it must have been wonderful that Jack took unpaid leave and cared for Emily during the second year of her life. On the one hand, this option was infinitely better for Emily than being in institutional childcare. Nor would I ever want to diminish the value of that year for either for her or for Jack. However, for me, it was very difficult. I was in the luxurious position of having no concerns about her care and welfare. Yet, at work it felt completely wrong for me to be away from her. This was an experience I felt bodily which overrode any intellectual arguments to the contrary. Like many other aspects of motherhood, I was totally unprepared for this. I can only assume that there are countless 'working mothers' who are consumed at work by an overwhelming longing for their babies . . .

Cathy Sherry, a talented young Sydney lawyer and feminist activist for daycare during her student days, found her preconceptions dissolve on becoming a mother.

When I held my first daughter in my arms, my ideas were turned on their head. I suddenly discovered that I belonged to a large proportion of women who feel passionately about motherhood; for whom their children will always be the most important part of their lives; who find the prospect of leaving their babies and young children with a carer they do not know physically and emotionally distressing. I discovered that the ferocious desire to care for your own children has no correlation to educational level, intelligence or political convictions. Often, educated, left-wing feminists with many life options want to be mothers while they have the chance.

Most of my correspondents intended, in time, to go back to work. For some, that work was also experienced with passion, as a vocation; but it was one that just for a time they wished to delay. Sherry wrote in that same article:

Work is still important to me. I laughed with recognition when I read a recent essay by fellow . . . writer Joanna Murray-Smith. She wrote, 'I play with the baby then put him to bed and run to the desk. I need him to sleep in order to write, but curiously the intensity of love keeps my mind sharp.' That sounds familiar.

They would agree with Anne Roiphe in her memoir *A Mother's Eye*, who observed with wisdom that this period of intensity will come to an end; and when it does it is 'better not to have the sum of one's worth in the bank of motherhood'.

Listening to women: the Hakim thesis

Feminism gains its moral authority from being universal—from speaking on behalf of *all women*. It loses its moral power if it is revealed to be acting mainly or exclusively on behalf of sectional interest groups: for example, if a highly educated, high-earning elite group interprets and insists on behalf of other women what their interests might be.

Cultural or post-modern feminism has long recognised that differences between women—rich or poor, black or white, lesbian or heterosexual—are often as important as the similarities. Catherine Hakim has taken that theme—differences among women—along a new path. Hakim's specialty is the sociology of work and, in particular, women's employment. A decade of working in the British Department of Employment as a labour market analyst persuaded Hakim that the facts radically contradicted what had become a 'monolithic consensus': that the rate of women's participation in paid work rates was climbing, that all women wanted to work, preferably full-time, and that the only barrier to them doing so was discrimination or the absence of childcare. Prior to that experience, Hakim, herself both childless and work-centred, accepted all the key tenets of the prevailing zeitgeist: 'We all believed it. It was a completely taken for granted assumption that the only thing that held women back from the labour market was discrimination.'

Hakim caused a minor academic thunderstorm when she gave a paper called 'Five Feminist Myths about Employment' at the London School of Economics. 'The room was overflowing, people were hanging out the windows,' she later recalled. It was published as a controversial article in the *British Journal of Sociology*, and no less than eleven feminists attacked it in the following issue.

Hakim questioned all the prevailing assumptions about women's work. She debunked the widespread conviction that men's and women's roles were becoming more symmetrical, with both partners in the labour force, and that women were converging on one desirable, homogeneous pattern—combining work and motherhood. Hakim's challenge to that thesis was based on its 'failure to predict.' It simply did not explain conflicting international data on contemporary women's preferences and behaviour.

In her landmark book *Work–Lifestyle Choices in the 21st Century*, Hakim refined and developed her thesis, based on 'hard hat' empirical work on women's preferences, pulling together a huge range of international data, including those regimes in Scandinavia and Eastern Europe which had promoted working motherhood. Grudgingly, even some of her critics began to admit the strength of her case. Professor Peter Elias, one of those who attacked her initial article in the *British Journal Of Sociology*, declared it 'the most important synthesis of women's work I have read this decade'.

Women's preferences in the new scenario

Hakim's argument is as follows.

We live in 'a new scenario'. This new scenario was ushered in by five transformations affecting modern Western societies. First, the equal opportunities revolution abolished the legislative framework that had engineered the breadwinner/homemaker family. Second, with the contraceptive revolution, control of fertility passed from men to women. Third, the decline of manual labour and the rise of the white-collar sector increased the number of jobs that suited women. Fourth, labour market deregulation increased part-time work, enabling women to work as secondary earners. Lastly, in the modern sensibility, inventing one's own life occurs in a world with 'no universal certainties' and 'no fixed model for the good life'.

The new scenario, a 'radical break with the past', means modern women not only face genuine choices about how they will live their lives, but make very different choices. The 'crucial finding' of systematic empirical work shows women's preferences are not homogenous but heterogenous; not the same but different, sometimes radically different, from one another. The capacity for *some* women to make radically new choices does not prevent others making different, autonomous choices.

Pulling together a huge range of international research, Hakim identified three broad preference groups. They exist in all societies. The first group consists of work-centred women, for whom paid work or competitive endeavour in the public realm is the chief source of meaning, pleasure, identity and honour. Depending on whether state policies support or hinder them, they constitute between 10 and 30 per cent of all women. It is here that voluntarily childless women with a single-minded career focus are concentrated. This group also includes mothers who demonstrate new levels of continuous work commitment, return earlier after childbirth, are orientated to career success, and have an attachment to the labour force that represents a qualitatively different attitude from the past. Their attitudes are much closer to or even identical with those of career-focused men. Among this group the much-vaunted 'baby versus briefcase' dilemmas are located.

The polar opposite—also constituting between 10 and 30 per cent of all women depending on government policy—are home-centred women, for whom family life is the chief source of pleasure, identity, meaning and honour. In their life histories and expressed preferences, even before marriage or children, home-centred women show little desire for employment, working little or not at all unless they have to. They often have larger families.

Hakim offers a higher and lower estimate according to whether women's preferences are supported or denied by government and the broader culture. Societies in which the lower estimates, of around 10 per cent, hold good, give some women's preferences little or no support, whether we are talking about childless career women under the old gender regime, or homemakers in Sweden's new regime.

Between 60 and 80 per cent of women fall into the third and largest group, which Hakim calls 'adaptive'. 'Adaptive' women shape their working life around the demands of family life. They have multiple goals and want the best of both worlds. Very responsive to different family policies, they usually seek to combine work and family in two clear patterns. Some combine work and family across the life cycle by doing it in sequence—a substantial work or career break followed by gradual re-entry. Others do so by combining work and family throughout, taking some leave and working part-time while children are young.

Hakim is not arguing—as some critics have suggested—that *only* preferences determine women's lives. The conditions of individual lives—whether or not a long-term partner is found, broken marriages, supportive or unsupportive partners, inflexible workplaces, good or bad policy frameworks, unexpected pleasure or dismay on motherhood—can all shape whether or not women's preferences are fulfilled. A significant proportion of women *do* want a life very close to the old male career pattern. For the first time in human history, such new ambitions are possible. What the evidence doesn't support, however, is the notion that a life where paid work is the *central life activity* is a *universal desire of all women*. For that reason, structural and attitudinal constraints are not the *sole* reason why women's lives still do not conform to the old male norm. Rather, many women still feel the pull of family, to the extent that they shape their lives around it.

In the new scenario, Hakim maintains, preferences become very important. After the equal opportunities revolution in a diverse, pluralist society, women have different values, different ways of seeing motherhood and careers, different ways of being in the world, and different life pathways.

Revolution? What revolution?

Central to Hakim's argument was a re-evaluation of the evidence about the rising number of women in paid work. Invariably, newspaper and academic articles trumpeting revolutionary change, and supposedly showing women's newfound attachment to the labour force, rely on the dramatic surge in women's workforce *participation rates.* Hakim is scathing about those writers who rely on data which use employment figures as vague and imprecise as 'more than one hour a week' to describe women's supposedly new-found attachment to the workforce. Such statistics are not nearly sophisticated enough to cater to the complexities of the new scenario and give a seriously misleading account of many women's priorities. Partisan scholarship inflates the ranks of women who seem 'work-centred' by including, wrongly, those whose attachment to the labour force is intermittent or even marginal. This lumps childless career women working eighty-hour weeks together with mothers working a couple of hours weekly while Dad minds the kids.

For example, the high-profile demographer Professor Peter McDonald, an advisor on the Australian Labor Party's 2004 tax and family policy, argued that Australian women's new-found attachment to the labour force justified scrapping an existing allowance to mothers at home, with assistance concentrated instead on dual-income families. His analysis relied on the rise in female labour market participation rates, from 43 per cent in 1979 to 55 per cent in October 2004.

Considering *the hours worked,* however, the Australian evidence is disconcerting for those declaring that tomorrow is already here. Professor Bob Gregory reported in July 2001 that the proportion of women in full-time work was similar to thirty years ago. In 2002, 47 per cent of working women are part-time. Only 22 per cent of partnered women aged thirty-five to thirty-nine worked full-time, compared to 78 per cent who worked part-time (39 per cent) or not at all (38 per cent). In 1998 only 8 per cent of employed mothers (not counting the half already out of the labour market) took six weeks of leave or less. In 2004, when the youngest child is aged under five, 49.8 per cent of mothers are in work, while the rest are at home. Two-thirds of those employed mothers of preschoolers worked part-time. On average, in 2002, part-timers worked sixteen hours a week.

The hours of formal childcare used in 2002 were modest and underline my points above. There are more children outside formal care than in such care. Only 7 per cent of babies under one were in formal care, down from 9 per cent in 2000. Among 0–4 year olds, 23 per cent of children were in long daycare, 6 per cent in family daycare. While slightly more children aged 0–12 attended childcare in 2002 (including before and after school care), the hours are modest and have not increased since 1993. The Bureau of Statistics reported:

> In both 2002 and 1993, 44 per cent of children in formal care received less than 10 hours per week of care, with a further 34 per cent receiving 10–19 hours. A relatively small proportion of children in formal care (9 per cent) received thirty hours or more care per week in 2002, down from 12 per cent in 1993. The median weekly hours of formal care in 2002 was twelve hours. Hours of care were higher for children in long daycare (a median of sixteen hours per week) than for children in before/after school care (four hours).

Australia is not untypical. Lisa Belkin, in a much discussed 2003 *New York Times* article, showed the complex reality behind high US female participation rates. New mothers returning to work fell from 59 per cent in 1998 to 55 per cent in 2000. Children cared for by at-home mothers increased 13 per cent in less than a decade.

> Look . . . at the Stanford class of '81. Fifty-seven percent of mothers in that class spent at least a year at home caring for their infant children in the first decade after graduation. One out of four have stayed home three or more years. Look at Harvard Business School. A survey of women from the classes of 1981, 1985 and 1991 found that only 38 per cent were working full-time . . . [Of] professional women . . . Between one-quarter and one-third are out of the workforce, depending on the study and the profession . . . Look, too, at the mothers who have not left completely but have scaled down or redefined their roles in the crucial career-building years (25 to 44). Two-thirds of those mothers work fewer than forty hours a week—in other words, part-time. Only 5 per cent work fifty or more hours weekly.

None of this is to deny the very real, even dramatic change among *some* mothers, especially those with high incomes, or with one child and a strong employment orientation. In 2000, of Australian families with incomes of over $2000 per week, 52 per cent used formal care, while 61 per cent used informal care. These forms of care can be used simultaneously—nanny care plus preschool for example. Or, to put it in Hakim's terms, the clear emergence of early return patterns among a minority of work-centred mothers of preschoolers is not a universal trend.

Hakim is *not* arguing that there is no change in women's work. Rather, she paints a more complex, fine-grained, accurate portrait, which recognises the real diversity in women's lives, and the continuing centrality of family for many. Hakim notes that it is 'foolish to assume that women's employment patterns necessarily reflect their preferences'. The largest single mismatch between desire and reality occurs between women in full-time jobs who want part-time work, while the best match is for those who are already working part-time.

What do women want?

Hakim argues that the answer to the question: 'What do women want?' is to be found in an extensive range of international data on women's preferences. Instead of elites imposing their own work-centred priorities on women, as universal and 'natural' desires, policy makers should 'ask them' what their priorities are and 'start taking them seriously when they tell us'.

Cohort studies following women's expressed preferences and behaviour over several decades show that their priorities are usually established early in life and remain reasonably consistent over the life course.

Home-centred, work-centred and adaptive women differ in their degrees of work attachment. A recent British survey found the highest percentage of employed women (63 per cent) among those expressing work-centred preferences. Adaptive women, who by contrast want a balance between family and work, are employed mainly part-time. Only around one-third of adaptive and home-centred women have full-time jobs. The majority of work-centred women are single; while the majority of home-centred and adaptive women are married or cohabiting. Fertility rates are higher among adaptive and home-centred women. In Australia, in the wealthy inner-city suburb of St Kilda, where childlessness and career women are common, the fertility rate is 0.8 children per woman.

In working-class, outer suburban Broadmeadows it is more than two children per woman.

The three main models of family life—egalitarian, traditional or compromise—attract no overwhelming consensus. Repeated Eurobarometer surveys show support for all three. 'With the possible exception of the homogeneous and hegemonic small Nordic countries, no single model of the family and sex roles attracts majority support in any European country.' Anglo-American liberal nations like Australia, Canada, New Zealand, the UK and the USA, have the *most* pluralistic, diverse and heterogenous attitudes to sex roles.

Surprisingly, more men than women favour completely symmetrical or egalitarian roles. Equally strikingly, for women the compromise position—of working as secondary earners while maintaining responsibility for family life—gains the highest individual support. This is especially true of married or cohabiting women.

Nor over the decades has there been any straightforward, uniform trajectory of opinion indicating ever-increasing support for more symmetrical roles for men and women. More usually, there is a honeymoon of enthusiasm, followed by a modest decline in support—possibly as parents discover just how difficult 'juggling' children, the second shift and full-time work for both partners really is.

Hakim challenges the 'equality as sameness' feminist assertion that work and public achievement is somehow intrinsically superior to work within the family. Entering imaginatively into the world of those living very different lives, Hakim says that for less educated women 'the birth of a baby . . . can give women as much joy and power as gaining an educational qualification'.

Noting that most 'adaptive and all home-centred women want to care for their children themselves, even if they also do a part-time job later on,' Hakim suggests policies like those of the maternal feminists; they should get 'public recognition for the family work they do' and some financial compensation: 'ultimately we have to pay all full-time mothers a wage for their time and efforts while their children are small.'

Barbara Pocock, author of *The Work/Life Collision*, makes the valuable point that the 'adaptive' group is complex, with women centring their main energies on family or work depending on their stage of the life cycle. 'Adaptives' can include women who are 'interrupted career women' —that is, who take time out but maintain strong employment and career goals as children get older, and those for whom employment always remains secondary. It also includes 'egalitarians', who don't accept the traditional sexual division of labour, but who share both income-earning and parenting. Ann Crittenden cites US polls over a number of years at America's Williams College, which found that women wanted 'marriage, children, a husband who shares childrearing and a fulfilling career on a part-time basis while the children are at home . . . They did not want themselves or their spouse to miss the parenting experience.' The women overwhelmingly wanted to work part-time while the children were under five. But they wanted their partners to do so too.

Preferences on caring for young children

The international data show a mismatch between parental preferences and the policies favoured by elite policy groups with respect to childcare. Hakim says 'research reports and policy papers of international bodies such as the European Commission (EC) and the International Labour Office (ILO) repeatedly endorse the proposition that *all* women want to work continuously throughout life'. Such elites favour the path preferred by *a tiny minority of any country*—full-time daycare and full-time work for mothers. Yet most parents are cautious or opposed to long daycare for the very youngest children. They favour full-time mothercare, or at most part-time work. Concern over infant and toddler care and majority preference for home care for the youngest children are universal—in *every* country where information is collected. To put the point even more bluntly: if the trajectory of public policy pushes families towards institutional childcare and punishes parental care, it is in clear violation of the principles of a democratic state.

Eurobarometer surveys have revealed strong preferences—over 70 per cent and in some countries over 80 per cent—for a mother's care for pre-school children. Over 80 per cent of French parents preferred financial support for home care rather than expanding childcare. Where maternal equity policies have been introduced in Scandinavia, giving a choice between home care allowances with job-protected leave, or a childcare place, they have been hugely popular. It is also an interesting indication of women's preferences. By the mid-1990s, three-quarters of Finnish women used home care allowances in preference to a childcare place.

Such results are consistent with recent Australian opinion data collected for the International Social Survey Program, a sophisticated survey in which questions approach the issues from different angles.

Reported in 2001 by Mariah Evans and Jonathan Kelley of the University of Melbourne, the survey showed 'a widespread preference for staying home' with preschoolers. Seventy-one per cent thought women should stay home, 27 per cent thought they should work part-time, and only 2 per cent believed women with children under six should work full-time. When asked to rate their *personal* preferences on working or staying home with young children (a different approach to the question above which uses the normative word 'should'), over 81 per cent gave strong and warm responses to staying home, and only 9 per cent gave warm responses to the idea of full-time work.

Reservations about early childcare are not part of a general disapproval of working mothers. More than 80 per cent of respondents in 2001 endorsed the view: 'I approve of a married women earning money in business and industry, even if she has a husband capable of supporting her.' Australians also have a healthy respect for the economic advantages that a working mother may bring. They 'widely endorse the idea that maternal employment is, in general, a major contribution to the family.' A clear majority agreed with the statement: 'A working mother can establish just as warm and secure a relationship with her children as a mother who does not work.'

However, only 30 per cent of Australians surveyed were in favour of full-time work for both parents. In 1984, 70 per cent agreed with the statement: 'It is more difficult to raise children successfully when both parents work full-time', and in 2001 'opinion on this issue is essentially unchanged'. Evans and Kelley conclude: 'Australians perceive the combination of successful mothering with substantial work commitment as possible, but a major struggle.'

For mothers of school-age children, employment is also the most widely held ideal, although part-time work is preferred by 75 per cent. Full-time employment is the ideal after children leave home. All in all, most Australians endorse as an ideal not the homemaker or work-centred life path, but the adaptive one.

Almost all of the concern over mothers working, then, is centred on the youngest children. About half of respondents agree with the statement 'A pre-school child is likely to suffer if their mother works', about one-third disagree, and just under one-fifth 'sit on the fence'. There was little change from 1989/90 to 2001. On childcare, the survey showed Australian concerns centred on teaching, attention and affection they thought might be missing: 'Only about a quarter of the population feel that little children get enough affection in daycare centres.' Given the opinions above on the financial benefits of working mothers to a family, as Evans and Kelley suggest: 'they know that forgoing income to devote time to childrearing is a major financial sacrifice. That makes it all the more impressive that large majorities think it is best for women to stay home with their small children.'

International data now consistently show only small variations on those themes. A survey of American parents in the year 2000 found two-thirds 'disagreed with the notion that the care children receive even at a "top notch daycare centre" is just as good as that they get at home with a parent'. Likewise, Newspoll data in 2001 showed 76 per cent of Australians believed children are better off at home with a parent than in paid childcare.

Helen Wilkinson of the British progressive think tank Demos, noting similar British attitudes, has argued that since attitudes to working motherhood radically change with older children, cautious attitudes towards childcare may represent 'perceptions of young children's needs rather any traditional attitudes'. Given the majority preference for home care for children in the early years it is, as Evans and Kelley have suggested, unconscionable in a democracy not to give this choice equal support.

Maternal depression

It is often argued that women must work because staying at home makes them depressed. Jessie Bernard's extraordinarily influential 1972 book, *The Future of Marriage*, argued that in marriage women's mental health declined, while men's improved. Marriage was good for men, Bernard concluded, but 'being a housewife makes women sick'. If this is true then there is reason for opposing the free play of preferences.

A study published in 2002 for the Australian Institute of Family Studies by sociologist David De Vaus showed that almost none of Bernard's propositions stand up in the light of contemporary data. De Vaus examined the 1997 National Survey of Mental Health and Well-being of Adults, the largest study of mental health ever conducted in Australia. As De Vaus pointed out, it offered a superb opportunity to test the Bernard thesis.

Married men and women were the *least likely* of any group to suffer mental health problems (around 13 per cent). Far from being a 'risk factor for depression' for women, marriage was a *protective factor* for mental health. Married women *do not* have worse mental health than married men. Their rates of disorder are the same, although women are more likely to suffer from anxiety or depression, men from substance and alcohol abuse. Married women have better, not worse, psychological health than unmarried women.

Being single, rather than being married, or working or not working, is the strongest risk factor for mental health problems for *both* sexes. Twice as many divorced women, or 22.3 per cent, suffered from an anxiety disorder, compared with 11 per cent of married women. Single, childless working women have almost double the rate of emotional disorders as married working mothers. De Vaus concluded: 'Workforce participation and the absence of children and marriage is associated with considerably greater risk of mood, anxiety, and substance use disorders among women.'

If suburbia was a graveyard of housewives' souls, Bernard thought children finished a woman off completely, delivering the final 'coup de grace'. Married full-time mothers, then, should be the sickest group of all. Yet this group is *much less at risk* of emotional disorders than any unmarried group, including working and non-working lone mothers, and single, childless, working women.

With regard to maternal depression, it also appears crucial to respect preferences in the new scenario. The careful studies of depression by George Brown and his colleagues, reported in the 1990s, showed part-time work to be a protection against depression. Mothers who were full-time in the workforce and mothers full-time at home showed equally high rates of depression, while solo mothers only developed depression if they worked full-time. Yet the truth is even more complex than that. Brown and his colleagues concluded that depression was least likely to occur if women were able to fulfil their preferences to work or not. Thus social policy should aim to help them to fulfil their desired role.

The failure of social engineering to alter women's preferences

It is often argued that discussions of women's 'choices' ignore how such decisions are not freely made but constrained by the weight of centuries of acculturation into traditional roles, as well as the absence of childcare and family-friendly workplaces. Arguments about cultural constraints ignore the evidence that those states in Eastern Europe and Scandinavia which have worked very hard to put institutional supports and the weight of collective opinion behind *working* motherhood did not succeed in establishing anything like a universal ideal. Forcible social engineering only alters behaviour in the short-term. The evidence Hakim presents shows that the three preference groups are tenacious and exist *despite all social engineering attempts to eradicate them.*

Sweden, even with all of its justly famous work/family policies, is not a utopian paradise of dual career couples working identical hours with equal career commitment. Rather, the dominant Swedish family type is the 'compromise' adaptive one. Women work as secondary earners; they still have the major share of responsibility for family life, and are far more likely than men to take advantage of family-friendly reforms like parental leave. Even when a period of 30 days leave was made exclusively available to fathers in the 1990s—if he didn't take it was lost and could not be transferred to the mother—only 11 per cent of fathers took leave. In attitudinal surveys, the majority of Swedes don't support 'symmetrical roles'. All this despite advertising campaigns, non-transferable leave components and the best, most generous system of benefits ever devised for both partners to work.

Moreover, when the Swedish Fathers' Commission mounted a campaign to give Swedish fathers a non-transferable component of three of the twelve months of parental leave available, the main opponents were not men!

'To the surprise of the commission the most vociferous protest came from women.' 'We had piles of letters and many, many phone calls from women . . . some said this is infringing on breastfeeding, even though the average for that is six months in Sweden.' Responses included, 'He can't handle the baby' and 'I am home and he is a farmer, why should he be at home?' The leave was to be taken in the last few months of the first year, at the height of mother–baby attachment. It had occurred to no one that a mother might not want to give up the 'baby moon period' simply to satisfy the ideologically pure position of shared care.

In communist Eastern Europe, despite universal childcare and paid maternity leave, many women longed to work part-time. The moment liberalisation occurred, the numbers working part-time expanded. Many women welcomed 'with a sigh of relief' the chance to shed the double or triple (with political activities and queuing!) burden and 'spend a few years home with children'. They resented being forced to work, and envied the more pluralist maternal cultures of the West, and Western women's choices to stay home or work. One consequence, historian Barbara Einhorn records, was the development, post-communism, of a real 'anti-feminist allergy'. While some women still feel work to be an important part of their identity, others are rebelling, embracing a new cult of motherhood. The group Prague Mothers, railing against 'feminism as sameness', argued that 'the communists said that in the first place a woman is a worker, then she should be active in political life, then in the third place have a family . . . we are sick and tired of equality. We want to be women in the first place and then to join other activities.' Others 'feel unable to see their mothers as role models, old before their time, worn out but without much career success to show for it.'

Sometimes it is women's own experiences of daycare as children that is a catalyst for different working patterns:

> The first generation of young mothers who had themselves spent long days in state nurseries often resisted imposing such a regime on their own children. Memories of being woken and taken, half asleep, by the hand in the dark of early morning, abound in fictional and documentary accounts. The impact of long days away from parents for very young children, the unfavourable child–carer ratios, which resulted in regimented days and a lack of individual attention, the frequent illnesses caught from other children—all these factors outweighed in the popular memory the advantages of early socialisation so eulogised by early socialist theoreticians.

Young children became so sick as a consequence of the very high infection rates of group care (also a problem in the West) that Hungarian women were given unlimited time off in their child's first year, then eighty-four days until the child's third birthday, and forty days until the age of six, to care for sick children. As in Sweden, then, the statistics on high workforce participation rates in Eastern Europe hid the reality—up to half of women with young children were at home on any one day, despite officially working full-time. It was also considered (as in Sweden) cheaper, in the end, to give paid parental leave to let parents care for very young children at home. The Hungarian sociologist Julia Szalai has calculated that the annual cost per child of parental leave was only about a third of the cost of equipping and staffing public nurseries. That extended leave was also granted because of fears over the birth rate. Policy makers clearly identified that the predominant one-child family pattern was due to the stress women felt in combining uninterrupted employment and motherhood. In Poland, Hungary and the Czech Republic, leave lasted until the child's third birthday.

The work-centred rule, OK?

The old breadwinner/homemaker regime was undoubtedly a coercive one, using state legislation, fiscal policy and everyday practices to enforce what in Hakim's terms looks like a minority preference. (No wonder there was so much female angst!) After the equal opportunity revolution, however, it is also possible for state policy to work in the interests of another minority group, the work-centred. Work-centred women are much more likely to achieve career success, making it into the policy-making elites. This self-selection process means a certain inevitable skewing towards their interests, with the elite cultural discourse reflecting preoccupations with the completely legitimate, but not universal, concerns of this group. Those working in feminist and government organisations like the Equal Opportunities Commission and the former Office of the Status of Women, as well as politicians, broadcasters, academics, opinion leaders and social commentators, are usually work-centred women. In a nice example, Anne Summers' book, *The End of Equality*, published in 2003, a restatement of the 'equality as sameness' position, was written by a childless career feminist, published by a childless career woman, and reviewed very favourably in three different newspapers by work-centred women with PhDs!

Hakim says that 'the position of women has been misrepresented by pundits because most pundits, whether they are academics, or journalists, tend to be work-centred women themselves'.

Sometimes this arises simply because of mixing with one's own peer group and rarely moving outside it. At other times it exemplifies a peculiar subset of feminism, what one might call 'no choice' or 'illiberal' feminism. De Beauvoir's earlier quoted comment—'No, after the revolution that choice will not be available'—is an example of the spirit and tone of what American philosopher Christina Hoff Sommers calls the 'new gender wardens', self-appointed commissars who patrol the boundaries of acceptable behaviour. Such people believe there is a right choice and a wrong one.

Linda Hirshman, interviewed for a 2004 CBS *Sixty Minutes* program, criticised the trend of high-achieving women choosing to stay home with small children:

> It's different to talk about their right than what's the right decision. As Mark Twain said, 'A man who chooses not to read is just as ignorant as a man who cannot read.' . . . I think there are better lives and worse lives.

The implicit assumption is that policies which suit the childless and the work-centred are implemented on behalf of all women. Engineering an outcome and denying choice fulfils a higher revolutionary goal. While the European parliament has recommended that the tax system should be neutral between single and dual-income families, others in the European commission like Allan Larsson, Hakim says, have 'effectively stated that commission policy was to outlaw the so-called "traditional". . . sexual division of labour'.

Hakim gives another telling example. When in the late 1990s the British Cabinet Office's Women's Unit organised a major research programme called 'Listening To Women', it found the usual conflicting views on work and family typical of all modern societies. Many valued motherhood and wanted it recognised and supported. The research was commissioned by the Blair government, which prided itself on developing 'evidence-based policies'. When its findings were published, deliciously entitled *Voices, Turning Listening into Action*, no mention was made of the diversity of opinion expressed! Instead, it emphasised 'education and training, access to paid work, job segregation, the pay gap, and childcare services for working mothers. There is virtually no mention of full-time homemakers and full-time parents, and there are no policies listed to support this group.' Hakim concludes: 'In practice, the focus of family and social policy has swung so far towards the working mother that there is now a systematic policy bias *against* non-working mothers in most modern societies.'

Patricia Hewitt, British Trade and Industry Secretary, admitted late in 2003:

> If I look back over the last six years I do think that we have given the impression that we think all mothers should be out to work, preferably full-time as soon as their children are a few months old. We have got to move to a position where as a society and as a Government we recognise and we value the unpaid work that people do within their families.

Apologising for a report by the women and equality unit in her department, which pronounced that non-working mothers did not 'benefit the nation', Hewitt interestingly now also expressed regrets about her own work-centred life: 'When I look back I wish I had worked part-time when my children were younger. I had a live-in nanny but I always loved being with my children, going to the primary school, and if I had my time again I would do more.'

Hakim repudiates the imperial ambitions of any gender wardens, old or new, to colonise all of womanhood. There can be no one-size-fits-all family policy. The logical conclusion of her divergence/polarisation thesis—and an argument of this book—is state neutrality on women's choices. She rejects the vanguardist temptation for an elite to decide, on behalf of other women, what constitutes the good life: 'Difference and diversity are now the key features of the female population . . . And in a civilised society difference and diversity are positively valued.'

The moral limits of choice

An early childhood specialist once raised a question at a childcare conference. 'Should a baby of a few weeks of age be in a childcare centre for fifty hours a week? Don't children have rights too?' One of the participants, a female politician, rounded on her, almost screaming: 'I haven't fought for women's rights for so long to listen to this!' Shaken and silenced, the early childhood specialist wondered aloud later if women's rights now mean that children have no rights at all? Has there been a simple exchange—women's for children's rights? It was an awkward, painful question.

Motherhood is not only, as Susan Johnson once put it, 'a show starring women centre stage'. What makes a woman a mother is a child. Motherhood is not just about the mother's experience, but also about the other half of that partnership—the child. Many contemporary discussions, to use the revealing title of one feminist text in literary theory, Elaine Tuttle Hansen's *Mother Without Child*, exclude the child's point of view, the needs and rights of the weaker child for care. It is certainly simpler and less politically tricky just not to consider them. Adults—women as well as men—are much more powerful than children. It is adults who write for newspapers, who are politicians and bureaucrats making policy. It is they who shape and control what is considered knowledge and what matters. Our societal conversations on these issues are often conducted as if only individual adult rights, or women's rights, matter. Almost the entire debate over paid maternity leave in Australia, for example, has taken place without infants' needs—especially for longer than the proposed fourteen weeks of care—being considered.

Catherine Hakim is unusual in acknowledging that in

the exclusive focus on women's [presumed interests] the conflicting interests of children receive virtually no attention, or are dismissed through claims that collective childcare is invariably of higher quality . . . as soon as the focus turns from working mothers to children, it becomes clear that no single, uniform approach to services for children, and hence family policy, is possible. Diversity is accepted as necessary and positive . . .

It was for that reason, Hakim points out, that the 1996 European Commission's childcare network included amongst its recommendations the need to actively promote choice between employment and caring for children at home, encouraging parents to remain home until the children are three.

In the next section, I move to a different window from that marked 'women's rights' to focus, with the same respect, on another point of view, that of the child. To do justice to their perspective we must get inside the skin of a child.

Part Two

Taking children seriously

6 Inside the skin of a child

'Simone Weil said that if one saw others as another perspective on the world, as one is oneself, one could not treat them unjustly. That means we must be open to the distinctive voice of others, and that in turn means we must encourage the conditions in which those voices can form and be heard.'
Raimond Gaita

Children and power

The remarkable English psychoanalyst Donald Winnicott once said that for eight children of an ordinary family, there are eight different families. What he meant was this. Alongside their common, shared family history, each child of the same family has so distinct and unique an experience, particular to them, that one might say they each have their own history.

The social movements shaped by the cultural revolution of the 1960s, like the offspring of an ordinary family, share elements in common but also have distinctive, sometimes conflicting stories to tell. Great gains—derived from the newfound impulse to tell history from 'below'—were made in social history, integrating the history of women and of different racial groups into mainstream history. That inclusive impulse also found its way into a new field: the history of childhood. The narratives of hitherto marginal groups offer fascinating and diverse windows on family life in times past.

The stories within those different windows sometimes converge, but often do not. Each story has its own integrity, but the interests of such groups can be in tension, and sometimes at odds with one another. Feminists have exposed the patriarchal fallacy that there is always an identity of interests between men and women, or between women and the family; in the same way there is not always an easy identity of interest between women and children.

The discourse about children emerged hesitantly, uncertainly, throughout the twentieth century, to come into the light of the public realm, running parallel to—but often overshadowed by—the struggles over race and gender. Like feminism and the struggle against racism, it has at its core something deep and humane. Like feminism, it was a new discourse about an old, old story, just as ancient as that of male dominance. The subjects of that story, however, are not women but children.

This new discourse dealt with the same theme: the powerlessness of a vulnerable group. It depended upon the same kind of 'putting one self in the shoes of another'—overcoming difference and extending our empathy, imagination and the capacity for identification—except this time with a child. It created a new history of childhood, invigorated our awareness and sensitivity to the treatment of children by parents, schools and institutions, and started a new movement for children's rights. Like other political movements, the new awareness of children brought into the open injustices hitherto invisible. It, too, penetrated the force field of privacy and secrecy behind which the lies, misconduct and dark secrets of the dominant group could shelter and flourish. It pointed out the moral carelessness involved when a less powerful group is objectified and treated as The Other—as lesser, inferior—and thus not within that human constituency to whom equal respect need be granted. It punctured forever the notion that injustice matters less because it's not happening to 'chaps like us'.

That age-old hierarchy is presently, painfully, uncertainly, and only in certain domains, being overturned. Just as feminism brought into the public awareness sexual harassment, so the movement for children's rights focussed our attention on the previously ignored issue of child sexual abuse. Like feminism, the movement is capable of throwing up subversive cultural flashpoints, which destabilise the existing social order. In 2003, the widespread perception that the Governor-General of Australia, Peter Hollingworth, was indulgent of paedophiles engulfed him in a scandal, and forced his resignation. Explosive affairs such as these, which can destabilise powerful institutions, derive energy and impetus from this new and radical discourse about the place of children in the social order.

I argued in previous chapters that, at its best, feminism is about justice. It calls us to a certain kind of attentiveness, and forces awareness of the moral carelessness possible when the needs of a vulnerable group are rendered invisible. It is about recognising the person and not constructing them as an Other who is lesser, an inferior whose needs and desires are of less importance than men's. Feminism, like the struggle against racism, may sometimes be foolish or even reprehensible, but has at its centre ideas of profound moral seriousness. But so does the discourse about children. For it, too, confronts us with those who are vulnerable and powerless. Unlike women, however, children are usually politically mute. Consider, for example, the following instances of moral carelessness towards children in the contemporary misuse of the 'lessons' from the history of childhood.

The Good Old Days: Lessons from the history of childhood

Historians such as Lloyd de Mause present evidence that the story of childhood was a 'long nightmare from which we are only just beginning to awake'. They tell of past brutality, indifference, neglect and cruelty. In the world we have lost, they argue, there was an almost complete lack of empathy for children. It reveals the dark side of parenting, of beatings, abandonment and even infanticide, of unspeakable cruelties perpetrated in the name of virtue, of neglect and indifference. Children were farmed out to wet nurses in the countryside, to be retrieved when past the most tiresome, troublesome part of infancy at age two or three. The infants of the poor might die while their mothers fed from their own bodies the children of the rich. Children of the well to do, having been given away to wet nurses for several years, came to bond and love those women as their own mothers, only to suffer terrible grief when returned to their birth mother. Large numbers of babies were left to die on the roads and the alleyways, abandoned by the parents who were too poor to care for them.

Yet a common response to concerns over the effect on children of poor quality childcare is an appeal to the past. Children, the argument goes, have always had 'shared care' and just as often had it tough. The economist Juliet Schor, bewailing the pressure on modern mothers, looks back to the time when

Children were hardly 'raised' in today's sense of the term ... past parent–child relationships appear to have been much less emotional. What is seen today as a deep biological bond between parent and child, particularly mother and child, is very much a social construction. For the most part children were not 'cared for' by their parents. The rich had little to do with their offspring until they were grown. Infants were given to wet nurses, despite widespread evidence of neglect and markedly lower chances of survival. Older children were sent off to school . . .

Babies were swaddled so that they 'may not trouble those that have the care of [them]. However harmful these practises may have been for children, they were convenient for their elders.' In the late nineteenth-century they could be drugged with opium: 'The young 'uns all lay about on the floor,' said one woman who was in the habit of dosing her children with it, 'like dead 'uns, and there's no bother with 'em.'

Schor describes child neglect, citing babies and children 'routinely left unattended for long periods of time'. For the poor and labouring classes, when times got tough 'infanticide and abandonment were not unusual. Time for mothering was an unaffordable luxury, and the children were frequently left alone.'

Schor admits that:

> Parental indifference was not merely the result of infant mortality. It was also a cause. Historians now realise that one reason many children died is that their parents did not, or could not, take sufficient pains to keep them alive. Neglect and abuse were dangerous, in both rich and poor families.

Rising standards of mothering were responsible for dramatically improving child survival rates, happiness and wellbeing: 'Children benefited from all this attention . . . But the burden that it placed on the new American housewife was immense.' That clash of interest is also the focus of Carl Degler at the end of his history of American women. What, he wonders, will the social revolution mean for children? Perhaps work, as suggested by so many feminists, should be radically restructured? As attractive as this idea is, he concludes that 'if something so fundamental as restructuring a whole economy is necessary' then we must call into question the 'proposal's practicality, at least for the immediate future'. Perhaps men will step in to fill the gap as women withdraw such full-time investment in the family? On this point Degler is particularly firm. He thinks not; he concludes 'optimism' about how far men are prepared to have two jobs, sharing the 'second shift', 'has a thin basis in fact'. So what is to be done?

Degler finds the answer in history. Calmly, placidly, without compunction, he tells us that looking at the

> longer history of the family, one possible solution for the future of women and the family suggests itself. It is that we may well be at a point in the

history of the family where *the high level of child care*, to which two centuries of the modern family have accustomed us, *can no longer be sustained*.

That too, is the sentiment of two well known child developmentalists, Kathleen Sternberg and Michael Lamb, also supporters of the feminist revolution, who suggest we should look to enlightened Asian societies, where, we are told, 'it is not unreasonable to emphasise *custodial* aspects of care designed largely to *ensure survival* until the age of reason begins (six or seven years) . . . These differing belief systems have major implications for child care practises and the *seriousness of concerns about the quality of care*.'

If women are to do better, children will just have to get less. Such a Faustian bargain depends on the withdrawal of empathy from children, whose feelings and needs are seen as of less significance than adults, by recourse to ideas of what historically has been considered 'natural' for children.

What is so interesting, however, is the radical disjuncture between these arguments about 'what is natural' for children—that is, taking the 'lessons' of the past to justify present and future practice—and how we think about 'the natural' in relation to adults. Given that the history of childhood contains so much injustice, history does *not* establish 'what is natural'—and right—for children any more than do past relations between male and female. What such arguments justify for one group of citizens—children—is precisely the opposite of what a modern progressive society argues in relation to other groups—women, blacks or Jews. For a generation or more we have recognised the humane necessity for a radical break with past treatment that was once regarded as 'natural'—the subjugation of women or, the domination of white over black, the persecution of the Jews. We acknowledge, rather, the need for treatment that is *just*. If one is interested in humane, just treatment of children, then one cannot appeal to ages more barbarous than our own in order to justify our practice.

| The Missing Child In Liberal Theory

The quality of being politically voiceless is what makes thinking about children and justice difficult and our responsibility so heavy. There is no real possibility of creating, publicly at least, Habermas's equal speech situation; one attentive to the distortions possible when one participant is more powerful than the other, where the effort is to develop a conversation that treats all contributions with equal respect. After all, it is adults, not children, who write the books of child psychology and parenting manuals, who speak on behalf of what we claim as their best interests. It is adults and not children who make work and family policies and individual decisions about childcare—but it is children who inhabit childcare centres and spend the time there.

Moreover, although the 1960s 'liberation' movements developed a powerful language of rights, notions of responsibility were often sorely underdeveloped. There are good grounds for questioning how well children do in a libertarian paradise. There is very good evidence that in contemporary society, whether due to rising inequality, patterns of parental over- or under-work, family fragmentation, rising rates of fatherlessness and sole parenthood, loss of connected communities or many combinations thereof, despite greater economic prosperity than ever before, child wellbeing is dramatically declining—especially in emotional and psychological health. Fiona Stanley spent her time as *Australian of the Year* highlighting the troubling fact that our children are doing worse across a range of different indices. She highlighted an epidemic of emotional and behavioural disorders, and increased rates of depression, anxiety and teenage suicide.

The American report published in 2003, *Hardwired to Connect*, found the same story. One-fifth of American children aged from 9 to 17 now have a diagnosable mental disorder or addiction. Eight per cent of adolescents suffer from clinical depression. One-fifth report having seriously considered suicide. Child psychiatric patients present with much higher levels of anxiety than did those of the 1950s. It is not just the poor. Affluent children are also affected. Most tellingly, many immigrant children, despite their disadvantaged position, initially have lower rates of emotional health problems than American-born children. They gradually begin to exhibit the same difficulties as the native-born.

It is children's predicament in a world dominated by the assumptions of liberal individualism which has prompted many, from all over the present political and moral map, to try to rethink their previously held positions. Such writers have joined what feminist and political theorist Jean Elshtain calls the 'ranks of the nervous.' John O'Neill in *The Missing Child in Liberal Theory* argued that the adult rights focus of liberal theory is inadequate, leading to a 'duty-free society' in which children are especially vulnerable. Instead, O'Neill suggests, children need an intergenerational covenant of care by committed adults with a sense of obligation.

As Simone Weil suggests, it would be harder to behave unjustly if one 'saw others as another perspective on the world, as one is oneself'. But how do we, in relation to children, 'encourage the conditions in which those voices can form and be heard,' as Gaita says so eloquently? Let us begin by listening to how perceptive writers illuminate, in their remembrance of things past, the child's point of view.

Such, such were the joys

In an essay on the extraordinary Polish hero Janusz Korczak, who went to his death in the Nazi gas chambers alongside the children from his orphanage rather than abandon them, Bruno Bettelheim remarked:

> those who like Korczak single-mindedly devote themselves to making a better world for children are usually motivated by their own unhappy childhood. What they suffer makes such a lasting impression that all their lives they try to come to terms with it by working to change things so that other children will not have to suffer a similar fate.

Bettelheim was clearly speaking autobiographically. Much the same kind of 'coming to terms with suffering' can be seen in the work of great children's authors like Roald Dahl, or writers on the experience of childhood like Charles Dickens and George Orwell. Ordinary mortals may suffer a kind of amnesia about childhood and the suffering it may entail, or veil it in a misty-eyed sentimentality, but these writers have such vivid, precise recollections that they are able effortlessly to call up the emotional space that was their childhood. Their imaginations have no difficulty in slipping inside the skin of a child.

Much of the intensity of childhood derives from the fact that it is an encounter with life *for the very first time*. It is that which gives a child's experience that quality of being 'tout court', as representing the whole of the world, of showing *all* of reality, of revealing *what the world is like*. That is one reason we find it so terrible that a child is abused or beaten or hungry or terrified or neglected, because the child's suffering can so easily be mistaken by that child for the whole of the world and not a part. The child does not yet have the distancing, controlling, regulating mechanisms of memory or alternative comparative experiences by which we, as adults, can ward off or soften something terrible. It is that freshness, that openness deriving from the 'firstness' of their experience of the world that so disarms us in watching children and gives childhood an especial intensity and heightened sensitivity. It is what makes a child so utterly, vividly alive to the world's joys, pleasures and exhilarations as well as so vulnerable to humiliation, disappointment and loss. The playwright Dennis Potter once spoke about that intensity, the firstness, of childhood experience. He rembered receiving a simple gift of a pen, and he exulted in 'the penness of that pen'.

Then there is their smallness and our bigness. One blow of our hand, one violent shake and we can kill them. Inga Clendinnen, with her characteristic perceptiveness, writes of how Hilary Mantel's account of her early life

> explodes our sentimental notions of childhood, replacing them with a stack of bladed memories and probably unanswerable questions. What is childhood? Lewis Carroll's 'nest of gladness'; edenic prelude before bread, sweat and tears? Or the dooming time when fatal dies are cast, with everything to follow as sad iteration? . . . I doubt that anyone is suited to being small, powerless and ignored, especially at the time when, all character and no experience, we must somehow learn to survive in a world run by dangerously unpredictable and wholly disingenuous giants.

Clendinnen also contrasts Mantel's sharp, hard insight that damage can be irreparable, with our contemporary predilection for survivor memoirs that turn on a consolation myth of resilience—'the human as a high quality tennis ball bouncing back no matter how hard you whack it'. One way of distancing ourselves from the discomfort of confronting our own power over children is to create a myth of an independent, resilient child who, like the cat with nine lives, always lands on its feet.

There is a universal childhood terror of separation, neglect and abandonment. Such an imagination is deep in Charles Dickens's many stories of abandoned and neglected children. The psychoanalyst Leonard Shengold, in one of a number of arresting and perceptive essays on the effect of childhood neglect and abuse, draws attention to Dickens's 'obsessive interest' in such themes. Dickens's novels also feature the adult counterpart to the abandoned child—unfeeling, affectless or indifferent parents. They all share what E.M. Forster called the 'undeveloped heart', a characteristic 'especially applicable to the English' by which was meant 'an inability to care enough about another person, a deficiency of the capacity for love, joy and empathy . . . the parent's underdeveloped heart . . . expressed not only by indifference but also by hatred and cruelty'.

The pivotal experience for Dickens was being separated from his family at age ten when his father went to a debtors prison. Sent to work in a bleak, cold, rat-infested blacking factory, Charles toiled long and hard, pasting labels on the jars of tar used for cleaning boots and fire grates. He was continually humiliated for his social airs and graces. He ate one meal a week with his family, but for the rest of the week mostly went hungry. Dickens felt forgotten, abandoned: 'I might have easily been, for any care that was taken of me, a little robber or vagabond.' Even his father, to whom he had been closest, 'appeared to have utterly lost' interest in his education, 'and to have utterly put from him the notion that I had any claim upon him'.

Dickens wrote later: 'even after my descent into the poor little drudge . . . no one had compassion enough on me—a child of singular ability, quick, eager, delicate, and soon hurt, bodily or mentally . . . My mother and father were quite satisfied.' It was even more occasion for bitterness when his father eventually tried to retrieve him but his mother resisted. It was his mother who exemplified for Dickens the unempathic 'under-developed heart'. 'I never afterwards forgot, I never shall forget, that my mother was warm for having me sent back.' When he did return home, it was as if it never happened. The door was shut upon the subject; his parents were 'stricken dumb'. 'I never heard the least allusion to it . . . from either of them.' But it haunted him,

> The deep remembrance of the sense I had of being utterly neglected and hopeless; of the shame I felt in my position; of the misery it was to my young heart to believe that day by day, what I had learned, and delighted in . . . was passing away from me. My whole nature was so penetrated with the grief and humiliations . . . even now, famous and caressed and happy, I often forget in my dreams I have a dear wife and children . . . and wander desolately back to that time in my life.

A child's vulnerability is also the leitmotif of George Orwell's wonderful essay about the horrors of boarding school. 'Such, such were the Joys' was written at the same time that he was working on his nightmare vision of the future, *1984*. Much ink has been spilt upon the novel's connections with the political past, present and future, but less has been said of its connections to Orwell's own private, past nightmares in childhood. Of that commonplace English upper-class practice of sending a child off to boarding school, Orwell wrote, 'Your home might be far from perfect, but at least it was a place ruled by love rather than fear . . . At eight years old you were suddenly taken out of this warm nest and flung into a world of force and fraud and secrecy, like a goldfish into a tank full of pike.'

As Shengold suggests there are many unconscious connections between Orwell's alarming school headmaster in 'Such, such were the Joys' and *1984's* menacing character O'Brien. O'Brien ultimately rules over Winston by getting inside his head and both divining and exploiting his worst fear—being devoured alive by rats. Reduced to an abject, terror-filled state, Winston cannot resist and is forced in the end to submit to an arbitrary, vicious authority in a totalitarian world. Winston's ultimate submission is in the self-erasure of forgetting his own point of view, of identifying completely with O'Brien's way of seeing, of thinking what O'Brien wants him to think. In 'Such, such were the joys', Orwell tells of a vicious beating.

> Look what you've made me do!' he said furiously, holding up the broken crop . . . The second beating had not hurt very much either. Fright and shame had anaesthetised me. I was crying partly because I felt that this was expected of me, partly from genuine repentance, but partly *because of a deeper grief which is peculiar to childhood . . . a sense of desolate loneliness and helplessness, of being locked up not only in a hostile world but in a world of good and evil where the rules were such that it was actually not possible for me to keep them . . .* I had a conviction of folly and weakness, such as I do not remember to have felt before . . . I accepted the broken riding crop as my own crime. I can still recall my feeling as I saw the handle lying on the carpet—the feeling of having done an ill-bred, clumsy thing, and ruined an expensive object. *I* had broken it: so Sim told me and so I believed. This acceptance of guilt lay unnoticed in my memory for twenty or thirty years. [emphasis added]

Submission to O'Brien and Sim occurs in an arbitrary world of Machiavellian power—the 'tank full of pike'—where the fragile goldfish can only be eaten. In Orwell's memoir, being separated at boarding school means there is no one—the imperfect parents who 'at least followed the rule of love'—to protect him. He is alone, left to his own devices. And those devices, of a sensitive child, are not enough. Thus, undergirding Orwell's story is not just the fear of being annihilated by a powerful Other, the whip-wielding Sim or the rat-wielding O'Brien, but that other, fundamental terror of childhood, the fear of separation and abandonment.

For Roald Dahl the boarding school was also an element in triggering a lifelong preoccupation with children warding off and defeating nightmare bullies like the headmistress figure from hell, the Trunchbull in *Matilda*, as well as his many consoling, antidote stories about benign, stupid giants like *The BFG*.

Boarding school, and the preoccupation with children's terror of separation and abandonment, are also examined by one of a handful of truly important child psychiatrists of the twentieth century, John Bowlby. At the age of eight, Bowlby, like most of his class, experienced 'the traditional first step in the time-honoured barbarism required to produce English gentleman', i.e. he was sent to boarding school. It was an experience about which he spoke little, except to say with characteristic brevity and directness that he would not send his dog to a boarding school at that age.

The child's point of view

'Bowlby's *Separation: Anxiety and Anger* would be at home next to Dickens's novels or Kipling's or Orwell's . . . It belongs in the tradition of those great English writers of social conscience who plead for us to recognise that the miseries of childhood are serious and very real.' Elsa First

Bowlby's three-volume trilogy *Attachment, Separation and Loss* is a radical work, written with a brilliant imagination for the child's point of view. At a certain point, like the entry to those intriguing magic eye pictures, the cool English prose shifts, the gaze alters and one is looking as if through a different window on the world. One gains the capacity to see all kinds of layers and depths previously opaque or invisible to the eye. One slips inside a different world view, which turns one's own adult perspective upside down. One is In: inside the skin of a child.

It is a deeply unsettling experience. Quite suddenly, from the shadowy reaches of the memory of what it was like to be small and powerless, the vivid reality of childish joy, elation, love, but also misery, shame, frustration, the terror of abandonment, all begin to come to life, together with the fear of the great power of those huge beings—adults—one inhabits the world alongside and upon whom one so depends. It happens regardless of whether you stayed at home, as I did, or went to work, for the core, shared issue is our power over children, and our ability to affect their lives for good or ill.

Bowlby was, if you like, the Germaine Greer of children. He turns our careless assumptions about the way we currently arrange things upside down. It was Bowlby who more than anyone else penetrated the 'force field of privacy' around ordinary family life, exposed child abuse by mothers and fathers, and advocated listening to the testimony of children who bear truthful witness to horrifying family trauma, rather than to the adults who denied it. Bowlby alerted people to the ways in which children did not flourish in institutions like orphanages, and argued that adults should deal honestly and unflinchingly with mourning and grief in children.

All this, however, is not what he is most known for. Bowlby is one of those thinkers whose reputation precedes them. Hated more in ignorance than in knowledge—for few seem to actually have read his work—Bowlby's fame, or more precisely his infamy, comes from his work on children separated from their mothers for long periods in institutions.

We must, however, first clear away the clutter of some dead cultural baggage from a pervasive, widespread misunderstanding. It is a part of feminist folklore that Bowlby was to blame for the view that mothers must stay like sentries at their posts until the child reached the magical age of five, lest their child would become a delinquent or affectionless psychopath. In fact, Bowlby said no such thing. As Sarah Hrdy says:

> But wait a moment, . . . while we take a timeless tip on scholarship from George Eliot: 'It seems to me much better to read a man's own writing than to read what others say about him,' she wrote to a friend, 'especially when a man is first rate and the "others" are third rate.'

His concern at this time was *not* primarily directed at the *daily* separations of children of working mothers. Rather his focus was on *extreme* separations such as prolonged hospital stays of weeks, months or years, or similar time spent in orphanages. His first area of research interest was how prolonged separation—in situations of dramatic deprivation like those experienced by Romanian orphans, the Stolen Generations of Aboriginal children in Australia, or young patients in long-term hospital wards—might be linked to later psychological disturbance or delinquency.

Bowlby's views, however, were quoted out of their proper context and applied willy-nilly to day care, translated and dumbed down for the popular press. He was branded as patriarchy personified, a figure of hate for the emerging feminist movement. Ann Oakley's dismissal of Bowlby was not untypical. 'Bowlbyism', she felt, 'caught on because it was a very reactionary time for women'. He became 'that dreadful Dr B'.

The irony is that while Bowlby never considered *infant* daycare the ideal form of care, he did not suggest that the consequences which he argued might flow from *permanent* 'maternal deprivation' (i.e. landing in an orphanage in one's early years) would apply to the very different case of *daily* separations in childcare. Deborah Brennan, the Australian academic, feminist and childcare activist, in *The Politics of Australian Childcare: From Philanthropy to Feminism,* is one of the few to get this right. She notes that Bowlby actually used daycare children as a control group against which to measure the damaging effects of extreme, prolonged separations. Moreover, Bowlby thought it essential for a child in the three to five age bracket to leave mother and have at least some childcare or kindergarten experience with peers—without which the child would likely be too timid! Such important qualifications, however, unhappily usually escaped both the traditionalist and feminist protagonists entering the early debates over women working.

It is not my intention to dwell in this chapter on the debates over the long-term *consequences* of extreme or prolonged separation. For the moment I want to concentrate on what Bowlby showed about *the child's experience at the time.*

One of Bowlby's most original contributions was to elaborate the trauma of loss, particularly if suffered in early childhood. Perhaps unsurprisingly, Bowlby's childhood was marked by insecurity and loss, and his theoretical preoccupations might be seen as both an explication of, and reparation to, his own childhood.

Bowlby was born into a rather frosty English upper-class family, which was a kind of anti-metaphor for the qualities he came to feel were so essential for young children. Bowlby's father, a prominent baronet and surgeon to the king, was the prototype of an 'absent father'. His mother was known to boast that 'she *never* worried about her children, and left them mostly to their own devices'. The future architect of 'attachment theory' and interpreter of the ill effects of 'maternal deprivation', who argued that a child's 'warm and continuous relationship with their mother' was so important to their future psychological wellbeing, experienced the very form of childrearing whose virtues 1970s feminists often uncritically extolled: 'multiple mothering'. Bowlby was, unexceptionally for his class and generation, raised by a succession of nannies:

> Both parents set themselves utterly apart from their children, handing over their care to nannies and a governess. The children ate separately until each one reached the age of twelve, when, if the child still lived at home, he or

she was permitted to join the parents for dessert. The nannydom consisted of a head nanny, herself a somewhat cold creature and the only stable figure in the children's lives, and an assortment of under nannies, mainly young girls who did not stay long.

Significantly for a thinker whose leitmotif was the dangers of disrupting bonds of attachment of the very young child, Bowlby was apparently very attached to one of these young nannies and was heartbroken when she left.

Children and loss

'The great terror of infancy is solitude.' William James

'What is grief but the lack of particular lips?' Inga Clendinnen

The first opportunity to explore the experience of separation and loss and their connection with depression and other psychological disturbances in adults came with children who had been dislocated from their families in World War Two. Anna Freud and Dorothy Burlingham, working in a wartime nursery for such children, were among the first to notice the profound effects of separation on children. Across the Atlantic some American researchers, such as David Levy, Loretta Bender, Harry Bakwin and Bill Goldfarb, but particularly René Spitz, had all begun to notice in different ways the bizarre and troubling behaviour of children raised in institutions, or shifted around from placement to placement. They showed the consequences of disruptions to the normal development of attachment. Language deficits and lowered IQ were only the tip of the iceberg. Like the Romanian orphans, the plight of these institutionalised babies was often shocking to behold. Depression, listlessness and a profound loss of hope resulted in a dramatic failure to thrive, infections, and in extreme cases emaciation and even death. This institutional 'failure to thrive' was widespread enough to be given the name 'hospitalism'.

Sometimes children began to recover, after going through what appeared to be a period of intense misery and mourning, but they seemed strangely transformed. On the surface they seemed to have recovered their spirits, and seemed charming and even indiscriminately affectionate. The psychologist Stella Chess, who worked in one of the early units, remarked: 'They were affectionate to everybody. The foster parents would find that they would call someone Daddy who they saw for the first time in the street.' Yet underneath they seemed indifferent, lost to any deep emotion. They proved incapable of developing deep attachments even when placed in stable adoption homes, and seemed, in fact, 'to lack any feeling for others at all'.

The children displayed 'incorrigible behaviour problems including sexual aggressiveness, fantastic lying, stealing, temper tantrums, immature or infantile demands, and failure to make meaningful friendships'. Worse, none seemed to respond to psychotherapy. One researcher, Levy, concluded that they suffered from an emotional starvation so severe that they lacked the capacity for normal human feelings.

It was not long before researchers began to link this phenomenon to the failure of hospitals and institutions to provide loving interactions with a stable person who was committed to the child, interactions which happen as a matter of course in a normal good-enough family.

Bowlby also had decided to study separation. There were two main reasons. The first was the desire to study a child's real-life experience as a possible source of troubled behaviour. Bowlby had graduated at a time when psychoanalysis seemed the only alternative to a sanitised version of childhood as a paradise of uncomplicated happiness and untroubled innocence. At first Bowlby was attracted to the psychoanalyst Melanie Klein for her insights into the power of infant emotional life, and her recognition of the capacity of young children, denied at the time, to experience emotions like grief, mourning and depression. Over time, however, he became disillusioned with the Kleinian emphasis on the child's fantasy world—as if the actual realities of their lives had no bearing on the inner psychic life. His post-war work with disturbed children dislocated from their families, and his work at child guidance clinics, underscored the lesson that direct observation of children and their lives, past and present, held as much of a key to understanding psychological difficulties as exploring the memories of adults on the psychoanalyst's couch.

For Klein and her school there was no easy continuity between psychic reality and experiential reality. Joan Riviere expressed it like this: 'Psychoanalysis . . . is not concerned with the real world nor with the child's or adult's adaptation to the real world. It is concerned simply and solely with the imaginings of the childish mind, the phantasied pleasures and the dreaded retributions.'

It was this self-referential quality, the lack of interest in the child or parent's real experience, that infuriated Bowlby. Klein was supervising him in the treatment of a hyperactive little boy suffering from anxiety. Bowlby immediately noticed that his mother, who brought him each day, was 'an extremely anxious distressed woman, who was wringing her hands, in a very tense, unhappy state'. Bowlby found Klein's reaction maddeningly frustrating. 'I was forbidden by Melanie Klein to talk to this poor woman. It was just something that wasn't done, mustn't be done. Well, I found this a rather painful situation really.' Bowlby felt the need to move to a family therapy model, to treat not just the little boy, but the mother and the whole family ecology. A few months into treatment, Bowlby recorded:

> After three months the news reached me that the mother had been taken to a mental hospital—she had a state of anxiety or depression or both, which didn't surprise me. And when I came to report this to Melanie Klein her response was, 'What a nuisance, we shall have to find another case . . . The fact that the poor woman had had a breakdown was of no clinical interest to her whatever. So this horrified me to be quite frank. And from that point on my mission in life was to demonstrate that real life experiences have a very important effect on development.

Bowlby's frustration with Klein was not far from the analogy that Maurice Eagle once drew between psychoanalysis and an illustrative story told by Francis Bacon, 'of monks arguing, on purely theoretical grounds, about the number of teeth in a horse's mouth. When a novice suggests they look in the horse's mouth, he is thrashed soundly for his blatant disrespect.'

If one wished to examine the environment of young children, a lengthy separation was an obvious and clear-cut place to start, whereas other variables like quality of care in the home were less accessible to scientific exploration. Bowlby's interest in the question of separation was aroused after he studied some young delinquents. Many of the young thieves demonstrated the curious detached quality that Bender, Levy and others had noticed, which Bowlby christened 'affectionless'. The thieves had appalling home backgrounds with disturbed and abusive parents, but this was no different to the non-thieving control group. Convinced that severe parental failings had consequences for the emotional disturbances children suffered, Bowlby decided to investigate another factor which was easier to document—prolonged early separation.

Fourteen of his forty-four young thieves typified the 'affectionless character'. Most strikingly for Bowlby, all but two of those had been subjected to prolonged early separations. One child, Derek, came from an ordinary, good-enough family without the gross parental negligence or abuse of the other children. At eighteen months, however, he had been hospitalised for nine months. It was standard procedure at this time for children not to see their parents, and he remained in hospital without seeing his mother or father the entire time. Coming home he 'seemed a stranger', even calling his mother 'nurse'. His mother recorded, 'It seemed like looking after someone else's baby.' He remained always 'strangely detached, unmoved by either affection or punishment. His mother described him as hard boiled.' Others who had been through a prolonged separation suffered from terrible and unquenchable longings, like the adult patient who took her morning tea in a baby's bottle. Just as later researchers would show the importance of attachment in the emergence of empathy—so crucial for the moral development of children—these young thieves had little empathy or feeling for others: 'None of them seemed to have any sense of the meaning of what they had done. They could not say why they stole, and they seemed impervious to the wrong they had done others.'

Behind the hostility and detachment, however, Bowlby felt, there was a tragedy: feelings of love so tormented by loss that they suffer repression and are turned back upon the self, never to be risked again. Love at its deepest makes us profoundly vulnerable, and the consequence of its loss for these children was a deep and unreachable depression: 'Behind the mask of indifference is bottomless misery and behind the apparent callousness despair.'

The child as other

'I don't really think of children as people.' A father to Penelope Leach

From the outset, researchers who suggested ill effects from what came to be called 'maternal deprivation' met not with approval but with fury. This came from two sources. First, there was a resistance to any criticism of the upper-class English system of childrearing, the main aim of which was the cultivation of the stiff upper lip—institutionalised separation from parents via nannies, boarding schools and a cool emotional climate which emphasised control over feelings and suppression of dependency needs. Second, the administrators, doctors and nurses who looked after children in institutions resented any criticism of their institutions, and felt that to allow parents visiting rights would disrupt their smooth routines.

It is now commonplace to allow parents to stay with children in hospitals. Yet before the 1950s the suggestion that children might suffer as a result of long separations—even for several months—was met with scepticism, indifference and, most interestingly, rage. As Robert Karen has observed, professionals caring for children found any number of ways to dodge the issue: 'It was temporary. It was hereditary. It wasn't really so bad. And the studies that suggested otherwise were flawed and should thus be dismissed. The resistance to seeing the pain of deprived, neglected or abused children has a long history.'

A colleague of Bowlby's at the Tavistock, James Robertson, had become interested in the question of separation of the very young child while working with Anna Freud. Bowlby employed Robertson as a field worker. Bowlby's sense of the importance of continuity of care for young children and the dangers of disrupting the bonds of attachment had depended on inferences and on reconstructions of the past. There had not yet been first-hand observations of children undergoing separation. Observing long-stay children's hospital wards, where parents were still only allowed occasional visits, Robertson was, from the outset, profoundly affected by the extent of the misery and distress that he saw. The older children seemed to adapt well enough, but the youngest children 'sat in their cots desolate and tearful and deeply silent'. With no understanding and little time sense to help them, they

> were overwhelmed. If a nurse stopped beside a silent toddler, he would usually burst into tears at the human contact and the nurse would be rebuked for making him unhappy. A quiet ward was prized above all else . . . the nurses . . . were intent on avoiding provoking tears.

The nurses were assigned to particular tasks, so had no opportunity to build up a relationship with a distressed child. Robertson found that one dangerously ill child had been assigned a special nurse, but she was ordered to stand behind him out of sight. 'That was the usual practice, the escorting matron told me, because if the child saw the nurse he would "make demands".' There was much emphasis upon the 'settled child', which could mean a despairing, apathetic child, or even one who had become emotionally detached from his parents—so long as they were quiet. The children were seen not as people, as individuals who were suffering, but as *problems of management*. Parents' visiting days brought wards that 'rang with the cries of young patients who had been quiet until their parents appeared. These visits did not so much cause upset as reveal the distress hidden by the quiet exterior of the ominously named "settled" children.'

Robertson's concerns were 'smilingly put aside as those of a sentimental psychologist.' Following the children home, however, he found lasting behavioural disturbances: clinging, temper tantrums, regressions like nightmares, bed-wetting and sleep disturbances, fear of strangers and aggression directed against the mother 'as if blaming her'. Sometimes parents felt they were getting back a different child. One mother recorded,

> I could hardly believe it was the same wee darling boy. He had lost so much weight, his face was pinched and haggard as if he'd been so miserable, and he could do nothing but hang on to me, and hug me tight. I'll never forget his first words to me—'Mummy, I thought you were never coming back for me.'

Hospital staff attributed such behaviour to the fact that mothers were so much less competent and professional than the trained nurses at handling children! Sir James Spence, a distinguished professor of child health, inquired loftily, 'What is wrong with emotional upset?' He cited Wordsworth, who, he said, 'suffered from emotional upset, yet look at the poems he produced.' He did, however, think that Robertson's work was preferable to the even 'more dangerous attitudes' of Dr Bowlby. Walking through the wards with Spence on his round, Robertson felt that he could detect everything he had observed elsewhere: the sequence of protest, despair, detachment. Robertson asked why the parents were only allowed two hours of visiting a week. The eminent professor patted Robertson's knee kindly and said, 'I know how much these children need. Twice a week is enough.'

In long-term stays, children did eventually adapt to the institution, but at an extraordinary psychological cost. Visiting long-term hospital wards for young TB sufferers, Robertson observed children who no longer protested or despaired, but had moved into the phase he began to call denial/detachment. They were cheerful, no longer sought attention, and could not care less which nurse was on duty. The picture appeared disarmingly reassuring, yet Robertson noticed puzzling qualities. The first was an indiscriminate friendliness that had struck observers like Bender and Levy in America. Visitors were charmed, but Robertson was less sanguine. When visited by their parents they seemed indifferent, as if denying the need for any relationships. Neither crying nor clinging, they seemed only interested in the presents their parents brought, not in the parents themselves. 'They searched bags and stuffed chocolate into their mouths. "Don't be greedy," perplexed parents would say.' Robertson felt that 'feeling for their parents had died because of the passage of time and had been replaced by hunger for sweet things which did not disappoint.'

Robertson watched children destroy toys which had been brought by parents, as if in anger against the parents. He watched a little girl called Mary move from despair to detachment. When her mother brought her a doll, 'using hands and teeth' she silently 'rent it apart'. Going home at three and a half, Mary 'squirmed out of her mother's embrace, then stood as if not knowing what affection was about'. No longer fitting into the 'reciprocity of family life', Mary was 'self centred' and 'intent on looking after herself; for more than a year her needs had not been met by others', defeating family members and teachers by her ruthlessness.

While convinced of the importance of alerting people to the dangers of prolonged separations, Robertson was deeply frustrated by the resistance he encountered from professionals. It was a resistance much deeper than mere unfamiliarity with distress: rather, he felt, people were putting up unconscious defences against recognising what they were choosing not to see. 'I was up against a blank wall.' He realised that his task was to pierce the extraordinary resistance on the part of paediatric nurses and doctors to seeing the distress in front of their noses. Robertson decided on the medium of film.

Robertson's film record moved and persuaded as the accounts of Bender, Levy and Bowlby had not. Robertson's primitive footage was at times unbearably painful to watch. The film record of one little child, 'John', disintegrating over a period of fourteen days is shockingly, powerfully moving. Bowlby, recording these reactions, had an extraordinary imagination for what it was that young children felt, and depicted their terror of abandonment with great delicacy and power. The children, upon separation in the extreme circumstances of hospitalisation among strangers, or being put into residential care, reacted with panic. They sobbed inconsolably or beat their fists against the bars of the cot, turning eagerly towards any sight or sound that might have been the missing parents. Some turned away from comfort, violently rejecting any alternative figure. Worse was when they became listless:

> The active physical movements diminish or come to an end, and he may cry monotonously or intermittently. He is withdrawn and inactive, makes no demands on people or the environment, and appears to be in a state of deep

mourning. This is a quiet stage, and sometimes erroneously is presumed to indicate a diminution of distress.

What then follows appeared to be recovery, but Bowlby and Robertson thought it was in fact detachment. Although children may begin to take an interest in their surroundings and accept care and food, their reaction on being reunited with their mother revealed a transformation of the relationship from intimacy to disengagement: 'So far from greeting her he may hardly seem to know her; so from clinging there is a listless turning away. He seems to have lost all interest in her.' These stages in the child's integration of separation Robertson and Bowlby termed 'protest, despair and detachment'.

The reaction to the films was extraordinary. Bowlby and Robertson were writers of social conscience, as Elsa First points out, struggling to make adults *see* the truth that the miseries of childhood can be 'serious and very real'. It was the invisibility of children's suffering to adults that they had to break through: the construction of the child as Other, with feelings and needs supposed to be quite different and lesser than that of adults.

When Robertson's most famous film, *A Two Year Old Goes to Hospital*, was first screened, the reaction in London was overwhelmingly negative. He had 'slandered paediatrics' and 'lacked objectivity'. The child, the professionals said, was 'an atypical child of atypical parents'. All their young patients were happy; there were only happy children's wards. The poignant remarks the little girl made about missing her mother were supposed to have been invented by Robertson, so the Tavistock Clinic had to hire the headmaster of a school for the deaf to lip-read the film! One professor of child health complained to the chairman of the clinic. He was particularly offended by a sequence that showed the little girl's twitching fingers. Such a shot of twitching fingers was 'unfair'. The film, they all said, should be withdrawn. It was decided not to release it; it was simply too explosive.

In Belfast and Glasgow, the abuse was repeated. Robertson recalled later that 'such was the emotional confusion created by the film in usually civilised men that they had abandoned the usual courtesies'. Walking home after one such torrid meeting, 'I heard the patter of running feet behind me. It was the matron. Catching up she said breathlessly, "Yon may be true of a wee English lassie, but it's not true of a Scottish bairn!"'

The quiet testimony of the films, however, did in the end pierce people's defences. One paediatrician remarked that at first 'I was angry, but after the film I really heard children crying for the first time.' An old nurse admitted: 'This film brings back to me the first child I ever nursed in hospital . . . He grieved for his mother and it simply broke my heart. After that I never saw grief again until I saw this film.' That professionals screened out grief and repressed all knowledge of the distress they were witnessing was not of course news to Robertson.

It was Bowlby then, that 'Terrible Dr B', and Robertson who revolutionised the practices of hospitals such that parents could stay with young children. The pitfalls of residential care were also accepted, reluctantly, after films like *John, aged 17 months, in foster care for 10 days*, and it is now standard practice to place orphaned children or children in need of care in foster homes rather than institutions, or to assign them to particular caregivers with whom they can form some ongoing bond.

Nobody could argue that the direction of these reforms was not in a humane direction. So complete was the victory of Robertson and Bowlby that it is now commonplace for parents to have unrestricted visiting rights to hospitals. These days if children go into hospital, parents stay with them as a matter of routine. Yet it is worth reflecting on that era's pervasive attitudes to children: the idea that a child simply did not possess an emotional life. Children were thought of as resilient, shallow creatures only a little above animals in the great chain of being, incapable of deep feeling, which meant that they could settle happily with anyone as long as they were kind. Such myths served the interests of an adult-centred world. It was a mixture of those deep habits of mind, and of course unconscious guilt, which fired the ferocity of the resistance.

The sequences of emotions observed by Bowlby and Robertson—protest, despair and detachment—raised issues of central interest to psychiatry. Protest raised the issue of separation anxiety implicated in conditions like agoraphobia. Despair intimated the grief and mourning of depression. Detachment had resonances with repression and defence. Only in understanding these issues, *together* rather than separately, is their significance for psychopathology realised. As a clinician, Bowlby had often confronted the centrality of experiences of separation and loss, whether recent or from the distant past, in the origin of many of the clinical conditions that his patients experienced.

The central question preoccupying the empirically minded Bowlby, after Robertson's studies of separation, was why the child's reaction was so intense.

'Why should a child be distressed in his mother's absence? What is he afraid of? Why should he be anxious when she is missing and cannot be found? Why is he apprehensive lest she leave him again?'

What Bowlby built over the next four decades, along with others, was the most important, empirically based account of child emotional development we have, now supported by the most recent findings of neurobiology. Contemplating children's reaction to prolonged separation was merely the beginning point. The main game was always to establish the outlines of a general theory. The suffering brought about by separation anxiety was, as Bowlby recorded, so 'widespread and common' that he conceptualised it as the key that might open the door to what was, in the late 1940s, the still opaque mystery of a child's emotional development. 'That being so, let us grasp the key at hand and see what door it opens.'

7 First love: its light and shadow

Werner Herzog's powerful film *The Enigma of Kaspar Hauser* depicts a true story. In the early nineteenth century, a young man was found wandering through the streets of Nuremberg, dazed and disoriented. Kept from earliest infancy to late adolescence chained to a wall in a dark cellar, Kaspar had been deprived for his entire childhood of any human relationships except for occasional visits from his mysterious jailor.

Kaspar had the body of a man but 'seemed not to know how to walk'. He had no recognisable emotional life, 'betrayed neither fear, nor astonishment, nor confusion: he rather showed an almost brutish dullness,' not even anger at his tormentor who had kept him so imprisoned. He had to be taught to walk, talk and toilet himself: all the simple skills a young child learns in an ordinary family. Initially showing unusual intellectual promise (some speaking of genius), his early deprivation, however, meant he soon lapsed into 'a kind of obsessive compulsive automaton . . . this chasm, which crime has torn in his life, cannot anymore be filled up; that time, in which he omitted to live, can never be brought back . . . How long soever he may live, he must for ever remain a man without a childhood and boyhood, a monstrous being . . .' For Kaspar it was simply too late.

A *cause célèbre* at the time, the story of Kaspar Hauser has profound resonances with our knowledge, at the beginning of the twenty-first century, that early childhood is a 'critical period'. The Canadian child advocate Fraser Mustard, author of a ground-breaking report, *The Early Years Study: Reversing the Real Brain Drain*, gives another vivid example of the critical period phenomenon. The Nobel Prize-winning work of David Hubel and Torstein Wiesel showed that when children who had been born with cataracts had them removed the operation could not restore normal vision. Adults, on the other hand, undergoing the same procedure, did regain normal sight. Hubel and Wiesel concluded that there is a critical period when the infant brain needs the stimulation from the eye to establish the necessary nerve connections. For those children surgical intervention came too late.

The New Continent

Bowlby and Robertson's observations ultimately opened a door onto an extraordinarily fertile new field. Fifty years later we stand at the threshold of what Daniel Stern has described as 'an exciting new continent' of infant mental health. New knowledge from several disciplines—attachment theory, neurobiology and psychoanalysis—is converging, refining our understandings of what children need in order to flourish. All of it underlines the importance of early childhood. In the first few years of life, a child may begin a pathway that is hopeful or ominous. During this 'critical period' children develop profoundly important attachments to their parents and an 'internal working model' of themselves and others—whether other people are essentially benign or malign. As Ron Lally once expressed it, in the early years children are putting on spectacles with which they come to view the world ever after. Or, as the remarkable Melbourne psychoanalyst 'Mama' Geroe put it to one of her patients: life can be lived in the light—or shadow—of those first relationships.

Brain development, according to the *Early Years* report, 'is especially rapid and extensive in the first year of life than . . . previously realised' and '. . . is much more vulnerable to environmental influence than we ever suspected . . . environmental influence is long lasting . . .' That means that if 'there has been extreme neglect through the critical periods—a child who is rarely touched or talked to or soothed—it may be very difficult to make up for the effects of severe deprivation later on.' Underlying levels of cortisol production and stress reactivity may be 'set', and as a consequence levels of anxiety and anger will also be 'set'. An adverse early environment may affect aspects of later physical as well as mental health. This clear new evidence concerning the significant neurobiological changes to the under-lying structure and chemistry of the brain as a result of early deprivation, neglect and/or abuse has also begun to transform our thinking when dealing with delinquency, violence and criminal behaviour. To begin expensive reparative programs by the time children have reached adoles-cence may well be shutting the stable door after the horse has bolted. Prevention will be better than cure.

So powerful, persuasive and important is this 'new continent' of knowledge about early childhood that in nations like Australia, America,

Canada and Britain, governments are all, in different ways, trying to integrate into bipartisan policy elements of these new findings about children's development.

That said, the early childhood story can easily be misrepresented. It can be conscripted by conservatives to prove that 'every mother must stay at home' or by an alliance of ideological feminism and the burgeoning daycare establishment to imply that 'every mother must leave her child in the hands of the childcare professionals'. Both readings are terrible distortions.

The new knowledge illuminates the likely consequences of maternal depression as well as the inadequacies of contemporary childcare. It underscores the importance of improving the conditions of stay-at-home *and* working motherhood *and* parenting generally, *and* the quality of childcare. It is potentially politically radical because it reveals the deeply layered interplay between social and economic factors and their translation into intergenerational cycles of deprivation, abuse and neglect. Above all, by taking the child's point of view it jettisons rigid ideological positions of both the traditionalist and feminist kinds. Instead, this new knowledge contains a moral imperative. We must use it to do something genuinely creative, and form social policies that will start children on a hopeful life trajectory. It must include all children, all parents and all caregivers.

There are other important points about the early childhood story. First, while early experience is now recognised as a 'critical period', that does not mean anyone's life is determined in an absolute fixed way by age three! (The other extreme position is that early experience has *no* influence. Harvard University's Jerome Kagan maintains, 'Infant experience is very critical only if your mother goes after you with a frying pan.') As Sroufe argues, however, 'infinite elasticity and complete fixity' are not the only options. In

> sharp contrast to either of these positions . . . is a sophisticated sensitive period hypothesis. One's model of self, others and relationships begin to emerge in the first year and have some firmness even before leaving infancy. They become increasingly firm as their structuring is broadened and elaborated and as they are supported by more experience. By adolescence they are quite firm although new models of thinking here may also provide new opportunities for change.

Second, although attachment research began by looking at mothers and their babies, reflecting the ideologies of the 1950s, more recent attachment research includes attachment to fathers and other caregivers. Third, lest anyone be alarmed by the massive responsibilities of parents, all of the elements necessary for a child to flourish can be, and usually are, provided by imperfect but ordinary, good enough families. Parents do not need to be well educated or wealthy. Forget about enrolling the baby in the Better Baby Institute. So much has been discovered from observing and learning from what good enough mothers and fathers already do. So much comes from ordinary, day-to-day love, commitment, time and energy.

Learning from mothers

The study of separation anxiety opened the door to a new theoretical paradigm of children's emotional and social development, one that has profoundly shaped the direction of the discipline of developmental psychology. It partly reflected a seismic shift in emphasis within psychoanalysis. As psychoanalysis crossed the English channel with Freud in the flight from Nazism, there was at the same time a shift away from the emphasis on the father and the Oedipal triangle, to an exploration of the mystery of first relationships, particularly those between mother and baby.

The psychologist Allan Schore gives life to that shift by showing two images. The first is a photo of Freud. The image, of 'a man's face gazing inward', is a symbol of 'a single unit; an adult, conscious reflective mind attempting to understand the realm of the dynamic unconscious that forms in early childhood . . .' In contrast, the second image, of Mary Cassatt's painting 'Baby's First Caress', is an icon of a *relationship between two people*, '. . . the curve of their arms suggest a loop, the baby touches the mother's face, the mother's hand is on the baby's foot. But more than this, the heads are placed together: what unites them is the meeting of *direct glances between their eyes.*'

The fundamental 'drive' of the human infant is towards connectedness, towards forming relationships with other human partners. Winnicott, in his brilliant, whimsical, paradoxical way, expressed it thus: 'There is no such thing as a baby,' meaning a baby only develops in the context of a relationship with its caregivers.

It was this period of early relatedness—especially the mysteries of the mother–child relation—that preoccupied Bowlby. Bowlby utilised the insights gained from direct observation of how young children behave to 'extrapolate forwards', and to develop a general theory of child emotional development, now called attachment theory.

It is important to distinguish between the well-verified concept of 'attachment' and the popular, romantic—and unverified—notion of maternal 'bonding'. This idea, of a magical, instantaneous process of 'bonding' in the minutes and hours immediately after birth, is a myth. Sensible as updated hospital practices like 'rooming in' and the promotion of close contact are for breastfeeding and for parents to welcome and come to know their baby, the 'bonding' idea was based on some early and faulty research by Klaus and Kennell, which has not since been replicated. The task of attachment—the most important of the first year—is very far from instant. It may be, but often is not, love at first sight. More usually, like all human relationships, it takes time, and a lot of work. For the baby, it is not until the second half of the first year that the attachment behaviours consistent with 'falling in love' are clearly organised around one or a couple of clear 'attachment figures'—usually mum, but also dad and sometimes granny or another caregiver.

Bowlby's colleague Mary Ainsworth provided much-needed empirical evidence for the intuitions and inferences that his theory was first built upon. Inspired by Robertson's film observations ('It was Jimmy's work,' she would say later, 'that impressed me the most'), Ainsworth set up a research project first in Uganda, then in Baltimore, USA, spending many hours observing mothers and babies interacting. Despite the vast cultural differences, Ainsworth found similar attachment behaviour in both countries, 'suggesting that babies everywhere spoke the same attachment language'. She identified the key aspects of attachment behaviour: the development of differential crying (being comforted by mother but not others); the preference for the mother in times of stress; clinging; the mother as a secure base from which the baby explored the world; and distress on separation.

Ainsworth also went beyond separation issues to examine the connection between how you were raised and how you turn out: for example, the sensitivity of mothering and its effect on a child's inner emotional world. She observed that those mothers who were attentive, sensitive and promptly responsive to their children's signals had babies who at twelve months cried less and seemed more secure, and later became more cooperative. One of Ainsworth's central contributions was the idea of the 'secure base'—the way infants and toddlers use the emotional and physical availability of a parent as the basis from which to explore the world.

The secure base

One afternoon after primary school, the children gathered in the sandpit to play. Cathy, a toddler little sister, joined them. On this occasion, her mother went in to the classroom without telling her, to speak to the teacher. On noticing her disappearance, Cathy stopped playing and began to whimper, looking around anxiously. 'Mum?' she asked. 'Mum, there's Mum,' I said, pointing to the classroom. She began playing again, but quite close by, and the locus of her game was suddenly very small, for she had withdrawn to a tiny corner in the sandpit. She looked preoccupied. Every ten seconds or so she looked at me and said 'Mum?' I nodded sympathetically and said, 'Yes, Mum's in there,' pointing again. This went on for about five minutes, until she toddled over to check that mum was indeed there. She came out beaming. 'Mum,' she said, delighted. After that she went on playing, and only occasionally referred back to me with a questioning 'Mum?' at which I would reassure her. From that day forward she would run up to me and put her hand trustingly in mine, for I had become the next best thing to a transitional object: The Woman Who Knew Where Mum Was.

This vignette could come from any observational work of children who are walking or mobile but are not yet preschoolers. The same 'secure base' behaviour is displayed to fathers. The program *Baby It's You*, screened on ABC TV in 2003, showed a father sitting on a bench in a city square, reading a newspaper, while his vigorous, exploring baby crawls off with the speed of an Exocet missile, then returns, ventures away and returns, again and again.

Anderson's famous observations of toddlers in a London park shows that kind of venturing forth, returning and refuelling, as if towards and away from an invisible barrier. If the parent moves, however, the toddlers instantly drop their exploratory behaviour or play, and begin whining, demanding to be picked up and so on. In order for them to be mobile they need their mother or father, their protector, to be still. The more they are rebuffed or ignored, the more distressed, the less exploratory they become. The more they feel someone is ready and able to be attentive—that is the more they feel 'held' in someone's mind—the more they feel free to go.

Bowlby's explanation for this is in terms of evolutionary patterns—to seek contact and connectedness, he reminds us, is a part of our species being, which in order to deal with predators was also a social being. In

A Secure Base there is an elegant summary of the ways in which separation anxiety should be seen as heightened fear not in relation to some *objective* risk, but simply to *increased* risk. Bowlby's metaphor was that of a thermostat, switching on and off to maintain the set goal of heat. Similarly, children monitor and maintain contact with those they trust and love most, which allows the secure base from which they can explore.

But children do not remain toddlers forever. That separation anxiety, in time, is overcome. Some months later, Cathy was again in the sandpit. This time when her mother disappeared, she hardly looked up to see where she was, but continued playing happily. After a time she looked around, and when I told her where Mum was, she just nodded and kept playing. Not long after, her mother told me she thought Cathy was ready for some kind of creche or kindergarten experience, and she began at the local childcare centre without any difficulty.

The strange situation

In Uganda, Ainsworth found the secure base

> was so conspicuous. If the mother was there, the kid would roam all round the room and explore things, looking back at her and maybe giving her a smile, but focusing most of their attention on the environment. And just as soon as the mother got up to leave the room, the chances were the baby would shriek and absolutely stop any kind of exploratory behaviour.

In Baltimore, USA, however, despite the existence of a universal 'baby language', the pattern of a secure base was less clear. Babies were used to the mother coming and going from room to room, hence were less likely to be upset when they left the room. What kind of behaviours, then, indicated security of attachment?

Mindful of psychologist Harry Harlow's research—which indicated that rhesus monkeys were only able to explore a strange environment when accompanied by their mothers—Ainsworth designed the 'Strange Situation'. Bringing the babies to a university lab meant bringing them into a slightly stressful environment. First the baby is brought with the mother in a room with toys to invite exploration. Then a stranger joins them to see how the baby responds. Then the mother leaves. How does the baby respond to separation? Then the baby is left quite alone. The stranger returns, and then the mother. The reunion with the mother is assessed.

After over seventy hours of observation, Ainsworth categorised the parents into different groups depending on the sensitivity of care. Secure babies cried on separation but sought their mothers out immediately, were easily comforted by them, and returned to playing. There were other attachment patterns. One was termed Ambivalent: the baby expressed both distress but also great anger and an inability to draw comfort from the mother's return. Another was the Avoidant pattern, where the baby turned away, or seemed indifferent to the mother's return. Later research has added a Disorganised and Disorientated pattern, found in high proportions among abused and neglected children, where the response is one of confusion and contradiction—like freezing or circling.

'The thing that blew my mind was the avoidant response,' said Ainsworth. These babies were the group that appeared the most insecure at home but were blasé, almost indifferent, in the Strange Situation—in short, they looked precociously independent. At home these babies cried and showed more, not less, separation distress; were clingier, whinier and so on. Most importantly, they had mothers that the observers had rated as 'interfering, rejecting or neglectful'. Ainsworth made a lateral leap. She noticed these avoidant babies behaved in a fashion similar to the older children described by Bowlby and Robertson as being detached: coming home from hospital and ignoring the mother or pretending she wasn't there. This suggested that older and younger children are using the same coping mechanism, of shutting down attachment needs. Later tests would show that the avoidant babies were just as stressed as the other babies; their heart rates and cortisol levels rose in the strange situation, yet they displayed a curious shutdown. 'Already by the age of twelve months . . . [they] no longer express to their mothers one of their deepest emotions or the equally deep-seated desire for comfort and reassurance that accompanies it.'

Although Ainsworth did not intend the Strange Situation as an assessing technique, it soon became one. Instead of seventy-two hours of observation, the whole thing could be done in twenty minutes. Despite some vocal sceptics, attachment scholars were soon utilising the test or the insights derived from it. Over time it became clear that it was *behaviour on reunion*—whether or not babies asked for comfort and reassurance and how they did it—that was the most important indicator of inner emotional security, not the inevitable separation protest itself. Although the Strange Situation Assessment, courtesy of the daycare wars, has been the source of some controversy, the most recent, comprehensive, and sophisticated longitudinal study by the US

National Institute of Child Health and Development has validated the procedure.

The Strange Situation test is probably best seen as a window, but no more than that, into a child's emotional life at age one, utilising the language of gesture. Bowlby was amazed, viewing the videotapes of the Strange Situation, at how much was revealed of a child's internal emotional world and their capacity or incapacity to communicate their emotional needs freely to others.

Consider these gestures from children who have been physically abused. On being reunited with their mother in the Strange Situation, they might begin by reaching out or moving toward her, then suddenly freeze, or turn in confused circles, or even cover their faces with their hands in an apparent gesture of shame.

The Strange Situation has shown children to have different attachment classification systems with father and mother and even other caregivers; it shows a glimpse not of a child, or a mother or a father, but of a *relationship.*

The long-term implications of secure attachment

Ainsworth's work was soon supported by other systematic research studies. Alan Sroufe's work in Minnesota—a longitudinal study of different socio-economic groups—examined the later implications for development of the earlier attachment classifications. His studies showed that security of attachment has immense value for a child across a range of domains. Two-year-olds who had been assessed at eighteen months as secure were enthusiastic and persistent in solving easy tasks and effective in using maternal assistance when the tasks became more difficult. If psychotherapy is meant to put back the 'sparkle' into adults that harsh childrearing practices had taken out, these children had never lost the sparkle. In a study by Leah Albersheim, secure children showed more joyousness, persistence and responsiveness to instructions and less frustration. They expressed more positive emotions, more delight; they laughed, smiled and shared more pleasurable feelings with their mother. Confronted with the same task, their anxiously attached counterparts became whiny, collapsing under pressure.

Sroufe and his colleagues felt these studies had put them on to some central issue in early development. While early studies had been with a low-risk middle-class sample, they now moved to a 'poverty sample'. The children were assessed at birth doing prenatal measures of neurological, motor and cognitive tests. The mothers were also assessed by nurses, for example for their interest in the child. The study showed that the security of attachment could be largely predicted at birth. Answering Kagan's assertion that attachment classifications were really just a manifestation of inherited temperament, none of the infants' constitutional factors turned out to be important except for one neurological measure. The mothers' characteristics were more powerful. Depressed mothers and those rated by nurses as having a low interest in their baby before it was born, for example, were more likely to have anxiously attached children at one year. That finding—the relationship of attachment security to how babies are treated—was confirmed by a much later Dutch study by Dymphna van den Boom. Mothers whose babies had been assessed neonatally as having difficult, irritable temperaments were given supportive therapy to establish sensitive nurturing care. Sixty-eight per cent of those receiving therapeutic intervention established secure relationships compared with only 28 per cent of a control group who received no help. Temperament, then, makes a contribution, but does not determine outcome.

When the children in the poverty sample reached four-and-a-half to five, Sroufe enrolled them in a specially created nursery school on the Minnesota campus. None of the teachers knew the child's previously assessed attachment classification. Sroufe and his colleagues found that preschoolers who had been judged securely attached as infants were significantly more flexible, curious, and socially competent. They enjoyed themselves, confidently sought help when needed, rather than resorting to whiny tantrums to get attention. They were less aggressive, but could still be assertive about what they wanted. Secure children were also more empathetic, displaying sympathy when their peers were distressed. Such findings continued to hold in Sroufe's studies through the elementary years of schooling.

They were also more independent. This last finding on independence is important. The West is presently obsessed with hurrying early independence—usually for reasons of adult convenience—yet it was those children whose dependency needs as babies and toddlers were accepted and responded to promptly and sensitively who later became the most independent children. The preschoolers who had avoidant attachment relationships as infants—those forced to self-reliance too early, whose dependency needs were rebuffed or rejected—were more dependent, seeking out the teacher more often than securely attached children. However, they were least likely to seek attention or express dependency needs when they had been hurt or disappointed. Some 'expressed their needs for adult attention in bizarre ways'. One approached his teacher 'through a series of oblique angles'. 'That they were frequently sullen or oppositional and not inclined to seek help when injured or disappointed, however, spoke poignantly of their avoidant patterns.'

Children with an avoidant attachment pattern tended to be far less able to engage in fantasy play than securely attached children. Where they did engage in such play, it was often 'characterised by irresolvable conflict'. Avoidant children tended to victimise others, engaging in repeated acts of cruelty. Ambivalent children, with their desperate clinging and need for reassurance, kept coming back for more, almost as if they had no experience of not being treated badly. They were prepared to seek contact at any price; one approached one of his tormentors and begged: 'Why don't you tease me, I won't get mad.'

Sroufe and his colleagues found that in every case of victimisation, there was an avoidant and ambivalent pair, with the avoidant child doing the bullying, the ambivalent child submitting. None of the securely attached pairs showed any victimisation, refusing to let themselves be pulled into relationships with hurtful dynamics: 'they either found a way to make the relationship positive, withdrew, or met the aggression with just enough force to discourage it. *It was as if such behaviour was foreign to them and they would have nothing to do with it.*'

Teachers reacted very differently to each attachment style. They tended to treat secure children in a warm, matter-of-fact, age-appropriate way. They excused, indulged and infantilised the scattered and clingy, ambivalently attached children. They were controlling, cold and angry with the avoidantly attached children, describing them as 'mean, lying, everything is hers'. Watching all this, Sroufe and his colleagues, who knew each child's background, winced, feeling a great sense of loss and frustration. The avoidantly attached children began life by being rejected, and now had those harsh lessons reinforced by teachers' behaviour. As Sroufe put it, 'Whenever I see a teacher who looks as if she wants to pick a kid up by the shoulders and stuff him in the trash, I know that kid has an avoidant attachment history.'

Sroufe linked the behaviours to Ainsworth's extensive observations of children in the home. He felt strongly that the avoidant children's 'piteous behaviour pattern had its origin in the rebuffs the children had suffered . . .' Their experiences of emotional unavailability, rejection, or physical abuse at home meant it was natural to inflict it on others. So, thought Sroufe, did the empathy and sensitivity showed by secure children come from their family? 'How do you get an empathetic child?' asked Sroufe. 'You get an empathetic child not by trying to teach the child and admonish the child to be empathetic, you get an empathetic child by being empathetic with the child. The child's understanding of relation-ships can only be from the relationships he's experienced.' Ambivalent children 'by contrast seemed too preoccupied with their own needs to have any feelings left over with others, and avoidant children sometimes seemed to take pleasure in another child's misery . . . In the same situation a secure kid would get a teacher and bring the teacher to the child or stand by and look concerned.'

Following the sample through to adolescence, Sroufe found that security of attachment in infancy, despite coming from a sample marked by poverty, single parenthood and disadvantage, continued to show strong benefits. Again the notion that a close and strong early relation-ship with a mother will forever tie a child to her apron strings was shown to be false. By middle childhood, secure attachments meant a capacity for the intimate 'I and Thou' of friendship. At preadolescence, children made friends more easily, and spent less time with adults and more with their peers. Interpersonal sensitivity and empathy continued to develop. Seventy-six per cent of securely attached eleven-year-olds had friendships, compared with forty-five percent of insecurely attached children.

Insecure children's friendships were more marked by jealousy and possessiveness. They displayed more behaviour problems; those who were 'hostile, non-compliant, hyperactive, who tended to give up and cry, who displayed nervous habits, who were passive and withdrawn, or who were worried or unhappy—were usually children who had been anxiously attached to their mothers.'

Boys turned the sense of frustration associated with insecure attachment not inwards but outwards. Avoidantly attached boys were 'off the charts in every measure of aggression, assertion and control seeking'. They appeared hungry for attention and approval (their dependency scores were also highest) but sought attention in indirect ways, which were often disruptive and aggressive. Avoidant boys in whom aggression was 'particularly marked' were more likely to 'bully, lie, cheat, destroy things, brag, act cruelly, disrupt the class, swear, threaten, argue, throw temper tantrums, become defiant. Ambivalent boys, on the other hand, were more prone to be shy, apathetic, and withdrawn.'

The internal working model

'It was as if such behaviour was foreign to them and they would have nothing to do with it.' Robert Karen

One of the most interesting contributions emerging from this body of research was the idea of an internal working model of relationships that evolves—Lally's 'putting on spectacles with which to view the world'—in the early years.

Consider this. Talking on the phone to a friend I commented that in researching this book, I had been struck by how often we project our own basic mistrust or dislike onto the baby or the mother. One mother complained of her tiny baby, 'He looks daggers at me!'

I was remembering the gaze that had been such an important part of my own children's relatedness to me, or their father, beaming back extraordinary love to us. I remembered how my mother had said, 'She smiles at you with her whole being.' How absurd to think a baby was 'looking daggers' at his mother! A baby's gaze at his mother could not be anything but benign.

'Can you imagine', I said to him, laughing, 'the idea of a baby looking daggers at its mother!' To me it was a clear case of projective hostility. The phone went silent. Puzzled by his lack of responsiveness, I waited. There was a little pause and then he said, with a peculiar inflection, rather grimly, 'Maybe that baby *was* looking daggers at her!'

Suddenly, I remembered. His own mother had been intrusive and overbearing, but rather depressed at the same time. One phone call from her and his shoulders began to slump, and his normally cheerful demeanour gave way to irritable gloom. (And no wonder. His wife gave vivid descriptions of his mother furiously rifling through his bedroom cupboards, as if trying to divine the secret of his married existence.) That little black hole of silence and misunderstanding between us, that sudden disjunction, represented the collision of two very different internal working models of intimate attachment relationships. We were revealing our internal images of what we thought *mothers were like*.

Sroufe's study showed that secure children responded to victimisation or bullying by repelling it as something foreign to their experience. In revealing this, he was opening a door to a crucial contribution of attachment theory to developmental psychology. From the longitudinal work done by scholars like Sroufe, the question forms: why are there often such lasting consequences of these attachment patterns? Why are these patterns of behaviour so resistant to change?

Bowlby's answer to that was the formulation of the concept of an internal working model of relationships, of the self and others. This develops through what Stern describes as 'Repeated Interactions which are Generalised (or RIGs)'. What began as a pattern of interaction in relationships becomes generalised into expectations of the world, coded unconsciously, part of the structure of the mind. It becomes a kind of internal affective map of the self, of the other, of self with other.

The internal working model, deriving from interactions that are repeated and then generalised by the infant, 'reflects the child's relationship history, codifying the behaviours that belong to an intimate relationship, and defining how he will feel about himself when he is closely involved with another person.' This hypothesis has been amply confirmed by the now considerable body of empirical evidence reviewed at the beginning of this chapter.

Yet for the child with an insecure attachment, the 'internal working model' is 'a poor guide to reality': for example the child who, feeling unloved, comes to generalise and believe themselves to be unlovable, expecting rejection. Among insecure children, the internal model of relationships was particularly likely to become rigid, because of the suppression and banishment of emotions associated with dependency. In avoidant attachment the child may feel that their babyishness, their infantile nature, their dependency must be the reason for their parents' hostility. As a consequence they begin to deny, to screen out dependency needs, and to repress awareness of them altogether.

While the internal working model is *resistant* to change, it is not incapable of being revised. At several points—adolescence, marriage, and particularly on parenting—there is the possibility of reparation, change, growth and transformation.

Secure attachment helps what Daniel Goleman calls emotional intelligence. It builds the capacity for meta-cognition, or the capacity for self-reflection, for knowing the complexity of feelings, like having more than one feeling at a time, or that someone can feel one thing but say another; the capacity, as Peter Fonagy put it, of *thinking about thinking*. In contrast, anxiously attached children tend to not develop such capacities, as if the painfulness of emotions forces them to simply cut off thinking about feelings. As one child put it, 'if I started crying I would never stop'.

Fonagy suggested that in extreme cases, abused children could develop no 'theory of mind' because it was so unbearably painful to acknowledge the hostility or even hate that was in their parents' feelings towards them. One consequence was the incapacity to empathise, or recognise that one's actions might bring hurt and distress to another.

The micro world of the infant

The ways in which those patterns of love and hate, of secure or anxious attachment, might come into being have become the focus of some of the most exciting contemporary research into the first year of life. The 'previously unexplored continent' of new infancy research alerted people to the extraordinary intensity, richness and complexity of the 'micro world of the infant'. As people like Daniel Stern turned to slowing down videos of mother–infant interaction, they discovered that

> the world of intimate communication . . . in what was once dismissed as rather charming but meaningless babble turned out to be as rich and unexpected as the universe of 'cavorting beasties' that Anton van Leeuwenhoek observed when he put an ordinary drop of water under his newly invented microscope.

This research confirmed the sense that infants are socially responsive from the earliest days. They could pick out their own mother's breast milk pads from those of other mothers; conversely, mothers could identify their own infants' cries from other babies. Far from meaningless baby talk, mothers and infants were engaging from the beginning in lengthy and complex reciprocal exchanges. Even in the earliest months, when there is little control over movement, there is nonetheless a prolonged 'conversation', where infants respond, attune and take turns similar to that in conversations, and bring an interchange to an end by looking away.

> Gazing is a potent form of social communication. When watching the gazing patterns of mother and infant during this life period, one is watching two people with almost equal facility and control over the same social behaviour . . . infants exert major control over . . . contact with mother . . . they can avert their gaze, shut their eyes, stare past, become glassy eyed . . . reject, distance themselves from, or defend themselves against mother . . . reinitiate engagement and contact when they desire.

This work too showed the exceptional prescience and intuitive genius of D. W. Winnicott, whose metaphor of 'holding' turned out to stand for so much of what actually occurs between baby and mother. One of the most important interactions of all is to give the baby the space to be alone—securely 'held' so that the baby can drift off into reverie, into the state of 'going on being'. A baby can be alone in the presence of a loved adult, so secure in their love and holding that she can slip into her own world and discover herself. From this, Winnicott felt, came the capacity to be alone in adult life, for solitude as well as intimacy.

Among writers on the micro-world of the infant, Daniel Stern is of exceptional interest. He answers many of the questions frustrating those who see the limitations of the classifications of attachment styles. 'It's all very well,' commented a psychoanalytically inclined friend, 'this work—the mother has a secure baby, but what is she *like*?' Is she, like Manning Clark's mother, a 'frowner'? Is she a live wire who sees a moment without interaction as a moment lost? Is she responsive and sensitive enough to have a secure relationship with her baby, but also a bit melancholic?

In rich and revealing detail, Stern's brilliant *The Interpersonal World of the Infant*, now justly a classic, showed the shaping of human personality by these interactions, which occur long before the development of speech. A baby might come to see her world as a benign place, of being securely 'held' both psychically and physically. Her life has at its centre a warm hearth. Or that world might be felt to be unresponsive and indifferent, her emotional needs unnoticed or ignored, behind ice windows.

By the parents being so responsive, by identification with a baby's needs, the kind of 'reading' that makes up sensitive attunement, the baby may come to learn what she needs, and find that those needs are legitimate. She begins to learn to name feeling states. Far from the frantic intrusions of parents waving placards and mumbling the times tables under the influence of the competitive Mummy Olympics producing Superbabies, the capacity to 'pay attention' seems linked to the capacity to 'leave alone'. (Ironically, children of parents who respond also to the signal of 'enough' have children with much longer concentration spans.)

As adults, we have all experienced those moments where others increase and amplify the intensity of our joy by their enthusiastic, affirming response. Stern calls this a crescendo effect; emotions surge upward from pleasure to joy and then elation as mothers respond to a baby's smile with their own. Most of the communication is non-verbal, occurring especially through the gaze and smile, 'which can blast the infant into the next orbit of positive excitation'. Winnicott thought 'the main thing' was 'communication' between 'live bodies'.

Emotions come into being through our connection with others. We can, by sharing a response, slip inside an affective experience and then alter it. The feminist Julia Kristeva calls this a 'mother's translations'. A mother may do so to soothe an upset baby, sympathising warmly with the feeling state (Oh, poor darling are you cold, hungry, wet, dirty?), but with a voice that does not *reflect* the baby's stressed state but rather projects the mother's calm confidence and composure that the distress is temporary and will be overcome. (Sometimes easier said than done!) The baby is able to use the mother's calm emotional state to help contain her wilder feelings and return to the stable state offered by the stronger adult partner. But one can 'steal' a baby's response, too, by transforming it into something else, turning perhaps an act of aggression into some conventional bourgeois 'niceness'. I once heard a mother deny that her daughter had had a particularly vivid and terrible dream. 'Oh no, dear, you didn't dream such a nasty thing. You're imagining it.' Her daughter looked bewildered. What was true and what was not true? Is a mother so powerful she knows what I dream better than I do?

Stern's work showed how patterns of interaction enable parts of the self and soul to come alive and be acknowledged and accepted, in word or gesture; or be unattended, go underground, or be disconfirmed and banished. At worst, such misattunement opens the possibility for the development of a 'false self', one externally compliant with the world, but where authentic responses are lost and 'acceptable' responses substituted. The self is no longer the author of one's feelings.

Stern found a mother–baby 'dance' of extraordinary precision, a 'matching' of rhythm, contours of emotion, intensity, timing and imitation. There was even a kind of beat to these exchanges. Stern concluded:

> It is clear that interpersonal communion, as created by attunement, will play an important role in the infant's coming to recognise their feeling states are forms of human experience that are shareable with other humans. The converse is also true: feeling states that are never attuned to will be experienced only alone, isolated from the interpersonal context of shareable experience. *What is at stake here is nothing less than the shape of and extent of the shareable inner universe.* [emphasis added]

None of the research done on the micro-world of the infant need exclude fathers. Much of the work done on infant–father interactions shows how men interact with infants and children differently but in a way that's complementary to the way mothers behave, by extending the babies' exploratory play. As more men are drawn into an area not historically part of the role of father—direct infant care—my own observation is that they seem to become attuned in many of the ways Stern and others describe.

While I was writing this section, a friend and new father rang. He was looking after his seven-month-old baby. When the baby cried he said, apparently without looking, for the baby was in the next room, 'She has had a hard poo.' He knew his baby daughter's bodily rhythms well. He put down the phone, picked her up and tended to her. All crying instantly ceased. I could hear him making soothing, murmuring sounds. He brought her to the phone to sit on his lap, and I could hear a few squeaks of delight. The world was all right again. By the act of picking her up, which by seven months he and the mother will have done thousands of time, he is opening up her world to expect responsiveness, to expect the magic of a parent to soothe the internal discomfort. This baby has learned that the world is a good place.

But another baby might be left hanging, only responded to in moods that are jolly, but left alone and treated brusquely when sad, in pain, frustrated or angry. Such infants, when they take their needs to their parents, receive, as Bowlby put it, 'a dusty answer'. They learn something equally profound: that on our voyage in the world we float alone, on a sea of indifference.

If Bowlby's work opens us to the dark side of infant experience and the central terror of infancy—the fear of abandonment—Stern's work opens us to the impulse towards mastery and agency even in the tiniest baby, and reminds us that the baby is not just a passive recipient but a purposive actor, albeit an unequal one, in its own right, capable of meaningful reciprocal exchanges from the beginning of its life. Which brings me to an extremely important point.

Reparation: the importance of being a not so perfect mother

A mother, watching her children play in a sandpit, once remarked grimly to me that 'one false move as a mother and they've had it!' What the evidence shows, however, is that in an ordinary sample of non-high-risk mothers, around three-quarters of them will develop a secure attachment with their children. Given that mothers are not perfect, misattune as well as attune, that suggests a baby is reasonably resilient. In the general hubbub and messy scrum of a busy family life, there will be moments where baby waits or is misunderstood, when parents are tired, or cranky, or just get it plain wrong.

Does it matter? Must a mother be a Magical Mother who always knows what to do? How can mothers be magical when each baby is different and so much comes from simple trial and error, and particularly error? When the psychoanalyst Heinz Kohut speaks of the mother 'mirroring' back to the child who the child is—it is undoubtedly necessary for a baby to feel celebrated, that his mother and father glory in this particular baby—but does the child really need, like the narcissistic Bad Queen in the fairy tale 'Snow White', a mirror that must *always* answer back: '*You are the fairest of them all?*'

The answer is no. Every mother gets things wrong. The new thinking sees some degree of misattunement as important, perhaps *as important as attunement*. From those micro-moments of inattention, misunderstanding or mismatch of response comes the exceptionally important 'reparative moment'. Unless one wants to raise a tyrant, human beings need to know from earliest infancy that things don't always go their own way, and that when they don't, catastrophe will not strike. Rather, as the parent realises that the break has occurred and re-attunes to what the infant needs, consoling them and reconnecting with them, the baby has the essential experience of mastery—of going through a difficult, negative feeling state *but surviving and coming out the other side*. From the many moments of misattunement and reparation, within the general expectation that one will be cared for, comes the expectation that when things go wrong, *it can be repaired*. From such reparative moments, it is thought, comes the beginning of resilience.

For example, if a mother takes longer one day to come to the cot because an older child needs her, a baby might discover his own fingers to suck, and thus that he has the means of comforting and amusing himself for a little while. The most sensitive parents imaginable cannot entirely discover who a baby is and all of its desires, needs and preferences—his own true self. The baby, and later the child, must do that at least partly himself. If a mother or father flashed a toy in front of a baby's nose every time he grumbled, controlling and anticipating everything, he would be robbed of his own capacity for initiative. Even when parents are devoted and sensitive, the ordinary passage of life will mean the baby has to struggle a little bit. And he must struggle in order to learn that as well as confidently expecting to have people on his side, looking out for him, he can do things on his own behalf. Emphasising 'good enough' fathers or mothers does not mean wholesale neglect or outright abuse. But we are not perfect as parents and it is a great mercy that we are not, for no child will confront a perfect world answering their every need.

Emotional regulation and the origin of the self

Why is it that infants whose baby babble contains the sounds of every language known to human kind end up speaking only their mother's tongue? Why is there such a bias towards the influence of the early years? There is a neurobiological explanation: the phenomenon of neural pruning. Human infants are born with an overabundance of neurones. It is experience, especially repeated experience, which helps synapses connect, organising the evolving brain into certain neural pathways, and prunes unwanted, unused neurons. Repeated activation creates a well-worn neural pathway. It is a little like walking for the first time in an overgrown, untrodden field. Walk enough times along a particular route and the bias will be to seek out that path again. It's quicker, and offers advantages over ploughing through thickets of untested ground. With respect to language, as the sounds of one's mother tongue are repeatedly heard and learned, our capacity over time to learn other languages sharply declines.

When I first discovered the new infant research, I wondered if there was anyone—a new Bowlby perhaps—who was pulling together different fields, mining insights and the creative tension between disciplines. Then an Australian child psychiatrist, George Halasz, recommended to me a 700-page volume, *Affect Regulation and the Origin of the Self*, by the outstanding psychologist, neuroscientist and practising psychoanalyst Allan Schore. Schore's central contribution is in illuminating the neurobiology of all those aspects of attachment, attunement and interactions between a baby and its caregivers in the first two years of life. All that I have addressed so far in this chapter is fundamentally about the development of *emotional regulation*. The most important influence on the early environment is the emotional relationships with caregivers, especially the primary caregiver.

At first, the immature baby relies on a responsive, sensitive adult with a mature psychological organisation who can regulate their own emotions, and help soothe the intense negative feeling states that could easily overwhelm the baby (i.e. you calm a crying baby by cuddling or feeding, and not by screaming back at it!). A baby, says Schore, can only withstand short periods of intense negative feeling. The mother's presence, her milk, voice, smell, touch and rhythm of handling calms and soothes. Her actions help to 'downward regulate' chaotic emotional states due to overexcitement, fear, pain and hunger. She also 'upward regulates', arousing by gaze, feeding, speech, touch, offers of toys or change of scenery or shared excitement, 'pepping baby up', drawing baby out of flat, bored, sad, withdrawn, or depressive states. Over time, what begins with the baby utilising and depending on the adult's mature capacities gradually becomes internalised, helping the developing child to manage her own emotional regulation. Hence a preschooler in fantasy play may be heard to offer identical words of comfort to an 'injured' or 'sick' toy animal or doll to those that have been used to console them.

When asked in an interview about his new discoveries, Schore replied how important *pleasure* between mother and baby is. New brain imaging techniques (like PET and MRI scans) 'show that in mutual gaze the mother's face is triggering high levels of endogenous opiates in the child's growing brain'. We need not privilege the 'hard data' from neuroscience. Stern, too, speaks of how such interactions have what he calls vitality or crescendo effects. Emde talks of a baby's 'sparkling eyed pleasure' in the presence of the mother. The seventeenth-century French doctor Laurent Joubert, whose wife had had eleven children and nursed them all, gave this description of breastfeeding, recording the infant's sensual pleasure in it:

> Is there a better pastime than one with an infant who is endearing to his [mother] and strokes her as he suckles while with one hand he uncovers and handles the other breast and with the other grasps her hair or her necklace, playing with them. When with his feet he kicks at those who want to divert him, at the same moment with his loving eyes he gives a thousand little smiling glances . . . What a delight to see it!

In a weird way, the 'micro-world of the infant' places within the clumsy reach of science what Helen Garner describes as 'eros': that 'quick spark between people'—only in this case between mother and baby. It happens not because we have to remind ourselves to 'stimulate'—almost a guarantee of failure since there is no accompanying authentic emotion of real interest—but through love, pride, spontaneous lived moments. We touch a baby because her body is irresistible; it is impossible to change a nappy without blowing a raspberry on a little round belly. Or we pat her gently on the back as she wuffles into one's shoulder. It is impossible not to be delighted in some new skill, because a baby seems, with the positive distortion of parenthood, the most wondrous creature in the world. It is impossible not to comfort and soothe her because we identify so deeply with her that it is far more painful to see her distress than feel our own.

In turn, all these experiences have a neurobiological consequence. They change the brain. Policy makers were galvanised when shown photos of the shrunken brain of a severely neglected child, alongside the much larger one of a normal child. Responses to stress and fear can be permanently altered, threats perceived where there are none. Early childhood may shape the presence or absence of brain chemicals like dopamine, cortisol, opiates, serotonin, the capacity for pain and pleasure. Researchers like Felicity de Zulueta argue that later drug abuse may be an attempt by the individual to rectify early environmental trauma, to self-soothe and achieve emotional regulation by using chemicals like alcohol, nicotine, heroin and cocaine to alter brain deficits in the direction of a stable state.

The intense contemporary interest in attachment and emotional regulation has been sharpened as a result of the rise of numbers of conditions like Attention Deficit and Hyperactivity Disorder (ADHD), as well as narcissistic and borderline personality disorders. If in Freud's time it was the hysteric and sexual neurotic who typified the 'illness' of his time, it is these maladies that perplex and challenge our own generation of therapists. For example, the 'borderline personality disorder'— extremely difficult to treat with the chief characteristics of 'stable instability', aggressively hostile and chaotic emotional states—is quintessentially the incapacity to regulate emotions. And such disorders are thought to date not, as in Freud's time, to problems emerging from the later Oedipal period, but much earlier, to failures in the nurturing environment in infancy.

The motherhood constellation: who cares for the caregivers?

The psychoanalyst Harry Guntripp observed:

> If human infants are not surrounded by genuine love from birth, radiating outward into a truly caring family and social environment, then we pay for

our failure toward the next generation by having to live in a world torn with fear and hate ... The importance of security for babies and mothers outweighs every other issue.

If early childhood is so important, how can modern society be so foolish as to devalue and denigrate mothering? How can it be so careless as to make women 'pay the price of motherhood'? How can we be so short-sighted as to not extend our parental leave programs? How can we not cherish, respect and pay childcare workers what they are worth? How can we give them so many children to care for? How can we emphasise the market work of both parents at the expense of the extraordinarily important work they do nurturing their children?

We place a high valuation on how mothers 'perform', what clever, well-adjusted, high-achieving, money-making 'product' they 'produce', yet stay-at-home mothers often feel defensive as they try to sustain the meaning of what they do in the face of an indifferent, if not contemptuous society. When a woman returns to work, as she usually does, unlike the returned soldier there is no concession in training, income support or even respect for the essential societal service she has performed.

For working mothers the problems are no less grave, although of a different kind. So much of paid work has continued as if we can get away with integrating an entirely new group—mothers with young children—into jobs including demanding professions with an absolute minimum of accommodation to motherhood.

Part of this is our contemporary failure to provide a new version—which includes women's changed roles—of what Winnicott called the 'facilitating environment'. The mother's and father's efforts in 'holding' a child means they, too, in turn must be 'held'—by grandparents, other caregivers and the society at large. As Bowlby said, 'If a community values its children it must cherish its parents.' In a prescient passage, echoing feminist Marilyn Waring's *Counting For Nothing*, he wrote:

> Man and woman power devoted to the production of material goods counts as a plus in all our economic indices. Man and woman power devoted to the production of happy, healthy, self-reliant children in their own homes does not count at all. We have created a topsy turvy world ... Just as a society in which there is a chronic insufficiency of food takes a deplorably inadequate level of nutrition as the norm, so may a society in which parents of young children are left on their own with a chronic insufficiency of help take this state of affairs as its norm ...

What happens when such a nourishing environment is missing? The new research does not only show the bright side of the moon. Spinning out into ever-widening circles, the light cast by attachment theory began to illuminate the networks of relationships and the social context in which mothering occurs. There was a rich harvest of understanding, not only to the distorted and tragic world that a young child may inhabit, but also the quiet and terrible desperation with which some women lead their lives as young mothers.

8 The dark side of the moon

'If a child feels no emotional attachment to any human being, then we cannot expect any more remorse from him after killing a human than from someone who ran over a squirrel.' Bruce Perry

The roots of violence

Without attachment, a child psychotherapist once remarked to me, there can be no empathy. In 2003, Australians struggled to make sense of the bewildering crimes of a middle-class housewife, Kathleen Folbigg. Over a decade she had smothered to death four babies. Each child took a full, four, terrible minutes to die, struggling for air and for life. Incomprehensibly, the victims of Australia's worst female serial killer were her own children.

The desire for understanding is *not* the same impulse as that which allows people to evade responsibility for their actions. One can feel the enormity of a crime, the suffering of the victims, and the need for just punishment, as well as trying to make sense of it. To understand is not to exonerate. To try to answer why need not mean that 'the words of judgement crumble on our tongues', as Richard Hoggart once put it.

As Kathleen Folbigg's early life slowly emerged during the trial, I was immediately struck by the strong resonances of her strange personality with the case I am putting forward in these pages, especially the some-times terrible consequences of disrupted attachments.

Abuse, neglect and abandonment

Folbigg's first eighteen months—the critical period for forming emotional attachments—were almost unimaginably terrible. She suffered severe neglect and emotional deprivation, witnessed terrible violence and abusive attacks by her father on her mother, and was probably sexually abused herself. She had multiple separation experiences as she was repeatedly dumped on others, and finally, when her father murdered her mother, she was abandoned to a series of foster homes and an orphanage.

Kathleen Folbigg's father, 'Jack' Britton, was a hit man for notorious underworld figures like Robert Trimbole, with a predilection for breaking kneecaps. He had a 'vicious streak particularly with women'. He slashed his first wife's throat, and served eight months in jail. According to a family friend, Britton would hold a knife to his second wife's throat every morning and ask, 'Will I or won't I?'

The mother, Kathleen Donovan, was an alcoholic and addicted to gambling. She had already left her first husband and children. Her attachment to baby Kathleen seemed tenuous, and she continuously left her with others. After arguing with Britton over her heavy drinking, Donovan walked out, stealing his wallet and abandoning Kathleen.

Leaving Kathleen with friends, Britton asked her mother to return to the grief-stricken baby. 'I begged and pleaded with her to come back to me and the child. She refused point blank.' Moments before her death, Britton claimed, 'She said again she couldn't care less.' Overcome with rage, he stabbed her twenty-four times.

With the mother dead and the father finally behind bars, Kathleen was fostered with an aunt, Mrs Platt. During Folbigg's trial a revealing departmental report, written at this time, came to light. Mrs Platt was having trouble teaching her basic hygiene and acceptable behaviour. Kathleen was aggressive towards other children and prone to severe temper tantrums. She was preoccupied with her sexual organs, indulging in excessive sex play and masturbation, trying to insert various objects into her vagina. Referred to the Yagoona Child Health Clinic, a Dr Spencer assessed her and concluded that during infancy she had been sexually abused, possibly by her father. At three, Kathleen was withdrawn from Mrs Platt and sent to an orphanage, Bidura Children's Home. In a psychological assessment there, at this stage she was so disturbed as to be judged possibly intellectually disabled, although she was of above average intelligence. Ominously, she was emotionally detached from others: remote, restless, inattentive, and unresponsive when shown individual attention. She rarely smiled. Over the following months, however, she did perk up and became interested in her surroundings again.

Finally, she was sent to permanent foster parents, Deirdre and Neville Marlborough. The family lavished attention on the pretty, doll-faced child. Her foster-sister 'loved to dress her little sister in cute outfits'. Yet there were early intimations that the past had left a dark shadow. The child was strangely self-contained, always keeping her innermost feelings to herself. After the trial the foster family spoke of problems dating 'from earliest childhood'. Her foster-mother said, 'Kathy could look you in the face and lie, and you wouldn't be able to tell.'

Always curious about her past, she finally learned the terrible truth at fifteen, after tracking down her mother's brother. Her bonds with her foster family began to unravel. She left home, 'always seemed solitary', and, against the opposition of her foster-mother, married Craig Folbigg very young.

The compulsion to repeat

Several members of her new extended family noticed that Kathleen was rage-filled when thwarted, kicking a cat downstairs and viciously yanking a toddler out of a high chair for not eating enough. Her sister-in-law said, 'She had so much anger inside her if she couldn't get what she wanted.' As a mother, Folbigg was self-centred, uninterested in her children. Even after ostensibly losing three children to SIDS, she was indifferent to noises on the baby monitor, always wanting to turn it off. Preoccupied with her appearance, she came alive only when she was the centre of male attention. She was jealous of the love and care her children got from their father. 'He should be for me forever. Just because a baby is coming into our lives makes no difference really.'

Her diaries show the absence of any normal attachment to her children. She disliked the physical closeness of breastfeeding, putting the babies on the bottle as soon as they came home. Sarah, nicknamed the 'catnapper', only slept well when she was allowed the contact and comfort of co-sleeping, but it was with her father, Craig, that she slept. Kathleen departed to the spare room. In admitting 'scary feelings' in 'bonding' with the youngest, Laura, Folbigg wrote, 'maternal instinct is what they call it. I know now I never had it with the others.' In another entry she confesses, 'I gave nothing to the others.'

There are numerous diary entries showing a woman near the end of her tether. Her diary, while pregnant with her last child, is full of fear of what will happen: 'One day it will leave. The others did. But this one's not going in the same fashion. This time I'm prepared and know what to watch out for in myself changes in mood etc. Help I will get, if need be . . .' In another: 'I worry that my next child will suffer my psychological mood swings like the others did.' And again: '. . . stress made me do terrible things.' In another she muses: 'What sort of a mother am I? I've been a terrible one, that's what it boils down to . . . What scares me most will be when I'm alone with the baby. How do I overcome that? Defeat that?' And, 'With Sarah all I wanted was her to shut up and one day she did.'

Kathleen Folbigg, now completely estranged from her foster-family, did not have her own support networks. Craig Folbigg was a devoted father, with a strong family, although his mother had died early. His sister, a retired nurse with four older children, was a wonderfully patient alternative caregiver to the disabled Patrick, blinded and epileptic from an earlier smothering attempt. Psychologically, Craig was far better suited to looking after the children: tolerant, flexible and easy-going, taking great pleasure in their presence. But Craig's long working hours, often at least until 8 p.m. and with no clear, regular time of 'homecoming' when Kathleen could expect relief, left her isolated for long periods alone with the baby.

More important, however, than the lack of support, was the fact that her past had left her without the internal psychological resources necessary to care for a needy baby. She had no deep memories of being nurtured. Instead, she had a low stress threshold and an anger switch flicked permanently on high. Weeks after Sarah was born it was 'clear she is not coping'. When Sarah was two and a half months, Kathleen began to work weekends at BabyCo, an escape she looked forward to and depended upon. At first Craig looked after Sarah. Then he worked weekends too.

At home full-time again, Kathy became quickly 'very frustrated and domineering with Sarah'. Craig began to hear her angry frustration, and then increasingly 'a more disturbing noise. Kathy was growling . . .' This was the menacing, rage-filled growl he later imitated in court. Once he found Kathy pinning baby Sarah in a tight bear hug, patting her bottom harder and harder, the pats turning into blows. Not long after, she threw the child at Craig: 'You fucking deal with her.'

A few hours later, in the middle of the night, the baby was found dead.

Their last and longest-surviving child, Laura, was mercifully placid. As she became a toddler, however, she became more assertive and wilful. Craig dates the deterioration in their marital relationship, and in Kathleen's relationship with Laura, from this time. Folbigg's mental state and capacity to cope rapidly deteriorated. The diaries show an atmosphere of growing menace. Not long before Laura's death, Folbigg confesses to her diary:

Very depressed with myself. I've done it. I've lost it with her. I've yelled at her so angrily that it scared her she hasn't stopped crying. Got so bad I nearly purposely dropped her on the floor and left her. I was restrained enough to walk away. Went to my room and left her to cry . . . I feel like the worst mother in this earth. Scared that she'll leave me now like Sarah did. I know I was short tempered and cruel sometimes to her and she left with a bit of help. I actually seem to have a bond with Laura. It can't happen again.

Leading up to her death, Laura suffered from a cold, and was unusually grizzly and needy. The day before her death, Laura avoided all contact with her mother. Every time Kathleen came near her, Laura ran to cling to Craig. He asked Kathleen why. She admitted that the day before Laura had 'followed her around the house whingeing, moaning, and repeatedly saying, "Mum, Mum, Mum".' Losing her temper, Kathy had spun round shouting 'piss off' at her child, knocking her over as she did so. At this the baby had cowered, terrified, on the ground. Kathleen controlled herself and put the child to bed.

Craig heard,

Kathy losing patience . . . Then it came. A growl, a deep guttural roar. Craig had heard it increasingly, almost daily over recent months when Kathy was frustrated with Laura over bedtimes and mealtimes . . . it was a terrifying angry sound . . . she had the toddler's hands pinned under her own on the high chair trying to forcibly feed her. Laura's head was twisting and turning as she whined in protest . . . Laura dropped to the ground in abject terror, unable to move another step . . . hysterically shaking and sobbing.

Folbigg's police interview with the tenacious detective, Bernie Ryan, who brought her to justice, is a grey monotone, strikingly lifeless, emotionally flat and detached, curiously abstract, almost bureaucratic, as if she is speaking of someone else. It contains vague repetitive expressions; for example 'as such' and 'sort of', as if she did not ever quite know what had happened. The prosecutor, Mr Tedeschi, described her answers as 'glib, trite and evasive'. Quizzed by Ryan about diary entries on losing control, she said, 'I meant keeping in control as in not keeping in control as such, but sort of keeping control and learning to voice an objection or voice if I've got a problem. Instead of trying to handle everything myself, let other people sort of do it for me.'

Although there was much public and media tut-tutting about her going to the gym, in reality her escape only consisted of three half-hours a week. In Mr Tedeschi's summing up of the Crown case he is particularly severe on that fact that she may have '. . . deliberately sought to render them unconscious in an attempt to put them to sleep, either so she could get to sleep herself or that she could have some time to herself.' The gym, and its link to male attention, is one of the few things enabling her to stay sane: '. . . the gym was a pivotal part of me and now, because I can't go without taking Laura, it's put a damper on everything. I've had my one and only escape taken away from me.'

As she spirals deeper into depression, themes of isolation, self-hatred, fear of abandonment and feelings of worthlessness grow stronger in her diary. 'I have no past, no relatives to remind me, and I am it, so therefore the choice of this baby was to extend me, natural, and one I've made happily . . . Problem was with the other three kids I felt I didn't deserve to be extended, and that I was condemning them to a life with me . . .'

The past continued to haunt her:

Not sure why I'm so depressed lately. Seem to be suffering mood swings. I also have no energy lately either . . . why is family so important to me? I now have the start of my very own, but it doesn't seem good enough. I know Craig doesn't understand. He has the knowledge of stability and love from siblings and parents even if he chooses to ignore them. Me—I have no one but him. It seems to affect me so—why should it matter?

Finally, Folbigg seems without grief and without remorse. After Laura's funeral, she said, 'Thank Fuck that's over, now I can get on with things.' After each death, too, there was no further talk about the baby's life, no grieving, just a slate wiped clean. When once she watches a video of the dead Sarah, her tone is as flat and lifeless as if she were recalling a neighbour's dead cat. Craig's unquenchable grief she saw as an irritating fault. He couldn't 'lighten up'. She resented his inability to 'just move on'. Within weeks of her last surviving daughter's death she had left Craig and taken up with someone else.

On police tapes she rehearses emotion and quizzes Craig on her performance at an interview, 'Did I cry on the right spot?' 'You know, was I sounding pathetic enough for them? You know just stupid friggin' shit like that?'

In Justice Barr's summing up of the case his tone is one of sorrowful objectivity. He noted that although 'in the psychiatrist Dr Guiffruida's opinion, Folbigg was not psychotic', 'she dealt with the psychiatrist as if she was not responsible for the deaths of her children'. Justice Barr highlighted her first eighteen months: 'It is well established that children who are neglected and suffer serious physical trauma may suffer a profound disturbance of personality development.' That meant an

> incapacity to develop any meaningful emotional bonding or attachment, which in turn meant she could not care for and protect her own children . . . The abuse she had suffered as a baby had left her unable to form any normal loving relationships. She was unable to confide in her husband and he left her to cope because he did not know she was at the end of her tether.

The judge read some entries from her diaries to indicate her state of mind. They showed her fear of abandonment, her fears of being intrusive on others when needy, her compulsive self-sufficiency and incapacity to assert her own dependency needs, despite always promising herself to ask for help. He noted that, as one of the psychiatrists had attested, depression often manifests itself as hostility and anger. He also read the departmental report cited above which had come to light from over thirty years earlier, which revealed the likelihood that she had been sexually abused when a child. At this an audible, collective gasp of horror was heard in the courtroom.

Kathleen Folbigg, the judge concluded, had a 'bleak future'. Her condition, psychiatrists agreed, was largely untreatable. She must never be given the responsibility for caring for a child again.

Justice Barr sentenced Kathleen Folbigg to forty years imprisonment with a non-parole period of thirty years. She will not be freed before she reaches sixty-six years of age.

When the jury found Kathleen guilty, she lowered her head and wept. Her tears, her foster-sister Lea believed, were not of remorse for her dead babies. They were for herself.

On human mystery and the myth of the resilient child

What happens to a child if it has the misfortune to grow up in one of those families which the poet Randall Jarrell once described as 'God's concentration camps'? Not all children who are abused, neglected and abandoned grow up to be child killers like Kathleen Folbigg. In thinking about good and evil, we should acknowledge human mystery, an unfathomable element in all of us, a mystery that may afflict good parents too. ('Beware the bad seed!' I once heard a psychotherapist say with a portentous air.) As specialists in child trauma try to uncover the secrets of the 'resilient child' who triumphs over appalling circumstances, we all know someone who has been to hell and back in childhood but is nonetheless a decent, sometimes inspiring human being. Some children, through one good relationship, native spunk, fierce intelligence, a piece of good luck, some intrinsic goodness, have something that tilts the odds in their favour. They develop the capacity to see and judge their life for what it is and determine to leave it behind, lifting themselves out from under the chaos, violence and moral squalor. Sometimes they turn their terrible beginning into a source of empathy and creativity, a human forge in which, like Korczak, Bowlby and others, they transform their own suffering into helping others like themselves. We will never be reducible to the sum of our upbringing, for good or evil.

While people may be able to transcend a terrible childhood, a sensible society does not count upon it. The unequivocal message from our contemporary knowledge of early development is that children *are* vulnerable, and that there are circumstances *from which they are unlikely to recover*. The earlier and more extensive the trauma, the less likely the recovery is. The odds of a secure, well-cared-for child going seriously to the bad is very much less, just as the odds of a neglected or abused child doing so grow as the risk factors accumulate, sometimes to the point of behaviour as extreme as that of Kathleen Folbigg.

Bowlby once remarked that for a theory to have utility it must have explanatory power across a range of different circumstances. If attachment theory and the 'early childhood story' are in a deep sense a celebration of what ordinary, good-enough mothers and fathers do, it is also powerfully illuminating when things go wrong. The roots of violence such as Kathleen Folbigg's may well be found in the nursery.

Separation and abandonment

Anyone familiar with Bowlby and Robertson's famous studies of institutionalised children will see the striking consistency between Folbigg's early life and the suffering they described and its disturbing emotional consequences. There is evidence that Folbigg moved through the three stages that Robertson outlined: protest, despair and detachment. When her mother abandoned the baby Kathleen, her father speaks of her 'fretting' so badly she refused to eat. This disastrous beginning was not followed by an early placement in a stable foster home, but by repeated separations and further disruptions to any new attachments she may have formed. By the time the orphanage assessed her, some eighteen months later, this instability had taken its toll. She was a remote and unsmiling, blank-faced child, so unresponsive that they mistook her to be of low intelligence.

The third phase Robertson called 'detachment'. Here a child may show some recovery of spirits, getting interested in their surroundings again—as if loss had acted as a crucible and they had emerged quite changed on the other side, showing peculiar, eerie and ominous detachment. While they might now be precocious little charmers, well practised at getting attention from strangers, they also seemed indifferent to those closest to them. They seemed either incapable of attachment or only capable of the shallowest relationships. These children risked no more investment in other people; the only safe attachment was to the self. Such children seemed incapable of real affection or its counterpart, empathy.

Likewise we know that at the orphanage Kathleen after a time 'became interested in her surroundings again'. Her foster family mentioned 'problems from earliest childhood' and found her strangely cut off and self-contained. Robertson described children who could no longer risk or form real attachments; likewise, on feeling some kind of bond with Laura, Folbigg admitted she found it 'scary' and that she had 'felt nothing for the others'. Institutionalised children often lied with impunity and stole. Folbigg's foster-mother remarked on Kathy's barefaced lying. Robertson noted the precociously charming quality of the children used to getting a stranger's attention. Kathy, too, was a charmer, particularly coming alive in the admiration and company of men. Her husband, Craig Folbigg, and her new lover after Laura's death were both besotted by her.

Folbigg, however, did not only experience separation and abandonment. At least as serious was the prior environment of violence, chaotic neglect and abuse.

The body keeps the score: the myth of the resilient child

Robin Karr-Morse and Meredith Wiley's superb book *Ghosts from the Nursery: Tracing the Roots of Violence* tells a story of a terrible, inexplicable crime. School children were abducted at gunpoint, driven through the night and then buried alive. When they finally escaped to freedom, the doctors who examined them physically 'had no idea that anything serious was wrong'. No authority saw fit to get a psychologist or psychiatrist to even speak to the children: 'As incredible as the blindness to the psychic injuries of the Chowchilla children may seem to us now, at the time of the incident—just twenty years ago—we believed that children were resilient and would weather most trauma, given time.' As it turned out, as we now know, that complacent, self-comforting view— perhaps because the reality that children can be damaged forever is too horrible to contemplate—could not have been more wrong. When psychiatrist Dr Leonore Terr, after reading a newspaper article about how the abducted children all suffered 'terrible fears and nightmares', examined them, she found that every child was still 'seriously affected' five years later.

While we now understand that children can suffer from post-traumatic stress syndrome, or have long-term damage from a single episode of terrible trauma,

> we have yet to understand that when serious trauma occurs to babies and toddlers during their most explosive phase of brain development, the injury reverberates beyond anything we have imagined possible . . . When stress is especially severe or prolonged, permanent changes may occur in hormone levels that alter the brain's chemical profile . . . the result may be maladaptive behaviour patterns, including both aggression and depression. Children so traumatised come to perceive the world as a dangerous place.

As Bruce Perry explains, when a child perceives a threat, their sympathetic nervous system mobilises,

> goes into full swing, increasing blood pressure, heart rate, respiration, and muscle tone and creating a release of stored blood sugar. The child becomes hyper alert . . . If the threat is perceived frequently or is very intense, the systems contributing to hyperarousal will be sensitised, ready to flip on the least provocation.

But what happens if the child is too little—as a baby or toddler—to flee or fight? Suppose the danger is so prolonged or so terrifying because the source of protection (the parent) is also the source of alarm and terror? Like the bird that closes its eyes and feigns death in a cat's mouth, the last remaining survival response is that of 'freezing'—'the escape when there is no escape'. Expressed neurobiologically, 'freezing' activates the parasympathetic nervous system, which reduces blood pressure and heart rate, and begins shutting down into a self-protective state of withdrawal and conservation. The trauma is escaped internally, by disassociation—the sensation of being 'outside one's own body', viewing a scene from a higher, safer position. It is 'a submission and resignation to the inevitability of overwhelming, even psychically deadening danger'. A character in Margaret Atwood's *The Robber Bride* copes with sexual abuse as a child by disassociation. The most vulnerable people physically—women and children, particularly young children—are more prone to respond to intense threat by the 'freeze' and dissassociative response than men.

And as Perry explains, for children, if a 'state' is experienced enough times, it becomes a 'trait': a characteristic response to stress and an underlying pattern of brain organisation. As the popular Cyborg metaphor suggests, the brain will become 'hard wired' that way. Another child trauma specialist put it well: the body will keep the score.

The first two years of life are the period not only for forming key attachments but also for the maturation of the part of the brain, the orbitofrontal cortex, responsible for regulating our own emotions, like rage, anger, fear and so on, *but also for reading emotion in others*. If through neglect or abuse such early brain development is compromised, if no attachment is formed to others, then empathy, the capacity to feel or identify with another's pain, doesn't happen. Another person's intentions can be mistaken too, like a child flinching when an adult's arm is raised for entirely benign reasons.

Bruce Perry describes the child who murders in cold blood:

> The part of his brain which would have allowed him to feel connected to other human beings—empathy—simply does not develop. He has affective blindness. Just as the retarded child lacks the capacity to understand abstract cognitive capacity, the young murderer lacks the capacity to be connected to other human beings . . . Experiences or rather lack of critical experiences resulted in his affective blindness . . . If a child feels no emotional attachment to any human being, then we cannot expect any more remorse from him after killing a human than from someone who ran over a squirrel.

All this, of course, raises deep and profoundly important questions, as in the Folbigg case, linking the ways we raise children with their moral development and its absence, their capacity to understand good and evil. This is the negative counterpoint to the valuable empathy that securely attached children display.

Let the last words on the connection between our moral life and the world in which we grow up rest with a writer, Alexander Solzhenitsyn, in his description of children deprived of normal parental care in the Gulag camps: 'In their consciousness there was no demarcation line between what was permissible and what was not permissible, and no concept of good and evil. For them, everything that they desired was good and everything that hindered them was bad.'

On the origins of self hatred

The writer Kate Jennings, in an interview about her book *Snake*, said that it was about how a child, growing up unloved, comes to be unlovable. Jennings, with the antennae of the artist, expressed what psychologists, with their concept of an internal working model of self and others, were trying, in clumsier and less lyrical language, to elaborate.

But how does it happen?

Mary Main has pointed out that the avoidant infant is in a situation of irresolvable conflict.

> The infant cannot approach because of the parent's rejection, and cannot withdraw because of its own attachment. The situation is self-perpetuating because rebuff heightens alarm and hence heightens attachment, leading to increased rebuff, increased alarm and increased heightening of attachment . . . In other words, by repelling the infant the mother simultaneously attracts him.

Main's videotapes of avoidant toddlers showed the extraordinary lengths some children went to in avoiding contact on reunion with their mother. One child 'instead of approaching his mother, placed himself facing into a corner of the room, as though complying with a punishment, and then knelt down with his face to the floor'. These gestures were hardly random; videotapes of the mothers playing with these toddlers *in every case* 'showed them to differ from the mothers of non-avoidant toddlers; they appear "angry, inexpressive and disliking of physical contact with the infant" '. There was a quite palpable hostility from mother to child; 'some scolded in angry tones, some mocked, others spoke sarcastically to or about their child'. As Bowlby points out, 'an obvious possibility is that by keeping away from their mother like this a child is avoiding being treated in a hostile way again'.

'Put simply . . . the child, and later the adult, becomes afraid to allow himself to become attached to anyone for fear of a further rejection with all the agony, the anxiety, and the anger to which that would lead. As a result there is a massive block against his expressing or even feeling his natural desire for a close trusting relationship, for care, comfort, and love—which I regard as the subjective manifestations of a major system of instinctive behaviour.'

Folbigg had great difficulty in being close to anyone, or feeling legitimacy in her need for help. She could not form a normal attachment to her children. She had no therapeutic intervention or reworking of those childhood experiences. The neglect, abandonment and probable sexual abuse Folbigg endured as a young child made it very likely that she would have a disorganised or disorientated attachment, the category most closely associated with later psychiatric disturbance. Main, for example, described how a baby with such an attachment

> hunched her upper body and shoulders at hearing her mother's call, then broke into extravagant laugh-like screeches with an excited forward movement. Her braying laughter became a cry and distress–face with a new intake of breath as the infant hunched forward. Then suddenly she became silent, blank and dazed.

Abused and neglected children have extremely high rates of disorganised and disorientated attachments (some studies show around 80 to 90 per cent), which is highly correlated with the development of later personality disorders. One study found 91 per cent of patients with a borderline personality disorder report childhood abuse. It also strongly predicts later aggressive behaviour: 'emotional instability, including labile anger, anger regulation defects, high frequencies of dissociation.'

Folbigg also demonstrates disassociated, trance-like states. 'Sometimes I feel like it is a film scene, just practised and rehearsed, each actor perfect and surreal, times I don't fit in the play, have never fit, but keep attempting to anyway for fear of being isolated and alone.' People who are known to have a disorganised and disoriented attachment have been observed to use dissociative behaviours in later stages of life and are found in over 70 per cent of hostile, aggressive preschoolers. (Folbigg was very aggressive to peers at kindergarten age.) Subject to outbursts of sudden, intense, anger, Folbigg was aware that just under the surface there was a barely suppressed cauldron of unprocessed emotion: 'My brain has that much happening, unstored and unrecalled memories, just waiting. Heaven help the day they surface and I recall. That will be the day to lock me up and throw away the key.'

The untouchables

The British analyst Juliet Hopkins, interested in Winnicott's idea that a baby needs to feel securely 'held' psychically as well as physically, examined children who had been referred for therapy because their mothers could not bring themselves to physically touch or hold their baby or child.

Hopkins noted that mothers of avoidant infants manifested 'deep aversion to bodily contact which led them to rebuff their infants' attempts to initiate physical contact'. Like Kathleen Folbigg, they were often 'stiff and inexpressive, as if attempting to control their resentment'.

One patient, Clare, had a mother who 'had resented the child's arrival and had found her physically repellent as a baby'. Her mother had propped her up with her bottle rather than held her to feed, and 'confined her to a playpen all day'. Stoically independent, Clare was however inclined to get lost and was accident-prone, but never sought comfort when hurt. Clare explained to Hopkins, 'I never cry because if I started I would never stop.' Obsessed by lepers, Clare 'felt herself to be a leper whom no one wanted to touch because she would kill them . . . she was tortured by the longing to touch and be touched . . .'

'Laura', aged sixteen, whose mother also could not bear to touch her as a baby, suffered from an eating disorder and depression, and 'recounted a recurrent nightmare of finding herself alone in a desert, covered with a revolting skin disease'. She also had a collecting box for Hindu 'untouchables'. Her mother could, however, touch her younger daughter, and in therapy Laura represented herself as a repulsive tortoise and her sister as a cuddly rabbit.

Hopkins records: 'I have found it common for physically rejected children to dramatise or draw themselves as physically repellent or unstrokeable creatures, like tortoises, toads, crocodiles, and hedgehogs.'

Expressing the feelings of frozen withdrawal at the beginning of therapy, Laura's images were of icebergs, snow and refrigerators. In the second year of therapy she became:

obsessed with the image of the moth's fatal fascination for the candle flame. She wept as she expressed her horror at the moth's repeated return to the flame that burned it, and said that she experienced the pain of burning acutely on her own skin. This image of the moth and the candle flame is a dramatic reminder of Main's finding that, by repelling the infant, the mother simultaneously attracts him. For Laura it expressed the conflict between her burning desire to be loved by her alluring mother and the burning pain and rage associated with the continuous rejections which she had experienced.

It is unclear what a genetic determinist or those who, like Jerome Kagan, emphasise inborn temperament, or who argue that children are just 'born that way', might say to Hopkins's examples. Can a child be *born* feeling like a repulsive cockroach?

Ghosts in the nursery

'Those who cannot remember the past are condemned to repeat it.'
George Santayana

According to the infant psychotherapist Selma Fraiberg,

> In every nursery there are ghosts. They are the visitors from the unremembered past of the parents, the uninvited guests at the christening. Under favourable circumstance the unfriendly and unbidden spirits are banished from the nursery and return to their subterranean dwelling place . . . But how shall we explain another group of families who appear to be possessed by their ghosts? . . . While no one has issued an invitation, the ghosts take up residence and conduct the rehearsal of the family tragedy from a tattered script.

Mary Main's work on intergenerational patterns probed adults' 'internal working models' of relationships with loved ones. She identified four main patterns. Adults described as 'secure autonomous' were able to present a coherent picture of their parents, using 'fresh and lively language'. Their childhoods, while not 'perfect', were characterised by at least one parent providing a 'secure base'. These adults were capable of speaking of negative and positive elements in their parents, while keeping the elements in balance. They were capable of self-reflection and reflection on their relationships with others in ways that were open and expansive, and presented coherent narratives. There was little self-deception. Overwhelmingly, these adults had children with secure attachments.

Adults characterised as 'dismissing' resembled the avoidant patterns of insecurity. They steered clear of discussing attachment issues, and 'seemed unable or unwilling to take attachment issues seriously'. They were defensive and guarded, and did not expand on information in the relaxed way their secure counterparts did. They were reluctant to engage in looking inward, or were hostile to introspection. Interestingly, their parents were often exceptionally idealised, yet when pressed for specific examples their memories offered poignant contradictions of their rosy assessments:

> A dismissing mother said she had never been upset as a child. Never? she was asked. 'No, because nobody died.' As the interview progressed, however she revealed a number of painful facts. Her father had been upset that she wasn't a boy, and she overheard him say that the family would not have lost their farm if they had had a boy instead . . . she had often been left alone as a child and typically came home to an empty house. Finally it emerged her father was an alcoholic, that he beat her mother, and that one of those beatings, delivered when her mother was pregnant with her, caused her to be born with a crippled foot that required surgery.

Significantly, around three-quarters of dismissing adults had children who were avoidantly attached.

Unresolved issues from troubled childhoods dominated a third group, who Main described as 'preoccupied'. There was little sign of having 'worked through' painful memories; rather, these adults gave the impression of being still deeply enmeshed in destructive relationships with their parents. 'The childhoods . . . were often characterised by intense efforts to please, considerable anger and disappointment, and by role reversals in which the child had tried to parent the adult.' The narratives of these unhappy childhoods were incoherent, contradictory, often spoken about in the present tense, as if they were still locked in the past with wildly unpredictable and chaotic parents. Again, there was an overwhelming consistency between parents and their attachment patterns, with the majority of their children being ambivalently attached.

In one striking study, researchers found that they could work forwards in predicting attachment patterns by exploring the 'ghosts in the nursery', even before a baby was born. Peter Fonagy, Howard Steele and Miriam Steele were able to correctly predict the attachment classification of the offspring of expectant parents in 75 per cent of cases by interviewing mothers prior to birth. Arietta Slade's work with expectant mothers also found ghosts in the nursery, both benign and malign, which had taken up residence even before children were born. In an important corrective to the distorted tendency in modern Western societies to abhor anything that smacks of 'dependency' and to over-emphasise independence and 'self sufficiency', secure women were direct and assertive about their own needs to rely on others. They asked for help and support where needed. They were able to accept the child's dependence upon them, but also not idealise the difficulties they would face.

In contrast, 'dismissing' or 'preoccupied' mothers 'found it difficult to acknowledge pleasure from the knowledge of becoming a mother . . . their fantasies of what their babies would be like suggested that the baby had already become a figure in old struggles':

> a mother who's felt controlled by her mother her entire life is already preoccupied with whether she can control her foetus. Or a mother whose own mother pushed her aside is already convinced that her child won't have any needs, won't change her life, and will be autonomous early on. Chills go up and down your spine when you hear these things.

Abusive mothers

Bowlby, in a compassionate explication of why some mothers are violent, pointed to the role of extreme degrees of anxious attachment in child abuse. Such mothers are invariably prone to 'periods of intense anxiety punctuated by outbursts of violent anger'. Shown videotapes of crying infants, abusive mothers were less sympathetic and reacted with more anger. Like Folbigg, despite having strong dependency needs, they are socially isolated, 'distrustful' and 'unable or unwilling' to have intimate relationships. Such women yearned for care, but expected rejection. A significant minority were themselves battered as children; in one study two-fifths had suffered physical abuse.

A patient of Bowlby's, Mrs Q, struggled to control intense fits of rage, anxiety and depression after her son's birth, including the impulse to throw him out of the window. In therapy she revealed that her parents raged at and assaulted one another and threatened murder, her mother continually threatening to abandon the family. Twice Mrs Q returned from school to find her mother with her head in the gas oven. At other times her mother simply disappeared. Her mother terrorised her into not breathing a word of all this to anyone. She grew up petrified that if she did anything wrong her mother would disappear.

As Bowlby noted:

> for many of them the relationship of daughter to mother had been reversed and it was they who had been expected to care for the parent . . . thus whilst constantly yearning for the love and care she has never had, she has no confidence she will ever receive it. Small wonder then, when a woman with this background becomes a mother, that there are times, when instead of being ready to mother her child, she looks to the child to mother her. Small wonder, too, if when her child fails to oblige and starts crying she gets impatient and angry with it.

Can we see the distorted patterns of a Mrs Q or a Kathleen Folbigg in the making? In a daycare setting, abused children find it 'difficult to make relationships, either with caregivers or with other children, and also [are] very aggressive'. In one study, abused children assaulted other (non-abused) children at twice the rate of the controls. Some of the abused toddlers threatened adults, while none of the controls did. They were also

> notable for a particularly disagreeable type of aggression, termed 'harassment', meaning 'malicious behaviour with the sole intent of making the victim show distress'. Almost always it occurs suddenly without any evident cause, . . . such attacks coming unpredictably out of the blue, are frightening and invite retaliation. Clinical studies . . . report them to be directed towards an adult to whom the child is becoming attached.

While children with secure attachments commonly express empathy or concern when an age mate is distressed, abused youngsters showed little sympathy. Rather, their reactions were filled with anxiety or anger. One little toddler, a boy, hit a crying girl, saying over and over, 'Cut it out. Cut it out' his patting of her back turning quickly to beating, while hissing at her with bared teeth. (Remember Kathleen Folbigg's patting of Sarah, which turned into harder and harder pats, almost hitting, accompanied by a deep guttural growl?)

These observations of abused children show,

> with unmistakable clarity how early in life certain characteristic patterns of social behaviour—some hopeful, others ominous—become established.

They leave no doubts about what types of family experience influence development in one direction or another . . . All parents please note!

The bridge across the past

The writer Isak Dinesen thought that anything could be made bearable by being made into a story. A great many modern therapists would agree with her. If there is a tendency to repeat the deepest patterns of love and hate, there is also no simple reproduction. Different life phases—adolescence, adulthood, forming relationships, marriage, parenthood itself—offer new opportunities for growth and transcendence. The intimacy of a happy love relationship in adulthood opens the possibility of healing old wounds. Alongside those adults fortunate enough to have grown up in a secure home, there is the phenomenon of those who have developed what attachment researchers call 'earned security'.

Despite their terrible childhoods, which might include gross neglect or physical or emotional abuse, or parents with a mental illness, these mothers and fathers, through self-reflection, are able to tell their stories with honesty, fluency and coherency. Somehow they have found a way through their experiences to arrive at some kind of balance in understanding the past, and in forgiving the behaviour of their parents. What matters, as Dinesen thought, is the capacity to see one's life as a story. It is heartening to learn that these mothers, despite their troubled childhoods, are just as likely to have children with secure attachments as women with more fortunate pasts:

> however she may accomplish it, when a woman manages either to retain or regain access to such unhappy memories and reprocess them in such a way that she can come to terms with them, she is found to be no less able to respond to her child's attachment behaviour so he develops a secure attachment to her, than a woman whose childhood was a happy one.

On one occasion, when I was giving a talk, a woman present in the audience spoke movingly on how important she found it to look after her children well, to 'try to get things right', because she had suffered terribly from a parent with a mental illness. Over the course of writing this book, other extraordinarily painful and yet brave stories came to light. One person had a mother who was a depressed alcoholic who locked the children out of the house; the father (a workaholic) was almost never around and was abusive when he was. A family knew their adolescent daughter had an eating disorder but did nothing, even remaining indifferent once while she slept off an overdose for three days. And so on. But these children, despite such ominous beginnings, grew up to become very good mothers. Such stories are surprisingly common.

Those Bowlby described as 'exceptional women' differed not in their experiences but in the meanings they made of them. By facing the past they gained control over it, unlike those who were unconscious of the role their parents were still playing in their lives. For these mothers, the painful and sometimes shocking experiences of their own childhood did not lead to a repetition of these experiences with their children, but to a conscious effort to establish something different. The experience of nurturing acted as a healing process; giving a better childhood to one's own children created the possibility of a new beginning. Watching their children grow up happy and well cared for offered the deepest kind of healing, a reparation to the child within themselves and to their own past. Parenthood need not be an unconscious and monstrous repetition of an old tragedy, but something transcendent, a bridge across the past.

The dead mother: maternal depression and its consequences

The French psychoanalyst André Green has written a brilliant essay called 'The Dead Mother'. Green's 'dead mother' is of course, meant metaphorically to capture the child's experience of a mother who is depressed; she is physically present but emotionally absent. The phrase 'dead mother' Green uses to convey the centrality of mourning in the child's response to maternal depression. Maternal depression destroys the child's internal image of their mother, 'brutally transforming' her from a 'source of vitality for the child, into a distant figure, toneless, practically inanimate' who 'deeply impregnates' the emerging spirit of the child, 'weighing on the destiny' of their capacity for love, for life, for a viable selfhood.

The mother who

was absorbed, either in herself or with something else, unreachable without an echo, but always sad. A silent mother, even if talkative. When she was present she remained indifferent, even when she was plying the child with her reproaches . . . The dead mother had taken away with her . . . the major portion of the love [her child feels for her]; her look, her tone of voice, her smell, the memory of her caress . . . She had been buried alive, but her tomb itself had disappeared. The hole that gaped in its place made solitude dreadful, as though the subject ran the risk of being sunk in it . . .

At the centre of the child's being, where there was warmth there is now a cold core, like a dead star in the centre of a universe. The mother's depression is 'experienced by the child as a catastrophe; because without any warning signal, love has been lost at one blow'. It involves for Green, most importantly 'the loss of *meaning*, for the baby [cannot] account for what has happened'. At first the child attempts to 'repair, to reanimate, to interest and distract her, to give her a renewed taste for life, to make her smile and laugh'. Soon a different defence is deployed; so as not to lose emotional contact with her, the child attunes and enters into the cold, frozen, stellar affective space she is residing in. He identifies with the emotional quality of the 'dead' or depressed mother, and mirrors or adopts her qualities.

While Green writes of maternal depression in a wonderfully evocative way, he also shows the limitations of extrapolating backwards, or reconstructing the past from adult patients' memories. Daniel Stern's superb observational work shows maternal depression to be part of the evolving conversation and interactions between mother and baby. Stern's outstanding contribution, as shown in the last chapter, is the subtle concept of 'attunement', derived from extremely fine observations of mothers and babies interacting on slowed-down videos. He shows us that the baby experiences a mother's depression not as Green conceptualises it, as one single catastrophic 'life event', but as a pattern of micro-events. The baby, far from being passive, in every interaction tries to influence its mother. Psychologist Edward Tronick asked mothers to create a 'still face', mimicking the expressionless, lifeless face often showed by depressed mothers. The babies in Tronick's experiment reacted to a still face with profound distress, alternating with attempts to reanimate their mother's face. The baby 'is often very creative with humour and invention. When none of this works he turns away . . . and then turns back to try again.'

Stern pointed out that the response is not always mourning. If occasionally the child succeeds in bringing its beloved mother back to life, since infrequent reinforcement is the most ferocious stimulant of all, the child tries again and again. The child learns to sparkle, to be the live wire. This is the best, the only way of making the contact with mother they so desperately need, of being truly with her. Breathing life into mother becomes almost addictive. The child becomes a walking antidepressant, a creative signal reader and performer. Stern shows that the 'effects' of one mother's depression on her daughter, Susie, is to make her into Little Miss Sparkle Plenty—a life-giver, a real spark plug in any gathering. Stern suggests, however, drawing from psychotherapeutic work with adult patients, that having a severely depressed mother may shape the future choice of a lover, the spark plug choosing—to their own detriment—someone who needs frequent reanimation.

Prolonged maternal depression can have serious, long-term consequences for children's development—particularly since the symptoms so often include hostility to the child and sometimes overt violence.

Single mothers within marriages

As a society we must *both* understand the internal 'ghosts in the nursery' *and* move out to the social and wider political context of maternal depression. We need to consider the portrait of the 'father-absent, patriarchal family where children are imploded onto unsupported mothers' painted by feminist therapist Deborah Leupnitz. While attachment theory first began with major separation experiences, it's a mistake to think that 'since absent mothers leads to unhappy children that ever-present mothers make for happy children'. Parenting is safest done not solo but in company. Mothers, however devoted, happy, competent, psychologically together and financially well resourced, will still need to seek both support and relief from others.

Although Bowlby was accused of forcing women to care alone for their babies, in fact he agreed with the emphasis that baby care should not be left to 'just one, isolated person'. His wife Ursula *always* employed another caregiver, who was usually present, usually a university student who came and went—not as the primary caregiver but to assist her with their children:

> I want to emphasise that, despite voices to the contrary, looking after babies and young children is no job for a single person. If the job is to be well done and the child's primary caregiver not to be too exhausted, the caregiver herself (or himself) needs a great deal of assistance. From whom that help comes may vary; very often it is the other parent: in many societies, including ours more often than is realised, it comes from a grandmother.

Others to be drawn in to help are adolescent girls and young women. In most societies throughout the world these facts have been, and still are, taken for granted and the society organised accordingly. Paradoxically it has taken the world's richest societies to ignore these basic facts.

Poverty is a crushingly obvious factor in maternal depression. Brown and Harris found depression among women at home with young children to be particularly common if they are working-class and have little help from their husband. A British specialist in maternal depression, Andrea Pound, pointed out that the devaluation of unpaid work like mothering in a market society doesn't help either.

> . . . it is not only the physical but also the psychological environment in which many women carry out their task that affects their emotional wellbeing and especially the 'esteem (or lack of it) ascribed to their child rearing activities'

> . . . In an increasingly mercantile society, unpaid work, no matter how skilled or necessary, can seem valueless. The loss of self esteem involved in feeling undervalued may play an important part in the development of depression in such a large proportion of young mothers in the general population.

There is also the issue of women's desire for a life beyond childrearing. The price of not respecting such preferences may be depression. In *I For Isobel*, Amy Witting wrote an unforgettable account of her experience of growing up as the daughter of a bitterly unhappy and abusive woman:

> Isobel's mother walked about white faced repeating 'Who'd be a mother? Who'd be a mother? You do everything for them, *you give up everything for them* and what do you get for it? Forgotten as soon as it suits them, they're gone without a thought. Heartless ungrateful children.' [emphasis added]

A martyr makes for very uncomfortable company. The clue as to *why* Isobel's mother, a stay-at-home mother of the 1930s, is so unhappy and so cruel is held in those bitter words 'you give up everything for them'. In the 'good old days' of the compulsory homemaker ideal, there was very little choice for a woman to be married or not, or to go back to work after children. We would do well, as a society, to remember what it was like, not just for the women, but also for the children who experienced the enforced company of a viciously unhappy mother who really wanted to be elsewhere. Witting, who later recalled her earliest memory as being held upside down with her head down the toilet bowl while her mother flushed it over her, said late in her life that her mother should have run a business or been a career woman.

For that reason I am more in favour of parental leave programs than stay-at-home motherhood—for they keep a profoundly important continuity with a woman's past and future identity. Motherhood is 'time out', not a permanent suburban cul de sac.

On the other hand, the feminist emphasis on paid work as the solution to maternal depression can be oversimplified. De Vaus's study showed a pattern strikingly consistent with what would be predicted from attachment theory; it was not the absence of employment that was the best predictor of anxiety and depressive symptoms, but being single (i.e. the absence of attachment relationships). Women working full-time with very young children are also at risk for depression. George Brown's studies showed that internal intergenerational psychic factors, like experiencing loss and separation in one's early life, make their contribution. Part-time work, rather than full-time stay-at-home motherhood or full-time work-ing motherhood, seemed to have a protective effect. Moreover, their overall conclusion was the importance of women fulfilling their pref-erences *either* for work *or* for being at home with their child.

Men's behaviour as partners and fathers has a powerful impact too. Some mothers are like single mothers within a marriage. Consider this case, from a research project examining the contribution of a mother's support networks to a child developing an insecure attachment. One mother is enmeshed in a tangle of unresolved grief and anger from her own childhood. We learn that she wakes up every morning in tears after a repetitive and terrible dream with themes from her childhood. The therapist asks, what does your husband say? 'He's never noticed,' she replies. In that one phrase we gain a flashing insight into the quiet desperation with which some women as mothers live their lives.

Many new mothers do not have the kin support that historically sustained childrearing. Instead, a modern mother is meant to rely on the father, who also happens to be absent at work for most of the day, and in some cases the best part of evenings as well. We are only just beginning, with paternity leave, to recognise the father's vitally important role; many workplaces still do not acknowledge that a father has any family responsibilities. The father may not regard childcare as his role, either, but expect the mother to cope, *feel it is her job*. And work may be for men (as it is for some women) a socially legitimated form of self-centredness.

The case for early intervention

Allan Schore, near the end of a recent book, expresses a growing consensus that to deal with the roots of violence one must begin in the nursery—the earlier the better. That is why Fraser Mustard and others suggest re-surrounding all parents with community support, affirmation, parenting advice, financial assistance, and, where necessary, high quality intervention programs. Fraser Mustard has a vision of community 'hubs', with 'spokes' of the wheel being outreach programs to all new parents, drawing them into convivial early childhood support networks. It is here that parents could meet, share resources and information, as well as seek and find, where needed, professional advice. Other creative, low-cost interventions, like the British Sure Start and Newpin, include home visiting programs which utilise the deep, acquired wisdom of experienced mothers, linking them with new mothers, especially those in difficulty. Other solutions include specialised intervention projects like the Perry Preschool which included an intensive, high quality daycare program and parenting support for severely disadvantaged and at risk children.

Surely here, then, in quality early childcare, is the answer to the basic question posed by women's emancipation—who will care for the kids?

Not so fast.

9 Electing a new child: truth, lies and the childcare debate

'If anything is incessantly and authoritatively acclaimed as the key to economic success, the solution to the demographic crisis, the basis for social justice and equality, the answer to every woman's dream, a great business opportunity, the remedy for poverty, welfare dependency, crime, educational failure and the basis for children's success, it is childcare. For the last ten years or more this has been hammered home as the catch-all miracle solution to a host of complex problems, which will transform the nation and open the gates to Utopia.' Patricia Morgan

Bertolt Brecht once joked that the East German communist party had lost faith in the people, and must therefore elect a new people. In much the same way, I sometimes think this generation has not only lost faith in the old ideas of childhood, but is in the process of electing a new child. This child is the independent, competent child, whose qualities dovetail nicely with the needs of adults to be free. It is quite possible to see, in the now voluminous literature on childcare, the emergence of a new conception of the child and a new theoretical paradigm that reflects the interests of our age quite as surely as did the old models of dependency and attachment. If, in the History of Childhood, one finds developmental goals and qualities ascribed to children reflecting the deepest values of each age—for the Romans valour; for the Puritans purity, piety and obedience; for the Victorians innocence and vulnerability; and so on—it is distinctive to our age to see the enthusiasm for early independence and, an interesting word, *competence*.

The social science literature on childcare is a part of a larger cultural narrative. Professor Gay Ochiltree, author of *Childcare: Forty Years Research*, argues in her review of the literature that previous research has been flawed by its link to the 'spirit of the times'. Unhappily, Ochiltree—who was once described by a journalist as the 'working mother's Bex'—speaks as if once we lived in times cloaked in darkness by ideology, but now live in times illuminated by objectivity, as if postmodernism and political correctness have ushered in a new Age of Truthtelling.

We should examine earlier thinkers like John Bowlby for their intrinsic merits and defects, and see how far those ideas were shaped by the spirit of their times, but we should also examine current work and observe how deeply shaped *it* is by ideology, by the spirit of our own time. It is quite remarkable, in an age so fond of 'deconstructing', that we do not deconstruct our own dogmas. Our forensic gaze, so sharply honed by the work of Michel Foucault, is turned without pity onto the past, yet grows hazy with sentimentality when confronting the present. We read of the 'cult of motherhood' and of the 'psychologically vulnerable child' as artefacts of their time, but never of our own ideologies of the 'cult of quality childcare' and 'the independent, resilient and competent child'. We avoid examining the ways in which our contemporary ideas about motherhood and childhood might also—to use Marx's sense of ideology—be representing and concealing an interest.

Touch it and you die

In the mid 1990s in late summer, just after dawn, my husband and I were talking, as we do every morning, over coffee. The house lay in that stillness before the day takes shape. My younger daughter had just settled into school. He asked me what I was going to do next. When I told him his response was swift and adamant. 'Don't do it. Listen, I've been involved in some of the nastiest controversies in public life for the last twenty years, and I wouldn't dream of touching that issue. *Anything but that topic!*' From someone who had always waded so fearlessly into public controversy, this was surprising.

When I discussed my plans with friends they variously warned that I would be defamed or my children attacked, suggested silent phone numbers, advised publishing under a pseudonym or hiring a defamation lawyer or leaving the country immediately after the article was published, or better still, not publishing at all. 'You'll cop it,' they all wailed. My mother only turned pale and fell silent.

One would think that I had suggested sky diving without a parachute, or going on a walking tour of post-war Baghdad! It was neither of these things. I wanted to gently question the direction of our childcare policies, in particular those concerning early infant daycare.

Like the old force field of privacy around the dark secrets of family life such as child abuse, a force field of ideology now protects and places beyond scrutiny an important new industry. As American commentator Brian Robertson remarks:

> It is a truism among politicians and pundits that reform of the social security system is the 'third rail' of American politics: touch it and you die. In academic circles the same principle applies to evidence that daycare has detrimental effects on children. It is understood you simply don't go there if you know what's good for you.

Psychologist Robert Karen reports this revealing exchange:

> I asked one researcher what he would do, given what he now knows, if he were a young man just starting a family . . . about he and his wife's both working full-time through the child's first year? There was an extended silence . . . 'Well, what if a young couple should ask you your opinion: Should we try to work it out so that one of us can stay home during much of the child's first year? . . . Another protracted silence. 'No, I wouldn't have an opinion.'
>
> 'You wouldn't have an opinion or you wouldn't have one for publication?'
>
> 'I wouldn't have one for publication.'

In Britain, when Penelope Leach took part in a TV program which:

> painted a bleak picture of a day at an expensive private London nursery . . . the National Children's Bureau took her off their mailing list, and the director of the program was hauled up in front of the Broadcasting Complaints Commission . . . you would think you had uttered a heresy.

The word heresy, with its connotations of breaking through an absolute, religious belief, is a very accurate description.

In Australia, anyone challenging early childcare as an unquestioned and highly desirable part of modern life risks being considered to be in companionship with the Taliban and clitoridectomies. Michael Leunig was once a cherished figure on the progressive side of politics, beloved for his cartoon depictions of psychological vulnerability and the dehumanisation of modern life. His cartoon 'Thoughts of a Baby lying in Childcare' in 1995 transformed him from a loved to a hated figure. All sorts of unpleasant discoveries about Leunig's 'true' character were made. When Leunig returned to the subject of childcare in 2000, he was a 'misogynist with his head up his arse'—to quote the thoughtful contribution from Professor Don Edgar, the former head of the Australian Institute of Family Studies (AIFS). When Australian researcher Kay Margetts reported her study finding that over thirty hours of care meant poorer adjustment to school, she was attacked on every media outlet. Margetts also received negative feedback from staff; it was even suggested that she should be 'disciplined' for publishing this research.

Three nations, same bullying pattern.

It is enough to make any prudent person who desires a pleasant life keep silent.

Which, of course, is precisely what is intended.

Why persist?

The European path to women's equality

When conflict over childcare was most bitter in the US, Britain and Australia, Scandinavian nations, which also promoted women's employment as a central public policy aim, were quietly junking infant daycare and turning to paid parental leave for infants and toddlers. As Australian Institute of Family Studies researchers Irene Wolcott and Helen Glezer noted:

> Swedish policy, . . . which provides financial compensation for parental leave almost up to a child's second birthday, does this to both promote parental care in the home for infants, a situation considered desirable for the physical and emotional health of young children and their parents, and gender equity. Extended parental leave provisions may lessen the public cost of the most expensive form of childcare—that is infant care. In Sweden for example, it is unusual for children under eighteen months to be in public childcare . . .

As Pam Meadows says, 'Although use of formal daycare is well established in Sweden, in practice its use is concentrated on children aged between three and seven years old.' British feminist Helen Wilkinson notes that the numbers of Swedish babies in childcare fell from 3000 to 200 when paid parental leave was introduced. Placing a baby in childcare at a few weeks of age—which in some US states is now mandatory for poor women on welfare-to-work policies—is rare in Sweden. Scandinavian daycare exists not within a long hours work culture where children are seen as 'lead weights in a worker's saddle bags', but within an overall

> context of a culture which believes time with family to be important. It is unlikely that a Swedish child would ever have to spend ten hours every day in daycare because the normal working day is shorter . . . and it is almost unheard of . . . for a parent not to stay home when a child is ill, needs a medical appointment or has a birthday or some event at school.

The worst 'rage in the nursery'—the polarised and often ugly debate that Robert Karen aptly dubbed 'the daycare wars'—occurred in the US where all of those aspects were absent. It took eleven years of political struggle to pass legislation to ensure a mere three months of unpaid family and medical leave. Karen wrote despairingly of the 'hard choices' parents, and women especially, had to make: 'What do you do if you are a single mother? . . . [or] two salaries are essential to meeting a mortgage? What do you do if you are a lawyer or a Wall street analyst or a professor on a tenure track? Will you be able to get your old job back?' In that context, it was unsurprising the debate turned so nasty: 'perhaps no debate in the history of the twentieth century's drawn-out conflicts on the proper ways to raise children generated more heat than that over working mothers and daycare.'

Outside the overheated ideological battleground of the True Believers in the traditional family or childcare zealots ('It's like a religion,' one high-level American policy advisor said wonderingly to me) however, is the terrain ordinary parents inhabit. Despite those well-meaning warnings from family and friends, the depth, honesty and intensity of the letters and responses I have received from parents over many years struggling with these issues were the genesis of this book. They encouraged me to feel that there was already a strong private space where parents grappled with those 'hard choices', such that it was extremely important to 'put the questions differently', to find alternatives. Maybe it *was* possible to open a conversation, and ultimately a social policy framework, that would help parents do things not just differently, but better. I wanted to take those two utterly valuable social goods, women's emancipation and child wellbeing, and try to put them together.

One final point. It is best to be precise about the argument. The focus of this chapter is not on kindergarten or childcare at the preschool ages of three to five. Most developmentalists (including Bowlby) and parents speak with similar warmth for good childcare or preschool (with the proviso of reasonable hours) at the age the Swedes primarily use it. Nor is it about the part-time, supplementary care that so many parents use. Rather, the issue in contention is early and extensive daycare for babies and toddlers under two.

What matters: the quality of care or who gives it?

Way back in the 1950s during the first research into the reactions of children to extreme separation experiences in hospitals and residential care, there was a very interesting dispute between Bowlby and James and Joyce Robertson. It was over the question of whether a substitute mother figure—we would now call it high quality childcare—would solve the problem of children and separation.

Joyce Robertson was a mother and a highly sensitive observer of children—her remarks at the end of their book prefigure Daniel Stern's now classic work on mother–infant attunement. She took on the role of substitute mother to several children undergoing a long separation. She visited them and they came to see her with their mother present. She took time to get to know them and their little ways, preferences and bed-time rituals before they came to stay. Joyce was, then, a trusted person by the time of separation. The transition into care was gradual, and the separation shock was lessened. While the Robertsons still warned against the hazards for a very young child of major separations, they felt that Bowlby had not acknowledged strongly enough the possibility of a workable alternative.

Bowlby didn't say that substitute care could *never* be done well. Bowlby's critics often accused him of monotropism—i.e. believing that *only* mothers could care for children. That, however, was untrue. Bowlby thought a child has, in a normal family, multiple attachments, to mother, father, siblings, and that these can include extended family members and a cherished caregiver. The reason he spoke mainly of mothers (apart from 1950s childrearing patterns) was that he thought a child had a hierarchy of relationships—the mother was usually (although by no means always) the most preferred figure, especially in times of fear, sickness or stress. But he acknowledged:

> the sheer inconvenience in practical life of the facts of the case as they seem
> actually to be in comparison with what things would be like were every

normal child to be happy and content with any caretaker whatever—provided she were kind. If children were only 'reasonable' in this regard, how much easier would life be!

Strangely enough, however, given the extraordinary power of his rendition of the stages of protest, despair and detachment, which moved a generation to reorganise hospital and foster care practices, it was Bowlby's own linguistic shift to the phrase 'attachment figure' or 'mother *or mother substitute*' which created the theoretical basis for the idea amongst post-Bowlbyian attachment scholars that while children must have their attachment needs answered, those needs might not necessarily be met exclusively by the mother and the mother only.

That highlights something else too. An attachment to a mother or father or substitute caregiver doesn't occur overnight. It takes many months as a baby's attachment behaviour is increasingly organised around their mother or a few special caregivers. Separation anxiety, for example, is typically at its height from 7 to 18 months. In the fiasco of misunderstanding over instant 'bonding' after birth, it is easy to overlook the time and hard work of loving attentiveness that means a child forms an attachment. A baby cannot simply flick a switch and 'bond' conveniently with someone new. An attachment relationship is 'earned'—it is the sensitivity and attentiveness of responding to a baby's signals that promotes a strong attachment. Knowing that a baby *can* form alternative attachments—one friend's mother mourned more when her nanny died than when her mother did—does not tell us how often or likely that is.

Attachment researchers, who have done so much work on maternal depression, child abuse and neglect, share common ground with those proposing, 'It's the quality of care that counts.' Their illuminations, in *The Dark Side of The Moon*, after all, provided support for the feminist contention that it is *not* just the person who gives the care (i.e. biological mother) who matters. On this point they are in agreement with quality-of-care advocates, as I am. There is, however, a central difference. As Bruno Bettelheim once put it, it is not just the quality of care that matters to a child, but *the person who gives it*. Michael Leunig put this more lyrically. Adopting the point of view of the infant, he alluded in an interview, to the 'specialness' of the mother–child relationship.

Leunig said:

What does a child feel when the mother is suddenly absent? The breast, the nipple, its whole world is taken away. The mother–baby relationship is a very particular one. It lies at the heart of our culture and I think we are losing this vital relationship. We've become ignorant about the psychological and emotional state of the infant, in the same way we were about the Aborigines when we used to take their children away . . . I'm just trying to open up the question, to be the voice of the infant.

A perceptive grandmother, an exceptionally sensitive caregiver, who looked after her two little grandchildren full-time while the mother worked, once told me of the eldest stopping dead in the middle of play and suddenly crying out for her mother's face. 'Where's that dear face? *Where is it?*'

That thought takes us to the heart of the view of those who are uneasy with the move to institutional childcare: right at the centre is the idea of *irreplaceability*, that a baby's love and attachment to their mother is an anti-commodity relationship. The thought that there is a fundamental *particularity* to love haunts, I think, all those who are never quite satisfied by the 'quality care' arguments.

That disagreement, over whether substitute childcare—so long as it is high quality—will do, is, of course, the nub of the vexed, painful and hotly debated issue of early non-maternal childcare.

Modern mothers and stone age babies

'Denial Is Not a River in Egypt' writes Sarah Hrdy, the maternal feminist and sociobiologist.

> Denial of infant needs runs like an invisible and insidious countercurrent through publications purporting to correct the 'river of mother-blame' coursing through our society . . . what a relief to deep six the whole attachment enterprise and replace it with a new superstition about innately flexible and resilient ready-formed personalities waiting to emerge, for whom 'good enough' care suffices in a world where it is considered crass to ask anyone to define what 'good enough' means . . .

Hrdy is not an opponent of non-maternal care, but she does take seriously 'meeting the eyes of love'; a baby's need to form stable, loving attachments. On the many dismissals of attachment theory by feminists she writes: 'Rarely has that overused phrase "throwing the baby out with the bathwater" applied so well.'

In an important point I shall return to in the conclusion, although attachment theory is often considered to be opposed to any alternative care, a childcare centre using such principles enabled Hrdy to work.

> When I was looking for infant daycare . . . the best place I found was the Harvard Yard Daycare Centre, whose program was designed by Berry Brazelton and other paediatricians heavily influenced by Bowlby . . . These paediatricians, identified by the critics of attachment theory as special enemies of working mothers, were among those who made it possible for me to continue to work part-time even while my children were infants. A condition of leaving a baby there was volunteering to work in the nursery, so that in addition to the very permanent staff . . . there was a fluctuating contingent of family members in a tiny village-like setting, with a high ratio of adults to infants.

Bowlby, she acknowledges, from his very first published paper in 1944, had specified 'mother' or '*mother figure*'. On his supposed refusal to countenance any carer other than a biological mother: 'No such views have been expressed by me . . .' However: 'The central reason Bowlby gave for opposing the notion of new mothers working outside the home was his purely practical observation that it is "very difficult to get people to look after other people's children".' 'This, alas,' writes Hrdy, 'is true. It is the crux of the matter.' As someone who believes human history shows that in nonmaternal care children can do 'just fine', Hrdy nonetheless thinks our contemporary method of

> grouping infants together—like bats in a communal nursery—for a certain number of hours every day under the supervision of *paid* alloparents [caregivers] who are not kin, but who are expected to act as if they are, is an evolutionary novelty, completely experimental.

The real childcare crisis: the quality of care

Let us leave aside, just for a moment, empirical evidence on the question of whether quality childcare will satisfactorily resolve all the issues. What is the quality of care widely available? Ron Lally, speaking to Jennifer Byrne on ABC television, explained the effects they were seeing in the US of poor quality childcare:

what we know is that there is a thermometer almost of chemicals called serotonin, cortisol, noradrenaline, that we are set with based on these experiences we have early on. And prolonged stress or fear, or not getting enough of your needs met very young, seem to set these chemicals at a level where the child views reality a bit differently. They'll see people acting in aggressive ways when they really aren't acting in aggressive ways, or they might be anxious to the point where their hearts might beat a little more. So what we are seeing is a wiring . . . based on interactions that children have early in life.

When Hrdy says that it is now considered 'crass to ask anyone to define what "good enough" care means', she is right.

So what is the quality of care widely available?

The ongoing study by the US National Institute of Child Health and Human Development (NICHD) following 1200 children from birth from the 1990s onward found only 12 per cent of US childcare settings were high quality, and their estimate of the national standard (since the sample was skewed towards above-average incomes) was that only 9 per cent were good quality, where positive caregiving was *highly characteristic*.

It is often claimed that no evidence from the US need concern us because Australian childcare is amongst the world's best practice. By the mid-1990s, journalist Adele Horin wrote of the 'hair-raising stories' told to the *Sydney Morning Herald* while she was researching a story on childcare. Horin interviewed Faye Pettit, a lecturer in early childhood whose work took her to many childcare centres. After lecturing for years that 'childcare was fantastic', Pettit resigned her job to look after her grandchild because she had seen 'so many terrible things', including at one centre babies dehydrating on a forty-degree day. When *Sydney Morning Herald* journalist Sally Loane investigated Australian childcare in 1996— after years of its dramatic expansion—she found mediocrity predominated. On national figures 63 per cent of centres achieved less than the highest standard of accreditation. Our journalists have continued to report (taking just a few examples) babies left at centres alone after staff have gone home, centres run by someone under arrest for possessing child pornography, children escaping and crawling onto a railway line, problems of neglect, hygiene and safety.

With respect to several crucial structural elements of care quality, Australia, in 2005, still does not do well. Our regulations permit, even in centres with the highest accreditation rating, ratios of caregivers to babies of one to five. One visiting developmentalist called it 'a license for neglect' and another, 'no-one's definition of high quality care.' The ratio recommended internationally is one to three. Penelope Leach thinks one to one is necessary for babies; some early childhood specialists I interviewed told me they thought one to two was needed. Despite accreditation procedures, the childcare industry confronts major difficulties in delivering high quality care.

One of the most important qualitative aspects of childcare quality given our knowledge of children and attachment is that the substitute caregivers should not change all the time. Caregiver turnover in Australia during the 1990s, Gay Ochiltree conceded, which in one estimate was 85.5 per cent over two years, was close to the American figures of 41 per cent per annum. It remains an acute problem. A recent Senate report *Childcare: Beyond 2001: Inquiry into future directions for childcare*, bluntly warned, 'the turnover rate amongst childcare workers is alarming and requires immediate action'. It also bewailed a 'childcare field characterised by limited career paths, low wages/income, poor working conditions and high turnover—resulting in loss of skills and experience and a critical shortage of workers/carers.'

Likewise, the implications of the increasing corporatisation of childcare cannot be underestimated. It is the influence of childcare corporates that is largely responsible, on issues like ratios of caregivers to children, which means Australia has become locked into accepting lower than internationally recognised standards. A 2004 *Background Briefing* report on ABC radio interviewed a childcare educator who supervised trainee childcare students, who said only one in ten for-profit centres—25 out of 250–300 centres she examined—were high enough quality to model good care for students. Because the major expense for childcare providers is labour, it is impossible to improve that unless there is further government subsidy.

I do not mean to suggest that Australia has no childcare of 'high quality', nor that there are not some exceptional people, who despite poor wages (less than parking lot attendants) and difficult working conditions carry out their work with dedication and skill. But if the argument is that poor quality childcare damages children, while high quality care benefits them, then too many of us are avoiding the obvious question: what is the quality of care most Australian babies in long daycare routinely get?

British commentator Patricia Morgan argues that the 'mantra of universal, affordable, high quality childcare has been achievable nowhere on earth'. We must face the first unpalatable fact. High quality care is *expensive* care. To make childcare both high quality *and* affordable for most parents, it must be more heavily subsidised by government than at present, *with the explicit intention of increasing care quality*.

Compared to what? Hoodwinking the public with show projects

Martin Krygier asked in his Boyer lectures, in a different context, a highly intelligent question: compared to what? When we moan about the shortcomings of Western democracies, we are comparing them to what and when? This question is no less applicable to childcare. Supporters of childcare often argue this point, with justice, in relation to severely disadvantaged children at risk of neglect or abuse.

However, the emphasis of daycare advocates on 'isolated and depressed' mothers moves well beyond honestly acknowledging the reality of a minority of women's circumstances, to a universalising pathology, as if mothering never goes well! Moreover, the poor quality of childcare routinely available means that in modern Western societies, invoking Krygier's question 'compared to what?' within a low-risk group might come up with a very different answer.

A more common comparison might be between, on the one hand, parents who, despite their inevitable mistakes, doubts and confusions, are doing a good job caring for their child, who love their child beyond reason, are prepared to do more for that child than anyone else on earth; and, on the other hand, mediocre or poor quality childcare.

One of the standard tricks of the propaganda machine promoting the 'daycare juggernaut', which utterly bamboozles ordinary parents (and politicians for that matter) is to compare results from 'show' projects for desperately underprivileged, at-risk children with the ordinary daycare routinely available to most parents. Ian Roberts, Director of the British Child Health Monitoring Unit, claimed, 'There *isn't a scrap of evidence* that putting children into daycare while their mothers go to work is bad for their health or education.' As it turned out, his blanket statement depended almost entirely on evidence from intervention projects with disadvantaged children. Removing children on a daily basis from drug-addicted, abusive or neglectful parents to a specialised, well-funded intervention project is not at all the same as children going from loving, attentive parental care to poor quality childcare. Childcare advocates are often guilty of conducting the debate as if every child at home is a child at risk, and every daycare centre is top notch. But it is a relative thing—just as you can take a child from a poor home situation and put them in a better one, you can put a child from a good family into a much worse circumstance.

An often-cited 'fact' is that for every one dollar invested in early childcare, seven dollars will be saved down the track in reduced delinquency, crime and enhanced educational achievements. This was a finding of a centrepiece show project of the childcare lobby: the Perry Preschool. Sometimes called the Ypsilanti study, the Perry Preschool did indeed have some excellent results. What such informants do not say is that this was utterly unrepresentative of normal daycare. It was a costly intervention consisting of specialist consultants who designed a high-quality, active learning program with individualised teaching in a daily two and a half hour classroom session for three- and four-year-olds, with advice and support to parents, including one and a half hours of home visits to each child and parent per week. It served the needs of fifty-eight children: 'Half of these were from families on welfare, homes in which the father was unemployed, or in families headed by single mothers, and the majority had IQs in the range of the borderline mentally retarded.'

As British writer on work and family issues, Jayne Buxton says, using 'showcase studies involving underprivileged children to hoodwink the general public about the benefits of full-time daycare for all children is irresponsible'.

The cortisol findings

The American psychoanalyst Sally Provence set up a model childcare centre, a pilot program at Yale University for low-income, disadvantaged families. It had expert staff with clinical training, superb adult–child ratios, constant meetings and consultations between staff, excellent facilities, a generous budget. As one commentator put it, it was as close to an ideal program as you could get. Provence did not take a position for or against daycare, but accepted that 'daycare is here to stay'. Provence's considered response, based on seven years of observations of young children in her ideal centre, however, was sobering:

> When adults have a fair capacity to be parents, their young children do
> best when cared for mainly by them ... Group care, even under the best
> circumstances, is stressful for very young children ... part-time will

ordinarily be better for the child than full-time . . . The child from one to three is not by nature a highly suitable member of a large group, whether of similar or diverse ages, and difficulties appear to magnify as the group increases in size . . . Length of day also is still very much the issue, for separation reactions become more acute as the day lengthens and fatigue decreases coping ability . . . when one is with them one is impressed that their feelings range from a sense of bewilderment to acute longing for mother and home . . . This seems to operate for most young children even when the staff–child ratio is favourable and the program is high-quality.

Provence's observation about the stress of group care, and concern over the 'length of day' in childcare, is given striking support by recent research into the physiological effects of centre-based care. In a number of studies since the late 1990s, researchers have discovered that many children experiencing a full day in centre-based care, compared with children not in childcare or in home-based childcare settings, have a significant increase in cortisol levels for the second half of the day.

Cortisol is a potent stress hormone, 'associated with experiences of fearfulness and vulnerability to stressors'. As child psychiatrist Stanley Greenspan explains: 'Significant rises in cortisol levels are associated with emotional and social disregulation and can be a sign of stress.' Normally it is highest in the morning and lowest in the afternoon. One recent study in 2003 into cortisol found the effect was particularly strong in the toddler age group, while other studies have found it also present, though less strongly, in ages three to four.

The 2003 study found that at childcare 35 per cent of infants and 71 per cent of toddlers showed *increases* in cortisol. In contrast when at home 71 per cent of infants and 64 per cent of toddlers showed *decreases*. Approximately 80 per cent of 3 to 4 year olds also showed increases in cortisol, showing that the stress of group care might not abate as quickly as we would like to think. However, it is also important to note that as well as children in parental care, one study Andrea Dettling and her colleagues conducted in 2000 showed children in highly responsive childminder care also had normal cortisol levels, indicating it is group care that is more stressful for the very young child.

The cortisol findings were of especial concern because the study group of children were enrolled in medium to very high quality centres. Quality of care was a mediating factor—in that the lower the quality the stronger the finding—but was also clearly still present in centres judged by careful measures to be excellent. (The centres studied had one caregiver to two or three babies, far better than the Australian childcare regulations allow: a recommended ratio of one to five.) Temperament was a factor too—shy children in the toddler age group were particularly vulnerable to the stress of dealing with the aggression of other, not yet fully socialised toddlers, and to feeling excluded. In another study they found it was not only shyness; children with poor self-control and aggression also experienced rises in cortisol as the day progressed.

How often we are told that childcare provides the opportunity to 'play with their friends!' Such optimistic accounts overlook the age of the child—infants and toddlers are some distance from older children's capacity for sustained cooperative play with peers. Andrea Dettling, Megan Gunnar and Bonny Donzella concluded in their 1999 study that 'Rather than reflecting children's pleasure in being with other children, it seems likely lower mid-morning cortisol concentration reflects something about the demands of the context and the child's attempts to cope with those demands.' They also noted that stressed NASA executives showed similar patterns!

In the journal of *Child Development* in June 2003, researchers warned that:

> Although there is currently no evidence that small increases in cortisol confer risk to the developing child, there are reasons to be attentive to the childcare cortisol findings described below. In research on animals there is strong evidence that early experiences shape the reactivity and regulation of neurobiological systems underlying fear, anxiety, and stress reactivity. The neurobiological changes . . . are believed to model . . . vulnerability to anxiety and depressive disorders. Animals who as infants have been exposed to conditions that activate . . . [cortisol] as adults exhibit heightened fearfulness and greater vulnerability to stressors . . . In addition, elevated cortisol levels impair immune functioning, thus increasing susceptibility to infectious disease . . .

New Australian research has also found evidence that even for older children in anything less than the highest quality childcare, elevated cortisol levels may be found. Researchers from Western Australia, Margaret Sims, Andrew Guilfoyle and Trevor Parry, studied 117 children from 16 centres of varying quality across Australia, aged three to six years. They noted that secure attachments, as well as 'touching, holding and responsive care in the early years', promote an individual's ability to manage stress in later life. In contrast:

Stress in infancy is particularly damaging, as high levels of cortisol impact on the development of a range of neurotransmitters (for example norepinephrine, epinephrine, dopamine) whose pathways in the brain are still being built. The outcome of this is long-term difficulties in self and emotional regulation.

Cortisol production increases in conditions of stress:

> Stress is created when the individual is threatened or feels insecure or uncertain ... Separation from the attachment figure is one of the key stressful events in early childhood. Children who attend childcare routinely experience stress through separation and research has commonly identified these children as 'at risk' for negative long term outcomes. Children in childcare are found to have elevated cortisol compared to children in the home environment.

The researchers acknowledged that those higher cortisol levels may have contributed to the pattern in the literature linking childcare attendance with aggression:

> High cortisol levels are likely to have contributed to the negative outcomes associated with childcare attendance demonstrated in much of the literature ... Children who attend childcare show higher levels of non-compliant and aggressive behaviour than children who are home-reared ... less positive parent–child relationships. Extensive use of childcare is found to be associated with behaviour problems in school, less well developed social skills including problems in relationships with peers and externalising problems.

In February 2005, Sims, Guilfoyle and Parry reported to the Australian Institute of Family Studies annual conference their first results. Even for these much older children, only at the highest level of care quality did children's cortisol levels decline. In centres deemed 'satisfactory' cortisol remained high or rose throughout the day.

Their results for infants and toddlers—which overseas research has shown to be an even greater problem—is yet to be reported.

In the US research, higher cortisol, even in good to excellent centres, also relates to inattentiveness in caregivers who have so many children to care for, and to the toddler's immersion for a full day in a peer group. A perceptive grandmother who looked after her toddler grandchild on a regular basis observed to me that she would often go off playing, but return for a quick hug, and plunge back into vigorous play. 'It's like she's recharging her batteries,' she remarked to me. 'It's as if she needs to know

I'm still there for her.' She was right. Schore reports work with mothers that shows that in the second year in the toddler phase, attunement is so synchronised that a mother continually modifies a child's emotional state—pepping up a baby or calming them down, often with just a glance lasting a micro-second. What seems clear is that this kind of emotional refuelling happens far less in many busy childcare centres. In group care an infant or toddler may go through the day—sometimes a long one—with very few intimate interactions.

Joint attention sequences

One aspect of early infant development which recent observational work illuminates is 'joint attention sequences'—sharing interest, excitement and engagement with an object or idea or experience with a caregiver. The formal, rather stilted language of developmental psychology is inadequate to what it needs to convey. A 'joint attention sequence' is also a special, shared emotional space where the parent's attention flows to where the child is—where they, at this moment, need it to go. It is a moment of connection and communion, where a child learns 'the extent and shape of the shareable inner universe'.

That does not mean other caregivers cannot enter into such interactions, given time and a relationship of genuine warmth and affection towards a particular child. But with one caregiver to five babies we are expecting far too much. One consequence is, as Greenspan says of US centres, 'Even in good daycare centres, we've seen many an eager, expectant eight-month-old baby give up and stare at the wall as his caregiver stops by his crib briefly but then hurries away to attend to a crying rival.'

Three separate investigations into these important interactions in Australian childcare found that while physical care needs were taken care of, there was an almost complete absence of joint attention sequences. In over thirty hours of videotape of caregivers and two infants, taken over eighteen months at two different centres, Berenice Nyland found almost none. In one instance, the entire extent of the 'joint attention sequences' during a whole day is for a caregiver asking children to put hats on to go outside, to point and say, 'Hat.' There was also a striking lack of intimacy, affection or physical touching. In an observational sequence over lunch, the mealtime is not, as it is meant to be, a social experience. There is no conversation, and no one notices that the subject child leaves the table having eaten very little.

In another investigation, Berenice Nyland, along with fellow researchers Sharne Rolfe and Romana Morda, found in over six hours of observation of caregiver–infant interactions, 'half of the attempts at connection by the infants resulted in failure'. Given the importance of 'turn taking' in those increasingly elaborate proto conversations that make up mother– infant attunement, it is of concern that for most childcare children in this study 'interactions were fleeting—characterised by only one turn'.

Unhappily, that is not an isolated finding. Another study by the School of Early Childhood Research at Queensland's University of Technology looked for joint attention in eight childcare programmes, randomly selected. They found the interactions in just two; in the others it was worry-ingly rare. Researcher Donna Berthelsen said: 'Often the kids would make bids for attention, and the caregivers would miss them or ignore them.'

Those concerns, it should be noted, are not particular to Australian or American centre-based childcare. In Britain, Trudy Marshall, then assistant director for daycare in a London borough, did over forty-eight hours of observation of the under twos in a local daycare centre. She found that 'the attention of adults flitted from child to child and rarely lasted more than thirty seconds with any single one. Signals about children's needs were missed, as were levels of distress and tiredness': 'to comfort a distressed child did not appear to play any part in the repertoire of adults in their daily care of children.' She argued, as a result of her observations, that at that level of care quality, 'sensitivity cannot be found and sustained in group care of infants under two'. Psychotherapist Dr Juliet Hopkins found similar fleeting, episodic attention in centre-based care.

There is something else. Nyland and others make very useful and important suggestions on training caregivers, and the child/carer ratios. Few, however, make the obvious point. Most parents have never heard of 'joint attention sequences'. But they do love their babies. As a consequence they are more likely to engage in those shared moments, all those 'joint attention sequences', simply because they gain profound pleasure out of being with and relating to their child. More training and instruction of caregivers, then, is only one possible response. The other is to give the parents back to the baby!

Social science and the abolition of meaning: the new discourse

The childcare discourse from the 1950s to the present begins by being child-centred and ends with a resolutely parent-centred viewpoint.

Whenever a child's point of view is expressed, a cultural flashpoint occurs.

There can be little doubt that 1950s men such as Bowlby and Winnicott were attentive to children. Bowlby also provided a superbly family-friendly workplace for working mothers at the Tavistock Institute. He gave them extensive leave, supported part-time work and held open their jobs. Professional women colleagues found him supportive—he instantly shifted meetings traditionally held in the afternoon to the morning to accommodate a female head of department with preschool children.

However, many of the complaints directed at male psychologists by professional women—that they were close to oblivious of what it might cost women to 'be there' with small children—were well founded. 'Men don't have to pay the bill with their careers,' remarked one psychoanalyst to me with real bitterness. Neglect of women's needs for fulfilment outside mothering were among the 'never saids' of the old discourse.

Refusing to assent to that flaw, however, surely need not mean that we should become complicit with a new obliviousness, in which the sole concern is parents' needs and desires, while children's needs that conflict with them become part of a new set of 'never saids', slowly but surely airbrushed out of existence. Let me give some instances taken from different decades to the present.

The first difference in emphasis in early work is on the child's emotional experience at the time rather than the long-term 'effects' on later psychological health. In *Separation*, first published in 1973, Bowlby tells the story of a child, 'Lottie', aged about two, beginning childcare that was described as 'benign'. Settled in gradually, she seems fine at first, but over time she protests more vigorously. She 'cried hard . . . her face hot and flushed'. She clings more to her mother, and begins wetting herself again. At childcare she now won't let her mother leave, and is always anxiously assuring her mother, 'I didn't cry.' Previously happy enough in short-term separations at home, now she expresses intense longing when her mother leaves her with someone else. Not until two years and nine months, six months later, is she happily settled in.

Bowlby remarks: 'it is evident from the account that both of Lottie's parents and the teacher were expecting far too much of a young child. Much pressure, it is clear, was put on her not to cry . . .' There are

> so many misconceptions about the norms of behaviour to be expected of young children when left, even briefly, in a strange place with strange people

. . . Again and again it is implied that a healthy normal child should not make a fuss when mother leaves, and that if he does it is an indication that either the mother spoils him or that he is suffering from pathological anxiety.

He concludes with the hope that once people understand the universality of attachment behaviour, 'such reactions will be seen in a new and more realistic light'. In other words, it is the child's emotional state that should be respected and adults should shape their expectations and actions accordingly. It is an uncompromisingly child-centred view. But that child-centred era was coming to a close.

Let me next look at a 'transitional position', an observational account published in 1980 by Jerome Bruner, while Professor of Psychology at Oxford, of childminding in Britain. The new era is beginning; Bruner is explicitly sympathetic to the desire of women to work.

I found Bruner's study particularly affecting because it is so similar to the family daycare I observed which first prompted my doubts about alternative care. A 'happy third' of children had the temperament that, Bruner suggests, would make them happy in any tolerable situation. Another third, however, were 'noticeably withdrawn, subdued, and conspicuously passive' in childcare. These children also had troubles—divorce or such like—at home. A second group, also withdrawn, passive and unresponsive in childcare, were lively at home, with a much warmer relationship with their mother than with the minder. Together, these 'risk' groups account for two-thirds of the sample. The differences, Bruner makes clear, are not due to difficulties caused by the caregivers, but in spite of their best efforts. Instead, they are to do with being 'minded': 'Minded children often pine, often withdraw, and often leave the minder unrequited in her effort to create a warm relationship. Minders are human; they respond as most ordinary people would to such a situation by letting it lie.'

In the period of observation nearly a third of the children made no approaches to the minder. There was little physical affection; more than half the minders never caressed the children in their care during the observation period. More than half the minders reported not spending time actively involved with the children in the preceding day. Most spoke kindly of their charges, a few with real affection, though *a full quarter had nothing good to say about the child*. No child was found to be livelier at the minder's home than at home. When asked, the mothers had *not a single negative remark about the minders*. When asked whether their child was happy, *100 percent replied in the affirmative.* This was not, Bruner emphasised, likely due to lack of concern but the opposite—their love for their children and the pain of leaving them led to an idealisation of the care situation.

The description of the children by the minders is the most telling part of Bruner's book. 'He's quiet . . . He's a gentle little boy and gets easily pushed around. Got a nervous disposition—if I tell him off he wets himself. He doesn't do naughty things, not like mine', or, 'Lovely little boy but not quite right—he walks around sucking his thumb and doesn't like cuddles or kisses. He's a bit like a little adult.' 'Very quiet . . . At first he wouldn't talk for weeks and weeks—just sat on the sofa and didn't answer.' The most worrying was perhaps this: 'After describing how insecure and unhappy the minded child was and how she wanted her mother all the time, the minder told the mother this and the mother said, "Oh Flora, you're a naughty girl".'

The researchers questioned whether child-minding 'offers the child a rich, loving and satisfying bond with one person, similar to the bond he has with his mother', and concluded that mothering is an activity particular to one's own children. 'Every bit of research that has been undertaken on this subject testifies to the contrary . . . An extension of domesticity to other children does not necessarily provide the child with a psychological home.'

Bruner concludes his study by a salutary warning of the likely generational consequences: '. . . the dangers should be made clear. There seems every reason for concluding on the basis of this study that the present practice of child-minding will increase maladjustment in the generation exposed to it.'

Somewhere in the 1980s, in that part of the cultural narrative shaped by the academic discourse on early childcare, the language begins to change. It becomes more abstract, technical, and submits everything to a kind of calculus increasingly remote from the experiences it is describing.

The word 'mother' begins to disappear, replaced by 'caregiver'. So, too, the word 'love' almost completely disappears; rather, phrases are used which express an ambivalence or even coldness to expressions of love as a form of irrationality—'emotionally involved', or even 'emotional outburst'—some euphemism which has rather a bad whiff to it. It is an increasing rarity to get 'inside the skin of a child'. No more little Lotties or Floras with their hot tears! Gay Ochiltree does mention Bruner's study in passing, but fails to mention the vivid portrait of children's distress.

Instead, Bruner's work is smoothly incorporated into a point about caregiver–child ratios.

By the 1990s a French researcher, Genevieve Balleyguier, acknowledges that children are very different when at home, in a nursery, or with a child-minder. The differences are because mothers have a '*more emotional attitude* than the substitutive caregiver'—an interesting way of expressing the fact that most mothers love their babies. As with Bruner there is clear evidence of passivity and withdrawal in the French childcare settings Balleyguier describes. There is, however, steadfast avoidance of the obvious inferences, a kind of flattening of meaning. Emotional expressiveness is characterised as 'tension' and 'irritability'. For Balleyguier, a mother's or father's love sounds a little dubious, since children are 'more tense' with their 'emotionally involved parents'. Here is a nine-month-old baby at home and at the nursery.

Situations	At home	At the nursery
Wakes by himself	Calls	Plays by himself
Time to eat	Restless	No reaction
Interrupted meal	Cries	No reaction
Caregiver passes by	Looks at her	Does not care
(*Caregiver at home means mother!*)		
Being dressed	Grumbles	Lets her
She refuses to take him	Cries	Accepts
Hindered to take something	Cries	Accepts
Mother/caregiver arrives	Laughs	Indifferent
Brother/child comes	Laughs	Indifferent
In bed	Tries to sit up	Does not try to sit up

By re-describing the emotional expressiveness at home as being 'more tense', Balleyguier never faces the meaning of the baby's apathetic state at the nursery.

It is not long before that coolness and passivity—the very aspect that so upset Bruner—moves from not being noticed, to being a childcare selling point. In her *Early Childcare: Forty Years Research*, Gay Ochiltree expresses enthusiastic endorsement of a Scandinavian expert whose research reveals the atmosphere at childcare to be one of 'affective neutrality' (meaning emotional neutrality) and involves the same peculiar ambivalence, even suspicion, of emotional expressiveness. 'In the home, children can express a range of emotions towards parents ranging from love to frustration and anger; such emotions are expressed less openly within the childcare setting.' Such 'dual socialisation' 'may be an advantage in social development'. The more 'emotionally neutral and instrumental' atmosphere of childcare contrasts with home where 'the specific function of the parents' is to be 'responsive to the child's emotional outbursts'.

If Balleyguier's euphemism for love is 'emotionally involved', it has here an even more unpleasant whiff to it; love is an *emotional outburst*. As Rosa Luxemburg remarked of the Bolsheviks, it makes a virtue out of necessity. To praise 'affective neutrality' is to cast one of the chief difficulties of childcare, *from a child's point of view*, as its leading virtue.

From paediatrician to parentician

There is in popular works too a decisive shift from an earlier child-centred perspective to a parent-centred one.

One letter about Michael Leunig's cartoon 'Thoughts of a Baby Lying in Childcare' argued that we should feel empathy for the feelings of pain women feel when they must leave their baby in childcare. The writer spoke of their sense of loss, how deeply they grieve. She was right. We should recognise how leaving a baby in childcare can be fraught with emotion for many women. Recognising how painful it can be is one reason why, understandably, people often prefer to avoid the childcare topic altogether. Yet Leunig's empathy for the loss or grief a baby might feel was dismissed by the same correspondent as 'sentimentalising, middle-class maundering'. The baby's point of view had dropped out altogether. My sense is that whenever a 'baby's point of view' is expressed a cultural flashpoint occurs, because it is subversive of this central transformation in the cultural narrative on childcare.

Gay Ochiltree speaks, disapprovingly, of a common image in Western society being a 'psychologically vulnerable child shaped by early experience with a mother'. This is historically true, but in much contemporary writing one can see a powerful new impulse towards psychological revisionism, reflecting a new 'spirit of the times'. A new conception of a child emerges—the child seems almost psychologically *invulnerable*: an image more appropriate to a free self-actualising adult. Painful experience or trauma is cheerfully countenanced as enhancing the child's ability to cope with the later slings and arrows of life, teaching a baby about 'strength and coping'. It is, in emotional terms, a little like the old idea of putting a child out in the cold to toughen it up, to harden its resistance. Besides, parents do not have to worry because babies are so tremendously resilient. If dropped, so to speak, they bounce. It is not so much the child who is vulnerable, or needs protection, as the parent, from feelings of guilt.

Take for example writing in the 1980s by T. Berry Brazelton, America's most popular paediatrician. After becoming 'a target of criticism', Brazelton dropped his earlier views on the dangers of too much early separation. He apologised to women for 'offending them'. The point here is not just that Brazelton is rightly reshaping in a post-feminist era his understanding to *include* what matters to the mother as an individual, alongside his understanding of what may matter to the child. In his book *Working and Caring* the child's point of view all but sank from sight.

A child's separation protests on going to childcare are a good sign that they are still gratifyingly attached to their parents. Brazelton says of one child, 'if he didn't fall apart, I'd be more worried than if he did . . . It shows how attached he is to his parents, despite all the time away from them.' 'The difficult thing' is not that 'falling apart' is hard on the baby, but that 'it compounds [the mother's] feelings of inadequacy and she wants to get away. Mothers . . . need constant reassurance. They constantly need to explore their feelings about leaving a baby to someone else.'

If in earlier thinkers, like Bowlby, attachment was seen from the baby's point of view as the adult providing a relationship of felt security for the child, by the mid-1980s the section in Brazelton's book dealing with attachment is called 'A Parent's Choice'. It is not so much the baby who needs to feel 'securely attached' as the parent: 'New mothers and fathers need different amounts of time to feel securely attached to their baby.'

At other moments babies are so 'competent' they possess the wisdom of little Buddhas, capable of a forward-thinking strategic vision, planning their days with a view to emotional economy. Brazelton's researchers observed and studied babies in daycare over an eight-hour stretch.

> They seemed to function at a rather low key all day . . . as if they were guarding themselves against getting too involved in any part of their day—until their parents came to get them at night. Then they let go! They cried loudly, almost angrily, saving up their strong emotions for the people who mattered to them. Their tired, 'disintegrated' parents ran headlong into this barrage. They felt guilty, blaming themselves, and took their baby's crying as

a personal response to having been left . . . *Parents are all too vulnerable*, and this tends to distance them from their babies. [emphasis added]

The new way of 'working and caring' was better for everyone, according to Brazelton, but particularly the children; among the 'joys and compensations' 'is to be home, safe together, snuggling with each other after a terrible day'. Parental nurturing or a mother's love was a little like Peter Rabbit's chamomile tea: a measured medicinal dose, a teaspoonful to be taken at bedtime. Brazelton even advised parents to practise rushing. On Sunday breakfasts 'you might try a game: "Now let's hurry like we do every day—rush, rush, rush—finish your toast—where's your mitten? Whew! Isn't it fun when we have time to make a nice breakfast?"'

Any questioning of complete freedom of action and choice for the adult was now out of bounds. There was a new taboo, expressed in a very 1980s commandment: Thou Shalt Not Make Parents Feel Guilty. Brazelton was no longer a paediatrician, but a parentician. (To be fair, as concern over widespread poor quality infant care mounted in the US, he did recover his balance, co-authoring with Stanley Greenspan *The Irreducible Needs of Children* in 2000.)

The technical literature too was affected by the new zeitgeist. In the mid-1990s, Alice Leibermann developed a new 'competency-based' paradigm that utilised new work on infant development to legitimate childcare. Daniel Stern's work could be read as revealing the importance of providing mothers and babies with the time and environment in which attunement can be fostered. Yet in Leibermann's chapter there is no mention of this mother-and-baby 'dance'. Instead we learn that the infant is 'actively discriminating and self-organising with an affectively continuous core self . . . able to evoke memories of the absent mother in moments of need and use these memories as bridges to her until she returns'.

The 'bridges' to the mother or parents, according to Barbara Karmelson, an expert on separation, might be, for example, photos in the daycare centre. When a child misses the mother or father they can be taken to a 'representation of the parent' (that is, a photo on the wall of the centre). They look at the photo. Or there are the technological solutions: 'audio tapes of the parent reading a favourite book for a toddler or pre-schooler, or just talking for an infant' (when the baby cries they turn on a tape of the mother's voice). Or there are 'objects' that serve as 'on-call parent substitutes': 'a photograph book with pictures of the child with the parent, or an object that belongs to the parent. To serve their purpose as on-call parent substitutes, these objects need to be available to the child throughout the day.'

Karmelson informs us that a 'strong, vigorous' separation protest indicates a 'healthy' attachment to parents. Separation anxiety has ceased to be something to respond to, as in the case of Lottie, but has a 'use value' for the parent, reassuring them that attachment has proceeded on a way that is 'healthy'.

Since separation anxiety may be viewed so positively from a developmental point of view, it changes the thinking on how one evaluates sadness and even depression. It becomes a 'transient distress period'. How 'transient' is transient? A Swedish researcher recorded the reactions of children placed in high quality Swedish daycare. 'In one study of children placed at daycare centres during the second half of their first year, Harsman found clear transient distress reaction which has disappeared *after five months*. At that time, group differences between the centre group and a home group were very small, although there were great individual differences. Some children recovered very quickly, while *others remained somewhat depressed* at the end of the observation period' [emphasis added].

A 1995 study of high quality Italian daycare with ratios of one caregiver to three babies, by Greta Fein from the University of Maryland, found some babies to have the despair-like reactions first described by Bowlby. Fein writes that 'mothers and teachers describe the first few weeks of childcare as highly stressful for infants'. The adjustment lasts up to six months. Some babies recover better than others, displaying more play and engagement with caregivers. But Fein did find some babies have 'despair like' reactions and were 'distressed, immobilized, and self-soothing at entry.' Others were 'detached, centred attention on toys, seemingly happy but socially unengaged after 6 months'.

Temperament, Fein thinks, plays a role, and also caregivers' reactions to infants' responses to childcare, since they give much more attention to babies who cry and fuss on entry—leaving the quieter ones to their own devices. Her article, however, with its abstract descriptions of babies, is an extraordinary contrast to the power with which Bowlby wrote about despair-like reactions of babies in hospitals and institutions. Then the knowledge that children felt despair was the basis of a passionate call to arms, the restoration of contact with parents and the transformation of that and subsequent generations' hospital and foster care practices. In contrast, Fein never questions whether some babies might be better off with their parents. There is no mention of alternative policies like parental leave. Instead, Fein says, 'the practical implications of these data are that those who work with young children must be trained to tune in to those who tune out'.

In part that shift is because the dominant voice shaping the discourse is now a highly educated career woman committed first and foremost to the ideal of maternal employment. Shahla Chehrazi's contribution to a book on childcare, 'Balancing Working and Parenting', was written because of her own desire to combine working and parenting. While some childcare advocates offer no qualifications such as length of day, speed of entry or temperamental differences, from Chehrazi we learn that 'length of day' and 'speed of entry into daycare' are turning out to be 'pivotal issues'. She also suggests we need to cherish mothers' separation responses because studies show that mothers with strong reactions to early separation had empathetic relationships with their babies, who in turn by age five were more empathetic with their peer group. Empathy is important, too, in assessing a baby's reaction to childcare. In one vignette a baby copes well with alternative care, even with several different caregivers, because of his strong relationship to his mother. In another example, however, even in the conditions of highest quality an abrupt return to full-time work results in a seven-month-old baby suffering a reaction severe enough to seek outside help:

> Mrs G . . . came to me because her baby was showing some signs of depression . . . the infant had lost her exuberance, joy and curiosity about her environment and had become passive and withdrawn . . . Mrs G . . . was surprised with the child's strong reaction to her returning to work in view of the fact that she was receiving quality care at home. A highly sensitive and devoted mother, she observed the signs of depression in her daughter, and her awareness and empathy helped the resolution of the infant's depression over the subsequent two months.

In this vignette we can see the profound loss within the discourse of the idea that from a baby's point of view it is not just the quality of care that counts but who gives it. What is troubling, too, is the acceptance— for all Chehrazi' s talk of empathy—of seeking therapy to resolve an infant's depression, rather than altering adult work patterns. In the 1950s a mother's depression could be part of the 'never saids' and the reasons why—frustration as a homemaker—an 'outside question'. Now, questioning early return to work is the 'outside question'. Chehrazi talks a lot about fathers, but what work of world-historic importance this father is doing that prevents him from helping out, even part-time, to save a baby from depression is outside the frame. At least, however, Chehrazi acknowledges that for some babies separation responses can be severe, and she urges respect for mothers' feelings of separation anxiety—this is part of the 'holding' relationship that is to be cherished, not eradicated.

By the twenty-first century, in an Australian study by Judith Ungerer and Linda Harrison, early separation is assumed to be both normative and desirable. Any ideas a mother has about her irreplaceability is part of her 'separation anxiety', which is treated less sympathetically than in Chehrazhi. That mothers in a childcare regime that has one caregiver to five babies might have some realistic concerns is not considered.

Some studies do find that parents who separate early from their babies are more likely to attribute resilience to a baby. Some babies *do* react well to sensitive, alternative care. Problem is, accepting at face value this 'parental leap of faith', as Sally Loane describes it, overlooks the frequent mismatch between parental perceptions of the childcare situation and the child's actual wellbeing. Bruner's study is but one example. Loane points out that when accreditation was introduced, about two-thirds of Australian childcare was found to be poor to mediocre, but in numerous surveys parents pronounced themselves 'very satisfied' with care quality. Loane instances cases where children were left wet or were beaten or neglected in centres, the parents, apparently oblivious. Sara Charlesworth and Leonie Morgan of the Victorian Work and Childcare Advisory Service, after surveying thousands of parents, found they generally are satisfied. 'They say, "I can live with it. The arrangements have to be very poor before they indicate they are dissatisfied".'

The startling disparity between parents' perceptions and the actual situation is also found in American studies. In one study of family daycare in 1994, which 'found 9 per cent of care settings good, 35 per cent poor, 56 per cent custodial', 92 per cent of parents said that if they had the chance to choose childcare arrangements again they'd choose their current arrangements. In another study of 46 daycare centres, only one met the recommended levels of group size, ratios and staff training. Yet when asked, 80 per cent of parents who used those centres said they'd enrol their child again 'without hesitation'.

Loane remarked: 'not only do we not shop around, we seem to be overwhelmingly satisfied with our undiscriminating choices ... I cannot think of another service where we are so cavalier. When we buy a new car we spend weeks ... reading about the various makes and styles ... Why then do we not take the same care with childcare?' Child psychiatrist

Stanley Greenspan used the same analogy in 2001 about American parents using childcare.

Yet at this point in the literature it is not uncommon to find mothers reluctant to use childcare for babies depicted as if they are problematic. One young mother who withdrew her child from a centre, was told by the centre director that she was a 'high anxiety/low-sharing mother'— very bad! In this there is a significant linguistic shift from mothers 'leaving' their babies to 'sharing' their babies. 'Sharing' is a nice word, even a feel-good word. 'Leaving' has an echo of abandonment. The word 'sharing' excludes a great deal of what the baby might feel. Who can complain about being 'shared'? The idea of the 'high sharing and low anxiety' new good mother is part of a new ideology, and new 'spirit of the times'. It not only supports but idealises early separation and creches for babies, and makes at-home mothers transgressors of the new world order and at least neurotic if not quite mentally ill!

No one, however, has taken the trajectory of idealising early separation and pathologising at-home mothers further—to the point of urging state intervention to prevent mothers making that choice—than the influential American psychologist Sandra Scarr.

The abolition of mothercare

Sandra Scarr believes infants are pretty much invulnerable by design: 'If our species had evolved to require scarce or unusual experiences for normal development to occur, humans would be extinct.' In response to the daycare wars in the late 1980s she observed to the *New York Times* that infants '. . . brains are Jell-O and their memories akin to those of decorticate rodents.' Perhaps unsurprisingly, then, Scarr proposes to *lower* existing childcare quality to make the price affordable. She asks, 'What is the *minimal expense* for childcare that will allow mothers to work and not do *permanent* damage to children?' [emphasis added]

As de Marneffe says, 'Avoiding "permanent damage" to one's child is not the standard most people would consider adequate when they are seeking childcare . . . for many mothers, leaving their children in even less good care than they already do is a recipe not for maternal freedom but despair.'

Brian Robertson makes the added point that there is also a clear conflict of interest between Scarr's advocacy of maternal employment, her positions as academic and editor of *American Psychologist*, and her close connection with one of America's largest for-profit daycare chains, Kindercare Inc, which has one of the worst records of care quality. From 1990 to 1994 Scarr was on the board of directors of Kindercare. Only when she was made CEO of Kindercare did she leave the University of Virginia, but she remained president of the American Psychological Association during 1996 to 1997. During that time she rejected articles for the Association's flagship publication *American Psychologist* which contained negative findings on daycare. If a research scientist gained financial benefits as CEO of a pharmaceutical company, it should be noted, we would immediately spot a conflict of interest.

Scarr advocated lowering the quality of care while she was serving as the CEO for Kindercare. So confident was she that she even began to argue for state intervention to prevent mothers from staying at home. In the bad old days working mothers were pathologised as neglectful, harmful, or 'unnatural'. Now she was attempting to pathologise mothers outside paid employment. In one article Scarr published in the *Brown University Child and Adolescent Behaviour Letter*, she argues that for the twenty-first century 'ideal children':

> Multiple attachments to others will become the ideal. Shyness and exclusive maternal attachment will be seen as dysfunctional. New treatments will be developed for children with exclusive maternal attachments (EMA syndrome) and those with low sociability scores.

Children in maternal care, of course, do have 'multiple' attachments—to fathers, grandmas, and siblings. Shyness is not pathology, but often partly a temperamental trait, and is exhibited in some childcare children too (as shown for example by the higher cortisol in the saliva of shyer daycare toddlers). Children with secure relationships to their mothers usually have very good friendship patterns by middle childhood. And so on.

The most important point, however, is the sheer coerciveness of Scarr's proposal. Remember Simone de Beauvoir's comment that after the revolution the choice to stay at home 'will not be permitted'? Scarr also looked forward to the time when 'experts will even claim that "being isolated at home with one adult and no peers" "is harmful" and "*should not be permitted*".' That coercive impulse is no mere theoretical issue. Lawrence Mead, the conservative architect of the US Welfare to Work policies for poor women, which force them to work and use childcare within a few months of a child's birth, utilised feminist arguments that daycare benefits children, just as work benefits women.

Groupthink: ideology masquerading as science

A discourse has certain logic, impetus and trajectory. Irving Janis, a political scientist, coined the phrase 'Groupthink' after looking at the reasons behind some disastrous foreign policy decisions made by expert advisory groups to the White House. At a certain point it becomes ever harder, perhaps impossible, to insert anything outside the assumptions of the dominant group. The very cohesion of the group makes it impossible to 'realistically appraise alternative courses of action . . . the danger [is] that independent critical thinking will be replaced by Groupthink . . .'

The ideological nature of Groupthink could not be more important in understanding a high level 'expert' workshop I attended on non-parental childcare convened by the Minister for Children and Youth Affairs, Larry Anthony, in early 2003. As it was Chatham House rules, I cannot divulge the identity of the participants. But I can give a gist of what occurred.

Between 2001 and 2002 the prestigious NICHD study group into early childcare and some Australian research had found problematic outcomes for those children in over 30 hours of childcare. In consequence the Minister invited experts in the field to examine whether 'early and extensive childcare in and of itself, is predictive of particular benefits and/or risks for children' and to 'debate the evidence and investigate various views on the impact of non-parental care'. As it was not an open conference with published presentations, its title was 'Closed Workshop on Non Parental Childcare'.

It turned out to be 'closed', however, in more ways than one.

The opening discussion was not a promising beginning, if the hope was a spirit of disinterested scientific inquiry. One early childhood professor went ballistic even at the suggestion of paid parental leave—since it implied that not all childcare was ideal. Others were outraged at the admission of negative evidence because 'it made parents feel guilty'. Childcare industry representatives present added a new addition to this theme: 'it made childcare providers feel guilty!' Others claimed the main children at risk were those outside childcare.

The lead speaker and visiting expert—whom I will call Dr X—began with a position statement that childcare was here to stay, and that demand for childcare places for children between the ages of 0 to 3 years was rising each year in the US. Since early childcare was a *fait accompli* the only task left was to improve its quality. Then, as he began reporting the latest US research, something exceedingly strange occurred. He accurately reported the data of the prestigious NICHD study—but inexplicably (since the conference was being held several years later in 2003) stopped at the late 1990s findings when the children were 36 months old. He omitted entirely the controversial 2001 findings when the children were 54 months old that over 30 hours of childcare raised aggression, which the group had been brought together to discuss. When the 2001 'quantity' findings were raised, Dr X waved them away—on the basis of a purported private conversation ('I had a long talk before leaving') with one of the NICHD researchers, who, he claimed, said the findings were 'washing out'.

I was puzzled. All participants had sent relevant research abstracts. I had sent a paper by Andrea Dettling on the higher cortisol findings, an article by NICHD member Jay Belsky in the 2001 *Journal of Child Psychology and Psychiatry* summarising international research into adverse effects of longer hours, and an advance copy of a peer reviewed NICHD article summarising and confirming the controversial 2001 findings on longer hours to be published only a few months later, in the June edition in 2003 of the journal *Child Development*. It was absolutely clear from that article that there was no 'washing out' of the quantity findings. Over morning tea I showed Dr X the forthcoming article and he seemed genuinely concerned and asked for a copy. Reading the abstract he asked me what 'no apparent threshold' meant and looked shocked when I told him that it meant that there was a direct relationship—the more hours the more problem behaviour—without any threshold under or over which it was without risk. A few participants who did not dare risk dissent on the floor of the meeting privately came up to me and agreed with parental leave options being important, citing their own child's difficulties with non-parental care when they were younger than two.

For the rest of the day the dominant group corralled the workshop into its comfort zone—how to give greater access to disadvantaged kids and how to improve care quality. It *was* admitted that the Australian ratio of one carer to five babies was painfully inadequate. No one showed any interest in the cortisol findings or the quantity findings, and the meeting steadfastly ignored a participant whose Australian research had found similar difficulties. Not even one question was addressed to her. It was all about holding the party line—that childcare was 'better than home', which meant getting increased government funding for childcare.

After the workshop, I checked, via my contacts in the NICHD, whether Dr M had indeed claimed that the findings were 'washing out'.

Dr M claimed to have not spoken to Dr X for six years, and acknowledged that the findings were not 'washing out'.

Some time after the conference came—in an Orwellian twist—a letter from the Minister, Larry Anthony, thanking the participants for explaining the 'benefits' of childcare. All mention of 'risks' had disappeared. To Dr X's credit, after *Child Development* in June 2003 published the two articles—one on higher cortisol in childcare children and the NICHD paper on the link between longer hours and aggression—he wrote to the group saying he did now 'have concerns' about childcare, sending those papers to conference participants to 'present the other side'. As an admission it was, however, too little and too late. The childcare juggernaut was already rushing onward. In the 2004 election, a non-means-tested 30 per cent rebate for childcare expenses was announced—but no paid parental leave. In 2005, having lost his seat at the 2004 election, the former Minister Larry Anthony, whom we had reported to, joined the board of the hugely profitable corporate childcare group, ABC Learning.

The prevailing consensus amongst the high-level experts gathered at the workshop reminded me of the words of the US feminist and psychologist Louise Silverstein (quoted approvingly by Ochiltree) when she wrote in *American Psychologist*, 'Psychologists must refuse to undertake any more research that looks for the negative consequences of [care] other than mothercare.' Instead, Silverstein argued, they should put their efforts solely into looking at the 'negative effects of not providing high-quality affordable day care.'

That ultimatum could not be more important in understanding the war of words over the long-term 'effects' of childcare.

10 The childcare wars . . . resolved

'. . . lay decision makers grope through darkness, like juries faced with rival psychologists called by prosecution and defence, neither of whom there is strong reason to believe.' Eric Hobsbawm

'I sometimes feel like I am in the old Soviet Union where only certain facts are allowed to be facts and only certain news allowed to be news.' Jay Belsky

To explore further the link between the 'spirit of the times' and the research it generates we must turn to the daycare wars over long-term 'effects'.

Advocates of infant daycare claim it has no negative impact on relationships with parents, promotes and accelerates independence, enhances school readiness, and increases social competence. In short, it gives children a head start. To quote Australia's June Wangman, echoing British childcare advocate Ian Roberts, 'There is no evidence from *any of the research* that childcare is detrimental to young children's development.' That should be a verifiable hypothesis.

The early investigations—let's call it the first wave—into the effects of daycare were limited in number, scope and sophistication, and displayed mixed results. They were often studies of intervention projects with disadvantaged children in high quality university-based centres. In 1978, Jay Belsky, a rising star of developmental psychology in America, published his first review of daycare, arguing that it did not pose any serious risks, and giving 'the green light' to daycare expansion.

By the 1980s, Belsky, now a respected figure in child psychology, was discovering that some, though not all, of the new evidence on daycare suggested that it might be more problematic than first thought. In this 'second wave of research' several factors had changed. Research techniques were now more refined and the studies were now of ordinary daycare.

At first, the new evidence mainly related to children who had begun extensive daycare (more than twenty hours a week) in their first year:

> the new data . . . described pre-schoolers with higher rates of avoidant (insecure) attachment; first graders who were more difficult, argumentative, and aggressive—hitting, kicking, swearing, shoving; and nine and ten-year-olds who were seen as troubled by their peers.

As Belsky put it in an interview, 'there was a slow, steady trickle of evidence. I would acknowledge the disconcerting evidence and, like everyone else, explain it away.' At first he resisted work like that of Judith Rubenstein and Carolee Howes which indicated that 'kids with infant daycare experience threw more temper tantrums, had more fears and that kind of thing'. Rubenstein and Howes wrote:

> this study reflected a more *anxious or angry* child. It should be emphasised that non-compliance and temper tantrums are more characteristic of two-year-old than three-year-old behaviour. Thus, we are considering the differences in the daycare children to reflect a delay in their negotiation of an age-appropriate developmental issue. [emphasis added]

'I felt like a pretzel,' Belsky explained, 'twisting and turning, trying to explain these things away.' He did an about-face. 'All of a sudden I realised, why am I spending all this time explaining away every piece of disconcerting evidence? A lot of energy was going into explaining away data, and every year there's more explaining to be done.' In the audience of one talk he gave was Edward Zigler, the eminent developmental psychologist who was one of the architects of Head Start—the project in which disadvantaged children were provided with high quality daycare. Independently, Zigler had been coming to a similar view, and asked Belsky to contribute to a book he was preparing on the importance of parental leave.

The trajectory of Zigler's writing on daycare has been one of increasing pessimism. Always a supporter of high quality care for older age groups, by the late 1980s he co-authored a book pressing for parental leave. His review of the literature led him 'to be less confident about the effects of infant daycare and less sanguine about it being the most major policy option available to working couples'.

By the early 1990s, in *Childcare Choices*, the tone is one of increasing anxiety. Zigler is clearly deeply worried by infants in daycare. They cannot tell their parents what is happening; it is a vulnerable time of life; attachment bonds are being formed; there are now clear, well-documented health risks in group care. 'Placing an infant in supplementary care at a few weeks of age is, we believe, an unwise practice which cannot be sanctioned by the research to date.' His tone in a later article is desperate: 'We are cannibalising children. Children are dying in the system, never mind achieving optimum development.'

Heartened by support from people like Zigler, in 1987 Belsky wrote his first, extremely cautious, rethink. It was packed with qualifications, as well as innocent alternative explanations. Belsky took care to indicate that not all studies show difficulties, as well as acknowledging the counter-evidence. In one such study, Andersson showed that Swedish children who began daycare in their first year were more confident and socially competent, by teachers' assessments, at ages eight and thirteen. Andersson's work, Belsky acknowledged, raised the question of whether a combination of lengthy parental leave and high quality care might resolve the difficulties he was finding. He also emphasised that the findings did not apply to all children, and thought a combination of factors, including as yet undetermined family factors, is also likely to be involved. (Otherwise why do some children appear affected and not others?) Nonetheless, Belsky inched towards the idea that full-time daycare in the first year might be a 'risk factor'.

The reaction from female psychologists was particularly bitter. Sandra Scarr asserted that he had 'an axe to grind'. Although no one had mentioned this while he was seen as a supporter of childcare, he was now discovered to have a number of unpleasant attributes: he was 'abrasive', part of a 'backlash against the women's movement'.

Pandemonium broke out. Poor Belsky! If he had hoped for a restrained and scholarly debate about social science data, he was, as they say, on a learning curve. If once he attended conferences amid a hubbub of approving companionship, 'Now I walk through a meeting like a ghost. Nobody sees me, nobody comes up to me . . . I'm a pariah. I violated the Eleventh Commandment of developmental psychology—Thou Shalt Not Speak Any Ill Of Daycare, Whatsoever, Ever.' At one meeting in New York the collective fury was so great, for a few moments he feared he might be shot. And eventually he did leave America, and went into effective intellectual exile at Birkbeck College, London. 'American universities for the most part wouldn't have me. That's impossible to prove but it's certainly a sense I got.'

He did have supporters. Dr Richie Poulton, a colleague from Otago University in Dunedin, New Zealand, who has done a six-year longitudinal study with Belsky, says his colleague has guts. 'It is admirable when someone has the courage of their professional convictions to stand steady and present the data faithfully.' Eleanor Szanton, a professional US childcare advocate, said, 'I think everybody feels now that Belsky did a service. It has made policy makers at least begin to consider parental leave.'

The most interesting and important exchange occurred between Belsky and Alison Clarke-Stewart, whose earlier book on daycare came with a preface thanking her son for spending his first thirteen months in childcare so she could write it. She later admitted to a journalist that her research *was* orientated to finding a positive result: 'I wanted to find out that childcare was good. I'm a working mother, but that's not the only reason. It made common sense to me.'

Clarke-Stewart conceded that there was a higher rate of insecurity of attachment for daycare children, though not as high as Belsky had found (36 per cent versus 41 per cent). In response to Belsky's interpretation, however, she argued it was not insecurity or avoidant behaviour being displayed but 'precocious independence'. Next, she reinterpreted the data concerning 'non-compliance' and aggression as a form of enhanced social competence, a modern and desirable kind of assertiveness.

> . . . children who have been in daycare beginning in infancy or later . . . think for themselves and that they want their own way. They are not willing to comply with adults' arbitrary rules. Children who have spent more time in daycare, then, may be more demanding and independent, more disobedient and aggressive, more bossy and bratty than children who stay at home.

Belsky countered Clarke-Stewart's arguments about the precocious independence of daycare babies by pointing out that her own data, along with studies by Kagan and others, showed that daycare babies were *as much or more* distressed by separation than home-reared children. Running a study himself with Julia Braungart explicitly to test the independence proposition, 'we found no support for it. The avoidant kids with daycare history were not spending more time playing and were not less stressed than avoidant kids without daycare history. In fact it was the reverse.' Belsky questioned whether the early reaching of developmental targets, that is, 'precocious independence', was always desirable.

Belsky defended the 'Strange Situation' technique for judging infant security by pointing to refinements in its use in the 1980s, and argued that the technique distinguished reliably between a range of child-rearing situations—25 to 30 per cent insecurity for a low risk sample, around 40 per cent for childcare, 50 per cent for children of clinically depressed mothers, and 65 per cent for maltreated infants. He pointed out that Clarke-Stewart, by dealing with the behavioural problems first and only then the question of security of attachment, was able to obscure the central causal connection—that behaviour problems have been shown to be the later consequence of insecurity of attachment. Moreover, Clarke-Stewart's lower figures for insecurity were questionable, since they were partly derived from unpublished data.

Belsky was criticised at the time (as anyone is who reports negative findings) with being excessively concerned with the infant–mother relationship and the Strange Situation. In fact, since there was evidence that showed no increased insecurity when children were cared for by their fathers rather than mothers, he shifted his focus from non-maternal to non-parental care. His argument, however, did *not* exclusively depend upon the Strange Situation technique, or on measures of the infant–mother relationship. It rested on the *combined* evidence of studies which showed *both* increased rates of insecure attachment among daycare children *as well* as evidence from unrelated studies showing increased problematic behaviour problems, on aggression and non-compliance. Questioning whether it was possible to interpret it as enhanced social competence, Belsky cited Ron Haskins, who found these children were

> more likely to use aggressive acts, kick and push than children in the control group. Second, they were more likely to threaten, swear and argue. Third, they demonstrated the propensities in several school settings—the playground, the hallway, the lunchroom, and the classroom. Fourth, teachers were more likely to rate these children as having aggressiveness as a serious deficit in social behaviour. Fifth, teachers viewed these children as less likely to use such strategies as walking away or discussion to avoid or extract themselves from situations that could lead to aggression.

It is a little difficult to interpret this as signifying a new kind of social competence or a useful kind of modern assertiveness.

Since the 1987 controversy, many other studies, though by no means all, have supported the findings that prompted Belsky's late 1980s reversal. The 'trickle' of evidence has become a 'steady stream'. Three major reviews of the evidence have found increased insecurity of attachment among daycare children: Belsky and Rovine (1988), Clarke-Stewart

(1989), and Michael Lamb (1992). A Canadian meta-analysis of all studies done since 1957 also found that more than twenty hours over a week in daycare 'had an unmistakeably negative effect' on 'attachment, socio-emotional development, and behavioural adjustment'. It's important not to exaggerate the results: in all of these the majority of daycare children—around 60 per cent—were securely attached. It was just that the rates were lower than for children at home.

With respect to behavioural and emotional adjustment, other, although by no means all, analyses in the US and Europe found similar problems for early, extensive and continuous care.

Deborah Vandell and Mary A. Corasaniti, studying all social classes, income levels and marital status, 'found third grade children who had had thirty or more hours of daycare begun some time in infancy scored the lowest in emotional wellbeing, work habits, peer relations and compliance'. Karen reports: 'Vandell had an arduous time getting this study published, more so than any of her other work, which surprised her, "because I'd never had such strong findings".'

Another study by Jack Bates in Indiana found that the more daycare a child had at any age, the more likely the child 'is to display problematic levels of aggression'. Bates also said there was nothing in his data 'to suggest middle-class families can be sanguine on this subject'. Goldberg et al. in 1996, after controlling for mother's education and the child's IQ, found 'total weekly employment hours predicted lower ego resiliency (i.e. capacity to handle new and stressful situations), adaptability, flexibility, and greater under-control of impulses'.

Peter Barglow found that when high quality full-time nanny care began in the first eight months, insecurity increased to 46 per cent compared with 29 per cent among home-reared children. It was a worrying finding because it was under such optimal conditions, with 'well-educated parents' 'deeply involved in parenting'. He found the effects fading over time, although there remained 'traces of adversity'.

Park and Honig found in 1991 that 'children who began full-time nonparental care in the first nine months of life and continued in full-time care thereafter were rated by teachers as, and observed to be, more hostile–aggressive (i.e. fights, destructiveness, kicks, hits) and noncompliant than age mates with less intensive and extensive care experience'. Youngblade, Kovacs, and Hoffman made similar findings in 1999.

It is often claimed that the only negative results are found in American daycare where care quality is poor. That is not so. Patricia Morgan fills an entire book, *Who Needs Parents?*, with a summary of negative evidence up to 1996, including a lot of material from Britain. Among the many results she cites from non-American research is the longitudinal British Child Health and Educational Study, which found the most favourable behavioural outcomes at age ten were for those who had no childcare experience, and the least favourable were associated with attending local authority childcare.

In the years following the publication of Patricia Morgan's book, many more studies have found the link between extensive care in infancy, especially group care, and more problematic child outcomes. Even in Scandinavia the link was found. Borge and Melhuish investigated a complete cohort from a single rural Norwegian community after controlling for socio-economic status, IQ and gender. 'Ten-year-old children were rated by teachers to show higher levels of problems when there has been a higher degree of maternal employment (i.e. hours and years), hence non-parental care, in the first few years.' In Australia, Ochiltree and Edgar also found increased non-compliance among those experiencing full-time daycare in the first year.

Not all research pointed to difficulties. Heather Joshi in Britain and Tiffany Field in the US found no such link, the latter study showing impressive attributes of daycare children similar to those found by Andersson. On security of attachment, an Australian study by Ungerer and Harrison made the unusual finding of greater security of attachment the longer the hours of childcare, although by school age children who had longer hours over the first two-and-a-half years had lower ratings academically.

Nonetheless, the literature on behavioural and emotional problems shows clear links to early and extensive daycare in infancy. The question, however, of whether all those results were due to care quality or the quantity of care remained. (A further possibility was that *both* quality and quantity mattered.) It was those questions that the National Institute of Child Health and Development (NICHD) set out to answer.

Quantity counts: the National Institute of Child Health and Development study

Twenty-eight eminent child psychologists (overwhelmingly women whose careers had depended on non-maternal childcare) formed a study group to settle the ongoing firestorm of controversy. It examined care quality, care quantity (age of entry and number of hours) and whether the behavioural problems noted were really assertiveness or aggression.

Explicitly designed not to depend on the now controversial Strange Situation, it utilised other finely tuned measures of mother–child interaction as well as childcare quality.

The study, which began in 1990, is one of the most comprehensive and sophisticated longitudinal studies of childcare ever undertaken. It involves more than 1,100 children from ten US cities. Both Clarke-Stewart and Belsky were involved. The stance of most of the researchers, it is fair to say, would be supportive of daycare.

The findings when the children were aged 0 to 3 were mixed and inconclusive. Poorer mothers and less sensitive mothers were more likely to have an insecurely attached infant. But there was good news too for the childcare lobby. Quality childcare, when compared with poor quality childcare, consistently showed advantages in children's cognitive and language development. Working mothers could take heart too. When the children were aged three, for example, no negative effect was found on mother–child attachment for kids with sensitive mothers in high quality care.

There were some important 'non results'. Parents remain the most important influence regardless of childcare. This means that our assumption that childcare will completely transform the lives of disadvantaged children is a form of magical thinking. We will need to work with parents, too. With respect to the cognitive benefits of high quality care, on one short-term memory item and a language measure, a little childcare goes a long way: 'cognitive outcomes are not promoted by more extensive exposure to higher quality care'.

The enthusiasts in the press who broadcast the findings about quality care often neglected, however, to mention that there were negative findings too. These supported Belsky's original formulation of childcare as a 'risk factor'. In the fine print there were all kinds of caveats. Mothers with strong beliefs about the benefits to their children of maternal employment were more likely to have insecure infants. Rather than childcare compensating for insensitive parenting, insecurity of attachment increased when mothers were low on 'sensitivity' and the childcare was for more than ten hours a week, or of relatively poor quality or unstable (i.e. more than one placement in childcare). Since the combined effects of childcare and insensitivity were worse than for insensitivity alone, 'the results', the group said, 'each support a cumulative risk model of development.'

All of us know working mothers who are sensitive and stay-at-home mothers who are not, and vice versa. That is, common sense and observation will tell you that there is more to a parent–child relationship than workforce status. The NICHD confirmed this, and found as well that sensitive parents tended to choose better quality care. But the study also found longer hours in childcare did negatively affect mother–infant sensitivity and attunement. The longer the hours of care, the more disharmonious was the relationship between mother and child; 'more time in care predicts less harmonious mother–infant interaction and less sensitive mothering at 6, 15, 24, and 36 months of age, even when quality of childcare and family selection variables are controlled'.

In the sanitised reports in the late 1990s (butchered by the powers that be, Belsky later said) that finally met the press, the releases led with good news about quality childcare, while the negative findings were buried in much later pages, and hurried over dismissively. By the time the press reported them, the caveats in the fine print had often disappeared altogether.

That is one reason why in 2001 the results released when the children were 54 months seemed so shocking. Again, high quality childcare was shown to have some cognitive benefits. But the 'quantity' effect on emotional and behavioural problems as the children got to kindergarten age was now worryingly clear. As the hours of childcare grew, so did the problems. At age four and a half, three times as many children—17 per cent—in over thirty hours of care showed more aggressive behavioural problems than children in care for less than ten hours (6 per cent). All variables like quality of care, type of care, time with peers, parent attributes and stability of care were carefully taken into account. Quantity, not quality, was the issue. The more time in care, the higher the problem behaviour.

On the specific question of whether the behavioural problems reflected 'assertiveness rather than aggression', they found

> not only that children with more hours of care were more likely to receive high ratings on items that could be considered to reflect assertiveness, such as bragging/boasting, demanding of lots of attention, and arguing a lot, and disobedience/defiance, such as talking out of turn, being disobedient at school, and being defiant, talking back to staff, but aggression as well, including getting into many fights, showing cruelty, bullying or meanness to others, physically attacking other people, and being explosive, showing unpredictable behaviour.

It was a minority of childcare children who displayed such behaviours. However, the researchers concluded: 'What should be very clear . . . is that the findings did not merely reflect the fact that children who spent more time in care were simply more assertive ... they were also more disobedient and defiant and aggressive and destructive.' The NICHD study put the issue of long hours in childcare firmly on the agenda.

Then something rather strange happened. Although all twenty-eight researchers were responsible for the data and the report, the 'intellectual property' of the NICHD report and the social ignominy of responsibility for the 'bad news' that their own research had generated, somehow passed to Belsky. It was as if he had authored and executed the entire report himself. He was even accused by principal investigator Sarah Friedman, in a revealing slip, of not 'toeing the party line' when he simply quoted from the report in a news conference. There were statements to the press about the dangers of researchers 'running away with the data'.

This last is interesting. To use a sporting metaphor: when the news is good for high quality daycare it sails through to the keeper without anyone putting a glove on it; but when evidence is negative the entire team and a significant portion of their supporters in the stadium descend to pulverise the hapless messenger! When the NICHD study showed benefits of high quality care, no researcher was criticised for 'running away with the evidence' or for making costly policy recommendations before findings were published and 'peer reviewed'. And in some instances—so long as the conclusions were positive and would lead to daycare's expansion—it was permissible to go running away *without* any evidence at all!

Sarah Friedman, for example, was asked by a Japanese paediatrician if the NICHD study had any information on the effect of daycare on children when they became parents themselves.

Friedman replied: 'Even though *I don't have the data* to demonstrate it, *I believe* that even when the mother is employed and the child is in childcare, there is ample opportunity for the mother to behave sensitively toward her child. *I also believe* the fact that mothers do interact with their children who are in childcare is sufficient for the transmission of sensitivity across generations.' [emphasis added]

If the results of childcare research are negative, even the most sophisticated quantitative study ever undertaken is rejected and a researcher pilloried for simply reporting the findings. If an academic's personal view is positive, plain old-fashioned belief—'even though I don't have the data to demonstrate it'—is good enough.

The Australian reaction was, likewise, depressingly predictable. As the journalist Michael Duffy once reported, the furious activity in response to any potentially negative finding is like watching 'white blood cells repelling an infection'. A flurry of ill-considered responses followed the NICHD findings. Experts when interviewed all angrily asserted that it was only and solely the 'quality of care which counts'. Professor Gay Ochiltree unwisely ventured her opinion that American relatives were not of the same quality as their Australian counterparts. (Apparently Aussie dads and grandmas are better than American ones!) *Sydney Morning Herald* journalist Adele Horin, who in 1999 had warmly praised the study and described Belsky as one of the 'world's most influential experts', suddenly reported the research to be dubious and Belsky to be an 'anti-childcare crusader'. Sarah Wise of the Australian Institute of Family Studies declared the study 'redundant' and, in an echo of Louise Silverstein, even questioned whether we should undertake such research.

The NICHD team reanalysed the data. Clarke-Stewart said, reasonably enough, that 'when you come out with a finding that is negative and scary, you want to make sure you have done every possible analysis'. Such sensitivity to *working* parents, however, is less impressive when it is realised that when the results are 'negative and scary' for *at-home* mothers, no one bothered with a re-analysis. They were treated as a non-constituency.

Belsky challenged his colleagues on the question of heightening fears of working parents:

> Two years ago we reported and subsequently published data showing that kids in high quality care outscored those in maternal care on cognitive assessments. The fact that we never ran a contrast to compare kids of mothers who remained at home and were highly sensitive to the high quality child-care group is appalling and was certainly irresponsible. I regard myself as guilty as everyone else for letting this get by. But the bigger point is that no one to my knowledge who is now accusing me of (yet again) making working mothers feel bad ever had a problem with making stay-at-home mothers feel bad.

In discussion with journalists some NICHD researchers maintained that 17 per cent of aggressive behavioural problems was about the 'norm' for society. This conveniently overlooked the fact that, as they knew perfectly well, the study sample was already skewed towards well-resourced parents—screening out at-risk groups. Many also blithely maintained, in the face of the evidence, that it was the quality of care, not the quantity, which counted, or that the study had not controlled for quality of care. Even Ed Zigler, revealing he had not read the study, said,

'That was the piece of that report that was most upsetting to me . . . Quality does matter . . .' (In fact that was one of the reasons why it was such a good study, and had been explicitly designed with the quality of care as a key variable to examine.) On the issue of aggression, *Time* magazine asked querulously, 'Should we even be worried at all? What about that adjective [aggressive], anyhow? Is a vice not sometimes a form of virtue?' The *Philadelphia Inquirer* echoed a widely touted interpretation: 'an aggressive kindergartner might just become a CEO . . . largely overlooked was the good news that children in high quality daycare are academically advanced . . . Make that a smart, articulate CEO.'

At this point in the cultural narrative that is the daycare debate, in which babies who have not yet been in the world a year, who cannot yet walk and talk, are praised for 'precocious independence', when aggressive and uncooperative behaviour is interpreted as an advanced form of social competence, I was reminded of Brecht's joke. It suddenly became clear to me that we have, in contemporary society, lost faith in the old child and elected a new one.

Game over: two British studies confirm NICHD finding

It was widely maintained that Belsky had misrepresented the 2001 findings. Things would be different after peer review and publication! When the NICHD published their summary paper in the journal *Child Development* in 2003, however, the results were utterly unchanged. Moreover, in that paper, the study group, after reviewing other contemporary evidence, conceded that 'When considered collectively the investigations just reviewed indicate that the timing and/or amount of early childcare have repeatedly, though not always, been related to problem behaviour in the early school years.'

The evidence on risks associated with longer hours of childcare has continued to gather. Other, later analyses of NICHD data continue to be troubling. In 2002, *Child Development* journal reported (using NICHD data) that there was a negative effect on school readiness, when mothers worked 30 hours or more by baby's sixth or ninth month. By 2004, (from as yet unpublished data) when the NICHD study children reached the third grade, the results showed a continuance of cognitive gains and academic functioning from better quality childcare. The statistical significance of externalising behaviour problems had declined by Grade 3; not due to *decreases* among childcare children, but due to the *increase* in behaviour problems among children with less childcare experience (until they resembled the childcare children). This led the investigators to call for more work on the effects on children of being in classrooms marked by high levels of aggression. Some new effects were detected. More time periods of centre care were associated with 'more conflictual relationships with teachers and mothers . . . More hours of child care were associated with poorer work habits and poorer social skills through third grade.'

In 2005 there was another addition to the NICHD study. Marinus van Ijzendoorn and his colleagues in the Netherlands examined the evidence on aggression and daycare again, this time using the criteria of 'non-familial' rather than non-maternal care. Utilising the evolutionary arguments of sociobiologists such as the feminist Sarah Hrdy, their hypothesis was that it would be *non-familial* child care, which was linked to aggression, rather than shared care by kin such as fathers and grandparents who also had a profound personal stake in the next generation.

This is no small matter at a time when so many young women want more egalitarian relationships of shared care with fathers. In the NICHD study more than 15 per cent of the children enjoyed father care for more than 10 hours a week. Van Ijzendoorn and his colleagues found the NICHD study linking childcare quantity and aggression was 'indeed robust' and that their re-analysis looking at non-familial care predicted even more strongly the link between increased 'problem behaviours and aggression in preschool, especially in boys'. By lumping fathers and grandparents in with commercial childcare, as part of 'non-maternal care', the NICHD had actually *underestimated* the link between more childcare and aggression.

It is not only the US based NICHD study that has linked early and extensive childcare with problems. In 2002 Melbourne University researcher Kay Margetts made similar findings. Children who spent more than 30 hours a week in childcare centres had significantly lower social skills, were less academically able and had more problem behaviours than other children. When *The Age* sought comment on the Margetts' study from Sarah Wise, the AIFS's principal childcare researcher, she questioned the validity of the findings, saying: 'The *only time* I have *ever heard* of long hours in childcare being harmful is where the quality of the care is poor.' [emphasis added] Wise had the previous year denounced the prestigious NICHD report showing exactly the same result for longer hours! It was an extraordinary moment in the daycare wars.

The most decisive contribution, however, was the results from two large, longitudinal British studies published and reported in 2003 and 2004 which again raised concerns about group care for the under-twos. In 2003, a new British study—a government-funded study by the University of London's Institute of Education—concluded that 'high levels of group care before the age of three (and particularly before the age of two) were associated with higher levels of antisocial behaviour at age three'. It also found that while higher quality of care could reduce the 'antisocial/worried behaviour', it could not eliminate it.

One of the key researchers in that project was Professor Ted Melhuish from London University, an internationally respected British scholar on childcare and early development, described in the Guardian newspaper as a man who:

> picks his words carefully. He is probably the most respected academic in the field of childcare in the UK; he worked on the EPPE study, and is heading the £16m evaluation of the government's flagship programme for pre-school children, Sure Start. He has just completed a review of all the international research on childcare for the National Audit Office, which found other studies, such as one from Norway, substantiating the Anglo–American research.

In September 2004 the British press was reporting another study, 'the trends being observed to add to a growing body of evidence,' this time from an Oxford University study, the Families, Children and Childcare project, co-directed by Kathy Sylva and childcare expert Penelope Leach, which followed 1,201 British toddlers from birth to school age. Again, this study found difficulties for the under-twos who had experienced infant daycare, in some instances for as little as twelve hours per week. The less time infants spent in daycare, the better. Leach pointed out that for the under twos, apart from parental leave options, one to one childminder or nanny care was less risky.

> We know from research that staff in nurseries tend to be firstly, more detached—less sensitive and responsive—towards the children and there is more 'flatness of affect', a subtle but very important characteristic which means that there is no differentiation in response to a child, a sort of blandness. Somewhere after two years, as the children begin to relate more to each other than to the adult, then high-quality, group-based care becomes an unequivocal benefit.

When one news headline used the word 'thugs', Belsky corrected them. The findings are modest and do not apply to every child. There is no need to catastrophise the results, but in modern societies, on every health issue, the agreed principle is that a person adopting a recommended course of action should know the risks as well as the suggested benefits. Not to inform a person of a risk, however small, is grounds for litigation. One parent involved in the NICHD study appeared on Rush Limbaugh's radio program saying, 'Why wasn't I told?' It was a fair question.

Journalist Rebecca Abrams noted that the press release for the London University study had excitedly announced good news about preschool for older children, but coyly did not mention the finding on babies. She found it, after wading through forty-five paragraphs.

> It's time to be honest with ourselves and face facts . . . The true emotional and psychological effects of neglectful or insensitive care in infancy may not show up at four or five, but 20 or 30 years down the line, in our relationships with our children, friends, husbands and wives . . . [in] the capacity to think, to empathise, to love . . . [in] the kind of society we're creating for the future . . . parents need easy access to unbiased information. An effective taboo on talking and thinking about children's needs, especially in the first year of life, is not what any of us need. On this issue at least, the time has surely come for speaking on the record.

Thankfully, the evidence on early infant childcare has had an effect, finally, on British policy makers. Patricia Hewitt, who had once described mothers who did not return to work in their child's first two years as a 'real problem'—now favours extending paid leave from six months to one year and jettisoning an earlier emphasis on early return for mothers and infant daycare. One headline read, 'If you want what's best, wait until she's two.' Noting that children who had long hours of care at the beginning of their first year of life were 'at risk even in a good nursery', Belsky commented to the journalist:

> I am delighted that this [the Blair] government seems to be listening to the research. I'm an American and I can tell you that President George W. Bush is not listening. The attitude there is, data be damned . . . The [Blair] government is showing a sophisticated appreciation of the fact that children at different ages need different things. From the age of two or three, children in nurseries with good-quality education programmes can thrive.

Belsky concluded that the NICHD and all the other research since the late 1980s 'should encourage the expansion of parental leaves, preferably paid, ideally as lengthy as they are in some Scandinavian countries.' Part-time employment should be used to reduce the time spent by infants, toddlers and preschoolers in care, and

> tax policies should support families . . . reducing the economic coercion that necessitates many to leave the care of their children to others when they would rather not . . . Finally, given the clear benefits of high quality childcare, its expansion seems called for as well. Of significance is that all of these conclusions could be justified on humanitarian grounds alone.

He pointed out that such changes would be consistent with most parents' preferences, and observed, 'One of the interesting questions that only history will answer is whether the cost of such leaves will prove less than the consequences of their absence.'

Ted Melhuish agrees. He has been advising the British government that unless you compromise on quality, 'for the first 18 months to two years of life, the cost of good-quality care is potentially very high, and is comparable in cost to paid parental leave for two years . . . To improve the responsiveness of group care requires maintaining very high staff–infant ratios and keeping staff turnover down to an absolute minimum: both are very expensive . . .'

Melhuish also highlights the experience of Sweden, which he suggests shows what parents will do if given a real choice: 'The Swedish case is very revealing—there was high-quality infant care available to all and heavily subsidised. It was widely used in the 70s and 80s, but in the early 90s, parental leave was increased and now there is remarkably little use of childcare under 18 months. Parents voted with their feet.'

That is also the argument of this book. Again and again in the literature, not in every study but in too many to ignore, the question of *time* away from parents, especially during infancy, comes up. Parents' preferences on childcare, which I outlined earlier, are uncannily close to the path of least risk: later entry, part-time at first, more when children were older.

Trouble is, the True Believers attempting to shut down awareness of issues like age and speed of entry and length of hours in daycare are very powerful. They have, thus far, largely succeeded. Many academics have now staked their reputations on claims that childcare is not just 'safe' but 'better'. For those wanting to increase places or raise the quality of care, to admit such complexities makes presenting one's argument to government for funding so much harder. 'Childcare's fantastic . . . so long as it's expensive, high quality, part-time care and preferably not the first year . . .' is harder to sell. Better to stick with the blanket line that childcare benefits all children, and 'for one dollar invested in childcare, seven dollars will be returned'—and take no prisoners when meeting opposition. The major stakeholders and beneficiaries now include the billion-dollar for-profit daycare industry. Even socially conservative governments now won't seriously oppose *their* interests—whether in raising care quality, increasing staff and paying them decently.

The mantra 'It's only the Quality of Care that Counts' has worked as a societal alibi, and prevented us from asking the important questions. Childcare centres explicitly for sick children have begun opening their doors. A new 48-hour for-profit centre opened in Melbourne in 2003, offering not just 12 hours of care, not just 24 hours, but the option of depositing children for a full 48 hours, even sleeping nights there.

Come to think of it, why not corporate-funded orphanages for the first few years of life? If it is truly only the 'quality of care that counts', why not?

★   ★   ★

Much of the pain, anguish and anger outlined above occur because we have presently constructed things such that, as Hrdy said, women's talent is usually played out in domains designed for men that have 'no tolerance for children'. If we are 'in denial' it is because of that brute, unfair fact. But we could do things differently.

We can continue to support parents' preferences to raise very young children at home and be generous with assistance with retraining on their return to the labour force. It is a societal madness if we do not support mothers who desire and want to care for their own children, both while they are mothering and afterwards.

Yet that need not be the only solution. In the post Bowlbyian world, the other ideal of the early feminist movement, for shared parenting, is also being proposed. The eminent child psychiatrist Stanley Greenspan, in response to what he sees as the dangers of daycare and to protect women's employment, advocates a new model of shared parenting—the 'four-thirds model'—where both parents work a two-thirds schedule to reduce the amount of time infants and toddlers spend in childcare.

Likewise, the neuroscientist Allan Schore, in an interview with British psychotherapist Roz Carroll, reviewing the evidence on the importance of early attachment, confessed how worried he was by increasing social trends to use poor quality infant daycare. He contrasted the generous European leave schemes with the US practice of sending mothers back to work when the baby is six weeks.

> [this] is the point whereby the face to face joy interactions just begin. Parents now have this terrible dilemma of how to face this problem without any social support at all, or any programmes at all. In addition the level of day care here is on the average sub-optimal, the people in it are paid very poorly, they're not trained enough . . . the first word that comes is scandal . . . we as adults in our society should definitely have some shame about how we are avoiding this problem and about how little attention we're paying to our futures.

In Crittenden's maternal feminist account, she interviews a Swedish family living just such an alternative. They live in a neighbourhood with one of the highest densities of children in Europe—there is no 'hard choice' between a careerless motherhood and a motherless career. Karin had been at home with her toddler, on paid leave from her job at 75 per cent of her full salary. She is presently 'introducing him to daycare, staying with him a couple of hours every day until he was happy in the group.' When he is settled Karin plans to return to an 80 per cent schedule. The father is about to do likewise. That means three days a week of care. And the toddlers can go home early, via a state guaranteed right for parents to work a six-hour day until the child is eight. In the daycare centre Crittenden visits, by 4 p.m. almost all of the children have gone home.

Karin cites other couples where the mother has taken the first year, the father the second year, of leave. Yet others take three years of leave, with the right to return to their previous job. Rather than special childcare centres for sick kids, Scandinavia gives up to 120 paid sick days per child per year. Either parent or a grandparent can take the carers' leave and payment.

We are not yet putting our full energies into that possibility, of giving those 'crazy about the kid' the chance to honour and practise that love, while not forever foreclosing the world of opportunity that paid work offers by extended paid leave programs and the right to part-time work. It is an alternative and humane path through the feminist revolution, which maintains an attentiveness to the needs of children, which 'takes them seriously'. It has already shown itself to be practical and workable in other nations. Yet it is already in competition with a much darker path.

The New Politics Of Attachment

Many attachment scholars raise the question of whether we are moving towards a society that is weakening the ties that bind. If patterns of love and attachment, the capacity for intimacy and autonomy, are deeply shaped by the earliest relationships, they may also vary widely from culture to culture. History shows that many childrearing environments, which scholars call the Environment of Evolutionary Adaptiveness (EEA), were perishingly harsh. Although the 'secure' attachment pattern is so attractive, and offers children and society many advantages, in some harsh circumstances might not insecure attachment be more adaptive—by making a child one of life's little survivors? A secure child, having had their emotional needs met by responsive adults, has high expectations; they expect to be treated well. In contrast, 'patterns of rearing that are negative, inconsiderate and coercive lead children to behave in ways that are self centred'. More suited to a dog-eat-dog world.

When the going gets tough in 'the foraging context' writes Hrdy, developing the point:

> it might be highly adaptive for an avoidantly-attached individual to learn to downplay love, to dismiss the importance of close human relationships . . . Rather than rely on those around him, the most advantageous course open might be for the child to become self-reliant and avoid developing empathetic feelings for others around him . . .

So what is this new 'EEA?' Robert Karen calls it the 'Avoidant Society.' Like the 'avoidant' adult, it is cooler, impatient if not hostile to the display of dependency needs in children and the vulnerable, attracted to ideas of self-sufficiency and independence, and is dismissive of attachment needs. Another way of looking at the harsh new world, however, is to see them as imperatives for survival in the hyper-individualist paradise of the new capitalism. A good childhood, in the dog-eat-dog world of late commodity capitalism, gives children unreasonable expectations. Here we must cut to the chase.

Western societies are undergoing profound transformations, in the nature of the family, in women's roles, but most deeply, with globalisation, in the nature of consumer capitalism. The new capitalism has created economic conditions inimical to a flourishing family life among both overworked elites and the working poor.

We face two very different paths through those difficulties. One path, suggested by this book, argues for the recognition that some children are getting a raw deal. Admitting children have emotional needs for protection, nurturance and love requires reparation. It demands action on an individual and public level to create the tools for a convivial childhood. It means tackling adequate parental leave provisions, involving fathers as well as mothers in family life, economic support for families, efforts on the part of government and business to help parents manage a reasonable family and work balance, investment in early childcare. It requires commitment, effort, sacrifice and money. It is a radical transformative vision.

There is, however, quite another path. The postmodern world will not adapt to children, but rather children must adapt—submit—to the new world order.

Childhood is sped up, if not declared obsolete. An unhappy childhood? All the better to toughen them up. Thus Judith Rich Harris, in her bestselling book, *The Nurture Assumption: Why Children Turn Out the Way They Do*, debunks the idea that parental nurture matters at all, 'Kids are not that fragile. They are tougher than you think. They have to be, because the world out there does not handle them with kid gloves . . . out on the playground it's "You shithead!" '

Cui Bono? Who benefits? It is the oldest political question. Feminists have plausibly argued a connection between early industrialising capitalism and the cult of protective motherhood and the vulnerable child. But capitalism has moved on, reaching into its bag of inventive new tricks to maintain itself. The new capitalism, however, requires a quite different ideology—not just of motherhood but of childhood. A new child must be invented. These agreeable creatures, bearing more than a little resemblance to the wives and mothers under patriarchy, conveniently enough, never have needs of their own which compete and conflict with the needs of the employer, or adult desires for self-fulfilment. Children who grow up fast are not childlike but little adults and tough ones at that—street-wise, sassy, competent, capable of surviving on their own. They do not need too much parental time or nurture. Quite suddenly, the new childcare discourse—that children don't need mothers but 'professional' caregivers, that childcare is 'better than home' and that children lose nothing by society institutionalising their care from the earliest weeks and months of life—can be seen for what it is. The ideology of childhood that the new capitalism has to have.

Part Three

Hard times: motherhood

under the new capitalism

'Late Capitalism has decided that it is better for all adults to work rather than for one designated gender to stay home with the children. It has decided that most children will spend at least part of their early childhood with people outside their families who are hired to care for them, often in institutional settings.' Jan Smiley.

11 Affluenza: the new ethic of work and spend

Truffle country

I am standing in a supermarket aisle in the country town where I grew up. I am shopping for my elderly mother, wondering which packet soup to choose. From time to time matters pertaining to the 'ethic of care'— my mother has just had an operation—spill over and can no longer be contained within ordinary time.

This enormous barn of a supermarket is a timeless world. As in a casino, there are no clocks. Piped music with a leisurely beat encourages me to move slowly. I feel vaguely confused but also mesmerised. A kind of shopper's enchantment has overtaken me and I notice my pace has slowed to a dawdle. Is it the piped music? Or all that choice? I am drifting around in a kind of dream, dazzled by the minor decisions I must make, the attractiveness of it all. And I am buying far more than the modest items on my mother's frugal list. I need tomato soup. Confronting me, however, are a bewildering number of new varieties—gourmet with noodles, spicy, with and without croutons. But no plain, old, garden variety tomato soup. Finally I find it and move on to the next item, only to discover a further cornucopia of choice.

The aisle billows out into a huge fresh food area. In the delicatessen there are expensive packaged meals, promising to save the hard-pressed working mother's labour: 'Just microwave and serve'. I pause to admire a fruit salad with different coloured melons attractively cut into balls. In an international cuisine area, there is every possible permutation of pasta, rice and noodle. Bottled herbs dangle in golden oils. An entire wall is devoted to different breads. In a large seafood bar, Atlantic salmon and lobsters are gracefully arranged next to an unruly tumble of globular grey squids.

I walk out with my overloaded trolley through the mall swarming with Sunday shoppers. There are hip clothing stores for teenagers overflowing with designer logo clothing: Mambo, Ripcurl and Nike. Brand names are emblazoned boldly so as to register, before any witness, how much the wearer has spent on them. A teenager is explaining to his anxious, harried mother just why he '*needs*' a pair of Oakley sunglasses costing $150. She is half mutinous, half submissive. I pause to mull over some shoes and eavesdrop on a cherubic pre-teen campaigning for brand-name sneakers priced at $130. She tries moral blackmail. '*Everyone* at school has them,' she sniffs with an injured air.

A bedding shop nearby has, centre stage, a four-poster bed wearing a frilly petticoat. I count eight silky pillows cascading down the eiderdown, and fancy bolsters tied with ribbons. The linen and napery have names aimed at a new elite with pretensions to aristocracy; 'Country Manor', 'Baronial Table Ware' and even 'The Linen *Collection*', as if sheets can be a work of art. Outside in bright sunshine, I search for my car in an enormous car park, larger than the famous century-old green park with its leafy oaks that languishes, rather neglected, down the road. I trundle past dinky little cafés and an enormous chain store selling home furnishings. My eye is caught by a mortgage advertisement in a bank window telling customers that its repayment rates will allow mothers the choice of staying home with their baby a few months longer. A specialty butcher's shop displays pickled lambs' brains. I pause, staring around in amazement. I am remembering times past.

When my mother first arrived in this country town many years ago, the groceries arrived once a week on our kitchen table in a small cardboard box. As we had no car, the local grocery store proprietor, wearing an apron and sporting a pencil behind one ear, delivered it. His entire shop would have fitted into one corner of the supermarket. I remember the Spartan quality of the meals: the narrow, monotonous, English fodder served up by accomplished country cooks who, the saying went, could make a pound of mince last a fortnight. I remember how housewives rejected the fragrant loaves of continental rye bread as too dark, sticking firmly to the safer, known quantity of Tip Top white sliced.

I remember the dreariness of the local shopping emporiums, and how there was one decent café in the entire town. Back then, the churches, pubs and sporting fields on every corner were the centre of community life. I remember modest dwellings with outdoor toilets, beds with one flock pillow, and the children's havens: large backyards. I also remember our freedom as children to roam—a gift bestowed by a powerful maternal tradition, because houses, indeed entire neighbourhoods, were not empty but full of women.

But I also remember the toll that gift might take. I see my mother, no stranger to sorrow, sitting at a kitchen table under a bright fluorescent light trying to help a depressed housewife who was twisting a wet, yellow handkerchief around and around in despairing fingers. And I remember a popular song about women in country towns, 'The Girls in My Town', a haunting dirge of lost opportunity and human flourishing denied, trailing after me like a threat as I made my escape to university.

On my way home there is a new housing estate where business is booming. For a moment I think that backyards have shrunk. Then I realise that the blocks are the same size as ever; but the houses have grown so much, their plump sides squeeze out almost to the very edge of the block. The Great Australian Backyard—the child's paradise—is disappearing. A real estate billboard advertises a house with rumpus and billiard room, several bathrooms, many bedrooms, and a study. The modest cottages of my childhood would fit within their walls several times over, even perhaps into the handsome two- and three-car garages housing the ubiquitous four-wheel-drive vehicles. There are also many childcare centres with fetching names—like Brighter Horizons Family Services and Little Moppet's Earlybird Learning Centre, offering places for babies of a few weeks to children of school age—open from 6.30 a.m. to 7.30 p.m.

Home again, I go on a walk along a glorious ridge road, looking out on the houses dotted over the countryside. The newest ones are on a grand scale: landscaped gardens, several bathrooms, tennis courts, and garden pavilions. Outside one I pause as two dogs whoosh out and hurl themselves at the fence. There is a strange young woman—not the householder so a babysitter presumably—with twins, about two years old, in matching pink outfits. I realise with a shock that this house, which I have walked past almost daily, actually has children in it. The children walk gingerly, as if their backyard is unfamiliar. I have never seen them in it before, only glimpsed cars flashing past early and late, travelling to the city and back. The twins must be at some city childcare centre from dawn till dusk. That is the price one must pay for sustaining the mortgage that bestows the tennis court, the pavilion, the swimming pool that the family hardly ever have the time to use.

Walking along, I reflect on a comment by one childcare advocate who said that 'two incomes are needed nowadays, not just for luxuries but for the necessities of life'. For a considerable portion of my old town, dependent on poorly paid casual labour, the word 'necessity' aptly describes their circumstances under the new capitalism. A shake-out of those losing out economically has seen city dwellers come here in search of cheaper rents. A roof over one's head, a place to sleep, food on the table: these things surely are *necessities*. For sole parents like my mother, or in the case of the working poor, it is a woman's paid work that lifts a family out of poverty. Yet incredibly, these are the families who are statistically *least likely* to be using childcare. Even in Australia, where childcare for those on low incomes is subsidised, in the year 2000 only 16 per cent of children whose family income was less than $400 a week used formal care. That includes before and after school care, occasional care and preschool, so long daycare only accounts for part of that 16 per cent. What is striking—and it is the same the world over—is that use of formal care steadily and consistently rises with income. Among dual income families with incomes over $2000 a week, 61 per cent used some type of childcare. There is a simple correlation—the more mum and dad earn, the more likely they are to use childcare. Across the Western world it is the wealthiest who are most likely to use childcare, and most likely to use it for the longest hours. In the US, for example, during the period of the feminist revolution, between 1960 and 1990 the labour force participation of mothers with children under six increased by over 270 per cent for women with husbands in the top income quartile, compared to around 110 per cent for women whose husbands were in the bottom quartile.

To describe all I have seen in truffle country, to describe it all as *'necessity'* is to draw too wide a bow. Is it *necessity* to have billiard rooms? Is it *necessity* to have eight down-filled pillows? Is it a *necessity* to wash in quite so many places?

Anyone who thinks that the great movement of women into the workforce, the dismantling of the old meanings of motherhood, the transformation in the landscape of childhood, is solely about women's emancipation—on women's own terms—is living with their eyes wide shut.

The new capitalism

The contemporary redefinition of motherhood is profoundly shaped by the new capitalism. It is indissolubly connected to the transformation of Anglo-American economies from those based on production, especially manufacturing, to those based on the provision of services and on high consumption. The new 'necessity' for a family to have more than one adult earning is inseparable from 'affluenza': the luxury fever of conspicuous consumption. The new ideal of the dual-earning 'symmetrical family' is inseparable from the process that critic Frederic Jameson alluded to as the essence of the new capitalism: the commercialisation of the private realm, the transformation of even private relations into commodities bought and sold in the marketplace, 'the extension of commodification into hitherto uncommodified areas'.

No ground has proved more fertile for commercialisation, for the extension of the cash nexus, than the private realm being vacated by women. The market now largely provides for elder care. A mother's love is transformed into the profit-based, commodity service of childcare, largely provided by giant corporate childcare chains. Childhood under the new capitalism is being profoundly reshaped—if early capitalism introduced mass compulsory schooling, the new capitalism has seen the extension of institutional life over early childhood. All this may gain ideological legitimacy from feminism and the rhetoric of women's emancipation—but its practical realities derive from the work-and-spend ethic of the new turbo-charged capitalism.

The American conservative Irving Kristol has observed that 'radical feminism today is a far more potent enemy of capitalism than radical trade unionism'. My sense is rather of the easy incorporation of main-stream feminism into the emerging new capitalism. One strand of feminism—a hard-line 'equality as sameness' strand emphasising paid work—was selected out as being the most compatible with the new ethos. That process partly defused the genuinely emancipatory potential of feminism, and ensured that the mainstream agenda would occur not on women's terms but on existing economic terms, the terms of the new capitalism.

Both liberal feminism and economic liberalism shared, as Jean Bethke Elshtain puts it, 'an insistence on the overall benefits of self interest'. Both were ambivalent, if not hostile, to different expressions of altruism, one to a public manifestation of altruism—the welfare state—and the other to a private expression of altruism—motherhood. There is no intrinsic contradiction between the needs of corporate capitalism and the needs of the upper-middle-class professional couple. As Elshtain pointed out, Betty Friedan's *The Feminine Mystique* is a 'paean of praise to what Americans themselves call the "rat race": she just wants women to join it.' Though 1970s feminism originated in the neo-Marxism of the New Left, there sprang up, during the 1980s and after, a natural alliance—a kind of companionate marriage—between feminism and corporate capitalism.

The ultimate aims of these idea systems may be different, but each has benefited from the existence of the other.

Feminists have pointed out that the conditions of early capitalism required an ideology of 'separate spheres'. The 'dark satanic mills'—the soulless, dehumanising conditions of the early factory system which gave rise to Marx's critique of capitalism—created the need for an 'angel in the house', the woman at home who provided a 'haven in the heartless world'. An ideology or 'cult' of motherhood, and a perception of children as vulnerable and in need of a mother's full-time care, emerged.

The needs, conditions, and requirements of the new capitalism, however, are very different. The new economy needs the radical downsizing and devaluation of motherhood. It requires not the cult of motherhood but the cult of the creche. And in the process the old idea of the dependent, vulnerable child must be revised and a new one invented—the independent and resilient child who does not need much parental time or nurture.

Let me put it this way. Had there been no feminist movement, the time bind of the two-income family and the new economy would have demanded a downsizing—a new minimalist version—of motherhood, and its counterpart, a new ideology of childhood. Had there existed no feminist movement, the new capitalism would still need a rationale for the extension of the market into the private realm, for the substitution of market services for family relations. The needs of the new capitalism are best served neither by at-home motherhood, nor by shared parenting, but by two parents in the workforce maximising family income. If feminism had not arisen, it would have had to have been invented. Or to put it another way, as the American social theorist Philip Selznick did, feminism saved capitalism.

If it was ironic that some feminists, given feminism's origins in the New Left of the 1960s and 1970s, have embraced the values of a hyper-individualist capitalism, the irony for social conservatism is that the embrace of a radical free market philosophy has radically undermined the economic foundations of the traditional family! There is a very real contradiction between support for a laissez faire global economy and traditional family values. Anthony Giddens puts it thus: that its two halves, market fundamentalism and social conservatism, are in fundamental tension. 'Individualism and choice are supposed to stop abruptly at the boundaries of the family and national identity. But nothing is more dissolving of tradition than the permanent revolution of market forces.'

During the economic restructuring of the 1980s, single-income families plummeted to the group just above the poverty line. The important family story of this period of turbo-charged capitalism is that it has thrown up—even demanded—a new family type. Even when presided over by social conservatives like John Howard, the imperatives of the new economy are at least in tension, but more often in direct conflict with the single-income male breadwinner model. Rather, it is the dual-earner family, which is better placed to survive the new capitalism. Job insecurity, reduced farm incomes, the disappearance of manufacturing jobs, declining male full-time work, the hollowing out of middle incomes, as well as high consumption patterns and spiralling house prices, all give impetus to the growth of the two-income family. More than half of all Australian families with dependent children now have two parents in the workforce.

There has been a radical shakeout of class position *according to family type*. Simply put, families did better or worse according to the time spent with children. As the *Australian Financial Review* concluded in their 2001 survey of the new rich, 'the presence of children is largely inconsistent with wealth'. Nearly 67 per cent of the top five per cent of richest households have no children. Childless couples have moved to the top of the wealth table. Dual-income families with children come next, followed by single-income families, with sole parents and families with both parents unemployed at the bottom of the economic heap. Rising family inequality is recognised in a wide variety of studies in Britain, the US and Australia. Now, prosperity is inextricably tied up with two incomes and female employment.

Luxury fever and the paradox of 'progress'

'A house may be large or small; as long as the surrounding houses are equally small, it satisfies all of our social demands for a dwelling. But if a palace arises beside our little house, the little house shrinks to a hut.'
Karl Marx

What, then, are the constituent parts of the new capitalism that we need to consider?

First, in the new economy consumption is absolutely central. It is a shift not just of economic activity but of sensibility, away from the ethic of delayed gratification as part of the old Protestant work ethic under a production-based economy, and towards the hedonism of a high consumption, service-orientated economy. As the sociologist Zygmunt Bauman observes, the producer/soldier ethic has been replaced by the consumer ethic of the hedonistic sensation-gatherer. Those on the wrong side of globalisation, like the unemployed, are transgressors not only of the work ethic but also of the ethic of spending. They are flawed consumers. Winners spend a lot, losers don't.

Children absorb these lessons early, being initiated not into the sobriety of thrift by elders, but into buying badges of belonging that signify acceptance into the cult of consumption. Like a child blackmailing her mother for designer clothes, youngsters feel deprived because the formation of identity—who I am—becomes inseparable from what I can afford to buy.

According to one of America's most astute economic observers, Robert Frank, the West is in the grip of a spectacular luxury fever. That, too, is the theme of Clive Hamilton's sharp-eyed and provocative book *Growth Fetish,* which showed how Australia was succumbing to the seductions of overconsumption. The overconsumption thesis was a critique first developed by American economist Juliet Schor in *The Overworked American* and *The Overspent American.* The thesis is a radical break with the Old Left's preoccupation with inequality and deprivation. While poverty still exists (Hamilton estimates it at around 10 to 20 per cent of the population), the old paradigm obscures a fundamental fact. Our society is more troubled by problems of overabundance.

In the emergence of the first *mass* affluent class in history (by the year 2000), the US had over five million millionaires, living, according to commentator Dinesh D'Souza, 'like the barons and dukes and aristocrats of old'. With some 25 million overseas vacations a year, as Gregg Easterbrook, author of *The Progress Paradox*, quips, '70 percent of the nation are members of the jet set'.

Between 1993 and 2000, Australia's millionaires increased almost threefold, to 208,000. Ordinary people watched open-mouthed in astonishment as they were admonished to tighten *their* belts and ride through a period of economic restructuring which saw executive salaries, part of a Winner-Take-All phenomenon, skyrocket. By 1998 the chief executive of Westpac was earning, through salary and share dividends, $142,000 *per week.* The top 20 per cent of income-earners, women included, began to form an overclass whose prosperity pulled sharply away from a stagnating middle, while the incomes—before welfare transfers—of those at the bottom declined. In Australia the top 20 per cent of baby boomers own over half the assets of that age group. (One Australian newspaper detailing the changes to the wealth tables used a racing metaphor—the new overclass were showing the rest of society 'a clean pair of heels'.)

'Luxury fever' does not only affect millionaires. 'Affluenza' or luxury fever is a competitive phenomenon—a kind of consumer arms race—and leaves few untouched. Expectations for patterns of consumption, the house one should aspire to, the education children should have, the toys, clothes, sporting and cultural interests that they 'need' to 'compete' with their peers, the sense in which a 'successful' identity is bestowed by material goods or even particular brands, is not particular to wealthy elites. Nor is the frenetic work-and-spend cycle that can leave family life impoverished. Many families devote ever more family hours to paid work but still cannot afford the domestic help that eases the lives of the wealthy.

Like the homes I observed in my old country town, new houses in the US are now twice as big as those built in the 1950s and have twice as many bathrooms as those of the 1970s. In Australia in the early 2000s, as average dwelling size swelled to 250 square metres, the average number of people within shrank to 2.6. The average Sydney mortgage in 2002 was around $1200 a month. This was partly due to the upward competitive pressure of investment by overclass members in real estate, but also through the immodest scale on which houses were now built. For all the rhetoric around women's choices, that almost guarantees two parents working full time.

In Australia, annual sales of the luxury four-wheel-drive vehicles that took up so much garage space in my old country town doubled from 1995 to 2000, up from 47,000 to 100,000 a year, four times the increase in the rest of the market. Clive Hamilton has some other arresting examples of the 'consumer arms race' phenomena—in barbecues, houses, and personal appliances, even cosmetic surgery. Ever larger, grander, more complex models, including the Grand Turbo barbecue, which weighed in at $6990, replaced the 1980s 150-brick barbecue, for example, assembled at home. Oakley X Metal XX 'eyewear' (sunglasses) retailed at $570 in 2002. Rental of extra storage space to stash all this stuff also ballooned, with a thousand self-storage sites dotted around Australia.

At the core of the overconsumption thesis, however, is not just a puritanical critique of 'affluenza' or the emptiness of materialism. Rather, a consumer arms race pursuing vantage positions of status and success ends by damaging the environment, our health and wellbeing, and—the focus of this book—the tenor of family life. As Hamilton points out, every examination, in every country, shows that beyond a certain benchmark of poverty and deprivation, people's sense of wellbeing does *not* increase with greater personal or societal wealth. There is no natural point of satiation. Hamilton points to the 'insatiate' nature of consumer demands:

> Real incomes in Australia have risen by around 300 per cent since the 1950s yet most Australians do not believe that they can afford to buy everything that they need. The notion of Howard's battlers is broad enough to include people earning up to $80,000 per annum and, according to the Australian Labor Party, average Australians are doing it tough.

Interestingly, it is the richest households that are the least likely to agree that Australia is too materialistic. Instead, human competitiveness gives rise to feelings of relative deprivation, which fuel a pointless pursuit of all things bigger and better. It is not our absolute relation to poverty that matters, but our relation to those in our social circle. If our peers have larger houses, then we feel deprived or less successful.

That is the 'paradox of progress'. What makes sense for the individual—to gain a competitive edge—ends by reducing the quality of life of the many. It leads to pressure on space and on the environment. Competitive housing markets mean stress on families, who must maintain a higher work effort to service mortgages, and commute in choked, overpopulated cities swelled to gargantuan proportions.

Robert Frank's term 'luxury fever', however, is in a way misleading. It applies well to the top 20 per cent. For most, it is far from a life of ease that enables them to acquire some of the good things of life. They live their lives nowadays, via television, glossy magazines and depiction of luxury lifestyles, advertising and those programs where advertising and programming blur into one, with the constant arousal of restless, insatiable, unquenchable desire. They live with their noses pressed up against the windowpane of plenty. Those further down the social pile have consumption patterns fuelled by an explosion of credit card debt. Australia's credit card debt has increased four-fold between 1998 and 2004. The average US family owes more than $5000 of unpaid credit card debt, at interest rates of between 17 and 20 per cent. Patterns of conspicuous consumption have a trickle-down effect. The stagnating middle class has kept pace with consumption and servicing debt by sending two adults into the workforce, and devoting ever more family time to paid work. Family income growth in America has still slowed, despite a greater paid work effort by families. A middle-class family's annual work hours grew by 10 per cent in eighteen years (for all family members), up from 3,020 in 1979, to 3,206 in 1989 and to 3,335 by 1997.

The power of employers was greatly enhanced by the new 'flexible' capitalism; the deregulation of industries saw the profound weakening of the unions; while increased competition under globalisation forced savage trimmings of the workforce. Elizabeth Warren and Amelia Warren Tyagi's book, *The Two Income Trap: Why Middle Class Mothers and Fathers are Going Broke*, exposes the catastrophic effect of galloping mortgages on ordinary American families. If either parent was downsized in the newly volatile labour market, bankruptcy often followed. Here is the central point about affluenza. A consumer arms race may make sense for an individual. Once everyone participates in such a game, the cost in terms of stress, commuting times, the effort put into paid work to pay for the larger houses (never mind women's work in cleaning them) dramatically reduces the time and energy required for a decent family life.

Risk society: no long term

While in my old home town I visited an old friend. Jenny's first piece of news is that her family has been dealt a blow by the cold winds of economic change. Her husband has been 'downsized' from a job that would once have promised life-long tenure. Age has seen the erosion of any competitive edge he might have, and at fifty-four, after trying hopelessly to get other jobs, he has retreated, bewildered and humiliated. For a time he felt that he was on the scrap heap. Now he is working very long hours, seven days a week, despite ill health, trying to transform his modest termination package into a small and not very prosperous business.

While his previous employer, a telephone company, has seen an extraordinary shedding of labour, its executives were awarded astronomical salary packages. Its share prices have risen. The shattering of his life has been just one small blip in the process. Richard Sennett has described in *The Corrosion of Character* how 'perfectly viable businesses are gutted or abandoned, capable employees set adrift rather than rewarded, simply because the organisation must prove to the market that it was capable of change'. A hand grenade of insecurity has been thrown into the previous assumptions about life narratives shaped around a predictable life-long career path. The consequence is a new and treacherous work culture of 'no long term'. Business schools, like the Harvard professor John Kotter, urge their students to 'work on the outside rather than the inside' of organisations. In a workplace marked by 'the strength of weak ties' (where fleeting forms of association are more useful to people than long-term connections) 'detachment and superficial cooperativeness' were 'better armour' than personal qualities like reciprocity, mutual commitment, trust and loyalty.

One of the men Sennett describes, Rico, erupts: 'You can't imagine how stupid I feel when I talk to my kids about commitment. It's an abstract virtue to them; they don't see it anywhere.' Rico is disquieted, uneasy with the way his working life gives him little to offer in the way of a parental role model. He 'cannot instil in his children worthwhile values'. Instead, for

> this modern couple, the problem is just the reverse; how can they protect family relations from succumbing to the short-term behaviour . . . the weaknesses of loyalty and commitment, which mark the modern workplace. In place of the chameleon values of the new economy, the family—as Rico sees it—should emphasise instead formal obligation, trustworthiness, commitment, and purpose . . . long term virtues.

Rico wants to prevent the intrusion of market-style relationships into his family. As Sennett puts it, the new short-term capitalism threatens a corrosion of character:

> how can long-term purposes be pursued in a short-term society? How can durable social relations be sustained? How can a human being develop a narrative of identity and life history in a society composed of episodes and fragments? The conditions of the new economy feed instead on experience which drifts in time, from place to place, from job to job.

Social commentator Hugh Mackay described the dislocation of men who went into the workforce during the 1960s and 1970s 'with a pretty debonair feeling. They believed they could have what they wanted . . . the escalator was always going straight up.' There was no hint that the halcyon days of the post-war 'golden age of capitalism' were to be so radically shaken up, so radically transformed under a resurgence of laissez faire economics.

During the 1980s and 1990s, working life shrank from both ends. Due to the expansion of higher education, young people entered it later. For older workers an entrenched culture of prejudice and a ruthless sense of their expendability meant they were the first to go in downsizing. The sociologist Manuel Castells thus predicted in the 1990s that in America and Western Europe 'the actual working lifetime could be shortened to about thirty years (from twenty-four to fifty-four), out of a real lifetime span of seventy-five to eighty years ... the productive part of life is compressed to less than half the biological lifespan, with older workers leaving the scene long before they are physically or mentally unfit'. It was seen most vividly in relation to men.

Overall, the full-time, life-long male employment of the breadwinner era has sharply declined. The numbers of men working full-time in Australia dropped from about 80 per cent in the 1970s to below 60 per cent in 1996. The proportion of men aged sixty to sixty-four in full-time employment dropped from 75 per cent in 1966 to 34 per cent in 1996. One effect of the compression of the working life, according to Sennett, is an increased social prejudice against age. 'If you're in advertising you're dead after thirty. Age is a killer. A Wall Street executive says, "Employers think that [if you are over forty] you can't think any more. Over fifty and [they think] you're burned out".' Likewise when Cheryl Kernot did a report for the ALP on the over-45s, she was 'overwhelmed by the stories ... from anguished men ... and the damage caused to their health, their finances and their family relationships by these retrenchments'. In October 1999, Drake Management Consulting surveyed 500 senior executives and human resources managers nationwide. *Not one* said they would employ managers in their fifties. This group would also be the first to go in the case of downsizing.

By the late 1990s fewer than two workers in every five worked a 'standard' eight-hour day, forty-hour week. In November 2000 a study for the charity organisation the Smith Family, by researchers from the National Centre for Economic and Social modelling, shows a 40 per cent increase in children growing up in 'working poor families' from 1995; 'one in five poor Australians now lives in a family where wages and salaries are the main income source ... In Australia today, having a job no longer guarantees that you or your family will not be in poverty.'

The capacity of young adults to achieve the 'Great Australian Dream' of owning a home was also negatively affected by the new culture of part-time work and job insecurity. The Committee for Economic Development report released in 2002 noted that many in Generation X had to abandon hopes of buying their own home. 'Australia has one of the highest rates of non-standard work (casual, part-time or unstable tenure) in the world,' explained one of the report's authors, Linda Hancock. Like Sennett's book, the report suggested that increased social risk created a prevailing attitude of uncertainty about 'what will happen'.

A pervasive, nagging anxiety accompanies even those who have escaped downsizing. Apprehension about *what might happen,* Sennett tells us, is deeply intertwined with the new capitalism. As a *New York Times* writer put it: 'job apprehension has intruded everywhere, diluting self-worth, splintering families, fragmenting communities, and altering the chemistry of workplaces'.

There is no easy path for the downsized. As the British psychiatrist Anthony Clare observed, the culture of work means that 'there is no point in telling these executives who have lost their jobs to cultivate wider interests. Late twentieth-century capitalism demands that people give their all to the company.'

Don't marry a millionaire, become one!

After a time the conversation with Jenny passes to her children and their various doings. Unlike her husband, one of her daughters, Sarah, has been doing well in a new job in marketing computer systems. Only in her early twenties, she has a salary that her father did not achieve in a lifetime of honourable effort.

There's a billboard advertising financial advice which exhorts young women not to marry a millionaire but to become one. Similarly, the new capitalism undoubtedly offers for a minority of women historically unprecedented financial rewards that their stay-at-home mothers would not have dreamt of. Some highly skilled, highly educated women are doing very well under the new capitalism.

Yet there is an issue surfacing here too. Sarah works fourteen- to sixteen-hour days. Although the new capitalism sold the message very successfully that *to have a life* meant to have a *work* life, my friend is proud of her daughter but also anxious that she hardly 'has a life'. She means a private, intimate life, rich in love. Sarah now wants children, yet how will she find a partner, let alone have any family life, with those kinds of hours? And once a mother she will probably not have, as many of her male workplace competitors still have, the comfort of a loving, supportive stay-at-home partner to smooth her passage through life. Nor is her work culture kind to those who cut back or take time out. Being there is everything.

And there is something else. Not long ago Sarah got wind of the fact that her present department was about to be reshuffled, and her present position abolished. In a series of clever moves she offered her services, in advance of being downsized, to a rival IT company, played off her old company against the new and got herself rehired at her old company in a different department at a better salary. But it was a close call.

Such insecurity of course profoundly affects family life—partly in the willingness to commit to partnerships or children, to risk taking time out of the workforce. At one level it encourages the 'collaborative' family, maximising paid work for both partners to buffer against the likelihood of loss of one or other income. Given the mounting number of young women who are childless and will remain so, it is also likely to be affecting their decision to have either fewer or no children.

For women, the radically insecure work world has other profound consequences. If a working life is made or lost between the ages of twenty-five and thirty-five, then career building often collides with raising small children. Suzanne Franks notes the urgency of young women's career plans; there is much to be done and quite possibly very little time to do it. Work insecurity makes it less likely that women, unless protected by legislation, push for or utilise extended leave entitlements, or shorter working days, or 'family friendly' work arrangements. Women who spend time at home with young children face a world of work on their return where age does not bestow authority or wisdom. As Sennett says, 'the passage of time seems to hollow us out, where experience seems a shameful citation'.

Work has changed in other ways too. Under the new capitalism there is an overworked core of permanent full-timers (the minority) who put in long hours, often in return for higher status and salaries. They coordinate the periphery—the majority of workers who work part-time or lurch between temporary contracts. For those who have permanent secure work, the returns financially and in terms of status are high—for women never higher. But so is the price. Long hours were widely recognised as increasing under globalisation and the move to a leaner, more efficient workplace.

Support for working women at home was hardly improved by the insecurity at work and the long hours culture. Just as men were being expected to pitch in more at home, many commentators have concluded that for many middle-class families the 'five o'clock dad' was a thing of the past. Many 'in principle' egalitarian men *in practice* worked hours longer and more inhospitable than their more traditional fathers.

It is a profound mistake to imagine that no one on their deathbed wishes they had spent more time in the office. If we take 'the office' not to represent just the humdrum location itself, but a metaphor for all work, and even more broadly as a symbol of all our worldly accomplishments in life, some of us are more dependent on 'the office' than we care to admit. There is a sharp contrast, for example, between the overclass members and the rest on the work–family balance. Those earning over $100,000 were less likely to have taken their annual leave entitlements (65 per cent compared with an average of 58 per cent) and more than twice as likely to cite business or work for the failure to take holidays, and were more likely to prefer a pay increase to less time at work. More than half of these were managers and administrators. Economic commentator Ross Gittins, analysing the ABS data in 2003, found long hours twice as likely among men as women, and among self-employed (57 per cent work fifty hours or more, compared with 23 per cent of employees), and among 'occupations involving high levels of responsibility, high earnings and no awards or agreements specifying standard hours', especially managers. Among such employees 'almost two-thirds said they preferred to continue working the same hours for the same pay. Only 11 per cent said they would prefer to work fewer hours for less pay, and these were pretty much offset by the 8 per cent who would prefer to work longer hours for more pay.'

Often occupational success at the highest levels is contingent on accepting the same logic as the old ideal of the good mother—being there. Always. One woman working for a large multinational firm recorded:

> Over the past decade the expectations of full-time working hours have become so enormous that I could never undertake a full-time job. It would mean being available at all times including weekends. It is impossible to compete with men who are able to offer this total flexibility. And being part-time means that it takes many years to build up credibility and to develop a reputation for being reliable.

My friend Jenny is now the main breadwinner in her family. While such a position is supposed to be privileged in our society, she feels a marked ambivalence about it. Some women relish being the 'first' career in a family. Others have mixed feelings on losing their 'choice' to cut back working hours while the kids are little, or to retire early to pursue other dreams when they are independent. All Jenny's hopes for more freedom to pursue her own private passions once the kids were grown, she now ruefully observes receding into the horizon of a future potential self, who has what she does not have—time. Her husband's downsizing means she must, as men have traditionally done, 'stay the course' and stoically soldier on, driven on by the responsibility, the burden of earning. It does alter the old division of labour, but it does not have the feel of the ease or confidence of the kind implied by 'choice'.

Work: the new sacred

'More and more, work enlists all good conscience on its side. The desire for joy already calls itself a 'need to recuperate' and is beginning to be ashamed of itself. One owes it to one's health—that is what people say when they are caught on an excursion into the country. Soon we may well reach the point where people can no longer give in to the desire for a vita contemplativa (that is, taking a walk with ideas and friends) without self contempt and a bad conscience.' Friedrich Nietzsche

Ulrich Beck's thesis is the triumph of the 'dominion of work'—a new 'totalitarian value cycle of work', to the exclusion of all else, which is ironically occurring at a time when full-time, life-long work is shrinking. The title of a recent book summed it up: *Better Than Sex: How a Whole Generation Became Hooked on Work*.

So all-pervasive is the sway that Work has over our imagination, it is hard to conceptualise an alternative. Beck recalls older societies where the values were different. In Ancient Greece, freedom meant the freedom *not* to have to work. 'Anyone who had to work was not only unfree; he did not count as a member of society . . . Society was even defined as an opposite world to the world of work.' Such was the fate of slaves and, of course, women. It was beyond the lowly realm of labour, of reproduction of the species that 'work' commenced, and beyond that the most significant realm—of 'freedom' and political life—began.

So deep were those distinctions that many European languages, Beck points out, evolved couplets like ponos/ergon, labor/opus, Mühe/Werk which indicate the old hierarchy of 'lower' and 'higher' realms of work— the realm of necessity or labour and the 'free, meaningful, active individuality'.

In early capitalism, the rise of the 'Protestant work ethic' was part of the bourgeois revolution, a revolt of the middle classes against corrupt and leisured nobility. Paid work was the way out of poverty, but also a way of being respectable. A wage integrated people who were poor, unruly, mad, bad or merely depressed into the social order. However, the intensity of the idealisation of Work, close to a secular religion, the source of all meaning and decency, is new. So little in life is opposed to it, 'to such an extent,' Beck argues, 'that almost no alternative remains . . . The biblical curse—that only those who work shall eat—has become the work morality grounding human existence; only those who work are truly human.'

This is not new for men, but it has certainly intensified. David Leser, in a moving account of men in the New Capitalism, 'From Rooster To Feather Duster', told a pitiful story about a downsized executive who kept getting up in the morning dressed in a suit, to spend the day rattling around the city rather than confess to his wife that he had been sacked. What's new, too, is how *all* adult citizens, including women, are now integrated into the sacralisation of paid work. It is absolutely clear, however, that only a fraction of meaningful, socially useful labour is paid.

Work in the sense of a central meaningful project, a vocation, can have depth, dignity and pride, and this should not surprise or concern us. No one need sentimentalise welfare dependency or the absence of work. Nor should it surprise or dismay us that for many women—for so long held away from the undoubted fulfilment and mastery that comes with developing one's talents, or the pride of providing both for oneself and for others economically—paid work should be a source of identity, meaning and honour. (I love paying for things with cheques from my writing!)

Yet when maternal feminists like Ann Crittenden and Nancy Folbre write about the unseen care economy, 'the dark matter in the universe of labour', they are describing something real. Women's unpaid non-market family work absolutely underpins paid work in the market economy. You can't leave home without it. So much socially useful, morally important work on behalf of communities and families is unpaid work. Voluntary work, elder care, unpaid household labour, being a mother—all these things are work—meaningful, purposive activities contributing to the commonweal. In fact 'work' is too paltry a term. They are honourable vocations. The upper middle classes in particular need to remember that only a minority of humankind have the great good fortune to be paid for doing work that they love.

What is peculiar to the new capitalism is how the ideal of valuable activity should be diminished so dispiritingly to *paid* work for every citizen. While there was a sentimental aspect to our sense of motherhood in times past, it is also true that such honouring kept a powerful sense that valuable aspects of life lay outside the cash nexus.

The cultural peculiarity of our love affair with Work, our sacralisation of work, cannot be overstated. For most of human history, and for the vast bulk of humanity still, work is a fate to escape from. It is often claimed that the 'the cult of motherhood' is a recent invention (and therefore can be dis-invented); yet our love affair with Work as the site of greatest status, power, and above all meaning, is what is really recent.

We should submit work to critical scrutiny. It can be a socially legitimated form of self-centredness—for men especially justifying absence from family obligations. Given what Beck calls the 'Brazilianisation' of the workforce into insecure, poorly paid and marginal jobs, the romanticisation of work as defining our worth and our meanings excludes large swathes of people. The shame of being excluded from the halo of paid work is illustrated by the humiliation that the unemployed or mothers at home feel, or by the way the retired nervously point to their 'busyness' with the anxious, defensive twitch of those at the receiving end of social judgement. According to one time-use expert, 'We have become walking résumés. If you're not doing something, you're not creating and defining who you are.'

The new fetish of paid work as the ultimate arbiter of one's worth has had profound consequences for mothers—whether in or out of the paid workforce—under the new capitalism.

12 The making of the New Capitalist Mother

'Scratch a new capitalist mother and you will find anxious references to performing motherhood expertly, efficiently and competently and the desire to do more exercise.' Julie Stephens

Charles Dickens' novel *Hard Times* was written during a period of dramatic economic expansion under nineteenth-century laissez faire capitalism. It is a depiction of the human costs of the elevation of one principle—economic calculus—above all other values, such that 'the whole of man's duty is to buy cheap and sell dear'. Karl Marx, wrote that there now existed

> no other nexus between man and man than naked self interest, than callous 'cash payment'. It has drowned the most heavenly ecstasies of religious fervour, of chivalrous enthusiasm, of philistine sentimentalism, in the icy water of egotistical calculation. It has resolved personal worth into exchange value . . .

All the Motherwars, and the identification of feminism with paid work and Progress, can blind us to a much deeper transformation at the heart of the new capitalism: what German social theorist Jurgen Habermas calls the colonisation of our life world by the values of the market. The penetration of the values and assumptions of the marketplace seeps inexorably into every cultural pore, every relationship, however intimate. As Raimond Gaita has commented, because of its connection to meaning, the language we use matters. If a certain kind of language—appropriate to the very different space of the marketplace—is used, then certain meanings will become dead to us. Market language radically alters the way we cast relations, love, intimacy, sex, motherlove and children in the life world. It fundamentally transforms the realm of *meaning*.

Consider, for example, the growing charge against the non-working mother of parasitism—of not being an economic contributor. Like mums on welfare, the charge is one of bludging: women at home *just do nothing*. Mothers, by investing in persons rather than things, may do work of great social value. Yet it takes only a few short steps from seeing a mother's work as having no *market* value, to the idea that it therefore *has no value, to such mothers as being people being without value*. That is not far off the barely concealed judgements behind the Labor Party Tax and Family package during the 2004 election, which penalised poorer families with a mother at home, and gave benefits to better-off families where the mother worked. One newspaper editorial said point blank: 'mothers are more valuable to society as workers than stay-at-home mums'. Another headline in 2005 screamed: 'Costello: Get Mums Working', delivering Treasurer Peter Costello's blunt message to single mothers to get back to work when their children reached school age. Ann Crittenden cites an American custody case where a mother had left work to look after her son who, having been 'a problem since kindergarten', had 'arrived at school with a gun in his backpack'. But the judge refused extra support from the father by arguing that a mother who did not work full time was 'a luxury that our world does not permit'.

That mothers 'do nothing' has inflexions of Richard Sennett's 'to be passive is to wither'. The sense is that one must keep moving, developing oneself. Children don't count on a curriculum vitae. The ethos of the new capitalist mother, writes Julie Stephens, is one of 'anxiety-ridden self-improvement'. There is very little sense that any 'self-improvement' might come from honouring the ethic of care. A mother at home, by putting the non-market identity of mothering first, has transgressed against just about every contemporary ethos: the ethic of self-fulfilment, of self-development, of being economically productive not dependent. They may be always busy with the many and varied tasks of looking after a family, but, in another way their life narrative is not now easily judged according to any inner standard—of living true to an ideal, a vocation centring on the ethic of care, however they might like to see it. 'I feel shame about being at home as a mother', one interviewee with postgraduate qualifications remarked to Barbara Pocock. 'For that six hours when they are at school, I don't sit down. I feel anxious. I have to be productive.' Instead, by the light of the values of paid market work, of a life story shaped around a career trajectory, they appear to have halted. Stopped dead. To have achieved the shameful status of being stationary, when around them, everywhere, women as well as men are 'on the move', upwards on the career ladder.

Barbara Pocock puts it very well: 'Those who respect full-time mothering and those who do it, work against the grain of society where so much of personal worth, value and self is shaped by a worker identity established through the market.' To have a proper, respectable middle-class identity now, for women as much as men, depends upon the narrative of work, the story of a career. I meet young women who go back to work they don't even like very much, because of the fear of that shameful status, of feeling obliterated by having no market identity. One recent Australian study found that 'Being fit and in control are key concepts for pregnant and postpartum women of the dual-earning middle class.' It is now 'unthinkable', says Robert Karen, 'for a middle-class woman in America now not to have a job'. 'Unthinkable' is a very interesting word. The sociologist Peter Berger has pointed out how our 'thinking as usual' constitutes the 'social construction of reality,' what we regard as fact and fiction. It becomes 'naturalised', invisible, beyond the reach of reflection and critique. It is of course culturally bound. To invoke a home-making 'career' or attempt to professionalise it as a 'domestic engineer' is to simply reveal how one set of values has lost out to another—the attributes of the higher realm of paid work, 'up amongst the men' must be used to dignify, to retrieve and bestow respectability, to redeem the lowly labour of reproduction, of being 'down among the children.' The newly 'unthinkable' quality of the homemaker's life is at least as much an 'achievement' of the new capitalism as it is of feminism.

Working motherhood is also shaped by the logic of the market. In one Australian study of high-earning women with a strongly individualist ethos, doing very well in the new capitalism, one said, 'We've always had a full-time place at creche whether we use it or not because we can't afford not to have it. Everything's ordered and organised for work.' Another mother said: 'People who don't work and live this life do not understand what it is like to have to run your household like a business, your partner like a business. Everything's run like a business because you can't afford in any way or form to get it wrong because there's a chain reaction.'

British economist Heather Joshi, while giving birth, calculated between contractions, not about the new human being—her child—that she was about to meet but just how much women lose economically through taking time out for motherhood. She concluded that 'lifetime earnings would be 57 per cent lower than if they had not taken a break'. As the power and coherence of a market identity grows, motherhood becomes a loss and a lack, something to surmount. Baroness Margaret

Thatcher, architect of the resurgence of free market principles in Britain, was reported to have looked down on her newborn twins and determined 'not to be overcome by this. Like a hostile foreign power or the enemy within, motherhood was a force to be reckoned with, wrestled with and finally overcome.' She claimed her children only ever got sick on weekends.

The feminist Julie Kristeva has written about the particular qualities of 'women's time', while others have explored the nature of maternal time, the messy, but also spontaneous, unbounded and free flowing qualities of life with children. That is in sharp contradiction with a capitalist society that places great pressure on mothers to get themselves and their children, as speedily as possible, onto a schedule of efficient time management. Jules Henry has noted that 'The cultural configuration of time demands our submission, it requires that we renounce impulses that interfere with it. This is the austerity of time . . . Although most people in our culture restrain the desire to wander from the compelling path of time, they are naturally unaware of the enormous amount of training they need as children to prevent them from doing so.'

In the Truby King era in the 1940s, for example, there was an application of industrial principles to the home—an attempt to make housewifery 'scientific', with housewives depicted as 'domestic engineers' doing 'everything by the clock', households run on efficient business-like principles. Infant-feeding schedules, where babies were fed at four-hourly intervals, however hungry, enforced submission to the austerity of industrial time at an early age. That impulse is also behind the growing use, particularly among young urban professionals, of the harsh new contemporary technique of 'controlled crying' (leaving the baby to cry). By such methods it is hoped to force children to sleep through the night. As one young mother said to me, 'I need him on a sleep schedule because I *have to get back to work.*' For centuries mothers have put babies to sleep in their arms while singing lullabies. The modern infant must put itself to sleep, and learn to manage its own needs for comfort.

Modern advice books exhort women, too, notes Arlie Hochschild, to develop an emotional asceticism. They must act as their own emotional investment counsellors, and *manage* their feelings of needing care from others. They must care for the self because no one else will. The new ideal was ultimately of *feeling less*, to better facilitate the survival of the self. The representation of the self in many advice books was of a lone post-modern cowgirl, who could depend or be depended upon by no one. The underlying ideal model was of *separateness and detachment*, not attachment or deep connection with others. That also applies to the mother–child relationship. For example, a recent literary text by Elaine Tuttle Hansen, *Mother Without Child*, tells us as if lifted from the annals of the new capitalism:

> . . . an important part of being a good mother by today's popular standards as experts and mothers will attest . . . the mother's work entails preparing the child, from the moment of birth, for independence from caretakers, and thus engaging in a relationship whose goal is greater disengagement, distance, or even dissolution.

Another aspect of the penetration of private life by market relations concerns the process whereby mothers, as well as fathers, are integrated into a new time consciousness, seeing time according to performance and achievement in the public realm.

> Male-styled careers introduce women to a new form of time consciousness; it is not age measured against beauty . . . but age measured against achievement . . . Time is objectified in the academic vita, which grows longer with each article and book, and not with each vegetable garden, camping trip, political meeting or child . . . What is won for the garden is lost to the vita.

Arlie Hochschild also remarks on the pressure on modern mothers to 'recycle the feeling rules' of middle-class corporate man in the 1950s. A good example is from *The Bitch in the House*, where Kristin van Ogtrop, much as a 1950s man might, describes herself as a whole lot nicer and more caring at the office than at home.

> Here are a few things people have said about me at the office: 'you're unflappable.' 'Are you ever in a bad mood?'. . . 'You're good at finessing things so people don't boil over.' Here are things people—OK, the members of my family—have said about me at home: 'Mommy is always grumpy.' 'Why are you so tense?' 'You're too mean to live in this house and I want you to go back to work for the rest of your life!'

Ruefully she observes, 'I had not become my mother, I was my father with ovaries.'

Peter Berger has shown that a core aspect of modernity is segmentation—separating our consciousness into different components. Berger points out that one component—work—is an emotionally inexpressive, 'cool' domain, of 'managed cheer,' where little of one's private life is meant to intrude, to better facilitate the smooth and efficient running of an enterprise. It is within another component, of family life, where we are to express, process and contain all the messy wilder emotions disavowed at work. Those divided worlds have profound implications for the colonisation of the private world by market relations—whereby the intensification and speed up of work came to dominate family life.

The time bind: the Taylorisation of family life

Last century an engineering genius called Frederick Taylor first attempted to apply the scientific management of time to enhance business efficiency and profitability. He studied a steel worker, Schmidt, measuring precisely the arc of his shovel swing, the speed to the last second of each swing, the weight of each scoop, and the number of rest periods needed. By scientific calculation, by controlling every aspect of his movements, Taylor could increase the quantity Schmidt shovelled fourfold. Thus the time and motion study was invented. This rationalisation of processes to create greater efficiency within organisations we now often call Taylorisation.

An extraordinary surge of Taylorisation has occurred within the new capitalism, intensifying work but also home life. Hochschild has found family life is now undergoing a process whereby a 'low grade' cult of efficiency has leapt the fence from the workplace and come home. Family life is being Taylorised.

Central to the new capitalism is a seismic value shift 'when work becomes home and home becomes work'. It is this value shift that is the focus of Hochschild's brilliant book *The Time Bind*. An astute social observer, she gets inside the social relations of the new capitalism. On investigating an American IT company she calls 'Amerco', she found that even with family-friendly policies the 'emotional magnets between home and workplace were in the process of being reversed.' People, women included, fled the domestic mess and the dirty laundry and the unfinished quarrels to the 'managed cheer of work'.

It went deeper with some families than with others. The more extreme version of people '"marrying" their work', 'investing in work the emotional significance once reserved for family', accounted for about a fifth of her company families, and a less extreme version in which it was still an 'important theme' took in over one-half of all her 'Amerco' families. Hochschild's point is that this may be a change destined to affect us all.

The culture of paid work and the value we attribute to it has expanded at the expense of family culture. Thus when women do more market work, the labour of the 'shadow care economy'—the 'invisible heart' as Folbre called it—is most often not replaced by men doing more on the home front. Hence what we are looking at is not a reformulation but an emptying of the family nest. The child-centred feminist Julie Stephens recorded, 'As one notable feminist commentator and researcher said on ABC Radio's *Life Matters*, she wouldn't be able to choose between her children and her work.' Work is the more powerful culture, creating a kind of 'psychological necessity' to put work first. One mother said to me wistfully, about the temptation of letting her children spend too many hours in after-school care, 'You feel so *important* at work . . .' Hochschild says:

> The more women and men do what they do in exchange for money and the more their work is honoured, the more, almost by definition, private life is devalued and its boundaries shrink. For women as well as men, work in the marketplace is less often a simple economic fact than a complex cultural value. If in the early part of the century it was considered unfortunate that a woman had to work, it is now thought surprising when she doesn't.

That value shift—where home becomes work and work becomes home—has profound consequences for family life, especially since it is true for increasing numbers of women as well as men. What Hochschild found was that the social world that held sway—work—imparted deep patterning to time. There was no longer an 'angel in the house'—the Victorian or early-twentieth-century housewife living outside the austerity of industrial time, smoothing the passage of her family through the vicissitudes of birth, schooling, work, sickness, old age and death, providing the 'haven' in the heartless world. *The Time Bind* explores how deeply the industrial workplace patterns and even the speed of industrial time have intruded on family life, and contributed in turn to emptying the home as a place of pleasure, restoration and leisure.

The more collective family hours are put into paid work, the more rushed, harried and strained—the more locked into the time bind—the private realm becomes. Over time the 'juggling act' is so intense that the cultural valuing of work over family gains further strength by the sheer pleasurelessness of the 'sped up' family realm—trying to do in one quarter of the time what housewives used to take all day to do. The home becomes an unpleasant pressure cooker of unresolved emotions, a place to escape from into the quiet, more controlled pace of work, promising time free of interruptions and domestic arguments over unwashed dishes.

The rigidity of paid work, but particularly the internalisation of its norms and demands as pre-eminent, meant that the agents promoting the speed-up, submitting themselves to a regime of self-surveillance, monitoring their home performance and constantly looking for improvements, were the parents themselves. They accepted the 'austerity of industrial time'. Hochschild found exhausted working mothers sitting on bathtubs hurrying children while they answered e-mails and checked mobile phone messages, cribbing a little bit of time here and there, always with one eye on the clock, trying to make little efficiencies. There was a new sense of self-supervision. All the necessary activities of family life—the meals and nurturing, the conversations, the bedtime rituals—were jammed into an ever-smaller block of time. If the problem for the 1950s housewife might be too much time, this was a problem of too little time.

In a brilliant example of the way the logic of 'industrial time' and increased productivity had leapt the fence from work and come home, Hochschild says of the new popular idea of 'quality time' with children:

> quality time holds out the hope that scheduling intense periods of togetherness can compensate for an overall loss of time is such a way that the relationship will suffer no loss of quality. But this too is a way of transferring the cult of efficiency from office to home. Instead of nine hours a day with a child, we declare ourselves capable of getting the 'same result' with one more intensely focused total quality hour. As with Frederick Taylor and the hapless Schmidt, our family bonds are being recalibrated to achieve greater productivity in less time.

Amerco parents found themselves also spending time doing the 'third shift' of emotional 'work' repairing the damage caused—especially to children—by the time bind.

> When workers protest against a speed up, industrialists can replace them. But when children react against a speed up at home, parents have to deal with it. Children dawdle. They sulk. They ask for gifts. They tell their parents by

action and word, 'I don't like this.' They want to be having quality time when it's a quantity time of day ... Parents displace struggles for time they might have with managers onto children and spouses at home ... The emotional dirty work of adjusting children to the Taylorised home and making up to them for its stresses and strains is the most painful part of a growing third shift at home.

One mother remarked how on her returning from work, 'The marketing phone calls are still coming in at home. I leave work, and before I can get home, take a breath, and relax, the phone rings and I have to be "on" again.' Guilt adds to the burden of being home, she says wistfully. 'It seems like such a long stretch of time I haven't been there for them. All they see is the stress and anxiousness of my trying to get through the chores. They should remember laughter and not Mom crying because she can't figure out what's for dinner.' In comparison, the time away at work conferences is a real, uncomplicated pleasure. For this mother, 'I was away in New York last week with five colleagues. We sat down for lunch in this nice restaurant, nothing extravagant, and when the meal was put before me I sighed and said, 'It is so *nice to be here.*'

Marion Blum noted as early as the 1980s a pleasureless quality to the lives of the time-pressed dual career couples. The *New York Times* began reporting how Saturdays are for two-career families the equivalent of purgatory, citing a clinical psychologist who reported an 'anhedonic quality' to the lives of parents—a sense of joylessness and powerlessness and an inability to experience pure pleasure. In the late 1990s the same newspaper noted 'the quiet death of the dinner party'. A friend of Juliet Schor in *The Overworked American* noted, 'Most people I know have turned their ovens into planters.' Economist Staffan Lindner pointed to how leisure was getting more hectic as people crammed more into it: 'growing affluence would lead people to switch to those activities that could be done quickly ... long courtships, leisurely walks or lingering over the dinner table are likely to be things of the past. People would do more things at once and do them faster.' In the twenty-first century a new phenomenon, speed dating, where people meet for a few minutes and move on to the next prospective partner, makes the search for romantic love more efficient.

In a convivial community or family life, the build up of anticipation of a family ritual, the preparations, the actual event, the discussions and reflection on it afterwards during the lull that follows, are all deeply tied up with heightening emotional pleasure. Enjoyment is inextricably tied up with the uneven, erratic movement of time, the juxtaposition of busyness with slowness, of harvest time and fallow time. In the mad scramble to get everything done, what Hochschild calls 'framing'—a kind of invisible temporal architecture giving greater weight and meaning to events—disappears. (More than one parent I know has caught themselves 'speed reading' a bedtime story to their child.)

> As time becomes something to 'save' at home as much or even more than at work, domestic life becomes quite literally a second shift; a cult of efficiency, once centred in the workplace, is allowed to set up shop and make itself comfortable at home. Efficiency has become both a means to an end—more home life—and a way of life, an end in itself . . . A surprising amount of family time has become a matter of efficiency, assembling people into prefabricated activity slots.

Australian television advertisements play on the time bind to sell goods—from packet dinners to those 'intelligent' appliances like washing machines which help the working mother out—because no one else will. Hochschild gives some American examples. One, for 'moms who have a lot of love but not a lot of time,' reads, 'Nicky is a very picky eater. With instant Quaker Oatmeal I can give him a terrific hot breakfast in just 90 seconds and I don't have to spend any time coaxing him to eat it!'

In families in which both parents work full time, the family time deficit can be acute. One response, by experts like Jonathan Gershuny, is to redefine parental time with children as 'face to face' time, rather like a business appointment. This conceals the decline in the 'quantity' of parental time children are really experiencing. As the British writer Jayne Buxton remarks, it is not only 'face to face interactions' that matter. 'My own would much rather have me around all day, even if I am cooking and doing loads of washing for much of it, than have me for just one "quality" hour at the end of every day.'

The Taylorisation of family life is experienced everywhere that the dual income family has taken root. Barbara Pocock describes many such Australian families in her *The Work/Life Collision*. Jayne Buxton describes the British version of the speed-up. Profiles of Supermothers gush about frantic busyness and houses which run like well-oiled machinery, while the women's own remarks seem strangely shaved of emotion, sounding more like excerpts from a time and motion expert. Tina Brown, the British editor of the *New Yorker* magazine and mother of two, rose at 5.30 for her daily run, dropped her daughter at school before a breakfast meeting at 8.15, worked until 5.45 when she left to have supper with the children and then worked until 12.30 a.m. She existed on five hours sleep a night. She never socialised with friends.

Reading about such lives—let alone living them—is enough to give one motion sickness. The overwhelming impression is of a woman on a stationary exercise bike pedalling furiously as if her life depended on it. Some people only feel half alive unless living like this, of course, but many others look back with regret once they get off the treadmill. Many women confessed to Buxton that they hated to maintain the mask of the superwoman but felt powerless to do otherwise. British journalist Yvonne Roberts is suspicious of the mantra of 'managed mothering' held by successful women:

> There is so much silence about this. You hear women talking about juggling and managing, pretending life runs smoothly, when it is in fact chaos behind the scenes. Exhaustion followed by a crisis, then a period of partial recovery, then renewed commitment to the treadmill, followed by more exhaustion. You never really recover. And eventually it all gives way.

The unquestioning obedience and submission to norms of work as the supreme overriding ethic is part and parcel of the new capitalism. It would be a great pity if earlier feminist critiques of 'the rat race' give way to a nearly exclusive emphasis on breaking glass ceilings, on succeeding on male terms, on rigid adherence to demanding work schedules, in which women are exhorted to compartmentalise their feelings about their children, downsize empathy or 'maternal thinking' and discipline such thoughts and 'feel less' in order to cope. That is increasingly true of even the very early nestling phase.

The Taylorisation of motherhood

'There was inefficiency, waste . . . What was needed was a simple product that moved from start to completion in a streamlined path.' Ray Kroc, founder of McDonald's

Not so long ago a lawyer of my acquaintance was on a phone conference and heard a strange squeaking noise. A fellow lawyer confessed. It was her baby, born seven hours ago, already being held by the nanny while she got on with the business of closing a big deal. Not even on this one day of her life was she out of the reach of work, that 'greedy institution'.

I have come across many examples of the phenomenon Melissa Benn dubbed 'premature returnism'. No time had been made for what Sheila Kitzinger has called the period of 'babymoon'—that time of special cherishing of the new human in our midst.

Such logic is also behind the rise of 'career caesareans'. In Australia as elsewhere, increasing numbers of women are disciplining the 'irrationality' of birth with its anarchic timing and the unpredictability of its progress. No messy waiting for baby to 'trigger' their own time of arrival, or for the contractions to dilate the uterus. No one knowing the history of women's reproductive health should romanticise 'natural' birth in the 'good old days', but the Taylorisation of birth is not about interventions undertaken to save lives, reduce pain or the risk to the baby. Instead, the 'career caesarean', during which a woman is unavailable on her mobile telephone for only a few hours, is organised for maximum control and efficiency. In the world of the nanosecond, just as the conveyor belt of cars moves swiftly through the drive-through service at McDonald's, modern mothers are borne in on the conveyor belt of birth, which efficiently carries women into the operating theatre, unzips them and dumps them back at work shortly thereafter.

In the Taylorised culture of instantaneity it is a virtue for a mother to return to work *ever faster*. Sally Loane writes of a journalist who didn't even tell her London-based employers she was pregnant: 'When I visited her in the hospital room, she was on the phone.' A business writer finished her weekly column as she went into labour with her first child, and another high-powered public relations executive resumed work from her hospital bed.

The ethos in the workplace is of a childless world. Small wonder then that Loane notes rather wistfully that the 'mantra of my generation was that motherhood wouldn't change our lives.' Her personal history in private girls schools, university and in the workplace deeply forged an identity, like men's, which was centred in paid work. She remembers 'struggling against allowing my pregnancies to show back at work ...' Loane squeezed back into 'sleek suits three months after giving birth', and 'perfected the art of the seamless entry and re-entry to work'.

The remarks of Gerry Harvey, chairman of electrical retail giant Harvey Norman, show how men can rapidly install such behaviour as a norm. Harvey told his wife, Katie, then the company's merchandising director, that he wanted her back at work within seven days of the birth of their second child. She was, and it was 'a damn good example for all those other women who have babies'. His wife 'slips them out and they are good solid kids'. Of women who take time out, Harvey said: 'career women who go off for three to six months may well not have that job when they come back because someone else will be slotted in there'. Likewise, Lawrence Mead, new right guru and architect of America's Welfare to Work policies, boasted (when visiting Australia) that most American mothers are back at work by six weeks after birth.

If the keynote of birth in a Taylorised society is on speedy delivery and efficient return—like the fast food factory itself—the hidden curriculum of the workplace is to shift from welcoming this new person to concealing children's presence and minimising their intrusions. The ideal employee is without human attachments or obligations—preferably childless. 'I was keen to prove I could have a baby and return to work— almost as if nothing had happened—as though this was a badge of honour.' Many commentators have suggested that subjecting central life experiences to 'speed-up' results in a flatter, less emotional, more superficial emotional style, rather like Frederic Jameson's suggestion that our post-modern culture is marked by the 'waning of emotion or affect'. Thus Loane found herself giving perfunctory unemotional, three-word answers to inquiries about her children's wellbeing at the babysitters: 'Oh, fine thanks.' 'It was not a subject over which I believed I should linger.'

Another mother, the owner–manager of a legal staff recruitment agency, Lisa Gasiz, described how the unpredictable chaos of being at home with a new baby, compared to the valued, predictable universe of work, was a 'shock'. 'No one had prepared me for what happens.' She 'never really stopped working . . . right up until she gave birth, and then began drafting résumés and taking calls from clients in hospital. Once she came home she worked by fax.' Work had a frisson, a status, an Eros home did not: '. . . the urge to come back is just too great', she says. 'It is almost exciting to be back.' For her next baby she 'will have another caesarean, put the baby straight on the bottle and be back at work . . .'

Compared to the brevity and businesslike quality, shorn of emotion, she expresses towards her baby, Gasiz describes relations with her workplace and clients in the language of attachment and connectedness: 'It's a competitive business and people expect a *personal service*. I was *distancing myself from my clients* . . .' [emphasis added]. It is not a problem to distance yourself from the messy and intimate care of a baby, or to hand the baby over to someone else, but it *is* a problem to distance yourself from clients, denying them the personal care *they* need. 'I didn't want to be out of it for too long . . . you *lose touch* very easily.' It is not seen as a problem to bottle feed rather than breastfeed because one might lose the 'touch' factor of skin-on-skin intimacy between mother and baby; it is a problem to 'lose touch' with clients. Sally Loane tells of mothers in corporate offices, Armani suit jackets flung open, pumping breast milk to give to the nanny to give to the baby. Here the emotional work of 'being there' for clients is privileged and paramount, while 'being there' or 'in touch' or not 'distancing oneself' from a child is relegated to one of the 'never saids' of the discourse. It has become an outside question.

In much of our public conversation, early returnism, often depicted in discussions of the lives of celebrity mothers like Cherie Blair, is embraced uncritically. Such a celebration moves in a simple way against the old cultural scripts that allowed so little movement for women outside motherhood, but it makes us slower to see that all this 'freedom' to return to work instantly—quite apart from the implications for children—is part of a much deeper submission to the 'totalitarianisation of work' and to the norms of Taylorisation. How little such patterns really are on women's own terms. How roughly, brutally, they move around birth, early infancy and the nestling phase! Melissa Benn remembers:

> As a new mother . . . I had been back to work within weeks of birth, resentfully taking transatlantic calls at some unearthly hour of the night on some article . . . This was at a time when all I wanted to do was to gaze at my new baby girl and not worry about money or the outside world, or whether I was still considered a serious person 'out there'.

Studies of mothers' separation responses show 'feelings of sadness, worry and guilt skyrocketed when mothers put children into childcare for the first time. The women remained highly anxious for about four weeks and did not fully recover for another eight months.' Such separation anxiety is usually redrawn as a 'problem of management', with advice on counselling the women into happiness rather than looking at the cause.

What began as a 'right' can quickly become an obligation. All the women above are affluent career women. A right asserted by the privileged often looks very different in the lives of the powerless. That is certainly true of welfare mothers forced to return to work and who can only afford lousy childcare. If some women *choose* to do it, it becomes quite possible to establish such 'choices' (like Gerry Harvey's wife cited above) as the proper 'norms'. Thus we can, with a clear conscience, pressure women to leave hospital before they are ready, in order to save governments money, and claim it is just one step on the way to women's emancipation.

Like workers responsible for the smooth delivery of objects along a conveyor belt, women's life narratives, particularly among the well educated, are increasingly constructed in terror of even a momentary deviation, let alone a disappearance down the motherhood cul de sac for a decade.

Kate Tully, Sydney-based author and journalist, spoke of:

> young women who put off having children because it would hinder their work . . . when they have a baby they worry about how to keep going ever upward and not skip a beat. There is very much a sense that they will lose their position on the career ladder. There's no appreciation that they might actually enjoy parenting, because they've never been allowed to consider it.

There is however a certain irrationality to all this rationality. During this period—before and after birth—a great deal of exceptionally important *emotional* work needs to be done by parents to establish those fundamental relationships essential to a child's future sense of themselves and the world. There is very good evidence that one cannot really 'speed it up' without consequences. 'If there is no space in the mother's mind for the baby, the baby will struggle with feelings of abandonment and rejection,' according to Dr Susan Taryan, 'unless you provide for the baby to have that intimate closeness from some other person, then there is no space for the baby to develop properly.' Brazelton and colleagues found that parents who returned to work early tended to distance themselves from their babies, not allowing themselves to get too attached to them. Instead, they were already consumed by the practical exigencies of getting back to work and arranging childcare. They disallow the natural fantasies, the dreams and the nightmares about who the child is, the essential acts of imagining which prepare us to open to the new human person among us. Their stance, Brazelton found, was already one of disengagement and detachment. Taryan could be echoing Jameson's argument about the 'waning of affect' when she suggests, 'I think there is going to be a price to pay for all this. We may be rearing a society in which warm feelings, contact and emotion are difficult for the next generation to handle.' Lurking behind all this are the modern mothers who are entering workplaces designed in the nineteenth century for men with wives at home.

Men, women and the hidden hierarchy of time

My old primary school headmaster used to take a five-minute walk home every day for a hot luncheon prepared by his wife. He walked slowly, as if lost in thought, with his hands crossed behind his back. He had a little bow tie and horn-rimmed spectacles that gleamed in the sun. In the afternoon, he always undid the last buttons of his waistcoat to accommodate his lunch. His role of the 'breadwinner' earned him a complete exemption from household humdrum. Only some yard tasks were 'his': a little lawnmowing, garden maintenance perhaps, and the occasional drying of dishes. At school, several secretaries acted as Time Sentries, swooped on any interloper who threatened, unauthorised, to intrude on His Time. His wife did the same at home, doing the 'everything else' in running the household, freeing him for paid labour, as well as screening telephone calls, and pressing the children not to 'disturb Daddy'.

My mother worked, so my main insight into the old regime came whenever I stayed with my grandmother, a housewife. The house (unlike mine!) was a model of order and grace. Meals arrived in a regular rhythm, never altered in forty years. The preparation of every dish of food, all the cups of tea, the removal of every cobweb and speck of dust, all the oven cleaning and washing was done by my grandmother. My main memory of my grandfather is of him either bowling or drinking with his mates at the local bowling club, or lying on a cane settee in the sunroom, having a nap. This was his life. He would not have washed a dish, cooked a meal, or even made a cup of tea in forty years. Only my grandmother's daughters and grandchildren would have helped her with the chores.

Staying with my grandmother was like floating back in time to a delicious infancy: the beds made for you in the morning, the soggy poached eggs for breakfast, the weak milk coffee at 11 a.m., the compulsory naps. (Even when we were in our twenties!) But with little education, my grandmother, who would have loved to run a small business, also did nothing else. Before my grandfather retired, between the two of them they would have divided—in a strict sexual division of labour—about one hundred hours of market and non-market work between them. What strikes me, however, looking back, is how much time they had to devote to tennis, golf, cricket, bowls, local dances and frequent card parties.

The plight of the dual income family is easily understood in comparison with my old headmaster and my grandfather. Much ink has been spilt on the *relative* problem of time—that working mothers spend far more time on household humdrum than their partners. The logic is that if men did more, and public policy changed, that relative problem of time, theoretically at least, is potentially soluble. Lurking darkly just behind, however, is the *absolute* problem—the tyranny even—of time. No social policy can alter the fact that there are only twenty-four hours in each day. The more one family member does, the more pressured the others will be. Two high-octane careers in one family means being time-stressed.

It is a matter of simple arithmetic. The traditional family, based on a rigid idea of male and female roles, also had a hidden temporal assumption—about how much *total* household time can be reasonably sustained without stress. Husbands worked for forty hours and spent about ten hours on home tasks; housewives worked a fifty-hour week—around one hundred total. Redistributing that time along egalitarian lines doesn't alter the brute fact that as total time goes up, so does stress. Robert Drago and Ping Tseng's 2003 study revealed that couples with sparklingly symmetrical work patterns of forty hours each nonetheless struggled under a much heavier overall workload—eighty-four hours' total paid work time—double the paid work component of the traditional family. These families are more maritally stressed, felt worse about parenting, had fewer children and continually complained about time stress!

Those 'separate spheres' have seen the evolution of not just high-octane careers but all full-time work being based on a presumed player off field, helping those 'on field'. It is partly a result of those separate spheres that male and female time is perceived differently. In the 'male' culture of work, men expect to *give*—attentiveness, energy, the psychological equivalent of 'holding'—at work. But they expect to *receive* all that at home from the woman in their life. Where both partners work, women need to challenge those domestic privileges, which often go on, unexamined, as a kind of male entitlement. Male and female time was not only complementary, it was also hierarchical. If paid work and the public role were valued more than family work, then the time of the gender identified most strongly with paid work—men—was also considered more important, valuable, perhaps even sacred.

The phenomenon of 'Don't disturb Daddy' is familiar to many of us. Men's boundaries are sensed and respected by others. A man can create a separate enclave even within his own home. We see this most easily with Dad reading the newspaper or watching news and sports on television; Dad 'working' at something either brought home or a household repair of some sort; Dad taking a nap and everyone being instructed by Mother to tiptoe around and not disturb him. There is an acceptance that men need privacy and that entering those invisible boundaries is a serious business with serious consequences for the intruder.

One of my friends, who works full-time, describes how on weekends she organises her one free day around the children, whereas her husband tended to organise the children around the leisure activities he wanted to do 'We're both available . . .' she says, but then she hesitates; 'but we're available in different ways'. There's an edge to her voice. Caitlin Flanagan writes of how mothers still keep the finger on the family pulse in ways men don't:

> Fathers are much more involved with their children's lives today than they were when I was growing up . . . but the interesting thing is that when you talk to moms about this, over and over they will tell you that no matter how equitably they divide the work with their husbands, they always feel that they are shouldering the larger burden. The mother is the one who's really got her eye on the ball, in terms of the dental appointments and the costumes for the school play and the cookies for the class party, and which child wants his sandwich cut in rectangles and which ones want it in triangles. A lot of moms—even some of the ones with super-involved husbands—feel that they're just not getting enough help, or the right kind of help from their husbands. A lot of moms feel angry about this.

I am reminded also of Ulrich Beck's point, that the values of the new capitalism bring contradictions with women's traditional role, valuing paid work and devaluing family work. But men are in a different situation. After all, the 'old father'—fatherhood enjoyed in small doses as a 'recreation'—held no obstacle to practising a busy, time-consuming career. The women's movement, of course, meant to change all that. But—and here's the irony—the fetishisation of paid work as a secular religion helps *undermine* women's traditional roles but *reinforces* men's old work role. That's even before you get to issues like the declining value of male real wages. Other aspects, too, of the new capitalism—the high risk society, the long hours culture, downsizing, the stigma attached to having no paid labour and so on—all work *to enhance* men's traditional roles.

Then there is the new freewheeling expressive individualism, the challenge to existing mores, the exhortation to 'chart one's own life course' and the 'just do it' culture. We are trying to *increase* men's obligations *in* a family, at a time when the very values that fuelled the women's liberation movement—freedom, autonomy for the individual—also offer men ways *out* of family obligation; they can 'choose' to be either devoted 'new' Dads or 'old husbands' who continue to live with unreconstructed domestic selfishness, or new cads, scarpering altogether and not paying child support. The same working mother tells me, with the hint of a cautionary tale, that another mother she knew put in a demand for more sharing of housework. Her husband presented her with a piece of paper upon which was written a cost–benefit analysis of their marriage. With this extra demand, the cost side of the ledger now, unhappily, outweighed the benefits. He walked out.

Thus despite the *public* support for women working, these *private* arrangements mean so many women sail into the headwinds of culture. Little wonder, then, that the new capitalist family must outsource some of its domestic labour. It is into this 'Time Bind' that another group of women enter, only this time at the servant's entrance.

Inequality: the new Victorian family

Fredric Jameson wrote about the 'extension of commodification into hitherto uncommodified areas'. Middle-class working women are now 'pioneers on the commodification frontier'. Simply put, one radical transformation in the new capitalism is about the commercialisation and contracting out of things that women used to do for love. 'The time-starved mother is increasingly forced more and more to choose between being a parent and buying a commodified version of parenthood from someone else,' says Arlie Hochschild. Although the emphasis from feminism has been on the exploitation of women's invisible labour, that labour can also be seen another way: as one of the last vestiges of a reciprocal relationship outside the cash nexus. It is an important transmitter of values, meanings and understandings outside market relationships. It was women's work, once outside paid work, that could be taken over, contracted out. But to do too much consumption from the 'time industry' while easing the burden of the second shift also contributed to a loss of identity, the sense that the pulse of a home, its heart, still beat strongly.

Mothers found themselves confused when trying to sort out how much of that change was a blessing and how much a curse. Despite their uncertainty, it seemed to fall to women more than men to set limits on commercial 'violations' of domestic life . . . to most Americans the mother still represents the heart and soul, the warmth and human kindness of family life, a brake on the forces of capitalism, and a protector of the family haven in what is still generally imagined as a heartless world. It is woman's symbolic role to preserve time for personal bonds, not spend money substituting for them . . .

A television program screened recently showed a woman walking about with a large sign on an apron. The sign read 'Wife'. She was part of a company that hires out 'wives' to busy executives: cleaning, dusting, washing and cooking, putting things away, and also the little 'wifely' activities like arranging fresh flowers. It was from a documentary on the new forms of 'outsourcing' family work. An article in the *Financial Review* looked at the revival of butlers. In yet another, an owner of a lawnmowing franchise reported that his clients—well-paid professionals—often have teams of domestic workers all present at once; while he manicured the lawns, someone else tackled the windows, another cleaned the house and nannies looked after the children. Sometimes people are so busy, so locked into the time bind, that there is no time to even to walk the pets. So a brightly coloured vehicle regularly visits, bearing the insignia 'Pampered Pets' and the distinctive number plate PAWS-4, to take pooches on their daily walk.

The market seizes the day

The story of hard times under the new capitalism is about more than just the time bind. The fates of rich and poor women have drawn radically apart. Women doing low-waged McJobs have made the new plum jobs for women possible. In her 2004 essay, 'How Serfdom Saved the Women's Movement', Caitlin Flanagan pointed out how professional women's problem of housework had been resolved: '. . . like magic, as though the fairy godmother of women's liberation had waved a starry wand, the whole problem got solved . . . [by] the forces of global capitalism'. Such realities posed moral dilemmas for a movement that prided itself on its egalitarianism. As Naomi Wolf bemoaned:

I never thought I would become one of those women who took up a foreordained place in a hierarchy of class and gender. Yet here we were, to my horror and complicity, shaping our new family structure along class and gender lines—daddy at work, mommy and caregiver from two different economic classes, sharing the baby work during the day.

As Flanagan dryly observes, 'She had wanted a revolution; what she got was a Venezuelan.'

Barbara Ehrenreich also has re-examined the politics of shitwork. In *Nickel and Dimed*, a moving book that quickly climbed onto the *New York Times* bestseller list, she writes about her year-long experiment of going down and out amongst America's working poor. The 'micro-defeat of feminism in the household opened a new door for women, only this time it was the servants' entrance'. Many of her friends in the women's movement, she noticed, began quietly hiring maids.

Disguising herself as an unskilled homemaker, washed up against the rocks of economic hardship by divorce, Ehrenreich scrounged a living of around $7 an hour. As a waitress in cheap eateries, working in a locked Alzheimer's ward, as a maid for the Merry Maids cleaning company, and stacking clothes in Wal-Mart, she gets inside the daily humiliations of working in what we cheerfully call 'service industries'.

Central to older-style feminism was the idea that 'housework was not only a relationship between a woman and a dust bunny or an unmade bed; it also defined a relationship between human beings . . . To make a mess that another person will deal with . . . is to exert domination in one of its more silent and intimate forms.' This relationship of dominance and submission was caught in an 'early German women's liberation cartoon [which] depicted a woman scrubbing on her hands and knees while her husband, apparently excited by her pose, approaches from behind her, unzipping his fly'.

Stepping through the servants' entrance, Ehrenreich was shocked by the hierarchy she found. As a maid she is either invisible, or female householders stare 'with arms folded' ready to point out an 'overlooked stain'. It is physically demanding work but maids must never sit down. Or get a glass of water. Or go to the toilet. Peculiar humiliations work as selling points. Merry Maids boast that their maids clean floors the old-fashioned way—on their hands and knees. Encountering her first shit-stained toilet she recoils at the 'unwanted intimacy'.

She worked at two exhausting, low-paid casual jobs at once. Among the American working poor, 7.8 million had two jobs in 1996, living from hand to mouth, lurching from one financial crisis to another, living in trailer parks. Welfare-to-work programs assume that if you work hard you'll get ahead. Yet Ehrenreich finds you can work 'harder than you thought possible—and still find yourself sinking into poverty'. She develops a new respect for those performing supposedly 'unskilled' jobs . . . 'the thinking behind welfare reform was that even the humblest jobs are morally uplifting and psychologically buoying. In reality they are likely to be fraught with insult and stress.'

Ehrenreich found that whereas a mother might once have spent time teaching a child chores as part of a contributive effort, 'these days in an elite household, parenting may centre on an awkward, one-sided conversation beginning with "How was school today?"' Such bullets of stiff and awkward exchanges of 'quality time' entail losses. 'A little "low quality time" spent washing the dishes or folding clothes together can provide a comfortable space for confidences—and give the child the dignity of knowing he or she is a participant in, not just the product of, the work of the home.' The affluent devote their lives to 'such ghostly pursuits as stock trading, image making and opinion polling'; meanwhile

> real work in the old-fashioned sense of labour that engages the hands as well as eye, that tires the body and directly alters the physical world—tends to vanish from sight . . . the moral challenge is, put simply, to make work visible again: not only the scrubbing and vacuuming, but all the hoeing, stacking, hammering, drilling, bending and lifting that goes into creating and maintaining a liveable habitat.

The import and export of motherlove

Nowhere is the process of commodification or commercialising relationships more dramatic than the emergence of a brisk international trade in motherlove. It transforms a mother's capacity for love into a commodity traded on the open market, part of the new 'free trade' between nations. It is a very unequal affair.

America's high rates of working motherhood absolutely depend upon an immigrant (often illegal) underclass. Hochschild, in a book on globalisation edited by Will Hutton and Anthony Giddens, continues her gentle probing of the post-feminist family. For all the hype about the 'genderquake' that is meant to have changed the world, the data Hochschild so tellingly supplies make the revolution sound more like a 'classquake'. Globalisation has brought about global 'care chains'. As the poor and the deprived migrate from poorer nations to richer ones, they tend the children of the wealthy, often abandoning their own. What happens when motherlove is a commodity, when poor women have nothing to sell but their capacity for motherlove? Hochschild emphasises the poignant outcome, not for the women who are globalisation's winners *but for the women who are its losers*. The emotional toll on the domestic worker, she suggests, is 'overwhelming.'

Some women from third world countries abandon their own children in order to care for first world mothers' children, and send the money home. They grieve intensely for their own children:

> The first two years I felt like I was going crazy . . . I was having intense psychological problems. I would catch myself gazing at nothing, thinking about my child. Every moment every second of the day, I felt like I was thinking about my baby. My youngest left when he was only two months old . . . you know whenever I receive a letter from my children, I cannot sleep I cry. It's good that my job is more demanding at night.

Such testimony leaves Hochschild, a feminist supporter, feeling she is looking at something she does not want to see—a tragedy within which there are winners (first world working mothers) and losers (the third world children and their mothers).

Hochschild points to the irony of first world mothers giving their emotional labour and care to employers as resource managers, rather than their children. They base their identities on careers, like men:

> Just as global capitalism creates a Third World supply of nannies it also creates a First World demand . . . First world women who hire nannies are themselves caught in a male career-pattern that has proved surprisingly resistant to change . . . doing professional work, competing with fellow professionals, getting credit for work, building a reputation, doing it while you are young, hoarding scarce time, and minimising family life by finding someone else to do it.

Children become 'beloved impediments' to careers, and the labour of raising them, whether by caregivers or mothers, while 'always low relative to the value of other kinds of labor, has, under the impact of globalisation, sunk lower still'.

Like *Nickel and Dimed*, Hochschild's enterprise extends beyond the mundane specifics of a domestic service worker's life. It goes to the very heart of feminism—that it gains its moral authority from the central claim that it is on behalf of all women, not just the privileged few. Neither she nor Flanagan opt for what Hochschild calls the sunshine modernist approach, of ignoring these unpalatable truths. But they also both argue we can't opt for a 'primordialist' one of wanting women to stay home, or of career women not using such services, or the women's movement will be derailed. What we can do, Hochschild suggests, as 'critical modernists', is to respect, pay and treat those women who do such important work justly. She is right. Ultimately, however, I'm with Barbara Ehrenreich, who says hiring a servant 'is not a relationship I want to have with another human being'.

That adds one more element to the case I am building here—to give first preference to policies like parental leave and flexibility, to allow parents more time to raise their own children, but also do their own shitwork. It should be possible not to imbibe too much from the commodification frontier. Then we really would have a chance of creating a new 'democratic family', one that's not based on exploitative relations with those poorer than oneself. It is, fundamentally, a matter of justice.

13 The McDonaldisation of childhood

'[McDonald's] has done everything to speed the way from secretion to excretion.' George Ritzer

'In a capitalist system . . . the price of female liberation is bought at the dialectically opposed cost of the oft eroded freedom of one's children.' Valerie Polakow

Alongside a desolate highway outlet coming into Melbourne is a McDonald's fast food restaurant. Directly opposite, in a very similar building, is a childcare centre, with a driveway pick up and drop off zone. Driving past one day, I started wondering. Could their external similarities of design be emblematic of a much deeper kinship? Is it possible that the organisational principles and the human relations inside the childcare centre, the atmosphere of managed cheer, the attitudes to time, work, and emotion, are being McDonaldised? More deeply, are the principles of rationalisation behind the highly efficient fast food industry being applied not just to the childcare centre opposite, but to many aspects of children's contemporary experience, right down to our very conception of childhood? Is the early feminist ideal—of 'care in the community'—being replaced in our market society by McChildcare?

George Ritzer's *The McDonaldisation of Society* depicts a central aspect of social relations under the new capitalism: the speed up of everyday life and its consequence, the destruction of deep relationships. Ritzer's preoccupation is the emptying of human meaning from our lives as we become increasingly dominated by one of the key processes of modernisation: rationalisation. To illustrate this process he uses a deft device. Rather than use, as the great sociologist Max Weber did, an abstract term like rationalisation, Ritzer uses the word McDonaldisation—part impishly, part metaphorically, part accurately.

The creator of the phenomenally successful McDonald's empire, Ray Kroc, was also a disciple of the efficiency genius Frederick Taylor. Utilising Tayloresque principles, Kroc industrialised, by efficient time use and assembly lines, the production of hamburgers. Ritzer's thesis is that McDonaldisation—rationalisation that creates greater economic efficiency—is incredibly successful because it possesses competitive advantages over rival ways of doing things. McDonald's is *a representative of a brilliantly successful and expanding principle of organisation*. Its core principles of efficiency, predictability, calculability and control are steadily colonising and seeping into all kinds of human activity—workplaces, leisure, and even intimacy and love.

Ritzer does not have some vague, aesthetic snobbery about McDonald's. Rather, he sees the organisational cleverness behind McDonald's expansion around the world. Piece by piece, Ritzer unfolds the darker story behind the golden arches. Wherever it takes over, McDonaldisation has a powerful downside, despite the 'broadly disseminated superlatives on its own behalf.' By way of analogy, the odd fast food meal will do in a time pinch—but a steady diet of nothing but high salt, high fat, high cholesterol McDonald's will lead to obesity, heart disease and early death. As an organising principle, McDonaldisation is insidious: depleting human variety and creativity, often destroying more humane, alternative ways of seeing and doing things. It promotes speed, convenience and quantity over quality, resulting in flattened, featureless and mediocre products. It succeeds ultimately because it is cheap.

Applied to human services and intimate relationships, McDonaldisation, with its emphasis on efficiency and maximising profits, has a human cost—dehumanisation. Human beings are not cars on assembly lines, sausages emerging from a factory or hamburgers in a bun. Consequently our very human desire is for experiences of birth, childhood, education, working, childbearing, childraising, ageing, dying and burying our loved ones, which resist and defy McDonaldisation. We risk dehumanisation when we submit.

Like Weber, Ritzer argues that people are being locked into one rationalised, over-controlled setting after another at leisure, work and home. 'Society would eventually become nothing more than a seamless web of rationalised structures, there would be no escape.' In such settings are places where 'the self was placed in confinement, its emotions controlled and its spirit subdued . . .' Rationalisation promises unproblematic dividends, but human beings are not easy clay to mould into the prefabricated shapes needed for McDonaldisation. Real people not only keep impeding the process, but end by being harmed. The problem, in short, is of the irrationality of rationality.

In the new capitalism, family functions are not only being transferred to the marketplace, they are also being McDonaldised. What follows here is an excavation—the retrieval and examination of what lies under the surface—of the McDonaldisation of childcare.

| McDonaldisation is everywhere

The process of McDonaldisation affects almost all of us. Some people freely choose one or all aspects of McDonaldisation. A woman has an elective caesarean because it is more efficient and predictable than natural birth, or prefers bottle feeding to breastfeeding because it is more calculable (you can 'see' what they're getting), or opts for McChildcare because one's child's life can be turned over to the 'professionals'. In general, however, there is not one virtuous camp which is unaffected, while a less virtuous group happily submits.

Rather, McDonaldisation is a deep cultural process penetrating and shaping all of us. Escaping it in one phase, we may submit in another. We may have hoped for a 'natural' birth but find medical intervention is essential, or want to breastfeed but find that we are unable to do so. We may find a wonderfully unMcDonaldised nanny, or share the parenting equally, or stay home while the children are young, only to find ourselves—as I did—caught up in McDonaldisation once children hit school. Or one part of our children's lives may be McDonaldised (sent to McChildcare) while we retrieve other parts, and by way of reparation offer them something very unMcDonaldised, like co-sleeping.

In all of these micro-defeats in the McDonaldised world, at least some of them beyond our control, we may experience feelings of unease, sadness, and loss, even grief. For most parents, 'There is a broader, vaguer unease that many parents share but most rarely voice: a sense of loss, even foreboding, arising from leaving much of their children's socialisation, education and acculturation to paid labour and the values of the market place.'

Munching the odd fast food meal does little harm, but a diet of little else does. Likewise, using small amounts of McDonaldised systems may have little impact, but being completely caught up in a life where we feel unable to resist submitting to the pace of a treadmill with its speed switch flicked permanently on high will affect us. Even in those moments, however, we can exercise our reflective capacity, try to see the processes for what they are, and engage in battle against them.

McDonaldisation versus the ethic of care

One day, dropping off my daughter at kindergarten, I arrived at the same time as the caregiver of a friend's child. She was fussing in a grandmotherly way over whether her young charge would concede defeat and wear his cardigan. The weather was cool but might fine up, in which case he would be hot with it on. Then again, there were darker clouds which suggested possible rain and he might get cold. On and on she went, all in great detail. 'I'll just wait a while,' she confided in a clucky tone, 'to settle him in. He doesn't like it if I go too quickly.' As we left she was still going on about that damn cardigan. I concluded that my friend's child was in exceptionally good—unMcDonaldised—hands.

It is sometimes said that mothers are boring. Having listened politely to teachers, nurses, lawyers, academics, journalists, and *especially* politicians, go on and on about work, I would say that anyone's obsessive interest in work can be rather tiresome for those outside it. There is however, some truth in the idea that mothers can be boring. In fact *all* attentive, loving caregivers, if we are honest, can be a little bit boring.

I have sat with grandmothers, caregivers and fathers as well as mothers, and listened with amusement and interest to the obsessive detail paid to the bodily and emotional care of children in their care. I have listened to mothers going into excruciating detail on whether or not to crust a Vegemite sandwich. I have been a patient audience to a lone father who held forth with disconcerting precision on all aspects of his child's daily bowel movements.

Obsession with our darling's details is, to those outside it, exceedingly tiresome. To the child who is the recipient, however, it is a part of the attentiveness of love. Most often associated with good mothering, it is the chief characteristic of any good nurturing care. It is all those little things, as Primo Levi put it, 'that mothers remember'. Most often displayed by mothers, it is not exclusive to them. It is as true of sensitive elder care, care for the sick or disabled, as it is of childcare. It is that attention to small preferences, habits, likes and dislikes, ways of being in the world, the sheer particularity of this one being, that is so important to the 'ethic of care'. It needs a shared history, knowledge built up over time, which helps the vulnerable to flourish. It requires the ability to get inside another's head, and to identify with their bodily and emotional state.

It is why we have had such a push in our more enlightened moments against institutionalisation—we know such places militate against the 'quality of care' they forever boast about, with consequent losses in the protection of human dignity among the vulnerable. As elder care and childcare are increasingly taken over by the market, we need to reflect on the ways that such places not only face the *traditional* problems of impersonal and insensitive care, but also are being *McDonaldised*. Greater efforts to efficiency, cost savings, budget cuts all lead to higher turnover and a higher ratio of inmates to staff. The consequence can be a whole system of institutionalised carelessness.

I have deliberately opened my discussion with my friend's caregiver because I am not arguing that childcare, just because a mother does not perform it, is always McDonaldised. Some people who are paid to care do cherish and respect the dignity of those they look after. But we should be able to recognise that the takeover of any form of personal care by the market can be problematic.

McChildcare

The child-centred feminist Julie Stephens wrote in *Arena*:

> A few years ago, a friend attended a parent evening at her toddler's creche. As a public relations exercise, the creche (of which she was an active member of the organising committee) decided to film the activities of the children over a day, and then speed up the film for the parents' entertainment. As the daily routine of the children unfolded on film, the initial amusement of parents was replaced by a deathly silence. It would seem that for these well-informed, middle-class parents, it was a shock to view the stark evidence of the regimentation, rigid conformity and institutionalised nature of their children's childcare experience. The film momentarily enabled a different reading of the childcare centre: not just as an environment full of stimulation, toys and activities and things parents would like to arrange for their children if only they had the time, but as something unfamiliar, as an institution first and foremost, with little resemblance to prevailing ideas of family and home.

What Stephens captures so well is the poignant disparity between parental hopes and the daily reality of an institution, even in a high quality setting.

It is made all the more difficult because for very young children what is 'irreducible and irreplaceable' is the way 'the spiralling strands of development that transform helpless newborns into sociable and socialised small people are plaited into their relationships with known, loved and loving adults.'

The common demand, as Patricia Morgan has pointed out, for universal, high quality and affordable childcare is a contradiction in terms. High quality care is expensive care because all good caregiving is labour-intensive and the largest component of any childcare centre's costs is salaries.

Childcare provided by the marketplace is an *organisational system with an inbuilt economic logic.* Rather than seventy-five or so mothers looking after one, two or three children each, McChildcare depends upon a very much reduced core of adults taking care of fifty or a hundred children. Instead of one mother looking after one baby (humans are not usually born in litters), one caregiver looks after five. Similar economies of scale occur as children move through toddler and preschool years. The amount of time and energy, the number of adults it takes to raise a child, childhood itself, is being rationalised.

McChildcare is more efficient and cost-effective, its economy of scale replacing costly, time-inefficient parental care by a commodity service. Just as the continued existence of McDonald's as a profitable enterprise requires a large quantity of hamburgers to be produced at the lowest possible cost, so too McChildcare takes on the largest number of children it can get away with—a veritable production line of early childhoods at the lowest possible cost.

Penelope Leach has pointed out:

> The more economy of scale a daycare institution offers, the worse the care will be for the children . . . childcare is so labour-intensive that any increase in salaries has a marked effect on total costs—and rapidly reverses economies of scale. Daycare centres are always expensive to run and the better they are the more they cost.

Sally Loane's *Who Cares* gives a pungent summary of the transfer of childrearing to the market during the 1980s and early 1990s. In many instances the welfare of children disappeared as a concern. The business pages and advertisements in property developer magazines salivated at the prospect of handsome profits. Queensland property developers were especially excitable. The *Courier Mail* noted that 'many potential childcare centre investors were told the profit would be fabulous, there would be virtually no night or weekend work, and all they had to do was rake the sandpit at weekends.' Some centres resorted to free haircuts and swimming lessons; one even offered a free frozen chook to entice non-working parents to put their children into care!

While the impersonality of mass institutional care is not restricted to the large for-profit childcare chains, it is most vividly seen there. Queensland businessman Eddy Groves presides over 'an aggressively expanding empire of childcare centres'. Groves's personal wealth, estimated in October 2004 at $175 million, was primarily made from childcare. Around 50 per cent of ABC Learning's income comes from taxpayer-provided funds via the Child Care Benefit.

Groves was poised in 2004 to merge with two other large chains. In an interview on *Background Briefing*, he boasted:

> The sheer growth of this company, when you look at where we came from in 2001, we had a market capital of about $25 million, and after this merger, the market capital I believe will be about $1 billion. And the fact of being able to do that in four or five years has been quite remarkable, so certainly there's been growth for people if they're looking to invest.
>
> Gerald Tooth: Where does the growth end?
>
> Eddy Groves: Well, I'm not sure that it does.

Groves is right. In 2001 he owned thirty-one centres in south-east Queensland. After floating the company on the Stock Exchange, by 2004 his merger with Childcare Centres of Australia and Peppercorn Management gave his business 750 centres across Australia. The implications of such market dominance cannot be overestimated. One early childhood specialist complained to me that Groves has the minister's ear, and that his market clout is such that none of the improvements in quality can occur without private sector approval.

Such corporatisation, according to the president of the New South Wales based Quality Childcare Association, representing 300 private long daycare centres, is 'inevitable.' Now that the private sector is the largest player, by 2002 outnumbering the community sector by 2750 to 1323 services, Australia is locked into accepting lower than internationally recognised standards—for example, the attempt to raise the number of caregivers to babies from the abysmally low one to five, nationally, was defeated. Moreover one article which quoted Groves noted that if there is one threat to profitability, it is the prospect of improving wages and conditions for staff!

In some instances, industry representatives explicitly opposed paid maternity leave. With almost entirely female labour, such paid leave was something to fear. Paid maternity leave is undoubtedly a threat in another way to a childcare business; women at home looking after babies on paid leave remove prospective clients.

One former childcare board member, Caroline Fewster, admitted sleepless nights after sitting on the board of a corporate childcare centre, forced to think about staffing levels not for children's wellbeing but as debits in a cost–benefit ledger:

> I've definitely experienced many tensions, and many ethical dilemmas in my time and it's a really difficult situation, in my experience . . . The hardest part was to constantly be reviewing ... the cost of the wages per week, constantly reviewing for profit, not for the service provision.

The market and the quality of care

The *Background Briefing* report also contained troubling evidence from childcare specialists and workers of the effect on the childcare floor of such priorities. Jennifer, a childcare educator who supervised trainee students in childcare, found that only one in ten ABC Learning centres—twenty-five out of 250–300 centres she examined—was of good enough quality to model care for students. In one centre, she saw

> Children's penises being compared on baby tables, and staff having a good giggle about how big one is and how small the other one is . . . Where does an infant have their dignity when they're lying on a change table completely naked and there's two women comparing the sizes of their penises? I mean seriously.

In another,

> . . . I witnessed staff saying to a toddler who was no more than sixteen months, 'You will lie on your bed, I don't care if your mother rocks you to sleep, that's not how we do it here'. And the toddler was extremely traumatised by the whole process. And that went on for something like thirty minutes . . . parents are so uninformed about what is good quality care, that they don't know what's going on in centres, and that's the scary part.

One childcare trainee said:

> They never washed the children's hands. They never had a program in the room. They only read about three books for children the whole time I was there. The only activities the children did were painting. There were maybe three times they did something different ... They never let the children decide what they want to eat, they talked in front of children about how their parents were on drugs and how dumb they were. One of the older children has autism and has very bad behaviour. The Director saw him doing something wrong so he picked him up by the collar of his shirt, and carried him across the playground by his shirt.

One childcare student said:

> ... I was told I need to yell at the children, I didn't. My personal philosophy is that children need to be in a loving, caring environment with support and challenges, not somewhere with no or poor supervision and where they leave children to cry alone when missing their parents.

Another trainee admitted she was glad the practical training was over: 'There were many occasions where I always broke into tears, because of the way the children were treated. At this centre, I felt trapped and uncomfortable.' In one survey of New South Wales childcare students, every single trainee said they would never place their own child in childcare after what they had seen.

While in the community-based sector wages constitute 80 per cent of the cost, in for-profit centres they make up 50 per cent.

Almost all advocates of quality childcare concede that it is dependent on the continuity of care, high staff to child ratios, good conditions, and decent pay to entice workers to stay. Yet Pam Cahir, national director of Early Childhood Australia, pointed out that in Australian childcare there are widespread staff shortages, high caregiver turnover, no career structures, 'conditions are terrible' and the pay poor (between $10 and $12 an hour). Unsurprisingly, 'the turnover of staff is enormous,' in some areas 30–40 per cent per year.

> I don't think it's appropriate or OK for parents to go to work on the back of the wages of poorly paid staff in childcare services, I don't think it's OK for services to have ratios of one to five for babies. I mean I can't imagine looking after five babies, I just think that's just an impossible task, and if you had quadruplets in this country you'd get support.

Efficiency

The principle of efficiency at the centre of the McDonaldisation of childcare leaves other fingerprints. Some US childcare centres have drive-by windows so that busy parents, as at McDonalds, don't have to get out of the car to drop off children or pick them up. I came across one advertisement for an Australian centre which promised greater efficiency in the drop-off time, as if dealing with parcel or product delivery, and said jokingly, 'depending on the number of kisses'. Another Australian centre suggested children could simply be plonked on a lift and a button pressed, rather than parents taking the time-consuming method of personally settling them in.

Space, that great luxury of an Australian childhood, so deeply present in written memoirs, is also subject to economies of scale. Prue Walsh, a play environment consultant, described some of the physical environments in creches, and decried the fact that more space was devoted to the childcare car parks than to space for playing.

> They are a tragedy. The legislation governing space and the environment is incomplete and there are too many developers without ethics as far as children's interests are concerned. They just want to cut costs and maximise profits. It has resulted in child ghettos and baby factories.

The implications of such economies of scale—more children to fewer adults—is vividly brought home in the decline of playing space for children from when they played in the great Australian backyard. Older-style kindergartens (the word literally translated means children's gardens) allocated 35 square metres of space per child. Now in childcare in Queensland, Victoria and New South Wales, metres per child have been subjected to a new calculus, and whittled down to 7 square metres.

Assembly lines are quite often present in eye-witness accounts of childcare. John Tainton, the executive director of the Lady Gowrie childcare centre in Brisbane, visited one centre which had been the recipient of an award for the best in the area. 'He was shocked by what he saw—rows of toddlers in highchairs being fed, their faces as blank as stone, and a stench of urine from the cot room which almost knocked him out.'

In *Child Care In Context*, there is a photo of Chinese babies at creche. They are in a circle, their little bare rumps planted on potties. Their faces are blank. They are being encouraged to defecate or urinate on command, to save the energies of caretakers who have so many to care for. Joint pottying is an efficient economy of scale. No author within the volume finds anything to fuss about in relation to that photo, rather they say, 'A daycare worker has to take care of more than ten children, so she cannot respond to the idiosyncrasies of any one child.' How ironic in a society so committed to adult individuality, the authors find nothing to object to in this enforcement of conformity—even over the children's bowel movements! For all the rhetoric about the 'naturalness' of 'care in the community', this looks like care via the assembly line, as care of children is contracted out and mass childrearing takes over. It looks wonderfully adapted to the market.

From McMuffins to McMumps: childcare for sick kids

Zygmunt Bauman argues that 'liberation rhetoric' often merely disguises what is really going on—the commercialisation of relationships previously outside the cash nexus. There is truth to his remark. All the arguments on behalf of 'care in the community' and 'shared care' were part of 'liberation rhetoric'. None of those early feminists, however, foresaw its current transformation where so much of childcare is provided by the market.

If workplaces are rigid, if there is no carer's leave, it forces compromises in parent's empathetic care—for example when the child is sick. None of this is a 'natural', inevitable part of working motherhood. Rather, it's how we, as nations, choose to 'do' working motherhood. Unlike Sweden, where parents have a generous allowance of time off to care for a sick child, neo-liberal nations all report versions of the 'Demazin Dump syndrome,' where children who are sick are dosed up with cough and fever suppressant, then left at childcare. One Sydney lawyer interviewed for *Sixty Minutes* candidly admitted: 'I know it's not the right thing to do, but when you've got a meeting with a client at nine o'clock in the morning that you just cannot cancel, I'm sorry, that child goes to childcare.'

The ethic of the new capitalism is to put work first. An efficient economy, a productive workplace need workers whose 'being there' work ethic is deeper and more pressing than a parental 'being there' home ethic.

In the populist *Herald Sun*, a front-page story in January 2004 called for 'sick rooms' at childcare centres: 'The call comes from researchers who have found working parents struggling to cope when their sick kids are banned from childcare.' The parents in this study felt guilty, not about sick kids in childcare, but about not 'being there' at work: 'Even where companies offer carers' leave, many parents feel guilty because of the impact on workmates.' It was only the childcare workers who articulated the old ideal of 'being there', saying sick kids prefer and need to be with their parents.

Children and the commodification of relationships

'The results of this high rate of turnover were evident when a three-year-old child had a temper tantrum at his daycare centre. His teacher could not console him, so she brought him into the director's office. The director held him on her lap and tried to comfort him, but he said that he wanted Kathy. "But Michael," said the director, "Kathy is your afternoon teacher." "Then I want Linda," he said. "Oh, Michael, you must remember, Linda teaches in another school now" "Then I want Cheryl." The director chuckled because Cheryl had been his first teacher at the centre, when he was two. "My goodness, Michael, you have a good memory . . ." "And", Michael said, "I even remember Debby." The director realised that the child had had ten major caretakers in two years. The total of ten did not even include student teachers aides, or volunteers.' Marion Blum, *The Daycare Dilemma*

Richard Sennett speaks of the 'no long term' of the workplace which promotes 'the strength of weak ties'. In order to survive such a world, 'detachment and superficial cooperativeness' are better armour than qualities like reciprocity, mutual commitment, trust and loyalty. Zygmunt Bauman, in a telling phrase, speaks of the 'permanent temporariness of a relationship and its readiness for cancellation at short notice'.

What are the implications for children of such a shifting sea of faces at the end of the cot? Precisely because it is not easy for a baby to be separated from their parents for most of their waking hours, every bit of evidence points to the importance of stability, continuity, and sensitivity in the substitute caregivers. That sensitivity is much more likely in a relationship where a shared history is built up. Yet such a shared history is impossible for children under these circumstances. Even those who claim that the deepest separation—that of mother and child—will not cause pain, will usually admit that the replaceability, the exchange of one caregiver after another when the child has become attached to them, will cause pain.

> The grieving of a baby who loses her one and only special person—her lone mother who dies, for example, or the lifelong foster mother from whom she is removed—is agonising to see because we know we are looking at a genuine tragedy. But the pain of separations we arrange and connive every time we change caregivers or leave a baby in the daycare centre that has seen new staff—again—or with an agency babysitter she has never seen, may not be as different as we assume . . . In the first six, nine, or even twelve months, that baby has no way of knowing that the parent who leaves her will come back . . . if each baby is not fully attached to each successive caregiver, she will spend many days in limbo; if she is fully attached, she will spend many more days in grief.

Centre-based care has inbuilt breakages in continuity and fragmentary experiences even when caregiver stability is high, as a baby shifts from the babies' room to the toddlers' room and then to the room for older preschoolers. For a twelve-hour day, morning and afternoon shifts will be needed, while replacement staff will be needed for holidays and sick leave.

Valerie Polakow, a child-centred feminist, noted in her exposé of American daycare that children in one for-profit centre she observed for months, seemed to be being integrated into a brave new world of short-term relationships in which others were treated instrumentally.

> I gradually became aware of and suspicious about a covert issue [which] lay beneath. How were the children being socialised into detachment? As they were unable to form meaningful relationships in time with any staff member, how, I wondered, did they perceive the world? They were separated from home fifty hours a week—an explicit detachment in itself—and yet there were no secondary attachments to compensate that were intimate or constant. Did this create a configuration of a world where relationships did not last, a world of inconstancy and uncertainty and confusion?'

This takes us to another aspect of late capitalism. Commodification, the 'no long term' of relationships and workplaces, means there is increasingly a loss of a shared history; there is often no coherent 'life narrative' for people. Instead, there are abrupt changes and severances when people and places, which have been special and important, disappear, often forever from a person's life. The consequence is a pervasive sense of fragmentation and disorientation.

In the childcare centre, with high turnover and low ratios of adults to children, as the research into joint attention sequences in Australian childcare showed, there can be a fragmentary, episodic quality of the attention children receive. One friend changed her little boy back to part-time care because in full-time childcare he was more aggressive. The way she put it was: 'He needs his parents to help him remember who he is.'

There is an echo, too, of Sennett's anguished question: 'how can long term purposes be pursued in a short term society? How can durable social relations be sustained? How can a human being develop a narrative of identity and life history in a society composed of episodes and fragments?'

One might describe the mother–child relationship as an anti-commodity relationship. Part of the story of a child is her capacity to attach powerfully—to 'fall in love with' particular, precious others. The kinds of emotional 'toughening' that must occur in order to cope with constant caregiver changes is a central aspect of childhood under the new capitalism. Most importantly, it makes children's universal, profound impulse to form loving attachments—that essence of humanness—very difficult.

What is so striking, reviewing the childcare literature, is how deeply and profoundly children do *not* adapt easily or well, or without protest, or without cost, to a world of rationalised childrearing. They will cry, beg, protest, sulk, and stage slow-downs—everything bar an all-out strike. And they will instantly state, if asked, their preference for a non-McDonaldised childhood.

> His first question every morning is, 'Is this a child care day?' He says, 'I just want to stay with you today, Mummy.' Is this an unreasonable thing for a four-year-old to ask? But we have to say, 'I'm sorry I can't have you all day long.' We are saying, grow up, *this is the real world.* We're the first generation of mothers *who've had to say this.* [emphasis added]

Consequently:

> Some parents avoid asking their children questions when they know they won't want to hear the answers. I conducted a small experiment with children I know who attended childcare. When I asked them whether they

would rather be at childcare or with mum, they all replied, not surprisingly, that they'd rather be with mummy. It doesn't do to ask too often.

Giving the illusion of quantity

Quantity is more often illusion than reality in a fast food restaurant. For example, the big, fluffy (and inexpensive) bun that surrounds the meat patty makes the burger look bigger than it is. Special scoops arrange the fries in such a way that a portion looks enormous. The bags and boxes seem to bulge at the top, overflowing with French fries.

Part of the smoke and mirrors of McDonaldisation is the trick that quantity means quality. We can see this illusion in the system of childcare. On the outside of a childcare centre there is often a list with little stars beside them such as:

- Highest accreditation for three years
- Professional, qualified staff
- Open long hours, 6 a.m. to 6 p.m.
- Babies welcome
- Qualified teachers running preschool program
- Individualised learning programs

Some of these items are clearly *against* the interest of children (like babies being taken at any age, for long hours) yet are presented as just one more impressive item on a hit list of virtues. Or take 'highest accreditation.' In fact this means accreditation for two-and-a-half years to the inadequate government regulations, and ratios that *guarantee* quality of care *less* than the highest international standards—for example, five babies to one caregiver. 'Professional' staff might mean an untrained seventeen-year-old. Accreditation also gives no control over central issues of quality like staff turnover or the quality of relationships in the centre.

In fact the 'broadly disseminated superlatives' on advertising billboards outside creches do resemble the photos in the front of the McDonald's driveway that give the *illusion that you are getting more than you are really getting*. One friend found her toddler's advertised 'individualised learning program' at creche, the 'artistic dimension', was putting her little paw in paint once every few months, and squishing it onto paper. The 'product' was then posted on the wall with a sign that said, 'Chloe likes experimenting with the colour green.' My friend commented later, 'It was weird. It seemed somehow a bigger and better, more "official" a learning experience than when she rummages in her big brother's paints all day, and I stick the pictures up all over the family room.'

Few people examine our assumption that what goes on within organised 'educational time' with 'certificated professionals' is superior to unstructured time with uncertificated parents. Parenting increasingly has a rickety, do-it-yourself whiff to it. Patricia Morgan examined several British studies on language and affection at home and in centres, and found:

> there were significant differences between the childcare groups, with mothers and relatives showing higher levels of affection toward the study child than childminders, who were in turn more affectionate than nursery [daycare] workers and . . . children in the home, relative and childminder group received significantly more vocal communication than the nursery group and . . . the home group received significantly more than the childminder group.

Another British study found that children at home spent far more time on a one-to-one basis with an adult, and that, despite fewer structured and organised activities, adult–child conversations at home 'were more frequent, more complex, more wide-ranging, longer and more evenly balanced . . . Such free-flowing conversation in nursery school has been found to be a rare event . . . the relatively superficial comments typical of pre-school staff: "that's nice", "lovely", "make him fatter" etc.' And, one might say, a superficiality reminiscent of the McDonald's 'Have a nice day.'

In other words there was, despite the 'broadly disseminated superlatives' offered on behalf of organised childcare, a hierarchy in matters of affection and in the complexity and richness of language favouring 'unofficial' non-market home care over its rival, market-provided 'official' childcare.

Another American study found that the adult–child ratios essential to high quality care were more likely to be found in the child's own home or in relative care.

Standardisation

The potato used in McDonald's is standardised. It is not too small or too big or a squiggly shape—but a product of engineering to create a neatness of fit between the potato and the institution of fast food. It must be the right size to allow long chips, so the fries can hang out of the box, to give the illusion of quantity. Whole fields, whole regions even, are filled with this one sort of potato. The standardised potato emerges within McDonaldisation because that system, with its premiums on efficiency, calculability and predictability, selects out one kind of potato which possesses certain competitive advantages.

There is in McChildcare the equivalent—a strong impulse towards a standardised child. The smooth operation of the institution is best served by the not too small, too sensitive, too shy, too quiet, too reserved, too dreamy, too sniffly, and especially not too attached child. Sally Loane wrote of how, in the interests of self-preservation, some children deliberately change their personality at the door of the childcare centre, to fit in to the group. Even children who were not outgoing felt obliged, apparently, to put on a gregarious 'performance'.

> From an early age they seem to want to fit in, to be popular. One child of five in childcare since he was a baby, adopts a different persona almost immediately, according to his mother. 'His face changes when he walks in, his voice rises in pitch, he starts telling jokes. He adapts to the environment and *becomes more like a childcare child . . . he's not comfortable with his childcare personality*, slipping back into his natural manner as a quiet, self-contained little boy at home, where he revels in a less structured, less ordered environment.'

Many early childhood professionals worry over the unintentional neglect in busy crowded centres of the shy 'good' children who are happiest doing things on their own. Faye Pettit, a former early childhood academic, spoke to Loane of her 'grave concerns about these shy, quiet more inhibited children. They can be ignored, and simply get lost in a busy centre . . .'

Antoinette Cross, Professor of Early Childhood at Macquarie University, commented on her 'constant worry' that 'In many centres infants who are not fussing are often left to their own devices for lengthy periods . . . what they are particularly missing out on is warm positive one-to-one interactions with nurturing.'

McDonaldising childhood

There are many contemporary trends that promise to transform the landscape of childhood, as Ritzer says of McDonaldisation, where children go from one rationalised, bureaucratised institutional setting—or following Weber's intuition—one 'iron cage' after another. In a way children are, to borrow the title of a recent book about childhood, *Raised in Captivity*. The process of McDonaldisation is not confined to people who use corporate childcare, or childcare practices. It pervades institutional schooling, and the ethos of the ambitious middle-class in particular, affecting stay-at-home parents too. Children spend less and less time in free play, in neighbourhood groups, roaming their backyards, creeks, parks and suburbs and more and more time in structured, educational, 'developmental' activities, swimming for toddlers, gymbaroo, dance, music lessons and organised sports lessons. There is less time to potter, dream and muse, or discover what you like or who you are, and more time spent in adult-organised activities based on boosting performance. No sooner does the child get interested in a leaf or a tadpole than the ambitious parent is 'at' them, transforming the uncolonised moment into one with an educational purpose. There is also the utopians' dream of the new landscape of childhood—to relieve busy parents of their tiresome childcare duties and allow them to progress up the career ladder that bit faster—from earliest infancy in institutional childcare in the hands of the professionals, 24 hour and then 48 hour childcare, 'wrap around' before- and after-school care, where a child 'works' a ten-hour day at school from 8 a.m. to 6 p.m., (one exclusive private school in Melbourne even had inquiries as to whether the after-care program was available on Christmas Eve!) then on to university, the corporation . . . where similar work patterns may be reproduced.

Another 'parent panic', even with stay-at-home parents, is to do with separation and dependency. The idea of childhood as a time 'for itself', *belonging to the child*, disappears. Instead, childhood is seen only as a preparation for something else, it *now belongs to the adults*. Given that it has no value *in itself*, it can be made more 'productive', sped up and gotten through rather more quickly, or McDonaldised.

One stay-at-home mother expressed this dilemma. To get him 'ready' to make it as a man and hold down a good job, her son had to be sent to university. To prepare for that he had go to school. But to 'get ready' for school he would have to go to kindergarten, and to 'get ready' for kindergarten, some time at a playgroup was not deemed enough, he had (according to his father) to be separated from his devoted mother and go to early childcare. There was a lot of visible anxiety, reflecting a very powerful discourse about masculinity and the widespread hostility to dependency in our culture.

Too much motherlove might interfere with the process of 'getting ready', which was conceptualised as a series of separations, each one larger than the last. So to get ready for kindergarten, although he still had a bottle and a blankie and was wearing nappies, in order to begin the great and arduous process of 'getting ready' for the moment some twenty or more years later when he would be launched into his ultimate destination, which was the workplace, he had to be sent to childcare. All this 'getting ready' was of course, perfectly rational, but the rationalisation of everyday life often leads, paradoxically, to irrationalities.

The irrationality that emerged was the child's tie to his mother, the particularity of his love for her. One can't love a child at speed, says Michael Leunig, and nor, it seems, can a child love his mother more efficiently—to be done with her all the quicker. The little boy, on being left, cried terribly. My friend 'confessed' to me her son's 'failure' to be left, and she felt very guilty about her decision to take him with her, even when he was so visibly upset. Father and childcare attendants were more than a little contemptuous of this joint 'failure'. Father in particular seemed inordinately concerned that if his son couldn't be a Little Man he might not, after all, make it as a Big Man. Aunties and grandmas had their say too. There seemed an awful lot of social 'static' collecting around the issue of whether this toddler would 'succeed' in being left. Everybody seemed very keen for him to go to childcare, although there was no pressing financial or even career reason why he should (his mother had a job she could return to at any time and she did not, presently, want to work). Father was only to pleased to take command of the situation.

On the appointed day, I saw Dad with his little son, not at creche. The little boy beamed at me and waved. Feigning innocence, I raised my eyebrows inquiringly. The father confessed in a guilty whisper that he had *no idea* his son got so upset.

There was no more talk of creche. Instead, he spent more time with his father at work—an idea that had never, previously, occurred to anyone. In due course, when the time was right, the little boy attended preschool in a childcare centre, and then school, without the slightest problem.

The irrationality of all this rational preparation in 'getting ready' is that of course children arrive at 'separation readiness' in their own good time. It is not a process that can be easily 'sped up' or McDonaldised or rationalised without irrationalities springing as a consequence—that is, without human pain.

| Love in a cool climate: the cultural logic of new capitalism

The sped up, fleeting nature of McDonaldised systems makes them superficial ones; 'people pass through McDonaldised systems without being touched by them.' The famous 'Have a nice day' is scripted for McDonald's employees the world over, not an authentic human interaction. Much of the human emotion, the atmosphere of managed cheer in McDonald's is 'simulated.'

This leads to another aspect which Jameson sees as central part of the 'cultural logic of post-modern societies'—'the waning of emotion or affect'. More simply it means the draining of emotional intensity, depth and commitment from our bonds with each other and the emptying of life of the rich, time-consuming traditions and rituals of family life that make existence worth living. Economic relations affect our social and intimate relationships profoundly. There is a politics of attachment associated with the new capitalism—the push away from intensity and long-term commitment, towards shallower, weaker, more replaceable ties. One might go further. It is those who 'just move on' who are best adapted to this brave new world, who do not feel the pull and indeed the limit of deep attachment.

The new conditions of motherhood mean that there are powerful incentives to invest less and hold back more. The opportunity cost of motherhood, Crittenden reminds us, is around $1 million dollars for a college-educated woman. It is in that context that we can read paediatrician T. Berry Brazelton's suggestion in *Working and Caring*, as he enters sympathetically into the dilemma of a woman who has to work and decides not to breastfeed in order to return to work early. 'If you are going to leave your baby to go back to work, you can't get too intimate with him. *It would lead him to expect more than he would get out of life.*'

In a high 'risk' society, of no long term, whether in relationships or at work, there are certain advantages to affable but shallow attachments—to colleagues, friends, wives, partners and even children.

'Travelling light,' as Bauman puts it, 'is now an asset of power . . . identities are more like spots of crust hardening time and again on top of volcanic lava which melt and dissolve again before they have time to cool and set.' When the time is right, or the company needs to downsize, when the marriage seems tiresome, or some new opportunity comes along—one just 'moves on.' Passionate, deep attachments to places, people, even one kind of job, make for a certain competitive disadvantage.

The social conservatives who hope for the cordoning off of 'market forces' from private life are certain to be disappointed. Instead, what I have tried to show here is the process whereby those values of the marketplace, far from being cordoned off, are able to seep into unexpected places, and colonise and reshape the private world. The real unleashing of 'animal spirits' tends much more to the dissolving of the ties that bind than to their strengthening. The new capitalism rewards those who attach themselves to nothing, not even their own ideas.

In such a world, narcissism is one solution:

> When the moral basis of life's meaning becomes so restricted and insecure, then the only reliable, ever-present object of nurturing attention is oneself . . . in making ourselves an object of love, to whom we can devote the care and attention of a parent, we transform our sense of ourselves—the remembering 'I' that links all our experience . . .

The fertility crisis: the irrationality of rationality

All this might seem bleak. But there is a delicious irony. One final example of the 'irrationality of rationality,' of the McDonaldisation of motherhood, offers us the way out.

Remember Nancy Folbre's race designed by the goddesses? One nation took a short-term view and assumed the race would not last long. It set every individual member to compete. Some citizens did well, but as time went on too many fell by the wayside. There was no one to care for the sick, injured and exhausted. Long-term, too few had children to replace them on the field. Before too long it was beset by a crisis of reproduction that ensured it would not win the race.

The first nation is Folbre's metaphor for the new capitalism. Short-term, it is a vibrant, economically vital and efficient society. Long-term, however, it cannot replace itself. We have taken the 'shadow' care economy for granted, and treated women, in and out of the workforce, carelessly. It has been economic folly, Folbre says, to treat 'children as pets'—expensive private indulgences like a yacht. For the care economy depends not only on altruism but also reciprocity. It has a gritty economic dimension. Children are not just a private matter, but also a crucial part of intergenerational reciprocity. It is through children that our society provides for the renewal and development of society as a whole, as well as collectively, through their taxes as adult workers, for all of us in old age.

And having children is just what we are not doing. Most Western nations face a crisis of reproduction.

Consider. In all Western nations, to a greater or lesser degree, fertility is in long-term decline. Except for New Zealand and America, none are near the replacement level of 2.1 children per woman per lifetime. The causes are complex and multiple, the cure uncertain. There is no doubt, however, about the central problem presented by declining fertility. It is the emergence of unfavourable ratios between workers and that part of the population dependent on government assistance. The taxes of an ever-shrinking group of workers must provide social security for a growing aged population.

In pro-family Catholic states like Italy and Spain, the fertility rate is 1.2 children per woman. At current fertility rates, Italians aged over 65 will outnumber children by seven to one by the year 2050. The Japanese are also worried. Their fertility rate of 1.32 children per woman means their population will be half its present level by 2100. Taxes would have to rise to at least 60 per cent of incomes just to fund current pensions and standards of health care. The Australian fertility rate was 1.75 children per woman in 2004.

It is this dramatic shift to low fertility societies, which, I suggest, changes everything. Moral suasion, the language of rights and needs, however morally powerful, is not enough. It is falling fertility that radically alters motherhood's terms of trade. It is this, above all else, which has produced the 'perfect storm' moment for a viable maternal feminist program, of new social policies aimed at providing 'tools for conviviality.' It is to this new social program that I now turn.

14 Conclusion

The gift of time: the road not taken

If an anthropologist from Mars descended to earth, she could be forgiven for thinking that in historical terms in rich modern societies we have won the equivalent of the lottery. She would be astonished to see the language of emotional scarcity and economic necessity amidst the evidence of so much abundance. She would wonder why fewer and fewer people living in rich nations feel able to 'afford' to have children. She would be amazed to hear from the richest society yet known to humankind, a famous paediatrician say of a woman that breastfeeding might teach her baby 'to expect more than he is going to get out of life'.

She would be bewildered by the way outstanding productivity gains over the last decades are persistently translated into an intensification of the work–spend cycle, and not into greater leisure time for families. She would be puzzled as to why ever-smaller families live in ever-larger houses with mortgages to match, necessitating such punishing working hours between two adults that no one has time to spend in them. She would wonder why more people do not 'downshift' and step out of the gilded cage of consumption.

As fertility falls and our society needs to keep on older workers, and as good health continues into our seventies, as average life expectancy increases to 85 years for women, she would be amazed by the Sophie's Choice still offered to women between a careerless motherhood and a childless career. She would see the pain of working lives still operating on the unforgiving temporal logic of the old breadwinner model, so that talented young women, our best and our brightest, still suffer under the cruel expectation that they must cram in education, career-building, marriage and children, all by their mid-thirties. She would be equally disturbed at how careless we are of those mothers who step off the treadmill to raise children: the airy 'Oh, it was her choice' as they 'pay the price of motherhood', deprived of chances to return to work, or only offered 'opportunities' humiliating to their talents and capacities. How can these people, our Martian would gasp, so treat those who reproduce and care for the generation that will look after these social policy delinquents in their old age? Finally, licking her pencil stub, she would make her concluding remarks. Why on earth, she would ask, do all these factors not create a new social movement—one that is *all about time*?

The cultural contradictions of the new capitalism

At the beginning of a new century, we have experienced a period of turbo-charged economic change. All that I have been describing as the 'new capitalism' has profoundly reshaped our social and family landscape. It depends less on assembly lines and factories and more on a highly skilled, well-educated workforce delivering human services. If the distinctive face of industrial age capitalism was the male factory worker, the representative face of the new capitalism is more likely a female service worker. This period of dynamic capitalism has thrown up a new type of family and a new set of problems. It may be stated simply. We are trying to have a new economy, a new workforce, based on old ways of doing things.

It is this tension between old family models and the new economy that makes discussions of work and family the great 'barbecue stopper', as John Howard declared it. If in the late nineteenth century the scarce commodity was money, in our age the scarce commodity for many families is time.

The new capitalism—like its nineteenth-century counterpart—has made little accommodation, thus far, to the distinctive needs of the new workforce. This time we do not face a crisis of production via the combined collective power of the worker and the strike. Strikes have all but disappeared. Women now have a choice whether or not to bear and rear children. Thus far we have assumed that we could remain largely indifferent to women's dual role as caregivers. We have, perhaps unconsciously, expected that we will continue to receive all the life-sustaining, nourishing labour of the shadow 'care economy', pretty much as we have always had it, for free. In the decades of the new capitalism we have behaved like the shortsighted nation in Folbre's race of the goddesses, which invited all to run and compete in the war of all against all. It is the most fundamental cultural contradiction. Most advanced Western nations face a crisis of reproduction, a new kind of strike, a birth strike. It is this factor, the dramatic shift to low fertility societies, which changes everything.

Low fertility, above all, means there is no turning back to old solutions. Instead, it opens the possibility of a new social conversation. The fertility crisis has given women a precious political bargaining chip. That presents an immense opportunity to press for a new societal deal that *improves the conditions of motherhood for all*. This is a political diamond dropped into women's laps by the cultural contradictions, by the irrationality of economic rationality. Here is a political weapon of great importance.

The new societal conversation

There is strong evidence that this new social conversation—all about time—is already beginning. Clive Hamilton's radical intervention *Growth Fetish* swept out of left field and into the centre of our cultural conversation, highlighting the significant proportion of Australians willing to 'downshift' to improve their quality of life, including choosing more time with family over greater material wealth.

Likewise, the landmark maternal feminist conference in Barnard College at Harvard in 2002 raised the possibility for a new alliance among women: recognising that central to women's experience in and out of the workforce is the devaluation of the work done by the shadow economy of care.

Australia took a small but important step forward with the adoption by both major political parties of *maternal equity policies*—an equal allowance of initially $3000 but eventually $5000 on the birth of a child, regardless of whether women work or not. It was also a sign of just how quickly the demographic problem can concentrate the minds of policy makers.

Another moment came in February 2004, when Treasurer Peter Costello spoke about the Federal Government's *Intergenerational Report*. 'Demography is destiny!' Costello declared, as he flagged radical changes to the way we phase out work and phase in retirement. Now the societal expectation will be that able-bodied members of the older generation who wish to, can work well into their sixties and seventies. The brute fact of an ageing, low-fertility society is already having its effect. Remember those men thrown on the scrap heap by economic restructuring—those roosters who became useless feather dusters? Attitudes to those older workers and the dead end to which many come to in their mid-fifties seemed to have changed overnight.

Long-term economic imperatives are driving those changes. The *Intergenerational Report* has calculated that the tax burden on the next generation will be 5 per cent of GDP by 2041–42, or a staggering $87 billion in today's dollars. The historical experience of other low-fertility societies shows that it is only a matter of time before the logic applied to older people to improve the ratio of working aged to dependents, will also be extended to young parents.

That sudden, unexpected rethinking of the situation of older workers is characteristic of the attitudinal change that will be necessary to enable us to restructure our working lives, giving women the precious time they need. We need not only to make work more flexible, releasing women from juggling full-time work with babies and toddlers, but also to redistribute working time *across the life cycle*. Reconceptualising a working life over a longer time frame, rather than cramming everything into the peak reproductive years, will have profound—and beneficial—implications for women. That longer time frame gives women the chance to have both motherhood and a career, if they wish, but in sequence rather than all at once.

It should be remembered that the group of women most likely, in Sylvia-Ann Hewlett's survey, to 'have it all', were those in occupations where they 'could bend the rules': all the self-employed entrepreneurs, business women, consultants, writers, editors and freelancers able to step outside normal working time. Hewlett also says: 'working mothers who participated in the survey made it abundantly clear that what they want most are work/life policies that confer on them what one woman called "the gift of time".' Almost all their suggestions are about softening the punishing austerity of corporate time frames. One high flyer Hewlett interviews was newly back at work after taking three years off to care for her son, made possible by IBM's personal leave program:

People don't believe me when I tell them my company offers a three-year personal leave of absence . . . I can't tell you how grateful I am to have had this kind of time out. Because of infertility problems it took me five years to conceive Kevin and he is likely to be our only child, so I was particularly eager to savour his babyhood. I breastfed him till he was eighteen months old, signed us both up for 'music together', and made friends in the neighbourhood. Most of all I avoided splitting myself in two. I knew so many new mothers who are tugged and pulled in all directions when they go back to work too soon. This three-year leave enabled Kevin and me to establish a bond so strong I feel we can withstand anything that comes down the pike.

We have been very good, argues Hewlett, at creating 'off ramps' from the workforce. The dependency/worker ratio will force us to become better at creating 'on ramps'. Recently, Victorian nursing shortages prompted the retraining and re-employment of older nurses no longer working—to the great approval of patients, who appreciated their well-honed human skills. There is no real reason why one could not have a flourishing, thirty-year career either between the ages of around 25 to 55, or the ages around 35 to 65. A new intergenerational covenant could allow a new 'late starter' path for men or women, where time out, the most intense work of care during childbearing years, does not carry the care penalty it does now.

Other proposals recently floated in the Australian community also concern the 'gift of time'. The ACTU suggested the extension of unpaid parental leave from one to two years (in keeping with European standards) and the right to work part-time after maternity leave ends. Unpaid leave during school holiday periods, essentially a new form of part-time work, could assist parents of older children.

While this book is not, strictly speaking, a social policy book, there are many policy elements to the 'road not taken' which help resolve the tensions and dilemmas outlined.

What we must do

In family policy the state should adopt what I term 'active neutrality'. In a post-feminist age, we must reject any enforced turning back to the old breadwinner/homemaker model. But we must also reject the idea of replacing the old coercive gender contract with a coercive new gender contract. Instead, the European Parliament's recommendation that the tax system should be neutral between single- and dual-income families is much more attractive. We should reject the ambitions of gender wardens, old and new, to colonise all of womanhood.

We should reject inactive state neutrality. State neutrality is not enough if it means inaction along the lines of the indifferent shrug of 'it was her choice' which currently greets so many women in Anglo-

American nations and ensures a minimum of support. Inactive neutrality in neo-liberal societies like the USA means that pluralism exists, but the state provides minimum support for any choice. Families struggle with the vagaries of non-family-friendly, full-time work. Children go into 'kennels for kids'—poor quality childcare provided by the market—in which indices of child wellbeing grow ever more worrying.

We should respect women's and parents' preferences, which are overwhelmingly for extended leave options and home care allowances. As Mariah Evans and Jonathan Kelley have commented, after their international survey of parental preferences, given the Australian majority preference for homecare for children in the early years, it is unconscionable in a democracy not to support it. With respect to fertility, Catherine Hakim also points to the desire for larger families among adaptive and home-centred women. It makes good policy sense, therefore, not simply to pitch every benefit at the work-centred group.

We should make working time more flexible, redistributing it across the lifecycle. Nations that have already faced low fertility, as in Eastern Europe, France and Scandinavia, have experimented with policy mixes to enable women, across the life cycle, to both work and have children. The evidence from those nations shows that state- or market-provided services, like childcare and nursing homes, are not enough. In every case it has been necessary to make more flexible the existing rigidities of working time: extended parental leave, home care allowances, the six-hour day in Sweden, and in France recently, the 35-hour week.

The emerging principle behind the French and Scandinavian strategy is the fair-minded, democratic one of maternal equity—the state being studiously neutral on women's different choices. A choice is offered between a childcare place and an equivalent cash benefit as a home care allowance. The Norwegian foreign minister, Janne Matlary, described the philosophy behind a new home care allowance as 'giving freedom of choice, nothing more, nothing less'. Explicitly designed to give equity between parents at home and those at work, it prompted the fiercest ideological debate in Norway since the 1970s. Although some feminist groups opposed the idea of choice, the policy proved very popular with the electorate. Parents caring for a young child under three are now paid the equivalent of the cost of a childcare place, around $US6000 per year. Many feminist commentators, such as Jane Waldfogel, see such policies as the way of the future.

Australia's present one year of parental leave should be expanded to two years, with the eventual aim of three years. In European countries, this is the most significant policy that helps parents balance work and family and aids fertility. It recognises the importance for many women of maintaining a long-term connection with the labour force, and the problems with childcare. There are few countries which have supported high women's workforce participation without introducing extended leave. Eastern Europe had to do so. Germany, Finland, France, and Sweden all offer such leave for the child's first three years, while Denmark offers two years, Austria two years full-time or four part-time. Accompanied by greater or lower income replacement, all give the right to return to the previous job. Mothers or fathers, or some combination of both, can take a career/job break followed by a return to their old job. Longer leave enables parents to structure early childrearing without losing their attachment to the labour force.

We should reduce the number of babies aged under one in childcare. Given the risks outlined for early infant daycare, while state policy should respect choice and remain neutral by offering equivalent allowances to those at work and at home, nonetheless we should encourage parental care in the first years of life, by providing job-protected leave and some income support.

All social policies should have a gender equity aspect, honouring and respecting that 'beautiful idea' of equality between the sexes. It would be unwise, however, to impose a rigid and foolish ideological grid upon intimate matters of the heart by any forced march into the future, for example, making 'mandatory' periods of leave for men. For children having *intentional* caregiving is crucial. It is no more intelligent to force a bitterly unhappy father upon a child than an unhappy mother. Nor is male and female 'symmetry' in workforce hours necessarily a 'beautiful set of numbers' if it ignores a family life overstretched and stressed beyond endurance. Instead, we should keep the whole thing alive, fluid and supple enough to be responsive to preference. Policy should create opportunity, but then let the cards fall where they may. Julia Kristeva once put the question of difference between men and women, with just the right touch, as a story 'to be continued . . .' Thus we should frame policy not to engineer, but to support newer *negotiated* family forms of shared caregiving between men and women, by giving practical policy tools for implementing such a life. At present anyone sharing the caregiving faces a dramatically reduced income, the risk of the care penalty for both father and mother—part-time work for both during the early years being interpreted as 'lack of work commitment'. In this way we might have more people overturning the old hierarchical patterns of relations between the sexes.

The neighbourhood 'hub and spokes' model of early childhood in the community, first proposed by the Canadian early childhood specialist Fraser Mustard, has great merit. The idea is to attempt to surround *all* parents and *all* children from birth with the elements of community that are presently missing. Beginning before birth, prenatal visits to every new parent would emphasise how much the bringing of new life will be valued and supported by their community. Those initial contacts could be followed up with postnatal visits linking them to vibrant neighbourhood centres. These could draw together maternal and infant nurses, other mothers and fathers, babysitting co-ops, toy libraries, playgroups, pre-school and childcare, as well as open preschools on the Swedish model (where parents come *with* their children), as well as professional outreach services, for example linking experienced mothers with new ones.

Improving childcare quality is not just a matter of throwing more resources and money at subsidising corporate childcare. Australian early childhood specialist Sharne Rolfe, like Ron Lally and Kay Margetts (all echoing the experience of Sarah Hrdy), argues that attachment theory has been wrongly opposed to childcare. In many sensitively chosen examples, Rolfe shows that attachment research provides the best shot in our locker to improve and achieve high quality childcare. Some parents will continue to use childcare, even with decent leave programs, either because they have to (single parenthood or poverty, for example) or because they want to (particularly the well educated, affluent middle classes, professional women who pay an 'opportunity cost' by not returning early to work.) Hence, if we are to take children seriously we need to consider how the circumstances of those in care can be improved. We should further develop the parent-run community childcare centre model initially proposed by the feminist movement, and consider them as 'best practice' centres similar to the 'teaching hospital' model.

Many of the 'best practice' and most recent innovations utilise insights drawn from attachment theory. Essentially they draw on what happens when things go well in a stable family with a primary caregiver. They involve a radical reorganisation of many of our contemporary work and childcare practices. Rolfe gives an example of a young couple taking their baby to the creche and spending hours with it there, letting the environment, caregivers and even the smell and feel of the nappy change table become familiar. The child is left at first only for a few hours, to make the experience more manageable. Rolfe points out, as does Shahla Chehrazi, that the transition to childcare is much kinder to the child when gradual. As the Swedish example shows, the quantity of time children spend should be minimised—part-time care will be better than full-time, and the length of day should be shorter. It makes a huge difference to a child to be collected at 3 p.m. rather than 7 p.m.

The 'quality' of substitute care is determined not simply structural matters like ratios and caregiver turnover, although of course they matter. Children do best, according to Ron Lally, when centre size and overall size of group is small. Caregivers will need to understand attachment principles. Because so much of a child's world is mediated through relationships, because their emotional, social and cognitive development are plaited together, it is the sensitivity and responsiveness of the *relationships* which matters most. There should be a 'primary care' model; one person should look after a baby, and a second person should be assigned to each child in the event of the first being ill or absent. Those people should stay with that group until they are three. Caregiving is a highly skilled job; hence they will need to be respected and paid well or we will never improve the endemic problem of caregiver turnover. All this, of course, radically reconfigures how we 'do' childcare.

Enola Aird made an impassioned speech at the Harvard conference on maternal feminism. She argued the need for a motherhood movement not only to improve working conditions for mothers, but also to go beyond the economics to improve living conditions for all mothers and all children and embrace the value of the non-quantifiable aspects of motherhood. 'We need', said Aird, 'to value the non-measurable of loving, nurturing, and caring for children . . . We need to tame the reach of the money world and extend the reach of the mother world.'

It is children's special vulnerability in a world dominated by the assumptions of radical individualism and the money world which is captured in Christopher Lasch's comment:

> To see the modern world from the point of view of a parent is to see it in the worst possible light. This perspective unmistakably reveals the unwholesomeness, not to put it more strongly, of our way of life: our obsession with sex, violence, and the pornography of 'making it'; our addictive dependence on drugs, 'entertainment' and the evening news; our impatience with anything that limits our sovereign freedom of choice, especially with the constraints of marital and familial ties; our preference for 'non binding commitments.'

A book about motherhood cannot 'put the questions differently' unless it goes beyond the impoverished language and reasoning of the new capitalism, or of the sovereign self. Motherhood is not just a state of being experienced by a single and isolated self. Maternal time, children's time, those values of the mother world, cannot be contained within the imperatives of either the new economy or the impoverished moral vision of radical individualism. Instead, what makes motherhood so complex, intoxicating, volatile, vexing, creative, engaging, so altogether more sparkling and interesting a state of being, what constitutes the 'voluptuous, ramshackle life of the mother' is that it is not a state experienced alone by a sovereign self, but is defined by a *relationship with another.*

We are engaged, when we become mothers, in a new way of being in the world that involves another human being, where once there was merely the long shadow of the letter I. 'Caritas', 'the loving kindness' of maternal feminism, must mean the inclusion of the child's interests—and not in the old 'children first' dialogue which meant putting women last while sentimentalising their 'sacrifice'. Rather, as a society we must do what mothers do, making all those 'little peering moments of attention', which reveal the lived experience of the other. In this way we can acknowledge children's needs *as they experience them*, as the basis of reinserting the 'missing child' back into liberal theory, of jettisoning forever an impoverished liberation rhetoric about adult rights that entirely leaves out children's rights.

Those affected most deeply by our decisions are, of course, children. It is children as subjects and future citizens who make the transformations of value, attitude and policy that I have sketched here so pressing and immediate. Yet, while they are very young, at least, they are wordless. We speak on behalf of them. As a consequence we bear a heavy moral responsibility, for they are in our power. Yet they will not remain forever without words. Let it not be the case that they come to look with disbelief at what they were given in their childhood, and to stare with stony and unforgiving eyes upon the road not taken.

Postscript
Up amongst the men

When my younger child started school, some people expressed anxiety at the change ahead for me. One acquaintance, after emphasising the *huge*, *huge* changes about to occur at my transition from being down among the children, said 'I'm sure you'll be able to . . .' she paused here and made a small gulping sound, after which the words came out in a strangled gasp, '*manage something*. Perhaps helping out at kindergarten . . .'

Another peered at me, squinting as if trying to divine whether any mental life after motherhood might conceivably be left. I had a sudden image of my mental apparatus, lying like old machinery, a disused harvester perhaps, in a farmer's field somewhere in a rural rust belt, long since left to seize up and decay. My acquaintance actually used the word *rehabilitation*. It was clear people thought this would be an arduous, lengthy process.

In the event, it took about ten minutes. I had taken my younger daughter to her first day of school. I settled her in, carefully concealing my sadness that this period of our lives together had come to an end. I wept briefly on the way home. But I was also happy. I had waited long enough. When I got home I settled my coffee cup in a firm, decided gesture, cracked my knuckles a few times and sat down to write. That first school term I wrote the first essay of this book. I have been writing ever since.

That time in motherland, however, shaped everything that followed. I hope this book shows that the opposition of motherhood to serious work and thought, the supposed contradiction between art and life, is wrong. Being a mother led me to a kind of deep reflection on so many parts of human existence that would not have come to life had I not had children. If we constitute mothering as a reflective enterprise, characterise maternal thinking as distinctive and different, then it is not opposed to but energises and informs thought. It was motherhood that made me search out less conventional feminist voices who wrote about the ethic of care. Being a mother also took me in new intellectual directions. It made me see freshly the power and depth of our attachments to one another, and opened for me an entirely new, fascinating area that forms the theoretical scaffolding of the second part of this book.

I found resuming work—the work itself—a great pleasure. I am now in a different place to when I wrote my first essay. I believe with Anne Roiphe that when that period of life comes to an end it is as well 'not to have the sum of one's worth in the bank of motherhood'. There was an irony. My *writing* about family work—the realm of what Nancy Folbre calls the invisible heart—was valued far more than the family work I did.

I am very glad I wrote that essay on early motherhood, because with one adult daughter and teenage years for the other, I am light years away from the emotional place where I wrote that. I could not write it now. Psychologists quite aptly describe the mothering of young children as a period of 'holding'—holding the wellbeing of another in one's head. The intensity of that time fades and one is beset with different preoccupations, but it fades the more deeply because some fundamental process of psychological separation has occurred. I am still very close to both my daughters—which is, as Helen Garner says, 'the most precious thing'. And it is part of life's greatest pleasures to see what kind of adults one's children become. But it is quite different to the early, aching anguish of love. When I read that first essay again, I feel astonished by it, and uncomfortable with the person I was. Splinters of memory bring a flash of something into focus, and then it is gone.

To be truthful about the complex, ambivalent feelings of motherhood one must often contradict one statement with another, and leave them there, letting their proximity to each other do the work. So let the intensity of being 'down among the children' rest alongside this.

With separation there is loss and relief, sorrow and joy. My most vivid memory of my 'letting go' phase was when I took a train from Melbourne to the Sydney Olympics. (From childhood I have adored trains.) As the train rattled forward I became aware of a sensation spreading over and suffusing me. It was oddly familiar but also strange. Then I realised. Like an old snakeskin I was re-inhabiting, climbing back inside a former self who had often travelled alone. The weirdest part was realising that a certain unconscious, *readiness* to jump up and answer a need, or laugh with or give comfort or counsel or talk, to *give* attention—was absent. That capacity to change whatever one is doing and respond, openly and freely to another, to shift whatever state you are in or where one's thoughts are and be attentive, to share another's emotional state. One does not achieve that perfectly of course, ever, and as children get older, they are more and more capable of withstanding and understanding times of preoccupation—after all, they have such moments of their own. Here I was, hermetically sealed in a silver bubble spearing its way to Sydney, and that underlying readiness to give attention, that 'holding' of another in one's head, was, for the moment, completely gone. In that intimation of what they call the empty nest, I felt both a dizzying sense of freedom but also an aching sense of loss. In the steady, thrumming rhythm of wheels upon steel I could hear the sound of the future.

One friend sent her beloved son to a new secondary school and said how she had wept when she saw his 'his tender little neck' strangled for the first time by the noose of a tie. Some people made disapproving, clucking noises at her revelation. Although some maintain that we are barely scrabbling our front hooves into the turf of freedom, our back hooves forever being dragged down by the weight of a patriarchal culture into the old cult of motherhood, people often frown or look queasy when I express the emotional, connected part of motherhood that is about maternal desire and love. Their faces lighten considerably if I speak of freedom on leaving motherland, and moving into the terrain of the sovereign self. There is a look of fleeting satisfaction, as if the world has been put right again.

We are more likely to tut-tut over 'sentimentalising motherhood' than about living a motherhood lite—a kind of affectless motherhood. In the elite discourse we are more comfortable with the expression of motherhood's dark side of rage and frustration. Cynicism about mothering is especially popular. This disdain of sentimentality is interesting because sentimentality is about a distortion, a prettifying of feelings, but cynicism is really, as Daphne de Marneffe astutely notes, the flip side of sentimentality because it involves denial too. The prevailing mood of cynicism goes much deeper than the gallows humour that women use to diffuse and get through the bodily discomforts of pregnancy or early motherhood. Cynicism's sin is not distant from the great moral hazard of envy—the puncturing, spoiling impulse to make everything ugly, to drag things down into the quagmire of resentment.

I sometimes think motherlove is like sex used to be: OK for procreation in the missionary position, all jolly and healthful like a hike in the woods, but making us uncomfortable if emotion or pleasure leaks out too visibly. And there are certainly those who would like to discipline and punish transgressors who, they consider, display too much emotion, or allow it to go beyond an orderly affair within a neat compartment which does not interfere with more appropriate, respectable enterprises, like paid work.

'Oh, motherhood can be *managed*, you know,' said one friend airily, as if talking about a well-run business meeting. 'It's just a matter of keeping your boundaries intact, and organisation.'

The mysterious pleasure of everyday life

There are people, women as well as men, who are work-centred. It really is central to their identity. But I am not one of them. I heard a woman say flatly at a dinner, amongst all the Supermen and Super-women boasting about their work schedules, 'I am not an energetic person.' I felt like hugging her. Deep down I think most of work is as G.K. Chesterton described it: 'the average man has to obey orders and do nothing else. He has to put one dull brick upon another dull brick, and do nothing else; he has to add one dull figure to another dull figure, and do nothing else.'

Caitlin Flanagan says: 'I come from a family that considered home life one of the great rewards and pleasures of life . . . Look at the great books—what does Odysseus dream of? Going home. If you don't have a really great home life—if you're not loved and cared for and wanted at home—you don't have anything at all . . . work is hard and draining, and home should be a pleasure. People are so confused about this—they think work is the pleasure and home is the burden.'

I remember when my kith and kin expected that I would have an academic career, and my heart quietly sank. I remember, as an apprentice academic at a university staff meeting, looking out the window to a sky shot with blue while they had moved onward from the photocopying allowance and onto the placement of the coffee urn, and thinking, 'I can't bear this!' And later, having morning tea amongst the tweed jackets with leather patches in the History common room, listening to bright men talk about their dull books while excitedly waving sticky buns in the air, I thought again, 'I can't bear this'.

Drusilla Modejska's *Stravinsky's Lunch* is a wonderful book. It is a remarkable achievement because it is a long, truthful meditation on women and art and life—or the ethic of care—not distorted by the corrosive acid of resentment. I have often wondered whether my book was the better or worse for being done slowly, over a long time, crammed in amongst the logjam and muddle of everyday life. Several men who had wives who took care of the 'everything else' advised me to adopt the male pattern of work: just go off for six weeks or months alone somewhere and get it done. Should I have 'worked like a man', as Simone de Beauvoir might have advised?

As I finished this book I had a chance to experience Stravinsky's lunch. First both my husband and I were, by chance, working frantically to finish major bits of writing. That is not how we normally do things; usually only one of us is working intensely, balanced by the other one who is not, to look after the 'everything else'. Usually he does more work and I do a little more of the 'everything else'. But he finished his deadline and we swapped places. He did the driving, picked up and washed and shopped. My elder daughter came home to stay for a while to help out and began cooking me lunches far more delicious than I suspect Mrs Stravinsky ever managed.

In a curious way, if ever I had fantasised whether I wanted to live the life of the male artist, working all hours and having my meals brought in on a tray and people tip-toeing and shushing around me, it was answered during this time.

I hated it. I don't want to work all day every day till all hours. I don't mind a short-term panic over a deadline, but I hate being under unrelenting pressure, long term, from work. I like a varied life, in which hard work is balanced by the humble, deep and pure pleasure of everyday life.

I longed to look out over the hills in the morning, sit in the garden, take a stroll, or watch the animals eating their breakfast. I longed to pick up our younger daughter from school and hear what her day was like, to shop and cook and linger over a meal. I yearned for the spontaneity and pleasure of shared plans with my daughters. I longed for escape from the austerity of industrial time, to spend a little while doing absolutely nothing, for that blissful calm, the emptying out feeling from which a thought, an idea begins to take shape and gain momentum, as slowly, slowly, creativity begins out of nothingness and spins into the kernel of what I will write next.

Nothing seemed convivial. It was working out on a treadmill compared with taking a walk in the beautiful countryside. My agent, Margaret Connolly, says she loves coming home after a writers' festival spent rubbing shoulders with the famous, to sort out socks and think about dinner because she feels grounded again. I felt out of touch with everything, and only kept going by focussing on the thought of a future self, who would reclaim the mundane but mysterious pleasure of every-day life.

Modjeska's beautifully written book sees the tension between art and motherhood, what women do in the domestic realm, but also shows how that creativity can also come out of a female way of being in the world. In my brief Stravinsky's lunch period, I noticed with interest, my writing got rather worse.

Sometimes our 'work–family balance'——to use the rather precarious-sounding contemporary phrase——hummed along very nicely. But there were times, actually every time we got close to the contemporary ideal of the 'dual-career couple', of feeling scattered, closer and closer to chaos, life crowded out by a too-muchness. There was pleasurelessness, too, in the sensation of finishing one task only to begin another, all over again.

One day I found myself kneeling in the mud by our ancient water tank, wiggling the plug with the special tweak that it needed to make our creaking water system work. It was Thursday and I had a Friday deadline and writer's block—I very rarely experience that horrifying freeze, except if I don't have enough time to do something—and I felt I didn't have enough time to do justice to the story. My daughter's lap-top had blown up, two days before a crucial university essay, losing all her work; my younger daughter had a music exam. My husband finished university teaching and took over the laptop drama, my editor gave me two more days, I worked furiously to finish the piece, cut several thousand words, then took over the various family crises (they had multi-plied), while he wrote a newspaper column on Sunday. I forget what or how we ate.

When my knees were in the mud, fingers wrapped around that plug, I bitterly reflected that, from the outside, our life together had never been this good. Our income was higher, and we had reached the apotheosis, the veritable pinnacle of favoured contemporary family patterns, the 'dual career couple'. (Actually, it felt more like a quadruple career family, as our daughters' lives had expanded too.) Everybody who earlier felt I had been doing 'nothing' now purred with contentment; I was finally, properly, doing 'something'.

But in this outwardly satisfactory state of affairs we often felt stretched and strained, sometimes beyond endurance.

And as I knelt I had a memory.

It was from a time when we had very little money beyond essentials. When I had no idea what the future *après* motherhood might hold.

I went to the old box of photos that I now had no time to order properly, and rummaged until I found it.

It was a photo of one of our daughters, near the spot where I had knelt. She is about two and a half, dressed in an old T-shirt of mine, just one small bare shoulder poking out. She is beaming, radiant with joy and triumph. The source of her pride is the flat wicker basket she holds of freshly harvested baby peas. The peas were the first from a vegetable garden she had helped make with her father.

And I ached for that period in our lives when we had time. Time to grow peas.

Endnotes

PART ONE: Feminism and the 'problem' of motherhood

1. Two paths to women's equality

Page 22: 'As the social theorist Zygmunt Bauman reminds us', Bauman, *Life in fragments.*

Page 24: 'It can hardly be doubted . . .', Gaita, *A common humanity*, p. 72.

Page 26: 'the way in which human beings . . .', Gaita, *A common humanity*, pp. 26–7.

2. Equality as sameness: the loneliness of the postmodern cowgirl

Page 31: De Beauvoir, *The second sex*, see especially chapter 1.

Page 33: 'conscious and free individual . . .', de Beauvoir quoted in de Marneffe, *Maternal desire*, pp. 27–8.

Page 33: Friedan and de Beauvoir conversation in Sommers, *Who stole feminism*, p. 257.

Page 34: '. . .I hardly saw one affirmation of the experience . . .' It was certainly not a reflection of all women's experience, judging by the many letters and responses I received after the publication of my first chapter, from women who shared my more positive experience of mothering.

Page 35: 'intense, unrelieved hostility . . .', Reiger, 'Maternal thinking and social activism'.

Page 36: 'we will be able to assume parental roles . . .', quoted in Rossi, 'A biosocial perspective on parenting', p. 15.

Page 41: '. . . one American commentator wondered . . .', Hymowitz, 'Fear and loathing in the daycare centre'.

Page 41: 'Feminists insisted that . . . children as well', Brennan, *The politics of Australian childcare*, p. 65.

Page 41: Margaret Mead quoted in Wolgast, *Equality and the rights of woman*, p. 107.

Page 43: 'Most women today . . .', de Marneffe, *Maternal desire*, p. 11.

Page 43: 'at the beginning of my thirties . . .', Murray-Smith, 'Too late for another Everest'.

Page 43: Hochschild, *The second shift* and *The time bind*; Schor, *The overworked American*; Tanner, *Crowded lives*; Pocock, *The work/life collision.*

Page 45: Hobsbawm, *Age of extremes*, pp. 334ff.

Page 45: 'permanent temporariness of a . . .', Bauman, *Post modernity and its discontents*, p. 148.

Page 45: male responses in National Marriage Project, *The State of Our Unions*. Available at <http://marriage.rutgers.edu>.

Page 46: Swedish women still childless: see Statistics Sweden, <http://www.scb.se.eng>, Population and Welfare; Population: Population Projections; Future Fertility.

Page 46: Australian research: see Birrell & Rapson, *A not so perfect match*; Birrell, Rapson & Hourigan, *Men and women apart: partnering in Australia*.

Page 49: Hochschild, 'The commercial spirit of intimate life and the abduction of feminism', see discussion pp. 13–29.

Page 50: 'recycle the feeling rules that once applied to middle class men . . .', Hochschild, 'The commercial spirit of intimate life and the abduction of feminism', p. 27.

Page 50: Waldfogel quoted in Crittenden, *The price of motherhood*, p. 44.

3. Meeting General Custer: maternal feminism and the ethic of care

Page 55: 'The experience of falling . . .', Greer, *The whole woman*, p. 197.

Page 56: 'dressed to the nines . . .', Buhle, *Feminism and its discontents*, pp. 338–9.

Page 59: Julie Olsen Edwards quoted in Ruddick, *Maternal thinking*, p. 70.

Page 59: Iris Murdoch quoted in Ruddick, *Maternal thinking*, p. 72.

Page 60: On mothers and cheerfulness: Spinoza quoted in Ruddick, *Maternal thinking*, pp. 74ff.

Page 62: Tim Winton interview is available at <http://www.abc.net.au/enoughrope/stories/s1227915.html>.

Page 64: 'the needs of your own children . . .', Peel, *The lowest rung*, pp. 157–63.

Page 65: Myra Strober quoted in Folbre, *The invisible heart*, p. 18.

Page 66: Iris Murdoch quoted in Sommers, *Who stole feminism*, p. 78.

Page 67: 'More and more women . . .', Peel, *The lowest rung*, p. 163.

Page 67: 'on top of demeaning work . . .', Bellah et al., *Habits of the heart*, p. 111.

Page 68: Flanagan, 'The mother's dilemma'.

4. The invisible heart: the shadow economy of care

Page 69: 'Today patriarchal coercion is unacceptable . . .', Folbre, *The invisible heart*, pp. 20–1.

Page 69: Parable is from Folbre, *The invisible heart*, pp. 22–3. This chapter also uses Crittenden, *The price of motherhood*. See also Burggraff, *The feminine economy and economic man*.

Page 70: 'What a terrible title!', Crittenden spoke at the conference held at Barnard College, Harvard University, 'Maternal feminism'.

Page 71: For the figure of 59 per cent of wealth see Crittenden, *The price of motherhood*, p. 71.

Page 71: For Gary Becker's 'potty' chair see Crittenden, *The price of motherhood*, pp. 75–6; see also, however, *Growth fetish*, Clive Hamilton's astute and very necessary points about the depletion of meaning inherent in Becker's approach to family economics.

Page 71: 'the dark matter in the universe of labor', see Crittenden, *The price of motherhood*, p. 47. For the 'disappearing' of mothers' labour see chapters 3 & 4.

Page 72: 'The moral elevation of the home . . .', Folbre, 'The unproductive housewife', p. 465.

Page 72: Harriet Beecher Stowe's remarks quoted in Crittenden, *The price of motherhood*, p. 53.

Page 72: 'the "unoccupied" class', see Crittenden, *The price of motherhood*, p. 61.

Page 73: 'As a woman does not work . . .', Crittenden, *The price of motherhood*, p. 4.

Page 73: Charlotte Perkins Gilman discussed in Crittenden, *The price of motherhood*, pp. 62–3.

Page 74: 'The first argued that only one road . . .', Crittenden, *The price of motherhood*, p. 63.

Page 75: Kuttner quoted in Folbre, *The invisible heart*, p. xi. See also Kuttner, *Everything for sale*.

Page 77: 'Even if the actual decision makers . . .', Folbre, *The invisible heart*, p. 49.

Page 79: Lawrence Sommers quoted in Crittenden, *The price of motherhood*, p. 110. See discussion of women's greater investment in family in Chapter 6, 'The dark little secrets of family life', third world figures pp. 121–2. Muhammad Yunus, founder of Grameen Bank in Bangladesh, which has a system of micro-lending to women, not men, on the basis of the knowledge that women are more likely to invest it in schemes for their children's well being.

Page 80: Harriet Beecher Stowe quoted in Folbre, *The invisible heart*, p. 18.

Page 81: 'Sarah Hrdy puts her finger on the necessary point', Crittenden, *The price of motherhood*, p. 128. The quotation is Crittenden's pithy summary of Hrdy's position, but see Hrdy, *Mother nature* for full discussion.

Page 81: 'story on motherhood', Cadzow, 'Kids? What kids?' p. 20.

Page 81: 'A conception of the "equivalence" of all citizens is needed . . .', from K. Reiger, *Our bodies, our babies*, p. 288. She also makes the point that there is not much mileage in proposals for increasing breast feeding without protections for time out of the labour force, income replacement (in the form of paid leave, and flexibility in working practices).

Page 83: On French and US mothers' earnings differentials see discussions in Crittenden, *The price of motherhood* and Folbre, *The invisible heart*. Figures from Crittenden, *The price of motherhood*, p. 90.

Page 84: 'We like to think that all women have choices today . . .', from Bauchner, 'A mother's place is in the women's movement'.

Page 84: Enola Aird interviewed by Judith Stadtman Tucker of Mothers Movement Online, available at <http://www.watchoutforchildren.org>.

Page 85: 'We will work to create a movement . . .', from statement by Enola Aird at Barnard conference 'Call to a Motherhood Movement'.

5. What do women want?

Page 87: Hakim, *Key Issues in Women's Work*, p. 215.

Page 87–8: quotes taken from John Stuart Mill, *The subjection of women*, Chapter 1.

Page 89: 'One such article in 2002', Sherry, 'A media vibe based on motherhood myth'.

Page 91: Sherry quotes, 'Parenting transcends politics'.

Page 92: 'We all believed it', Hakim quoted in Arndt, 'Myths and misconceptions'.

Page 93: Peter Elias's comments quoted in Arndt, 'Myths and misconceptions'.

Page 93: For Hakim's argument see her *Work–lifestyle choices* and 'Five feminist myths about women's employment'.

Page 93: 'a radical break with the past'. In fact one can overstate the discontinuity. For example, France's fertility rate was falling in the 19th century, well before the contraceptive revolution.

Page 95: 'more than one hour a week'—see, for example, McDonald, 'Family support policy in Australia: the need for a paradigm shift', Table 1, p. 18, and Hakim, *Key Issues in Women's Work*, p. 24.

Page 95: 'In 2002, 47 per cent of working women . . .', figures from the Hon. Kevin Andrews MP, Minister for Employment and Workplace Relations, an address to the Pursuing Opportunity and Prosperity Conference, University of Melbourne, 14 November 2003.

Page 95: 'In 1998 only 8 per cent of employed mothers', Australian Bureau of Statistics, *Australian social trends 2002*, Work–National summary tables.

Page 96: 'The hours of formal childcare . . .' and 'In both 2002 and 1993', from Australian Bureau of Statistics 'Formal childcare'.

Page 96: 'Look . . . at the Stanford Class of . . .', Belkin, 'The opt-out revolution'.

Page 97: 'In 2000, of Australian families . . .', Australian Bureau of Statistics, *Labour force status and other characteristics of families*.

Page 97: Cohort studies: see Hakim, *Work–lifestyle choices* for summaries, including Gerson, *Hard Choices*; Goldin, 'Career and family'.

Page 97: 'A recent British survey', Hakim, 'Taking women seriously', pp. 1–6; see also Hakim, 'Competing family models'.

Page 98: 'models of family life', see Hakim, *Work–lifestyle choices* especially chapters 4,5,6; see also Hakim, 'Models of the family'.

Page 98: For 'egalitarians' see examples of newer egalitarian patterns in Probert, 'Gender and choice'.

Page 99: 'Ann Crittenden cites US Polls' . . . see Crittenden, *The price of motherhood*, pp. 238–9. Supporting this, Bob Birrell, a sociologist at Monash University, told me that when he surveyed his students he also found strong support for egalitarian family patterns utilising shared parental care for young children, not institutional care.

Page 99: 'Eurobarometer surveys', see Hewitt, 'Nurseries for children or time for parents', pp. 68–70, and Morgan, *Who needs parents*, pp. 110–11, on British lone parents and low desire for childcare; also Robertson, *The daycare deception*. Note also Evans & Kelley, 'Changes in public attitudes' on Australian women's preferences for their own or family care, plus the Newspoll data reported in *The Weekend Australian*, 1–2 September 2001, p. 22, showing 76 per cent of Australians believe children are better off at home with a parent than in paid childcare.

Page 99: For home care allowances see Hakim, *Work–lifestyle choices*, chapter 8, especially p, 233; also Matlary, 'Celebrating the universal declaration of human rights' and Ilmakunnus, 'Public policy and child care choice'.

Page 101: 'A survey of American parents . . .', see Belsky, 'Developmental risk (still) associated with early child care', p. 846.

Page 101: Newspoll data in 2001 reported in *The Weekend Australian*, 1–2 September 2001, p. 22.

Page 101: De Vaus 'Marriage and mental health'; see also for supporting data Linda Waite's book *The case for marriage*.

Page 102: Brown & Bifulco, 'Motherhood, employment and the development of depression: a replication of a finding?'. See also discussion in Hakim, *Work–lifestyle choices*, pp. 181–4 and her bibliography for other articles. See also discussion in James, *Britain on the couch*.

Page 103: 'To the surprise of the commission . . .', from Crittenden, *The price of motherhood*, pp. 244–5.

Page 104: 'The first generation of young mothers . . .', Einhorn, *Cinderella goes to market*, p. 35.

Page 105: 'the position of women . . .', Hakim quoted in Arndt, 'Myths and misconceptions'.

Page 106: 'others in the European commission', see Hakim, *Work–lifestyle choices*, p. 238.

Page 106: Patricia Hewitt quoted in Sylvester, 'Working mothers demand choice to stay at home'.

Page 107: 'Difference and diversity', Hakim, *Key issues in women's work*, p. 215.

Page 107: 'the exclusive focus on women's . . .', Hakim, *Work–lifestyle choices*, p. 126 plus footnote 18 on that page.

PART TWO: Taking children seriously

6. Taking children seriously

Page 111: Simone Weil quoted in Gaita, *A common humanity*, p. 104.

Page 111: Winnicott, *Home is where we start from*, p. 40.

Page 113: 'long nightmare from which . . .', De Mause, *The history of childhood*.

Page 113–14: quotes from Schor, *The overworked American*, pp. 91–3.

Page 114: quotes from Degler, *At odds: women and the family from the revolution to the present*.

Page 115: 'It is not unreasonable to emphasise . . .', quoted in Ochiltree, *Effects of child care on young children: forty years* research, p. 17. The quotation is from Lamb & Sternberg, 'Socio cultural perspectives on nonparental childcare'.

Page 116: 'Fiona Stanley spent her time . . .', see interviews *Enough rope with Andrew Denton*.

Page 116: Commission on Children at Risk, *Hardwired to connect*.

Page 117: For Bettelheim's life see Sutton, *Bruno Bettelheim*.

Page 118: 'explodes our sentimental notions . . .', Clendinnen, 'The crack in the teapot: reading Hilary Mantel'.

Page 118: Shengold, *Soul murder: the effects of childhood abuse and deprivation*, pp. 192–3.

Page 119: 'Your home might have been far from perfect . . .', Orwell, 'Such, such were the Joys', pp. 331–69; see also analysis in Shengold, pp. 4–6.

Page 121: 'At the age of eight, Bowlby . . .', Karen, *Becoming attached*, p. 31. See also Holmes, *John Bowlby and attachment theory* for biographical details, p. 16.

Page 121: Elsa First is quoted on back cover of Bowlby, *Attachment and loss, vol 2; separation: anxiety and anger*.

Page 122: 'But wait a moment . . .', Hrdy, *Mother nature*.

Page 122: Gay Ochiltree, for example in her *Effects of childcare on young children: forty years research*, claims that Bowlby said mothers and children should not be separated for first 5 years of life. This is false. She also confuses him with a Freudian—when his work represents a substantial break with Freud.

Page 123: 'Deborah Brennan . . . is one of the few to get this right . . .', Brennan, *The politics of Australian childcare*, p. 59.

Page 124: William James quoted in Bowlby, *Attachment and loss, vol 2; separation, anxiety and anger*, p. 31.

Page 124: For a pithy summation of early work on maternal deprivation by Bender, Levy & Spitz, see Karen, *Becoming attached*, chapter 1.

Page 124: Stella Chess quoted in Karen. Karen himself said, 'they appear to lack any feelings for others at all . . .'. Loretta Bender said, 'The children displayed incorrigible behaviour problems . . .'. All quotes from Karen, *Becoming attached*, pp. 17–18.

Page 125: An account of his troubled relationship with Melanie Klein is in Karen, *Becoming attached*, chapter 3. Karen points out that while Bowlby rejected much of Klein's approach, she did have an impact on his imaginative evocation of the passionate intensity of a very young child's emotional life, and the centrality of mourning in response to loss. I would add that his early life prepared him unconsciously for receptivity and sensitivity to such a theme.

Page 125: Riviere quoted in Karen, *Becoming attached*, p. 32.

Page 126: 'I was forbidden by Melanie Klein to talk to this poor woman . . .', Bowlby interviewed by Karen, *Becoming attached*, pp. 45–6. For a more sympathetic and recent evaluation see Eagle, *Recent developments in psychoanalysis*. See also Fonagy, *Attachment theory and psychoanalysis*; Stern, *The interpersonal world of the infant*; and Kumin, *Pre-object relatedness*.

Page 127: 'None of them seemed . . .', are Robert Karen's words; see Karen, *Becoming attached*, p. 55, 'Behind the mask of indifference' is Bowlby's description, cited by Karen, p. 54.

Page 128: On Robertson and the separation studies see Bowlby, *Attachment and loss, vol 2; separation: anxiety and anger*, Robertson & Robertson, *Separation and the very young*. There is a superb account of all the debates in Karen, *Becoming attached*, chapter 6. Robertson's films are cited in Karen's bibliography.

Page 128: '. . .were overwhelmed . . .', from Robertson & Robertson, *Separation and the very young*, p. 11.

Page 129: 'I could hardly believe it was the same wee darling boy . . .', Karen, *Becoming attached*, p. 71.

Page 130: 'They searched bags and stuffed chocolate into their mouths . . .', Robertson & Robertson, *Separation and the very young*, p. 15.

Page 130: Mary described in Karen, *Becoming attached*, p. 75.

Page 130: 'The active physical movements diminish . . .', Bowlby, *Attachment and loss, vol 1; attachment*, p. 27.

7. First love: its light and shadow

Page 134: Anselm von Feurbach, *Kasper Hauser*, quoted in Shengold, *Soul murder*, p. 17.

Page 134: . . . *The Early Years Study* . . . This point is also made in *Hardwired to connect* report (Commission on Children at Risk et al.).

Page 135: Ron Lally, in interview with Jennifer Byrne *The 7.30 Report*, 6 November 1998, made this point based on US research; see also Schore, *Affect regulation and the origin of the self*.

Page 137: Photo of Freud and painting by Mary Cassatt in Schore, *Affect regulation and the repair of the self*, p. 5. Mary Cassatt's painting also graces the cover of Stern, *The interpersonal world of the infant*.

Page 137: There is no such thing as a baby see 'The fate of the transitional object' in Clare Winnicott et al. *Psycho-analytic explorations*, p. 54.

Page 138: 'the popular, romantic—and unverified . . .', first came from Klaus & Kennell, *Maternal–Infant bonding*; see Hrdy's useful discussion of this point in *Mother nature*, pp. 491ff, also her criticisms of Eyer, *Mother–infant bonding*, and Eyer, *Motherguilt*. See also Karen, *Becoming attached*, p. 453 note 8, for overstatement on bonding after birth.

Page 138: Mary Ainsworth interviewed in Karen, *Becoming attached*, p. 132.

Page 140: Mary Ainsworth quoted in Karen, *Becoming attached*, p. 146.

Page 141: 'avoidant babies were just as stressed', see Grossmann, 'Evolution and history of attachment research', pp. 111–13.

Page 141: '. . . already by the age of twelve months . . .', Bowlby, *A secure base*, p. 132.

Page 141: '. . . behaviour on reunion . . .', see Belsky, 'Developmental risks associated with infant daycare', pp. 44–5 and Siegel, *The developing mind*, p. 73.

Page 142: Leah Albersheim cited in Karen, *Becoming attached*, p. 180.

Page 143: van den Boom, 'Sensitivity and attachment', reported in Karen, *Becoming attached*, p. 304. See also her articles 'The influence of temperament and mothering on attachment and exploration: an experimental manipulation of sensitive responsiveness among lower class mothers with irritable infants' and 'Sensitivity and attachment: next steps for developmentalists'.

Page 144: 'Sroufe and his colleagues . . .', see Karen, *Becoming attached*, pp. 193–4, and Troy & Sroufe, 'Victimisation among preschoolers: role of attachment relationship theory'.

Page 145: Sroufe's comments on developing empathy in children in Karen, *Becoming attached*, pp. 194–5;199.

Page 147: For internal working models of the self see Bowlby, *Attachment and loss vol 1*, chapter 3. A simple outline is to be found in Karen, *Becoming attached*, chapter 15; see also Holmes, *John Bowlby and attachment theory*, pp. 78–9.

Page 147: 'Repeated Interactions which are Generalised', Stern, *The interpersonal world of the infant*, pp. 97–8; 114–19.

Page 147: '. . . reflects the child's relationship history . . .', Karen, *Becoming attached*, p. 205.

Page 147: '. . . a poor guide to reality . . .', Karen, *Becoming attached*, pp. 206ff.

Page 148: For the micro world of the infant see Stern *The interpersonal world of the infant* and *The motherhood constellation*, and Karen *Becoming attached*, chapter 23.

Page 148: '. . . the world of intimate communication . . .', Karen, *Becoming attached*, p. 347.

Page 148: 'Gazing is a potent form . . .', Stern, *The interpersonal world of the infant*, p. 21; see also Schore, *Affect regulation and the origin of the self*; and Schore, *Affect regulation and the repair of the self*, chapter 1.

Page 150: 'It is clear that interpersonal communion . . .', Stern, *The interpersonal world of the infant*, pp. 151–2.

Page 153: Emotional regulation and the origin of the self, see Schore *Affect regulation and the origin of the self*; *Affect dysregulation and disorders of the self*; *Affect regulation and the repair of the self* on the neurobiology of attachment patterns and effects on brain.

Page 154: '. . . in mutual gaze . . .', Schore, *Affect regulation and the repair of the self*, p. 14.

Page 154: 'sparkling eyed pleasure . . .', cited in Schore, *Affect regulation and the origin of the self*, p. 90.

Page 155: Felicity De Zulueta, *The traumatic roots of destructiveness*, pp. 192–3; see Myron Hofer 'Hidden regulators', p. 8; Van der Kolk et al., *Traumatic Stress*, p. 191.

Page 155: '. . . stable instability . . .', see Fonagy, 'Thinking about thinking', pp. 639–56. On ADHD see Halasz (ed.), Cries unheard; also Neven et al., *Rethinking ADHD*.

Page 155: 'If human infants . . . every other issue', Guntrip, *Psychoanalytic theory, therapy and the self*, p. 114.

Page 156: 'Man and woman power . . .', Bowlby, *A secure base*, pp. 2–3.

8. The dark side of the moon

Page 158: '. . . if a child feels no emotional attachment . . .', Perry cited in Karr-Morse & Wiley, *Ghosts from the nursery*, p. 199.

Page 158: For Kathleen Folbigg see contemporary newspaper coverage, plus Benns, *When the bough breaks*.

Page 159: 'I begged and pleaded with her . . .', Knowles, 'The girl who grew to kill'.

Page 160: 'Her foster-mother said . . .', Creer & Masters, 'The Folbigg murders'.

Page 163: 'Thank fuck that's over . . .', Glendinning, 'Folbigg baby coughed before dying, court told'.

Page 163: 'Did I cry on the right spot . . .' Benns, *When the bough breaks*, p. 208.

Page 164: 'incapacity to develop . . .' Benns, *When the bough breaks*, pp. 310–11.

Page 167: Californian Chowchilla kidnapping see Karr-Morse & Wiley, *Ghosts from the nursery*, pp. 153–6.

Page 167: Bruce Perry quoted in Karr-Morse & Wiley, *Ghosts from the nursery*, p. 162.

Page 168: Bruce Perry quoted in Karr-Morse & Wiley, *Ghosts from the nursery*, p. 199.

Page 169: Solzhenitsyn quoted in Appelbaum, *Gulag*.

Page 169: Mary Main quoted in Hopkins, 'Failure of the holding relationship', pp. 188–9.

Page 169: Videotapes described by Bowlby, *A secure base*, p. 55.

Page 170: '. . . hunched her upper body', Main & Solomon, 'Discovery of an insecure-disorganised/disorientated attachment pattern', pp. 188–9.

Page 170: Abused and neglected children, see Schore, *Affect dysregulation and disorders of the self*, p. 299.

Page 173: '. . . a dismissing mother . . .', Karen, *Becoming attached*, p. 365.

Page 174: 'a mother who's felt controlled . . .', Karen, *Becoming attached*, p. 367.

Page 175: Bowlby quotes, *A secure base*.

Page 176: 'however she may accomplish it . . .', Bowlby, *A secure base*, pp. 134–5.

Page 178: For Tronick's still face experiments, see Stern, *The motherhood constellation*, p. 102.

Page 179: 'Little Miss Sparkle Plenty', Stern, *The interpersonal world of the infant*, pp. 197ff.

Page 179: For maternal depression see above plus Murray, 'Personal and social influences on parenting and adult adjustment' pp. 41ff and Pound, 'Hope in the inner city', pp. 62ff.

Page 179: Leupnitz, *The family interpreted*. See also Holmes, *John Bowlby and attachment theory*, chapter 3 esp pp. 45–8 for feminist critiques.

Page 179: 'I want to emphasise that . . .', Bowlby, *A secure base*, p. 2.

Page 180: '. . . it is not only the physical . . .', in Pound, 'Attachment and maternal depression', p. 120; see also her essay 'Hope in the inner city'.

Page 181: On support networks and spousal relationships see Belsky & Nezworski, *The clinical implications of attachment*, pp. 41–94; see also Isabella, *Infant behaviour and development*.

Page 181: '. . . he's never noticed . . .', see Nezworski, Tolan & Belsky, 'Intervention in insecure infant attachment', p. 373.

Page 182: On need for early intervention, Schore, *Affect dysregulation and disorders of the self*, pp. 303ff.

Page 182: see McCain & Mustard, *The early years study*, for very useful suggestions.

9. Electing a new child: truth, lies and the childcare debate

Page 185: 'It is truism', from Robertson, *The daycare deception, what the child care establishment isn't telling us*, p. 42.

Page 185: Penelope Leach quoted in Buxton, *Ending the mother war*, p. 101.

Page 186: Edgar quoted in Manne, 'Zealots creche and burn in childcare defence'. Margetts's research reported in *The Age*, 22 May 2002, and on Australian Broadcasting Corporation (ABC) *The 7.30 Report*, 22 May 2002, 'Childcare research ignites fresh debate'. The reaction from researchers is from my personal communication with Margetts.

Page 186: 'Swedish policy, . . . which provides . . .', Wolcott & Glezer, *Work and family life: achieving integration*.

Page 187: '. . . context of a culture . . .', Buxton, *Ending the mother war*, p. 131.

Page 188: '. . . the sheer inconvenience in practical life . . .', Bowlby, *Attachment and loss, vol 2; separation: anxiety and anger*, p. 24.

Page 189: For Michael Leunig see Macken interview.

Page 189: 'What does a child feel . . .' Leunig quoted in Loane, *Who cares?*, p. 7.

Page 191: 'No such views have been expressed by me . . .', Bowlby quoted in Hrdy, *Mother nature*, p. 495.

Page 192: On quality of care, see also summary in Greenspan, *The four-thirds solution*, pp. 27–30; also Brazelton & Greenspan *The irreducible needs of children*; also Gerhardt, *Why love matters*.

Page 192: 'Pettit resigned her job . . .', Loane, *Who cares?*, pp. 326–8.

Page 192: '. . . found mediocrity predominated . . .', Loane, *Who cares*, pp. 145–52.

Page 192: '. . . a license for neglect . . .', Belsky personal communication to author regarding quality of care, 6 June 2005.

Page 193: '. . . no one's definition of high quality care . . .', Lally, interview on *The 7.30 Report*.

Page 193: 'the turnover rate . . .', Commonwealth Child Care Advisory Council (Australia), *Child care: beyond* 2001, executive summary.

Page 193: A 2004 *Background Briefing* report . . . Tooth, 'Child-care profits'.

Page 194: 'There isn't a scrap of evidence'. . .', Ian Roberts quoted in Buxton, *Ending the mother war*, pp. 121, 124.

Page 195: An often-cited 'fact' . . . this figure has now bumped up to $1 invested to $17 return <http://www.highscope.org/Research/PerryProject/perrymain.htm> and for cost benefit analysis <http://www.highscope.org/Research/PerryProject/Perry-SRCD-2003.pdf>.

Page 196: On higher cortisol in daycare children see Watamura et al., 'Morning-to-afternoon increases in cortisol concentrations' and Dettling et al., 'Cortisol levels of young children in full-day childcare centres'.

Page 196: 'at childcare 35 per cent . . .', Watamura et al., 'Morning-to-afternoon increases in cortisol concentrations' and Dettling et al., 'Cortisol levels of young children in full-day childcare centres'.

Page 196: Cortisol findings from Watamura et al., 'Morning-to-afternoon increases in cortisol concentrations'.

Page 197: 'Although there is currently no evidence . . .' Watamura et al., 'Morning-to-afternoon increases in cortisol concentrations'.

Page 197: 'New Australian research . . .', Sims et al., 'Children's well being in childcare'.

Page 199: on Joint Attention Sequences research see Nyland, 'The Australian child-care centre as a developmental niche'; also Rolfe et al., 'Quality in infant care: observations on joint attention'.

Page 200: 'half of the attempts . . .', Nyland, 'The Australian child-care centre as a developmental niche'.

Page 200: Berthelsen's research reported in Arndt, 'The chilling truth about childcare'.

Page 200: Trudy Marshall reported in Buxton, *Ending the mother war*, p. 120.

Page 204: Ochiltree on affective neutrality and Nordic expert and 'emotional outbursts', *Effects of child care on young children*, p. 113.

Page 208: In a 1995 study of high quality Italian daycare . . . , Fein, 'Infants in group care: patterns of despair and detachment', pp. 261–75.

Page 210: On parental leap of faith see Loane, *Who cares?*, ch 6 especially pp. 158–62.

Page 211: 'Greenspan used the same analogy . . .', Greenspan *The four-thirds solution*, p. 182.

Page 211: On Scarr's conflict of interest, Robertson, *The daycare deception*, pp. 105–10.

Page 212: 'Multiple attachments to others . . .', Scarr quoted in Robertson, *The daycare deception*, p. 109; quote is from Scarr, 'Research on day care should spur a new look at old ideas'.

Page 212: 'not be permitted', Scarr quoted in Robertson, The daycare deception, p. 110; quote is from Scarr, 'Research on day care should spur a new look at old ideas'.

Page 215: 'Psychologists must refuse . . .', Silverstein in Ochiltree, *Forty years research*, p. 116.

10. The childcare wars . . . resolved

Page 216: Jay Belsky quoted in Garrison, 'Researchers in child-care study clash over findings'; also quoted in Robertson, *The daycare deception*, p. 58.

Page 216: June Wangman in Arndt, 'Is childcare the new tobacco?'.

Page 217: '. . . the new data . . .' Karen, *Becoming attached*, p. 322.

Page 217: '. . . this study reflected a more anxious and angry child . . .', Rubenstein & Howes quoted in Belsky, 'Developmental risks associated with infant daycare', p. 53.

Page 217: '. . . I felt like a pretzel . . .', Sheryl Gay Stolberg, 'Public lives'; also cited Robertson, *The daycare deception*, p. 42.

Page 217: 'All of a sudden I realised . . .', Karen, *Becoming attached*, p. 322.

Page 217: Edward Zigler's doubts about infant daycare in Karen, *Becoming attached*, p. 325; see also Zigler & Frank, *The parental leave crisis* and Zigler & Lang, *Child care choices*.

Page 218: 'Now I walk through a meeting like a ghost ...', Belsky quoted in Karen *Becoming attached*, p. 332.

Page 218: 'American universities ... wouldn't have me ...', Legge, 'The voice that won't be silent'.

Page 219: Richie Poulton quoted in Legge 'The voice that won't be silent'; Eleanor Szanton quoted in Karen, *Becoming attached*, p. 333.

Page 219: debates between Belsky and Clarke-Stewart, see Belsky's articles: 'Infant daycare: a cause for concern?'; 'Developmental risks associated with infant daycare: attachment insecurity, non-compliance and aggression'; 'Consequences of childcare for children's development: a deconstructionist view'; and these by Clarke-Stewart: 'The "effects" of infant daycare reconsidered', and 'Infant daycare: maligned or malignant?'.

Page 219: 'I wanted to find that childcare was good ....', Alison Clarke-Stewart quoted in Robertson, *The daycare deception*, p. 58. She spoke to Zoellner, 'Daycare: study on putting your kids in daycare'.

Page 219: for figures on insecurity of attachment see Clarke-Stewart, 'Infant daycare: maligned or malignant?'.

Page 219: '... children who have been in daycare ...', Clarke-Stewart, 'Infant daycare: maligned or malignant?', p. 269.

Page 219: For 'precocious independence' and following discussion see Belsky, 'Developmental risks associated with infant daycare', p. 50.

Page 220: reviews of evidence (multi-study investigations) on attachment security: Belsky & Rovine, 'Non maternal care in the first year of life and the security of infant–parent attachment'; Clarke-Stewart, 'Infant daycare: maligned or malignant?'; Lamb, 'Nonmaternal care and the security of infant–mother: a reanalysis of the data'.

Page 221: For some of the other studies showing similar problems: Bates et al., 'Child-care history and kindergarten adjustment'; Goldberg et al., 'Employment and achievement'; Barglow et al., 'Effects of maternal absence'; Barglow et al., 'Offspring of Working Mothers'; Park et al., 'Infant child care patterns'; Youngblade et al., 'The effects of early maternal employment'.

Page 222: On problematic outcomes for extensive infant daycare experience, see summary of evidence in NICHD, 'Does amount of time spent in child care predict socioemotional adjustment during the transition to kindergarten?'; also Belsky, 'Developmental risks (still) associated with early child care', and, 'Quantity counts'.

Page 222: 'Even in Scandinavia the link was found ...', Borge & Melhuish, 'A longitudinal study of childhood behaviour problems, maternal employment, and day care in a rural Norwegian community'.

Page 222: on positive outcomes for children with extensive infant daycare experience: Joshi & Verropoulou, *Maternal employment and child outcomes*; Field, 'Quality infant day-care and grade school behavior and performance'; Harrison & Ungerer, 'Maternal employment and infant–mother attachment security at 12 months postpartum'.

Page 223: 'The study, which began in 1990 ...', NICHD, 'Familial factors associated with characteristics of nonmaternal care for infants'; NICHD, 'The effects of infant child care on infant–mother attachment security'; NICHD, 'Early child care and self-control, compliance and problem behaviour at 24 and 36 months'; NICHD, 'Child care and mother–child interaction in the first 3 years of life'.

Page 223: On infant attachment security see NICHD, 'The effects of infant child care on infant–mother attachment security'.

Page 223: For cognitive benefits of higher quality care, see NICHD, 'Does amount of time spent in child care predict socioemotional adjustment during the transition to kindergarten?'; also NICHD, 'The relation of child care to cognitive and language development'.

Page 223: For early childcare as 'risk factor' and for longer hours in care, see NICHD, 'Child care and mother–child interaction'; also NICHD, 'Child care and family predictors'.

Page 224: On the 2001 controversy see Robertson's chapter 2, 'An intolerable truth', in *The daycare deception*.

Page 224: For evidence on behavioural problems see NICHD, 'Does amount of time spent in child care'.

Page 224: '. . . not only that children with more hours of care . . .', from the NICHD draft paper in 2001 on quantity of childcare: 'Further explorations of the detected effects of quantity of early child care on socioemotional adjustment', NICHD Early Child Care Research Network, and see also final, peer reviewed, published version in NICHD, 'Does amount of time spent in child care predict socioemotional adjustment during the transition to kindergarten?. Note that the final published paper did not differ in its results from the draft paper, from which the controversy blew up, i.e. peer review could not alter or sanitise the data!

Page 225: On intellectual property passing from NICHD network to Belsky see Garrison, 'Researchers in child-care study'; also Robertson's account in Horin, 'Childcare gatekeepers', in which findings were alluded to as if Belsky was the sole researcher.

Page 225: For Sarah Friedman's accusation, see Sweeny, 'Jay Belsky doesn't play well with the others'.

Page 225: Sarah Friedman's comments to Japanese policy makers were made at a symposium entitled 'The child care paradox: choices in children's development-support for working mothers by learning from the NICHD study of early child care', hosted by the Childcare Research Network in Japan on 9 July 2000, available at <http://www.childresearch.net/RESOURCE/PRESEN/2000/SYMPO2000/KEYNOTE1.HTM>.

Page 226: See Manne, 'For our children's sake?' for summary of responses. Sarah Wise is quoted in Arndt, 'Is childcare the new tobacco?'.

Page 226: 'Two years ago . . .', Jay Belsky gave me permission to quote from this e-mail from Belsky to his colleagues. See also Belsky 'Sorry, but there is bad news on childcare'.

Page 227: For American comments on the aggression controversy see Robertson, *The daycare deception*, pp. 51–5.

Page 227: 'When considered collectively . . .', NICHD 'Early childcare and children's development in the primary grades', p. 30.

Page 227: on school readiness Brooks-Gunn et al., 'Maternal employment and child cognitive outcomes in the first three years of life: the NICHD study of early child care'.

Page 228: van Ijzendoorn et al., 'Does more non-maternal care lead to aggression', p. 2.

Page 228: Sarah Wise quoted in Arndt, 'Putting a spin on research'.

Page 229: British research by Melhuish et al., 'Social/behavioural and cognitive development'; also Sammons et al., 'Measuring the impact'.

Page 229: Information on new British studies also taken from Malik, 'Analysis: catch them young?' a discussion with Ed Melhuish, Sue Gerhardt and J. Belsky, BBC Radio 4, current affairs.

Page 229: 'picks his words carefully . . .', Bunting, 'Nursery tales'.

Page 229: '. . . the trends being observed . . .', from Bunting, 'Fear on nursery care forces rethink'.

Page 229: Oxford University study reported in Rumbelow, 'Maternity pay increase plan angers employers'.

Page 229: 'We know from research . . .', Bunting, 'Nursery tales'.

Page 230: parent on Rush Limbaugh reported by Legge, 'The voice that won't be silent'.

Page 230: On a 'real problem' see Sylvester, 'Working mothers demand choice to stay at home'.

Page 230: 'I am delighted . . .', from Griffith, 'If you want what's best, wait until she's two'.

Page 231: '. . . tax policies should support families . . .', from Belsky, 'Developmental risks (still) associated with early child care', p. 860.

Page 231: 'for the first 18 months . . .', Bunting, 'Nursery tales'.

Page 232: 'the four-thirds model', see Greenspan, *The four-thirds solution*.

Page 233: '[this] is the point whereby . . .', Schore, quoted in Carroll interview.

Page 233: 'introducing him to daycare . . .', Crittenden, *The price of motherhood*, p. 239ff.

Page 234: '. . . the Environment of Evolutionary Adaptiveness (EEA), were perishingly harsh . . .', see Belsky, 'Modern evolutionary theory and patterns of attachment', p. 142.

Page 234: '. . . patterns of rearing . . .', Belsky quoted in Hrdy, *Mother nature*, p. 525.

Page 234: '. . . it might be highly adapative . . .', Hrdy, *Mother nature*, p. 525.

Page 235: 'Kids are not that fragile . . .', Harris, *The nurture assumption*, p. 351.

PART THREE: Hard times: motherhood under the new capitalism

Page 237: Smiley, 'Money, marriage & monogamy'.

11. Affluenza: the new ethic of work and spend

Page 242: '. . . families with incomes of over $2000 per week . . .', see Australian Bureau of Statistics, *Labour force status and other characteristics of families*, and Australian Bureau of Statistics, Child Care.

Page 242: 'In America . . .', see Gill, *Posterity lost*; and Hakim, *Work–lifestyle choices in the 21st century*, p. 233 also notes that usage of home care allowances rather than childcare in Finland was twice as high among low-earning mothers compared to high-earning mothers, see Ilmakunnus, 'Public policy and child care choice'.

Page 244: 'Individualism and choice are supposed . . .', Giddens, *The third way: the renewal of social democracy*, p. 15.

Page 245: 'the presence of children . . .', Dwyer, 'The real face of Australian wealth'.

Page 245: Karl Marx quoted in Frank, Luxury fever, p. 122, see also Frank & Cook, *The winner take-all society*.

Page 246: On Australian millionaires, D'Souza 'Luxury fever'. For American millionaires see Frank, *Luxury fever*.

Page 247: On housing size see Lacey, 'Size does matter'; also Hamilton, 'Overconsumption in Australia'.

Page 247: 'Hamilton has some other arresting examples . . .', see Hamilton, *Growth fetish* and 'Overconsumption in Australia'.

Page 248: 'Real incomes in Australia have risen . . .', Hamilton cited in Denniss, 'Australia's affluence, consumption trends and indicators of progress'.

Page 249: 'Family income growth in America . . .', Faux & Mishel, 'Inequality and the global economy', p. 102; on Australian overwork see also Hamilton, *Growth Fetish*, pp. 157ff and *Overconsumption in Australia*, p. 8, who links overwork to overconsumption.

Page 249: On growth of income inequality, see Hutton & Giddens, *On the edge*, pp. 101ff.

Page 250: Hugh Mackay quoted in Leser, 'The lost men'.

Page 251: Manuel Castells cited by Sennett, *The corrosion of character*, p. 93.

Page 251: Figures on male employment see Leser, 'The lost men'.

Page 251: Cheryl Kernot on unemployed men over 45 in Leser, 'The lost men'.

Page 251: Drake personnel, October 1999 report cited in Leser, 'The lost men'.

Page 251: Smith Family study: Harding & Szukalska, 'Financial disadvantage in Australia—1999'.

Page 252: Linda Hancock quoted in Payten, 'Gen X destined to rent forever'. See also Wulff, 'Out with the old and in with the new?'.

Page 252: Anthony Clare quoted in Franks, *Having none of it*, p. 72.

Page 254: Those earning over $100,000 . . . , Denniss, 'Annual leave in Australia'.

Page 254: Economic commentator Ross Gittins, 'Strictly 9 to 5. That's most of us at work'.

Page 254: 'Over the past decade . . .' a British employee of a multinational quoted in Franks, *Having none of it*, pp. 85–6.

Page 255: Nietzsche cited in Beck, *The brave new world of work*, p. 61.

Page 255: quotes from Beck, *The brave new world of work*, pp. 11–13.

Page 257: Time-use expert cited in Schor, *The overworked American*, p. 23.

12. The making of the New Capitalist Mother

Page 258: Stephens, 'Beyond binaries in motherhood research', p. 97.

Page 258: Karl Marx: The communist manifesto in Tucker, *The Marx–Engels reader*.

Page 259: Costello's blunt message . . . Uren, 'Costello: get mums working'.

Page 259: 'the luxury our world does not permit', Crittenden, *The price of motherhood*, p. 5.

Page 259: 'anxiety ridden self-improvement', Stephens, 'Beyond binaries in motherhood research', p. 96.

Page 259: 'I feel shame . . .', interviewee to Barbara Pocock cited in Stephens, 'Beyond binaries in motherhood research', p. 97.

Page 260: Pocock puts it very well, 'Those who respect full time mothering', Pocock, *The work/life collision*, p. 89.

Page 260: 'Being fit and in control . . .', Australian study cited in Stephens, 'Beyond binaries in motherhood research', p. 97.

Page 260: working mothers' comments in Probert, 'Gender and choice'.

Page 260: 'lifetime earnings would be . . .', Joshi, cited in Benn, *Madonna and child*, p. 61.

Page 261: Margaret Thatcher in an interview with British celebrity doctor Miriam Stoppard, Benn, *Madonna and child*, p. 42.

Page 262: '. . . an important part of being . . .', Hansen, *Mother without child*, p. 21.

Page 262: 'Male-styled careers . . .', Hochschild, *The commercialisation of intimate life*, p. 13.

Page 262: 'Here are a few things . . .', van Ogtrop in Hanauer, *The bitch in the house*, pp. 161–2.

Page 262: Peter Berger et al., *The homeless mind*, esp. chapter 1.

Page 264: 'As one notable feminist . . .', Stephens, 'Motherhood and the market,' p. 35.

Page 267: declining parental time, Buxton, *Ending the mother war*, p. 87; critique of Gershuny pp. 87–8; 'My own would rather have me around all day . . .', p. 88.

Page 268: Ray Kroc quoted in Ritzer, *The McDonaldisation of society*, p. 42.

Page 269–70: Gerry Harvey and Lisa Gasiz reported in Bagnall, 'Unwilling child care conspirators'.

Page 271: 'As a new mother . . .', Benn, *Madonna and child*, p. 65.

Page 272: Kate Tully quoted in Loane, *Who cares?*, p. 41.

Page 272: Dr Susan Taryan quoted in Bagnall, 'Unwilling child care conspirators'.

Page 274: Drago & Tseng, 'Family structure, usual and preferred work hours and egalitarianism'.

Page 274: 'The phenomenon of "Don't Disturb Daddy" ... ', Orbach & Eichenbaum, What do women want?, pp. 56–7.

Page 275: 'Fathers are much more involved ...', Flanagan 'The mother's dilemma'.

Page 275: 'I am also reminded of Ulrich Beck's point ...', Beck, *The brave new world of work*.

Page 277: Naomi Wolf quote from Flanagan, 'Am I exploiting my nanny? Exchanges between Caitlin Flanagan, Sara Mosle, and Barbara Ehrenreich' on *Slate* at <http://slate.msn.com/id/2095545/entry/2095648/>.

Page 278–9: Ehrenreich, *Nickel and dimed*; see also her essay 'Maid to order'.

Page 279–80: Hochschild, 'Global care chains and emotional surplus value'.

13. The McDonaldisation of childhood

Page 282: [McDonald's] 'has done everything ...', Ritzer, *The McDonaldisation of society*, p. 42.

Page 283: '... the self was placed in confinement, its emotions controlled and its spirit subdued ...', from Ronald Takaki cited in Ritzer, *The McDonaldisation of society*, p. 25.

Page 284: 'There is a broader unease ...', Leach, *Children first*, p. 22.

Page 287: '... the spiralling strands of development that transform helpless newborns ...', Leach, *Children first*, p. 83.

Page 288: On ABC Learning, see Tooth, 'Child-care profits'.

Page 289: Caroline Fewster in Tooth, 'Child-care profits'.

Page 290: 'In one survey of New South Wales childcare students ...', Loane, *Who cares?*, p. 302.

Page 290: 'I don't think it's appropriate or OK ...', Pam Cahir in Tooth, 'Child-care profits'.

Page 291: Prue Walsh quoted in Loane, *Who cares?*, pp. 257–9.

Page 291: John Tainton quoted in Loane, *Who cares?*, pp. 125–6.

Page 291: 'Chinese babies at creche ...', Lamb, et al. *Child care in context*, see figure 11.5 Group Potty Training at the Radio and TV factory, Shanghai, p. 383, quote p. 382.

Page 292: 'liberation rhetoric' in Bauman, *Postmodernity and its discontents*, p. 146.

Page 292: 'I know it's not the right thing to do ...', Loane, *Who cares?*, p. 84.

Page 294: 'The grieving of a baby ...', Leach, *Children first*, p. 87.

Page 295: 'His first question every morning ...', Loane, *Who cares?*, p. 81.

Page 295: 'Some parents ...', Loane, *Who cares?*, p. 162.

Page 297: '... there were significant differences ...', Morgan, *Who needs parents?*, p. 33, reporting Melhuish; 'Research on daycare for young children in the United Kingdom'.

Page 298: Early childhood specialists Faye Pettit and Antoinette Cross quoted in Loane, *Who cares?*, p. 82.

Page 301: 'If you are going to leave your baby', Brazelton, *Working and caring*, p. 98.

Page 302: 'When the moral basis of life's meaning becomes so restricted and insecure . . .', Marris, 'The social construction of uncertainty'.

Bibliography

Abrams, Rebecca, 'Nurseries are safe and secure—but are they bad for your baby?', *The Daily Telegraph*, Weekend Section, 7 June 2003

Ainsworth, Mary, *Infancy in Uganda, infant care and the growth of love*, John Hopkins University Press, Baltimore, 1967

Ainsworth, Mary, M. C. Blehar, E. Waters & S. Wall, *Patterns of attachment: a psychological study of the strange situation*, Lawrence Erlbaum Associates, Hillsdale New Jersey, 1978

Aird, Enola, interviewed by Judith Stadtman Tucker of Mothers Movement Online. Available at <http://www.watchoutforchildren.org>

Anderson, J. W., 'Attachment behaviour out of doors' in N. Blurton Jones (ed.), *Ethological studies of child behaviour*, Cambridge University Press, Cambridge, 1972, pp. 199–215

Andersson, B. E., 'Effects of public daycare, a longitudinal study', *Child Development*, 1989, 60:857–66

Andersson, B. E., 'Effects of public day-care on cognitive and socio-emotional competence of thirteen year old children', *Child Development*, 1992, 63:20–36

Appelbaum, Anne, *Gulag: a history of the Soviet camp*, Allen Lane, London, 2003

Arndt, Bettina, 'Is childcare the new tobacco?', *Sydney Morning Herald*, 7 May 2001

Arndt, Bettina, 'Putting a spin on research', *The Age*, 23 May 2002

Arndt, Bettina, 'The chilling truth about childcare', *The Age*, 5 February 2003

Arndt, Bettina, profile of Catherine Hakim in 'Myths and misconceptions', *Sydney Morning Herald*, 7 February 2003

Atwood, Margaret, *The robber bride*, Anchor Books, New York, 1998

Australian Bureau of Statistics, *Child care*, Australian Bureau of Statistics, Canberra, 2000

Australian Bureau of Statistics, 'Formal childcare', *Australian social trends, family and community, No. 2*, Australian Bureau of Statistics, Canberra, 2002

Australian Bureau of Statistics, *Labour force status and other characteristics of families*, Australian Bureau of Statistics, Canberra, 2002

Australian Bureau of Statistics, *Australian social trends 2002*, Australian Bureau of Statistics, Canberra, 2002 (updated June 2003)

Badinter, Elizabeth, *Mother love: myth and reality*, Macmillan, New York, 1981

Bagnall, Diana, 'Unwilling child care conspirators', *The Bulletin*, 16 April 1996

Balleygueir, G., 'French research on daycare' in E. Melhuish & P. Moss (eds), *Daycare for young children: international perspectives*, Routledge, London, 1991, pp. 27–45

Barglow, P., 'Developmental follow-up of 6–7 year old children of mothers employed during their infancies', *Child Psychiatry and Human Development*, 1998, 29(1): 3–20

Barglow, P., P. Kavesh & L. Contreras, 'Offspring of working mothers: peer competence follow up', paper presented at Thirteenth Annual Congress of the International Association of Child and Adolescent Psychiatry and Allied Professions, July 1994

Barglow, P., B. Vaughn & N. Molitor, 'Effects of maternal absence due to employment on the quality of infant–mother attachment in a low-risk sample', *Child Development*, 1987, 58:945–54

Barnard College, conference: Maternal feminism: lessons for a 21st century motherhood movement, Harvard University, Massachusetts, 29 October 2002. Available at <http://www.watchoutforchildren.org/html/call to a motherhood movement.html>

Bates, J., & D. J. Marvinney, T. Kelly, K. Dodge, R. Bennett, & G. Pettit, 'Child-care history and kindergarten adjustment', *Developmental Psychology*, 1994, 30:690–700

Bauchner, Elizabeth, 'A mother's place is in the women's movement', *Women's News*, 3 October 2004. Available at <http://www.womensenews.org/article.cfm/dyn/aid/1744/context/archive>

Bauman, Zygmunt, *Life in fragments: essays in post-modern morality*, Polity Press, Oxford, 1995

Bauman, Zygmunt, *Post modernity and its discontents*, Polity Press, Cambridge, 1997

Bauman, Zygmunt, *Liquid modernity*, Polity Press, Cambridge, 2000

Bauman, Zygmunt, *The individualised society*, Polity Press, Cambridge, 2001; see esp essay 'Does love need reason' p. 163ff

Bauman, Zygmunt, *Liquid love*, Polity Press, Cambridge, 2003

Baydar, N., & J. Brooks-Gunn, 'Effects of maternal employment and child care arrangements on preschoolers' cognitive and behavioral outcomes: evidence from the children of the national longitudinal survey of youth', *Developmental Psychology*, 1991, 27:932–45

Beck, Ulrich, *Risk society*, Sage Publications, London, 1992

Beck, Ulrich, *The brave new world of work*, Polity Press, Frankfurt & New York, 2000

Belkin, Lisa, 'The opt-out revolution', *New York Times*, 26 October 2003, p. 42

Bellah, Robert, Richard Madsen, William Sullivan, Ann Swidler & Stephen Tipton, *Habits of the heart: individualism and commitment in American life*, University of California Press, Berkeley, 1996

Belsky, Jay, 'Infant daycare: a cause for concern?', *Zero to Three*, September 1986, pp. 1–7

Belsky, Jay, 'Developmental risks associated with infant daycare: attachment insecurity, non-compliance and aggression' in S. Chehrazi (ed.), *Psychosocial issues in daycare*, American Psychiatric Press, Washington, 1990, pp. 37–68

Belsky, Jay, 'Consequences of childcare for children's development: a deconstructionist view', in A. Booth (ed.), *Childcare in the 1990s: trends and consequences*, Lawrence Erlbaum Associates, Hillsdale New Jersey, 1992, pp. 83–94

Belsky, Jay, 'Attachment: theory and evidence', in M. Rutter, D. Hay, & S. Baron Cohen (eds), *Developmental principles and clinical issues in psychology and psychiatry*, Blackwell, Oxford, 1994, pp. 373–402

Belsky, Jay, 'The effects of infant day care reconsidered', *Early Childhood Research Quarterly*, 1998, 3:235–72

Belsky, Jay, 'Modern evolutionary theory and patterns of attachment', in J. Cassidy & P. R. Shaver, *Handbook of attachment theory, research and applications*, Guilford Press, New York, 1999, pp. 249–64

Belsky, Jay, 'Sorry, but there is bad news on child care', *The Age*, 8 May 2001, p. 15

Belsky, Jay, 'Developmental risks (still) associated with early child care', *Journal of Child Psychology and Psychiatry*, 2001, October:845–59

Belsky, Jay, 'Quantity counts: amount of child care and children's socioemotional development', *Journal of Developmental and Behavioral Pediatrics*, 2002, 23:167–70

Belsky, Jay, & J. Braungart, 'Are insecure–avoidant infants with extensive daycare experience less stressed by and more independent in the strange situation?', *Child Development*, 1991, 62:567–71

Belsky, Jay, & T. Nezworski, *The clinical implications of attachment*, Lawrence Erlbaum Associates, Hillsdale New Jersey, 1988

Belsky, Jay, & M. Rovine, 'Non maternal care in the first year of life and the security of infant–parent attachment', *Child Development*, 1988, 59:157–67

Belsky, Jay, & L. Steinberg, 'The effects of daycare: a critical review', *Child Development*, 1978, 49:929–49

Benjamin, Jessica, *The bonds of love: psychoanalysis, feminism and the problem of domination*, Pantheon Books, New York, 1988

Benn, Melissa, *Madonna and child: towards a new politics of motherhood*, Jonathan Cape, London, 1998

Benns, Mathew, *When the bough breaks: the true story of child killer Kathleen Folbigg*, Bantam Books, Australia & New Zealand, 2003

Berger, P., B. Berger & H. Kellner, *The homeless mind: modernization and consciousness*, Vintage Books, New York, 1974

Bernard, Jessie, *The future of marriage*, World, New York, 1972

Bettelheim, Bruno, *Children of the dream*, MacMillan, New York, 1969

Bettelheim, Bruno, 'Janusz Korczak, a tale for our time', in B. Bettelheim, *Recollections and reflections*, Thames & Hudson, London, 1990, pp. 191–206

Birrell, Robert, & Virginia Rapson, *A not so perfect match: the growing male/female divide, 1986–1996*, Centre for Population and Urban Research, Monash University, Melbourne, 1998

Birrell, Robert, Virginia Rapson & Claire Hourigan, *Men and women apart: partnering in Australia*, Australian Family Association and Centre for Population and Urban Research, Melbourne, March 2004

Bloom, Alan, *The closing of the American mind*, Simon & Schuster, New York, 1987

Blum, Marion, *The daycare dilemma: women and children first*, Lexington Books, Lexington Massachusetts, 1983

Borge, A., & E. Melhuish, 'A longitudinal study of childhood behaviour problems, maternal employment, and day care in a rural Norwegian community', *International Journal of Behavioral Development*, 1995, 18:23–42

Bowlby, John, 'Forty-four juvenile thieves: their characters and home-life', *International Journal of Psycho-Analysis*, 1944, 25:19–52, 107–27

Bowlby, John, *Attachment and loss, vol 1; attachment*, Penguin, London, 1971

Bowlby, John, *Attachment and loss, vol 2; separation: anxiety and anger*, Basic Books, USA, 1973

Bowlby, John, *Attachment and loss, vol 3; loss: sadness and depression*, Penguin Books, New York, 1981

Bowlby, John, *A secure base: clinical applications of attachment theory*, Routledge, London, 1988, reprints 1989, 1992, 1993, all quotes taken from 1993 edition

Brazelton, T. Berry, *Working and caring*, Addison–Wesley Publishing, Massachusetts, 1985

Brazelton, T. Berry & S. Greenspan, *The irreducible needs of children*, Harper Collins, New York, 2000

Brennan, Deborah, *The politics of Australian childcare: from philanthropy to feminism*, Cambridge University Press, New York & Melbourne, 1994

Brooks-Gunn, Jeanne, Wen-Jui Han & Jane Waldfogel, 'Maternal employment and child cognitive outcomes in the first three years of life: the NICHD study of early child care', *Child Development*, 2002, 73(4):1052–72

Brown, G., & A. Bifulco, 'Motherhood, employment and the development of depression: a replication of a finding?', *British Journal of Psychiatry*, 1990, 156:169–79

Bruner, Jerome, *Under five in Britain*, Grant Macintyre Ltd for Oxford Preschool Project, London, 1980

Buchanan, Rachel, 'He's not the boy next door', *The Age*, 24 June 2000, p. 9

Buhle, Mari Jo, *Feminism and its discontents: a century of struggle with psychoanalysis*, Harvard University Press, Cambridge Massachusetts, 1998

Bunting, Madeleine, 'Fear on nursery care forces rethink', *Guardian*, 8 July 2004 available at <http://www.guardian.co.uk/g2/story/0,3604,1256288,00.html>

Bunting, Madeleine, 'Nursery tales: are nurseries bad for our kids?', *Guardian*, 8 July 2004 available at <http://www.guardian.co.uk/g2/story/0,3604, 1256288,00.html>

Burggraff, Shirley, *The feminine economy and economic man*, Addison–Wesley, Boston, 1997

Burlingham, D., & A. Freud, *Young children in wartime London*, Allen & Unwin, London, 1942

Burlingham, D., & A. Freud, *Infants without families*, Allen & Unwin, London, 1944

Buxton, J., *Ending the mother war*, Pan Books, London, 1999

Cadzow, Jane, 'Kids? What kids?' *Good Weekend, Sydney Morning Herald*, 17 August 2002, p. 20

Carroll, John, 'Corporate carnivores', *Australian Quarterly*, August–September 2000, 72(4):18–20

Carroll, Roz, 'An interview with Allan Schore–the new American Bowlby', for UKCP (United Kingdom Council for Psychotherapists) available at <http://www.thinkbody.co.uk/papers/interview-with-allan-s.html>

Cassidy, J., & P. R. Shaver, *Handbook of attachment theory, research and applications*, The Guilford Press, New York, 1999

Chehrazi, S. (ed.), *Psychosocial issues in daycare*, American Psychiatric Press, Washington, 1990

Chodorow, Nancy, *The reproduction of mothering: psychoanalysis and the sociology of gender*, University of California Press, Berkeley, 1978

Clark, R., J. Hyde, M. Essex & M. Klein, 'Length of maternity leave and quality of mother–infant interactions', *Child Development*, 1997, 68: 364–83

Clarke-Stewart, Alison, 'The "effects" of infant daycare reconsidered', *Early Childhood Research Quarterly*, 1988, 3(3):293–318

Clarke-Stewart, Alison, 'Infant daycare: maligned or malignant? *American Psychologist*, 1989, 44(2):266–73

Clendinnen, Inga, *A tiger's eye: a memoir*, Text Publishing, Melbourne, 2000

Clendinnen, Inga, 'The crack in the teapot: reading Hilary Mantel', *Australian Book Review*, November 2003, 256:38

Commission on Children at Risk, YMCA of the USA, Dartmouth Medical School, & Institute for American Values, *Hardwired to connect: the new scientific case for authoritative communities*, A Report to the Nation from Commission on Children at Risk, YMCA of the USA, Dartmouth Medical School, & Institute for American Values, 2003

Commonwealth Child Care Advisory Council (Australia), *Child care: beyond 2001*, The Council, Canberra, 2001

Cook, P., *Early childcare: infants and nations at risk*, News Weekly Books, Melbourne, 1996

Creer, Katrina, & Clare Masters, 'The Folbigg murders', *The Sunday Telegraph*, 25 May 2003, p. 4

Crittenden, Ann, *The price of motherhood: why the most important job in the world is still the least valued*, Henry Holt & Company, New York, 2001

Cunningham, Sophie, 'Longing' in *Saturday Extra, The Age*, 30 March 2002, also available at <http://www.sophiecunningham.com/archives/000020.html>

Curthoys, Jean, *Feminist amnesia: the wake of women's liberation*, Routledge, London, 1997

Dahl, Roald, *The BFG*, Puffin, New York, 1982

Dahl, Roald, *Matilda*, Viking, New York, 1988

De Beauvoir, Simone, *The second sex*, Jonathan Cape, London, 1953

Degler, Carl, *At odds: women and the family from the revolution to the present*, Oxford University Press, Oxford & New York, 1980

De Marneffe, Daphne, *Maternal desire: on love, children and the inner life*, Little, Brown & Company, New York, 2004

De Mause, Lloyd (ed.), *The history of childhood*, Jason Aronson, Northvale New Jersey & London, 1995

Denniss, Richard, 'Annual leave in Australia', *Discussion paper 56*, The Australia Institute, Canberra, March 2003. Available at <www.tai.org.au>

Denniss, Richard, 'Australia's affluence, consumption trends and indicators of progress,' paper presented to Manning Clark House available at <http://www.manningclark.org.au/papers/affluence.htm>

Dettling, Andrea, Megan Gunnar & Bonny Donzella, 'Cortisol levels of young children in full-day childcare centres: relations with age and temperament', *Psychoneuroendocrinology*, 1999, 24:519–36

Dettling, Andrea, S. Parker, S. Lane, A. Sebanc, Megan Gunnar, 'Quality of care and temperament determine changes in cortisol concentrations over the day for young children in childcare', *Psychoneuroendocrinology*, 2000, 25:819–36

De Vaus, David, 'Marriage and mental health', *Family Matters* (the journal of the Australian Institute of Family Studies), Winter 2002, 62:26–32

De Zulueta, Felicity, *The traumatic roots of destructiveness: from pain to violence*, Jason Aronson, Northvale New Jersey & London, 1994 edition (first published 1993)

Dick, Diana, *Yesterday's babies–a history of baby care*, The Bodley Head, London, 1987

Dinesen, Isak, *Daguerreotypes and other essays*, University of Chicago Press, Chicago, 1979

Dinnerstein, Dorothy, *The mermaid and the minotaur: sexual arrangements and human malaise*, Harper & Row, New York, 1976

Dowrick, Stephanie, interview on motherhood available at <www.stephaniedowrick.com/biography/interview.html>

Drago, Robert, & Yi- Ping Tseng, 'Family structure, usual and preferred work hours and egalitarianism', paper delivered at HILDA conference, 10 March 2003 at Melbourne University's Institute of Applied Economic and Social Research

D'Souza, Dinesh, interviewed in 'Luxury fever', *Background Briefing*, ABC Radio, 6 April 2000. Available at <www.abc.net.au/rn/talks/bbing/stories/s98798.htm>

Dwyer, Carmel 'The real face of Australian wealth', *Australian Financial Review Magazine*, 27 July 2001

Eagle, M., *Recent developments in psychoanalysis: a critical evaluation*, Harvard University Press, London & Cambridge (Massachusetts), 1984

Easterbrook, Gregg, *The progress paradox, how life gets better while people feel worse*, Random House, New York, 2003

Eberstadt, Mary, *Home alone America: the hidden toll of day care, behavioral drugs, and other parent substitutes*, Penguin Group, New York, Toronto, London, Dublin, 2004

Egeland, B., & M. Heister, 'The long-term consequences of infant day-care and mother–infant attachment', *Child Development*, 1995, 66:74–85

Ehrenreich, Barbara, *The hearts of men*, an Anchor Book published by Doubleday, New York, 1983

Ehrenreich, Barbara, 'Maid to order—housecleaning services', *Harper's Magazine*, April 2000. Available at <www.findarticles.com/p/articles/mi_m1111/is_1799_300/ai_61291582>

Ehrenreich, Barbara, *Nickel and dimed: on (not) getting by in America*, Metropolitan Books, New York, 2001

Ehrensraft, Diane, *Spoiling childhood: how well meaning parents are giving children too much—but not what they need*, Guilford Press, New York & London, 1997

Einhorn, Barbara, *Cinderella goes to market: gender and women's movements in east central Europe*, Verso, London, 1993

Elshtain, Jean Bethke, *Public man, private woman: women in social and political thought*, Princeton University Press, Princeton New Jersey, 1981

Evans, M. D. R., & Jonathan Kelley, 'Employment for mothers of pre-school children: evidence from Australia and 23 other nations', *People and Place*, 2001, 9(3):28–40

Evans, M. D. R., & Jonathan Kelley, 'Changes in public attitudes to maternal employment: Australia 1984 to 2001', *People and Place*, 2002, 10(1):42–57

Eyer, Diane, *Mother–infant bonding: a scientific fiction*, Yale University Press, New Haven, 1992

Eyer, Diane, *Motherguilt: how our culture blames mothers for what's wrong with society*, Times Books, New York, 1996

Farganis, Sandra, *The social reconstruction of the feminine character*, Rowman & Littlefield, Maryland, 1996

Faux, Jeff & Larry Mishel, 'Inequality and the global economy' in Will Hutton & Anthony Giddens (eds), *On the edge: living with global capitalism*, Jonathan Cape, London, 2000, pp. 93–111

Fein, Greta, 'Infants in group care: patterns of despair and detachment', *Early Childhood Research Quarterly*, 1995, 10:261–75

Field, T., 'Quality infant day-care and grade school behavior and performance', *Child Development*, 1991, 62:863–70

Firestone, Shulamith, *The dialectic of sex: the case for feminist revolution*, Morrow, New York, 1970

Flanagan, Caitlin, 'The mother's dilemma', *Atlantic Unbound*, 12 February 2004

Flanagan, Caitlin, 'How serfdom saved the women's movement', *Atlantic Monthly*, March 2004. Available at <http://www.theatlantic.com/doc/200403/flanagan>

Flanagan, Caitlin, 'Am I exploiting my nanny? Exchanges between Flanagan, Sara Mosle, & Barbara Ehrenreich' on slate website at <http://slate.msn.com/id/2095545/entry/2095648/>

Folbre, Nancy, 'The unproductive housewife', *Signs: Journal of Women in Culture and Society*, 1991, 16(3):463–84

Folbre, Nancy, *The invisible heart: economics and family values*, New Press, New York, 2001

Fonagy, Peter, 'Thinking about thinking: some clinical and theoretical considerations in the treatment of a borderline patient', in *International Journal of Psychoanalysis*, 1991, 72:639–56

Fonagy, Peter, *Attachment theory and psychoanalysis*, Other Press, New York, 2001

Fonagy, Peter, & H. Steele, M. Steele, G. Moran & A. Higgett 'The capacity for understanding mental states: the reflective self in parent and its significance for security of attachment', *Infant mental health journal*, 1991, 13:200–17

Fonagy, Peter, & P. Target, 'Attachment and reflective function: their role in self organisation', *Development and Psychopathology*, 1997, 9:679–700

Fraiberg, S., & V. Adelson & V. Shapiro, 'Ghosts in the nursery: a psychoanalytic approach to the problems of impaired infant–mother relationships', *Journal of the American Academy of Child Psychiatry*, 1975,14:387–421

Frank, R., *Luxury fever: why money fails to satisfy in an era of excess*, Free Press, New York, 1999

Frank, R., & Phillip J. Cook, *The winner-take-all society*, Free Press, New York, 1995

Franks, S., *Having none of it: women, men and the future of work*, Granta, London, 1999

Freud, S., *Totem and taboo*, Lowe & Brydone, London, 1972 edition

Friedan, Betty, *The feminine mystique*, Dell, New York, 1964

Friedman, Sarah, comments to Japanese policy makers were at a 2000 symposium in Japan. On 9 July 2000 a symposium entitled 'The child care paradox: choices in children's development—support for working mothers by learning from the NICHD study of early child care', hosted by the Childcare Research Network

Gaita, Raimond, *Romulus my father*, Text Publishing, Melbourne, 1998

Gaita, Raimond, *A common humanity: thinking about love & truth & justice*, Text Publishing, Melbourne, 1999; Routledge, London & New York, 2000

Garner, Helen, *True Stories*, Text Publishing, Melbourne, 1996

Garrison, Jessica, 'Researchers in child-care study clash over findings', *Los Angeles Times*, 25 April 2001

Gelernter, David, 'Why mothers should stay home', *Commentary Magazine*, February 1996, 101(2):25–8

Gerhardt, Sue, *Why love matters*, Brunner & Routledge, Hove & New York, 2004

Gerson, K., *Hard choices: how women decide about work, career and motherhood*, University of California Press, Berkeley & Los Angeles, 1985

Giddens, Anthony, *The third way: the renewal of social democracy*, Polity Press, Cambridge, 1998

Giele, Janet Z., *Two paths to women's equality: temperance, suffrage, and the origins of modern feminism*, Twayne Publishers, New York, 1995

Gill, R. T., *Posterity lost: progress, ideology and the decline of the American family*, Rowan & Littlefield, New York & Oxford, 1997

Ginsborg, Paul, *Italy and its discontents, 1980–2000*, Penguin, London, 2003

Gittins, R., 'Strictly 9 to 5. That's most of us at work', *The Age*, 18 June 2003

Glendinning, Lee, 'Folbigg baby coughed before dying, court told', *Sydney Morning Herald*, 11 April 2003

Goldberg, S., R. Muir, & J. Kerr (eds), *Attachment theory: social, developmental, and clinical perspectives*, NJ Analytic Press, Hillsdale, 1995

Goldberg, W., E. Greenberger, & S. Nagel, 'Employment and achievement', *Child Development*, 1996, 67:1512–27

Goldin, C., 'Career and family: college women look to the past', in F. D. Blau & R. G. Ehrenberg (eds), *Gender and family issues in the workplace*, Russell Sage Foundation, New York, 1997, pp. 20–64

Goleman, Daniel, *Emotional intelligence*, Bloomsbury, Great Britain, 1996

Green, André, 'The dead mother' in André Green, *On private madness*, Karnac Books, London, 1997, pp. 142–73

Greenspan, Stanley, *The four-thirds solution, solving the childcare crisis in America today*, Perseus Books, Cambridge Massachusetts, 2001

Greer, Germaine, *The female eunuch*, Bantam Books, New York, 1972

Greer, Germaine, *Sex and destiny: the politics of human fertility*, Harper & Row, New York, 1984

Greer, Germaine, *The whole woman*, Doubleday, London & Sydney, 1999

Gregory, Bob, *Can this be the Promised Land? Work and welfare for the modern woman*, National Institute Public Lecture, Parliament House, Canberra, 5 June 2002

Griffith, Sian, 'If you want what's best, wait until she's two', *Sunday Times*, 11 July 2004

Grimshaw, P., & L. Strahan, *The half-open door: sixteen modern Australian women look at professional life and achievement*, Hale & Iremonger, Sydney, 1982

Grossmann, Klaus, 'Evolution and history of attachment research' in S. Goldberg, R. Muir, & J. Kerr (eds), *Attachment theory: social, developmental, and clinical perspectives*, NJ Analytic Press, Hillsdale, 1995, pp. 111–13

Gunn, J. Brooks, 'Maternal employment and child cognitive outcomes in the first three years of life: the NICHD study of early child care', *Child Development*, 2002, 73(4):1052–72

Guntrip, Harry J. S., *Psychoanalytic theory, therapy and the self: a basic guide to the human personality in Freud, Erickson, Klein, Sullivan, Fairbairn, Hartmann, Jacobson & Winnicott*, Basic Books, New York, 1971

Hakim, Catherine, 'Five feminist myths about women's employment', *British Journal of Sociology*, 1995, 46:429–55

Hakim, Catherine, *Key issues in women's work: female heterogeneity and the polarisation of women's employment*, Athlone Press, London, 1996

Hakim, Catherine, 'Models of the family: women's role and social policy: a new perspective from preference theory', *European Societies*, 1999, 1:33–58

Hakim, Catherine, *Work–lifestyle choices in the 21st century*, Oxford University Press, Oxford, 2001

Hakim, Catherine, 'Taking women seriously', *People and Place*, 2001, 9(4):1–6

Hakim, Catherine, 'Competing family models: competing social policies', paper delivered to Australian Institute of Family Studies conference, 12 March 2003

Halasz, George, 'Voltaire's bastards and the rights of the child: the manufacture of epidemics' in Psychiatrists Working Group, *She STILL won't be right, mate!*, Psychiatrists Working Group, Melbourne, 1999, pp. 186–99

Halasz, George (ed.), Peter Ellingsen, F. Salo Thompson & Anne Manne, *Cries unheard: a new look at attention deficit hyperactivity disorder*, Common Ground, Melbourne, 2002

Hamilton, Clive, 'Overconsumption in Australia: the rise of the middle-class battler', Discussion Paper no. 49, The Australia Institute, November 2002, available at <http://www.tai.org.au>

Hamilton, Clive, *Growth fetish*, Allen & Unwin, Sydney, 2003

Hanauer, Cathi (ed.), *The bitch in the house*, William Morrow, New York, 2002

Hansen, Elaine Tuttle, *Mother without child, contemporary fiction and the crisis of motherhood*, University of California Press, Berkeley & Los Angeles, 1997

Han Wen-Jui, Jane Waldfogel & Jeanne Brooks-Gunn, 'The effects of early maternal employment on later cognitive and behavioral outcomes', *Journal of Marriage and Family*, 2001, 63:336–54

Harding, Ann, & Aggie Szukalska, 'Financial disadvantage in Australia—1999: the unlucky Australians?', The Smith Family and the National Centre for Social and Economic Modelling (NATSEM) at the University of Canberra, November 2000

Harris, Judith Rich, *The nurture assumption: why children turn out the way they do*, Free Press, New York & London, 1998

Harrison, Linda, & Ungerer, J. 'Maternal employment and infant–mother attachment security at 12 months postpartum', *Developmental Psychology*, 2002, 38:758–73

Haskins, R., 'Public school aggression among children with varying day-care experience', *Child Development*, 1985, 56:689–703

Hausegger, Virginia, 'The sins of our feminist mothers', *The Age*, 22 July 2002

Held, Virginia, 'Non-contractual society', in Marsja Hame & Kai Nielson (eds), *Science, morality and feminist theory*, University of Calgary Press, Calgary, 1987, pp. 139–67

Held, Virginia, *Feminist morality: transforming culture, society and politics*, University of Chicago, Chicago, 1993

Henry, Jules, *The pathway to madness*, Random House, New York, 1971

Hewitt, Patricia, *About time: the revolution in work and family life*, Rivers Ovram Press, London, 1993

Hewlett, Sylvia Ann, *A lesser life: the myth of women's liberation in America*, William Morrow, New York, 1986

Hewlett, Sylvia Ann, *Creating a life, professional women and the quest for motherhood*, Talk Miramax Books, New York, 2002

Hobsbawm, Eric, *Age of extremes: a history of the world, 1914–1991*, Vintage Books, London, 1996

Hochschild, Arlie Russell, *The second shift: working parents and the revolution at home*, Viking, New York, 1989

Hochschild, Arlie Russell, 'The commercial spirit of intimate life and the abduction of feminism', *Theory, Culture and Society*, 1994, 112(2):1–24 (republished in slightly altered form in her *The commercialisation of intimate life*)

Hochschild, Arlie Russell, *The time bind: when work becomes home and home becomes work*, Metropolitan Books, New York, 1997

Hochschild, Arlie Russell, 'Global care chains and emotional surplus value', in Will Hutton & Anthony Giddens (eds.), *On the edge: living with global capitalism*, Jonathan Cape, London, 2000, pp. 130–46

Hochschild, Arlie Russell, *The commercialisation of intimate life: notes from home and work*, University of California Press, Berkeley, Los Angeles & London, 2003

Hodgson, Lucia, *Raised in captivity: why does America fail its children*, Graywolf Press, Minnesota, 1997

Hofer, Myron, 'Hidden regulators: implications for a new understanding of attachment, separation, and loss', in S. Goldberg, R. Muir & J. Kerr (eds), *Attachment theory: social, developmental, and clinical perspectives*, Analytic Press, Hillsdale New Jersey, 1995, pp. 203–32

Holmes, Jeremy, *John Bowlby and attachment theory*, Routledge, London, 1993

Holmes, Jeremy, *Attachment, intimacy and autonomy*, Jason Aronson, Northvale New Jersey & London, 1996

Hopkins, Juliet, 'Failure of the holding relationship: some effects of physical rejection on the child's attachment and inner experience' in C. Parks, J. Stevenson-Hinde & P. Marris (eds), *Attachment across the life cycle*, Routledge, London & New York, 1996 paperback edition, 187–98

Horin, A., 2001, 'Childcare aggression link rejected', *Sydney Morning Herald*, 21–22 April 2001

Howes, Carolee, D. Phillips & M. Whitebook, 'Thresholds of quality: implications for the social development of children in centre-based child care', *Child Development*, 1992, 63:449–60

Hrdy, Sarah Blaffer, *Mother nature, natural selection and the female of the species*, Chatto & Windus, London, 1999

Hughes, Nancy Schreper, *Death without weeping: the violence of everyday life in Brazil*, University of California Press, Berkeley, Los Angeles & London , 1992

Hulbert, Ann, *Raising America: experts and a century of advice about children*, Alfred Knopf, New York, 2003

Hutton, Will, and Anthony Giddens, *On the edge: living with global capitalism*, Jonathan Cape, London, 2000

Hymowitz, Kay, 'Fear and loathing in the daycare centre', *City Journal*, 2001, Summer 11. Available at <http://www.city-journal.org/html/11_3_fear_and_loathing.html>

Hymowitz, Kay, 'Ecstatic capitalism's brave new work ethic, *City Journal*, 2001, Winter 11(1). Available at <http://www.cityjournal.org/html/11_1_ecstatic_capitalisms.html>

Ilmakunnus, S., 'Public policy and child care choice' in I. Persson & C. Jonung (eds), *The economics of the family and family policies*, Routledge, London, 1997, pp. 179–93

James, Oliver, *Britain on the couch*, Arrow Books, London, 1998

Jameson, Fredric, *Postmodernism, or the cultural logic of late capitalism*, Duke University Press, Durham, 1997

Janis, Irving, *Groupthink*, Houghton Mifflin, Boston, 1982, 2nd edition

Johnson, Susan, *A better woman*, Random House, Sydney, 1999

Joshi, H., & G. Verropoulou, *Maternal employment and child outcomes*, Smith Institute, London, 2000

Kagan, Jerome, *Three seductive ideas*, Harvard University Press, Cambridge Massachusetts & London, 1998

Karen, Robert, *Becoming attached: first relationships and how they shape our capacity to love*, Oxford University Press, Oxford & New York, 1998

Karr-Morse, Robin, & Meredith Wiley, *Ghosts from the nursery: tracing the roots of violence*, Atlantic Monthly Press, New York, 1997

Kincheloe, J., 'The new childhood, home alone as way of life', in Henry Jenkins (ed.), *The children's culture reader*, New York University, New York, 1998, pp. 159–77

Klaus, M., & J. H. Kennell, *Maternal–infant bonding: the impact of early separation and loss on family development*, C.V. Mosby, St Louis, 1976

Knowles, Lorna, 'Nation's worst serial killer', *The Herald Sun*, 22 May 2003, p. 5

Knowles, Lorna, 'The girl who grew to kill', *Daily Telegraph*, 25 May 2003

Koren-Karie, Nina, 'Mother's attachment representations and choice of infant care: centre care vs. home', *Infant and child development*, 2001, 10:117–27

Kraemer, S., & J. Roberts, *The politics of attachment*, Free Association Books, London, 1996

Kristeva, Julie, 'About Chinese women', 'Women's time' and 'Sabat mater' all in Toril Moi (ed), *The Kristeva Reader*, Columbia Press, New York, 1986

Kristeva, Julie, *The crisis of the European subject*, translated by Susan Fairfield, Other Press, New York, 2000

Kristol, Irving, *The capitalist future*, Frances Boyer Lecture, American Enterprise Institute Annual Dinner (Washington), publication date: 4 December 1991

Krygier, Martin, *Between fear and hope: hybrid thoughts on public values*, Boyer Lectures, ABC Books, Sydney, 1997. The text of the radio lectures on which this book expands is available at <http://www.abc.net.au/rn/boyers/97boyer1.htm>.

Kumin, Ivri, *Pre-object relatedness: early attachment and the psychoanalytic situation*, Guilford Press, New York & London, 1996

Kuttner, R., *Everything for sale: the virtues and limits of markets*, University of Chicago Press, Chicago, 1996

Lacey, Stephen, 'This whopping life', *Spectrum*, *Sydney Morning Herald*, 8–9 March 2003

Lally, Ron, interviewed by Jennifer Byrne, *The 7.30 Report*, broadcast on the Australian Broadcasting Corporation (ABC), 6 November 1998

Lamb, M., 'Nonmaternal care and the security of infant–mother: a reanalysis of the data', *Infant Behaviour and Development*, 1992, 15:71–83

Lamb, M., & K. Sternberg, 'Socio cultural perspectives on nonparental childcare', in M. Lamb, K. Sternberg, P. Hwang, & A. Broberg (eds), *Child care in context*, Lawrence Erlbaum Associates, Hillsdale New Jersey, 1991, pp. 1–26

Leach, Penelope, *Children first: what our society must do—and is not doing—for our children today*, Michael Joseph, London, 1994

Leach, Penelope, 'Infant care from the infant's viewpoint: the views of some professionals', *Early Development and Parenting*, 1997, 6(2):47–58

Legge Kate, 'The voice that won't be silent—Belsky accuses his female collaborators of a Soviet style manipulation of the truth', *The Australian*, 12 May 2001, p. 9

Leser, David, 'The lost men', *Sydney Morning Herald, Good Weekend Magazine*, 25 March 2000

Leunig, Michael, 'Thoughts of a baby lying in childcare', cartoon in *The Age*, 26 July 1995. Available at <http://users.cyberone.com.au/myers/leunig-baby.jpg>

Leupnitz, Deborah, *The family interpreted*, Basic Books, New York, 1988

Loane, Sally, *Who cares? Guilt, hope and the childcare debate*, Mandarin Books, Melbourne, 1997

Longman, Phillip, *The empty cradle: how falling birthrates threaten world prosperity and what to do about it*, Basic Books, New York, 2004

Lyons-Ruth, Karlen & D. Jacobwitz, 'Attachment disorganisation, unresolved loss, relational violence, and lapses in behavioural and attentional strategies', in J. Cassidy & P. R. Shaver (eds), *Handbook of attachment*, Guilford, New York, 1999, pp. 520–54

Macken, Deirdre, interview with Michael Leunig, *Sydney Morning Herald*, 5 August 1995, p. 20 reported in S. Loane, *Who cares? Guilt, hope and the childcare debate*, Mandarin Books, Melbourne, 1997, p. 6

Main, M., & J. Solomon, 'Discovery of an insecure-disorganised/disorientated attachment pattern' in M. Greenberg, D. Cicchetti, & C. Cummings (eds), *Attachment in the preschool years*, University of Chicago Press, Chicago, 1990, pp. 121–60

Malik, Kenan, discussion with Ed Melhuish, Sue Gerhardt & Jay Belsky, BBC Radio 4, Current affairs, 'Analysis: catch them young?' Transcript of a recorded documentary, 26 Aug 2004

Manne, Anne, 'Electing a new child', *Quadrant Magazine*, Summer Jan/Feb 1996, pp. 8–19

Manne, Anne, 'Disposable childhood', *Australian Review of Books*, May 1998

Manne, Anne, 'Zealots creche and burn in childcare defence', *The Age*, 9 May 2000

Manne, Anne, 'For our children's sake', *The Age*, 1 May 2001, p. 13

Manne, Anne, 'Women's preferences, fertility and family policy: the case for diversity', *People and Place*, 2001, 9(4):6–25

Manne, Anne, 'Children, ADHD, and the contemporary conditions of childhood', in G. Halasz (ed.), *Cries unheard: a new look at attention deficit hyperactivity disorder*, Common Ground, Melbourne, 2002, pp. 7–28

Margetts, Kay, 'Child care arrangements, preschool, personal, family and school influences on children's adjustment', unpublished doctoral thesis, The University of Melbourne, Melbourne, 2001

Margetts, Kay, 'The developing child in today's world: issues and care in education', *Educare News*, 2002, 127(July):10–13

Margetts, Kay, 'Responsive caregiving: reducing stress in infant toddler care', *International Journal of Early Childhood*, 2005, 32(2):77–84

Marris, Peter, 'The social construction of uncertainty', in C. Parkes, J. Stevenson-Hinde & P. Marris (eds), *Attachment across the life cycle*, Routledge, London & New York, 1991, pp. 77–90

Marris, Peter, *The politics of uncertainty*, Routledge, New York & London, 1996

Marx, Karl, *The communist manifesto* in Robert C. Tucker (ed.), *The Marx–Engels reader*, W. W. Norton & Co, New York, 1972, pp. 469–500

Matlary, Janne Haaland, 'Celebrating the universal declaration of human rights: family rights and family policies', *Familia et Vita*, 1999, IV(1):5–14

McCain, Hon Margaret Norrie, & J. Fraser Mustard (co chairs), *The early years study: reversing the real brain drain*, Canadian Institute for Advanced Research, Toronto, April 1999

McCalman, Janet, *Struggletown: public and private life in Richmond, 1900–1965*, Melbourne University Press, Melbourne, 1984

McDonald, Peter, 'Contemporary fertility patterns in Australia: first data from the 1996 census', *People and Place*, 1998, 6(1):1–13

McDonald, Peter, 'Family support policy in Australia: the need for a paradigm shift', *People and Place*, 2001, 9(2):14–20

McDonald, Peter, 'Work–family policies are the right approach to the presentation of very low fertility', *People and Place*, 2001, 9(3):17–27

Mead, Lawrence, 'Welfare reform and the family: lessons from America', in P. Saunders (ed.) *Reforming the Australian welfare state*, Australian Institute of Family Studies, Melbourne, 2000, pp. 44–61

Meadows, Pam, *Women at work in Britain and Sweden*, National Institute of Economic and Social Research, London, 2000

Melhuish, E. C., 'Research on daycare for young children in the United Kingdom', in Melhuish E. C. & P. Moss (eds), *Daycare for young children: international perspectives*, Tavistock Routledge, London, 1991, pp. 142–60

Melhuish, E. C., K. Sylva, P. Sammons, I. Siraj-Blatchford & B. Taggart, 'Social/behavioural and cognitive development at 3–4 years in relation to family background', in Institute of Education/DfES, *The effective provision of pre-school education project, technical paper 7*, Institute of Education/DfES, London, 2001

Mill, John Stuart, *The subjection of women*, 1869. Chapter one available online at <http: //etext.library.adelaide.edu.au/m/mill/john_stuart/m645s/chapter1.html>

Modjeska, Drusilla, *Stravinsky's lunch*, Pan MacMillan, Sydney, 1999

Morgan, P., *Who needs parents: the effects of childcare and early education on children in Britain and the USA*, London IEA Health and Welfare Unit, 1996

Motherhood Project, Institute of American Values, Call to a Motherhood Movement, <http://www.watchoutforchildren.org/html/call_to_a_motherhood_movement.html>

Mothers and More: The network for sequencing women: <http://www.mothersandmore.org/>

Mothers Are Women (MAW) in Canada: <http://www.mothersarewomen.com/>

Mothers Movement Online: <http://www.mothersmovement.org/index.htm>

Mothers Ought to Have Equal Rights (MOTHERS): <http://www.mothersoughttohaveequalrights.org/>

Murdoch, Iris, *The Sovereignty of Good*, Schocken, New York, 1971

Murray, Lynne, 'Personal and social influences on parenting and adult adjustment' in Sebastian Kraemer & Jane Roberts (eds), *The politics of attachment*, Free Association Books, London, 1996, pp. 43–61

Murray, L., & P. Cooper (eds), *Post partum depression and child development*, Guilford, New York, 1997

Murray, Les, 'The steel', in *New Collected Poems*, Carcanet, Manchester, 2003

Murray-Smith, Joanna, 'Too late for another Everest', *Sunday Age*, 17 March 2002

National Marriage Project, *The state of our unions*, Rutgers University, New Jersey, 2002. Available at <http://marriage.rutgers.edu>

Neven, Ruth Schmidt, Vicki Anderson & Tim Godber, *Rethinking ADHD: integrated approaches to helping children at home and at school*, Allen & Unwin, Sydney, 2002

Nezworski, T., W. J. Tolan & Jay Belsky, 'Intervention in insecure infant attachment,' in Jay Belsky & T. Nezworski (eds.), *Clinical implications of attachment*, Lawrence Lawrence Erlbaum Associates, Hillsdale New Jersey & London, 1988, pp. 352–86

NICHD (National Institute of Child Health and Human Development), 'Employed first-time mothers: a typology of maternal responses to integrating parenting and employment', *Family Relations*, 1993, 4:3–20

NICHD (National Institute of Child Health and Human Development), Early Child Care Research Network, 'Familial factors associated with characteristics of nonmaternal care for infants', *Journal of Marriage and the Family*, 1997, 59:389–408

NICHD (National Institute of Child Health and Human Development), Early Child Care Research Network, 'The effects of infant child care on infant–mother attachment security', *Child Development*, 1997, 68(5):860–79

NICHD (National Institute of Child Health and Human Development), Early Child Care Research Network, 'Early child care and self-control, compliance and problem behaviour at 24 and 36 months', *Child Development*, 1998, 69:1145–70

NICHD (National Institute of Child Health and Human Development), Early Child Care Research Network, 'Child care and mother–child interaction in the first 3 years of life', *Developmental Psychology*, 1999, 35:1399–413

NICHD (National Institute of Child Health and Human Development), Early

Child Care Research Network, 'The relation of child care to cognitive and language development', *Child Development*, 2000, 71:958–78

NICHD (National Institute of Child Health and Human Development), Early Child Care Research Network, 'Characteristics and quality of child care for toddlers and preschoolers', *Applied Developmental Science*, 2000, 4(3): 116–135

NICHD (National Institute of Child Health and Human Development), Early Child Care Research Network, 'Child-care and family predictors of preschool attachment and stability from infancy', *Developmental Psychology*, 2001, 37(6):847–62

NICHD (National Institute of Child Health and Human Development), Early Child Care Research Network, 'Child care and children's peer interaction at 24 and 36 months', *Child Development*, 2001, 72(5):1478–1500

NICHD (National Institute of Child Health and Human Development), 'Does amount of time spent in child care predict socioemotional adjustment during the transition to kindergarten?', *Child Development*, 2003, 74:976–1005

NICHD (National Institute of Child Health and Human Development), 'Early child care and children's development in the primary grades: follow-up results from the NICHD study of early child care', draft paper, 26 October 2004

Nyland, Berenice, 'The Australian child-care centre as a developmental niche', paper given to Australian Institute of Family Studies conference, 8 February 2003

Ochiltree, G., *Effects of child care on young children: forty years research*, Early Childhood Study Paper No. 5, Australian Institute of Family Studies, Melbourne, 1994

Ochiltree, G., & D Edgar, *Today's child care: tomorrow's children*, Early Childhood Study Paper No 7, Australian Institute of Family Studies, Melbourne, 1995

O'Neill, John, *The missing child in liberal theory: towards a covenant theory of family, community, welfare and the civic state*, University of Toronto Press, Toronto, 1994

Orbach, Susie, 'The John Bowlby memorial lecture: the body in clinical practice, part one, "There is no such thing as a body" and part two, "When touch comes to therapy"', in Kate White (ed.), *Touch: attachment and the body*, Karnac Books, London, 2004, pp. 17–49

Orbach, Susie, & Luise Eichenbaum, *What do women want?*, Harper Collins, London, 1994

Orwell, G., 'Such, such were the joys', in Sonia Orwell & Ian Angus (eds), *The collected essays, journalism and letters of George Orwell, vol IV, in front of your nose, 1945–1950*, Secker & Warburg, London, 1968, pp. 330–69

Park, K., & Honig, A., 'Infant child care patterns and later teacher ratings of preschool behaviors', *Early Child Development and Care*, 1991, 68:89–96

Payten, Ian, 'Gen X destined to rent forever, *The Age*, 11 Feb 2002

Pearson, Alison, *I don't know how she does it!*, Chatto & Windus, London, 2002

Peel, Mark, *The lowest rung: voices of Australian poverty*, Cambridge University Press, Melbourne, 2003

Peterson, Peter G., *Running on empty: how the Democratic and Republican parties are bankrupting our future and what Americans can do about it*, Farrar, Straus & Giroux, New York, 2004

Pocock, Barbara, *The work/life collision*, Federation Press, Annandale, 2003

Polakow, Valerie, *The erosion of childhood*, University of Chicago Press, Chicago & London, 1992, first published 1982

Pollock, Linda, *Forgotten children: parent–child relations from 1500–1900*, Cambridge University Press, Cambridge, 1983

Popenoe, David, *Life without father*, Free Press, New York & London, 1996

Pound, Andrea, 'Attachment and maternal depression', in C. Parkes & J. Stevenson-Hinde (eds), *The place of attachment in human behaviour*, Basic Books, New York, 1982, chapter 6

Pound, Andrea, 'Hope in the inner city: towards a new deal' in S. Kraemer & J. Roberts (eds), *The politics of attachment*, Free Association Books, London, 1996, pp. 62–74

Probert, B., 'Gender and choice: the structure of opportunity' in Paul James, Walter Veit & Steve Wright (eds), *Work of the future*, Allen & Unwin, Sydney, 1997, pp. 181–97

Provence, Sally, *The challenge of daycare*, Yale University Press, New Haven, 1977

Pusey, Michael, *The experience of middle Australia: the dark side of economic reform*, Cambridge University Press, Melbourne, 2003

Putnam, Robert, *Bowling alone*, Simon & Schuster, New York, 2000

Razzell, P. E., & R. W. Wainwright, *The Victorian working class: selections from letters to the* Morning Chronicle, Frank Cass, London, 1973

Reiger, Kerreen, *Our bodies, our babies: the forgotten women's movement*, Melbourne University Press, Melbourne, 2001

Reiger, Kerreen, 'Maternal thinking and social activism', paper delivered at conference: Performing motherhood: ideology, agency and experience, La Trobe University, Melbourne, July 2002

Rich, Adrienne, *Of woman born: motherhood as experience and as institution*, Norton, New York, 1976

Ritzer, G., *The McDonaldisation of society*, Pine Forge Press, California, 2000

Roberts, Elizabeth, *A woman's place: an oral history of working class women, 1890–1940*, Blackwell, Oxford, 1996

Robertson, Brian C., *The daycare deception: what the child care establishment isn't telling us*, Encounter Books, San Francisco, 2003

Robertson, J., & J. Robertson, *Separation and the very young*, Free Association Books, London, 1989

Roe, Joy M., 'Interactions between three-month-old infants: a comparison between Greek mothers and institutional caregivers', *International Journal of Behavioural Development*, 1988, 11(3):359–67

Roiphe, Anne, *A mother's eye: motherhood and feminism*, Virago, London, 1996

Rolfe, S., *Rethinking attachment for early childhood practice: promoting security, autonomy and resilience in young children*, Allen & Unwin, Sydney, 2004

Rolfe, S., B. Nyland & R. Morda, 'Quality in infant care: observations on joint attention', *Australian Research in Early Childhood Education*, 2002, 9(1):86–96

Rossi, Alice, 'A biosocial perspective on parenting', *Daedalus*, 1977, Spring, 106:1–31

Rossi, Alice, *Sexuality across the life course*, University of Chicago Press, Chicago & London, 1994

Ruddick, Sara, *Maternal thinking: towards a politics of peace*, Beacon Press, Boston, 1995

Rumbelow, Helen, 'Maternity pay increase plan angers employers', *Health News*, 9 July 2004

Rutter, M., *Maternal deprivation reassessed*, Penguin, Harmondsworth, 1981

Sagi, A., N. Koren-Kari, M. Gini, Y. Ziv, & T. Joels, 'Shedding further light on the effects of various types and quality of early child care on infant–mother attachment relationship: the Haifa study of early child care', *Child Development*, 2002, 73(4):1166–86

Sammons, P., & R. Smees, B. Taggart, K. Sylva, E. C. Melhuish, I. Siraj-Blatchford & K. Elliot, 'Measuring the impact on children's social behavioural development over the pre-school years', *The effective provision of pre-school education project, technical paper 8b*, Institute of Education/DfES, London, 2003

Sammons, P., K. Sylva, E. C. Melhuish, I. Siraj-Blatchford, B. Taggart, & K. Elliot, 'Measuring the impact on children's social behavioural development over the pre-school years', *The effective provision of pre-school education project, technical paper 8a*, Institute of Education/DfES, London, 2002

Sandler, Joseph, Ann-Marie Sandler & Rosemary Davies (eds), *Clinical and observational psychoanalytic research: roots of a controversy*, Monograph no 5, Monograph series of the psychoanalytic unit of University College, London and The Anna Freud Center, Karnac Books, London, 2000

Scarr, Sandra, 'Research on day care should spur a new look at old ideas', *Brown University Child and Adolescent Behaviour Letter*, December 1997, 13:12

Scher, Anat, & Ofra Mayseless, 'Mothers of anxious/ambivalent infants: maternal characteristics and child-care context', *Child Development*, 2000, 71:1629–39

Schor, Juliet, *The overworked American: the unexpected decline of leisure*, Basic Books, New York, 1992

Schor, Juliet, *The overspent American: why we want what we don't need*, Harper Perennial, New York, 1998

Schor, Juliet, *Born to buy, the commercialised child and the new consumer culture*, Scribner, New York & London, 2004

Schore, Allan, *Affect regulation and the origin of the self: the neurobiology of emotional development*, Lawrence Erlbaum Associates, Hillsdale New Jersey, 1994

Schore, Allan, *Affect disregulation and disorders of the self*, Lawrence Erlbaum Associates, Hillsdale New Jersey, 2003

Schore, Allan, *Affect regulation and the repair of the self*, W. W. Norton & Co, New York & London, 2003

Sennett, R., *The corrosion of character: the personal consequences of work in the new capitalism*, W. W. Norton & Co, New York, 1998

Sennett, R., *Respect: the formation of character in an age of inequality*, The Penguin Press, London, 2003

Shengold, Leonard, *Soul murder: the effects of childhood abuse and deprivation*, Yale University Press, New York, 1989

Sherry, Cathy, 'Parenting transcends politics', *The Sunday Age*, 13 January 2002. Available at http://www.theage.com.au/news/state/2002/01/13/FFX4TIY 9CWC.html

Sherry, Cathy, 'A media vibe based on motherhood myth', *The Age*, 17 January 2002

Siegel, Daniel J., *The developing mind: how relationships and the brain interact to shape who we are*, Guilford Press, New York, 1999

Silverstein, L., 'Transforming the debate about child care and maternal employment', *American Psychologist*, 1991, 46:1025–32

Sims, Margaret, Andrew Guilfoyle & Trevor Parry, 'Children's well being in childcare', paper presented at the Australian Institute of Family Studies Conference, Melbourne, 9 February 2005

Sixty Minutes, 'Staying at home', broadcast on CBS 10 August 2004. Available at <http://www.cbsnews.com/stories/2004/10/08/60minutes/main648240. shtml>

Smiley, Jane, 'Money, marriage & monogamy', *Sydney Morning Herald, Good Weekend*, 6 January 2000

Solzhenitsyn, Alexander, *Lenin in Zurich*, translated by H. T. Willets, Bodley Head, London 1976

Sommers, Christina Hoff, *Who stole feminism?*, Simon & Schuster, New York, 1994

Sprengnether, Madelon, *The spectral mother: Freud, feminism and psychoanalysis*, Cornell University Press, Ithaca & London, 1990

Sroufe, A., 'Infant–caregiver attachment and patterns of adaptation in preschool: the roots of maladaptation and competence' in M. Perlmutter (ed.), *Minnesota symposium in child psychology vol 16*, Lawrence Erlbaum Associates, Hillsdale New Jersey, 1983, pp. 41–81

Sroufe, A., 'The role of infant–caregiver attachment,' in Jay Belsky & T. Nezworski, *The clinical implications of attachment*, Lawrence Erlbaum Associates, Hillsdale New Jersey, 1988, pp. 18–38

Stanley, Fiona, *Enough rope with Andrew Denton*, two interviews broadcast on the Australian Broadcast Corporation (ABC) 19 May 2003 & 6 October 2003. Also available at <http://www.abc.net.au/enoughrope/stories/s961001. htm>

Statistics Sweden, <http://www.scb.se.eng>, Population and Welfare: Population: Population Projections: Future Fertility

Stephens, Julie, 'Motherhood and the market', *Arena Magazine*, August/September, 2000, 48:35–7

Stephens, Julie, 'Eyes wide shut in the child-care debate', *Arena Magazine*, 2001, June–July (53):7–9

Stephens, Julie, 'Beyond binaries in motherhood research', *Family Matters* (the journal of the Australian Institute of Family Studies), Spring/Summer 2004/5, pp. 96–101

Stern, Daniel, *The interpersonal world of the infant: a view from psychoanalysis and developmental psychology*, Basic Books, New York, 1985

Stern, Daniel, *The motherhood constellation*, Basic Books, New York, 1995

Sternberg, K., & M. Lamb, C. Hwang, A. Brobert, R. Ketterlinus & B. Bookstein, 'Does out-of-home care affect compliance in preschoolers?', *International Journal of Behavioral Development*, 1991,14:45–65

Stolberg, Sheryl Gay, 'Public lives: another academic salvo in the nation's 'mommy wars', *New York Times*, 21 April 2001, p. A8

Stone, Lawrence, *The family, sex and marriage in England 1500–1800*, HarperCollins, New York, 1977

Summers, Anne, *End of equality: work, babies and women's choices in 21st century Australia*, Random House, Milsons Point NSW, 2003

Sutton, Nina, *Bruno Bettelheim: the other side of madness*, Gerald Duckworth & Co, Great Britain, 1995

Sweeny, Jennifer Foote, 'Jay Belsky doesn't play well with the others', *Salon*, 26 April 2001. Available at <http://dir.salon.com/mwt/feature/2001/04/26/belsky/index.html>

Sylvester, Rachel, 'Working mothers demand choice to stay at home', *Daily Telegraph*, 15 October 2003

Tanner, Lindsay, *Crowded lives*, Pluto Press, North Melbourne, 2003

Tooth, Gerald, 'Child-care profits', *Background Briefing*, ABC Radio National, 3 October 2004. Available at <http://www.abc.net.au/rn/talks/bbing/stories/s1214400.htm>

Tout, K., M. de Haan, E. Kipp Campbell & M. Gunnar, 'Social behavior correlates of adrenocortical activity in daycare', *Child Development*, 1998, 69:1247–62

Trebilcot, Joyce (ed.), *Mothering, essays in feminist theory*, Rowman & Allanheld, Totowa New Jersey, 1983

Trinca, H., & C. Fox, *Better than sex: how a whole generation became hooked on work*, Random House, Sydney, 2004

Troy, M., & A. Sroufe, 'Victimisation among preschoolers: role of attachment relationship theory', *Journal of American Academy of Child and Adolescent Psychiatry*, 1987, 26:166–72

Tucker, Robert C. (ed.), *The Marx–Engels reader*, W. W. Norton & Co., New York, 1972

Uren, David, 'Costello: get mums working', *The Australian*, 1April 2005, p. 1

Vandell, D. L., & M. A. Corasaniti, 'Childcare and the family: complex: contributors to child development', *New Directions for Child Development*, 1990, 49:23–37

van den Boom, Dymphna, 'The influence of temperament and mothering on attachment and exploration: an experimental manipulation of sensitive responsiveness among lower class mothers with irritable infants', *Child Development*,1994, 65:1457–77

van den Boom, Dymphna, 'Sensitivity and attachment: next steps for developmentalists', *Child Development*, 1997, July/August 68(4):592–95

van der Kolk, B., Alexander. C. McFarlane & Lars Weisaeth (eds), *Traumatic stress: the effects of overwhelming experience on mind, body and society*, Guilford, New York & London, 1996 van Ijzendoorn, M., P. Kroonenberg, D. Out, Y. Ransdorp, L. Aad, H. van der Maas, 'Does more non-maternal care lead to aggression? The NICHD study of early childcare and youth development on quantity of non-maternal care and aggression', draft paper April 2005

Varin, D., C. Crugnola, C. Ripamonti & P. Molina, 'Critical periods in the growth of attachment and the age of entry into day care', paper presented at the Annual Conference of the Developmental Section of the British Psychological Society, University of Portsmouth, UK, June 1994

Verhaeghe, Paul, *Love in the age of loneliness: three essays on drive and desire*, Other Press, New York, 1999

Violato, C., & C. Russell, 'Effects of non maternal care on child development: a meta analysis of published research', paper presented at 55th annual convention of the Canadian Psychological Association, 1994

Waite, Linda, & Maggie Gallagher, *The case for marriage: why married people are happier, healthier and better off financially*, Doubleday, New York, 2000

Waldfogel, Jane, Wen-Jui Han, & Jeanne Brooks-Gunn, 'The effects of early maternal employment on child cognitive development', *Demography*, 2000, 39(2):369–92

Waring, Marilyn, *Counting for nothing, what men value and what women are worth*, Allen & Unwin, Sydney, 1998

Warren, E., & A. Warren Tyagi, *The two income trap: why middle class mothers and fathers are going broke*, Basic Books, New York, 2003

Watamura, S. E., & B. Donzella, J. Alwin & M. R. Gunnar, 'Morning-to-afternoon increases in cortisol concentrations for infants and toddlers at child care: age differences and behavioural correlates', *Child Development*, Jul–Aug 2003, 74(4):1006–20

Wattenberg, Ben, *Fewer: how the new demography of depopulation will shape our future*, Ivan R. Dee, Chicago, 2004

Weil, Simone, *The need for roots, prelude to a declaration of duties towards mankind*, translation by Arthur Wills, Routledge Classics, Routledge, London & New York, 2001

Weitzman, Leonore, *The divorce revolution: the unexpected social and economic consequences for women and children in America*, Free Press, New York, 1986

Wilkinson, Helen, *Time out: the costs and benefits of paid parental leave*, Demos, London, 1997

Winnicott, Clare, Ray Shepherd & Madeleine Davis (eds), *Psycho-analytic explorations*, Harvard University Press, Cambridge, 1989

Winnicott, Donald, *Through paediatrics to psychoanalysis*, Hogarth, London, 1958

Winnicott, Donald, *The maturational processes and the facilitating environment*, International Universities Press, New York, 1965

Winnicott, Donald, *The family and individual development*, Basic Books, New York, 1966

Winnicott, Donald, *Home is where we start from*, W. W. Norton & Co, New York, 1986

Winton, Tim, *The riders*, Simon & Schuster, New York, 1994

Winton, Tim, *Enough rope with Andrew Denton*, broadcast on the Australian Broadcast Corporation (ABC) 25 October 2004. Available at <http://www.abc.net.au/enoughrope/stories/s1227915.html>

Witting, Amy, *I for Isobel*, Penguin, Melbourne, 1989

Wolcott, I., & H. Glezer, *Work and family life: achieving integration*, Australian Institute of Family Studies, Melbourne, 1995

Wolgast, Elizabeth, *Equality and the Rights of Woman*, Cornell University Press, Ithaca & London, 1980

Wulff, Maryann, 'Out with the old and in with the new? Housing's role in the new social settlement', *Future directions in Australian social policy: new ways of preventing Risk No 49*, Committee for Economic Development of Australia (CEDA), December 2001, pp. 257–66

Youngblade, L., D. Kovacs, & L. Hoffman, 'The effects of early maternal employment on 3rd and 4th grade children's social development', paper presented at the biennial meetings of the Society for Research in Child Development, Albuquerque, New Mexico, March 1999

Zigler, E., & M. Frank (eds), *The parental leave crisis: towards a national policy*, Yale University Press, New Haven, 1989

Zigler, E., & M. Lang, *Child care choices: balancing the needs of children, families and society*, Free Press, New York, 1991

Zinsmeister, Karl, 'The problem with daycare', *The American Enterprise*, May/June 1998. Available at <www.taemag.com/issues/issueID.128/toc.asp>

Zinsmeister, Karl, 'Why encouraging daycare is unwise', *The American Enterprise*, May/June 1998. Available at <www.taemag.com/issues/issueID.128/toc.asp>

Zoellner, Tom, 'Daycare: study on putting your kids in daycare', *Men's Health*, 1 September 1999

Selected further reading

General works

Raimond Gaita, *A common humanity: thinking about love & truth & justice*, Text Publishing, Melbourne, 1999; Routledge, London & New York, 2000. Essays on the nature of good and evil, justice and racism, which are original and profound, always drawing one back to what really matters. His original monthly essays in *Quadrant Magazine*, from which the wonderful essays in *A common humanity* are drawn, were called 'Turnings of attention'. By calling attention to what may previously have been in shadow, Gaita persistently enables us to see and act more humanely. And it is attentiveness that is at the heart of the attachment and maternal feminist project—to truly pay attention to another who is more vulnerable than the self.

Robert Bellah, Richard Madsen, William Sullivan, Ann Swidler & Stephen Tipton, *Habits of the heart: individualism and commitment in American life*, University of California Press, Berkeley, 1996. Shows the development of the ethos of self-fulfilment as the binding—and unstable—ideal for both sexes, a process which has only intensified since the book was published.

Empirical work on the family

Catherine Hakim, *Work–lifestyle choices in the 21st century*, Oxford University Press, Oxford, 2001. An exceptionally important empirical account of the diversity of women's preferences, and the consequent tensions and conflicts we now call the mother wars, and what policy frameworks might fairly resolve them. Although claimed by conservatives, she is in fact as serious as Crittenden and others on altering the economic disadvantages that flow from mothering. The strength of her case rests on the vast evidence she amasses from almost every continent across a range of work and family regimes with differing gender contracts. She also has an excellent bibliography.

Maternal feminism

Daphne de Marneffe, *Maternal desire: on love, children and the inner life*, Little, Brown and Company, New York, 2004. De Marneffe is a mother of three and a psychotherapist. Her book is a fresh, original and sophisticated contribution, and by far the most important answer to Chodorow from a very contemporary voice. She argues that maternal desire is as repressed today as sexual desire once was. She also shows how new insights from attachment research show up the limitations of earlier psychoanalytic accounts like those of Chodorow and Benjamin—which mistake patterns of relating as universal when in fact they are the consequence of insecure attachment.

Ann Crittenden, *The price of motherhood: why the most important job in the world is still the least valued*, Henry Holt & Company, New York, 2001. The most important and accessible contemporary account of what mothers do (in or out of the workforce)—both sympathetic to women's desire to mother, but also a portrait of their consequent economic disadvantage. The author is a mother, an economist and a Pulitzer Prize nominee.

Nancy Folbre, *The invisible heart: economics and family values*, New Press, New York, 2001. Along with Crittenden, this is the most important account of the work done by the shadow care economy, and how we must rethink our relation to it. Folbre values it, but does not forever consign women and women alone to caring. Her work, along with Crittenden's, marks a turning point in maternal or social feminism. Both books attempt to use the insights of difference or cultural feminism to surmount the problematic of sameness, without tacitly accepting the disadvantages flowing from caregiving.

Marilyn Waring, *Counting for nothing: what men value and what women are worth*, Allen & Unwin, Sydney, 1988

Germaine Greer, *Sex and destiny: the politics of human fertility*, Harper & Row, New York, 1984. Always cranky and independent and sometimes wild, Greer transcends a simplistic 'progressive' view of history. She is similar to the Frankfurt School theorists at times, with her intuitive insights into the dehumanising tendencies of the modern world.

Germaine Greer, *The whole woman*, Doubleday, London & Sydney, 1999. Argues that the liberation movement has settled for 'equality'—and a lifestyle feminism bent on admitting women to men's clubs. She admits she was wrong in earlier works not taking seriously women's 'falling in love' with their babies, and argues for state support for motherhood as a 'genuine career option'. She also says, 'Women's liberation must be mothers' liberation or it is nothing.' And that the 'immense rewardingness of children is the best-kept secret in the Western world'.

Sara Ruddick, *Maternal thinking: towards a politics of peace*, Beacon Press, Boston, 1995 (first published 1989). Perhaps the feminist classic of the moral and reflective work women do as mothers. Ruddick takes a philosophical and moral point of view, retrieving the value of what mothers do from the aggressive, repudiationist accounts of mothering by writers such as de Beauvoir.

Sylvia Ann Hewlett, *Creating a life: professional women and the quest for motherhood*, Talk Miramax Books, New York, 2002.

Sarah Blaffer Hrdy, *Mother nature: natural selection and the female of the species*, Chatto & Windus, London, 1999. A broad-ranging anthropological and historical work, giving evidence on past patterns of motherhood. Also contains an intelligent defence of attachment theory and the importance of attachment, in 'meeting the eyes of love', from a child's point of view.

Virginia Held, *Feminist morality: transforming culture, society and politics*, University of Chicago, Chicago, 1993.

Virginia Held, 'Non-contractual society,' in Marsja Hame and Kai Nielson (eds), *Science, morality and feminist theory*, University of Calgary Press, Calgary, 1987. Virginia Held argues against the prevailing assumptions behind contractarian liberalism, pointing to the moral impoverishment of those notions in applying to the relation of mother to child. Held also urges that rather than adapt the ethic of care to an individualist and market ethos, we should look to the ways the life practice and values of mothering might inform—and transform—the latter.

Children and attachment

John Bowlby, *Attachment and loss, vol 1; attachment*, Penguin, London, 1971.

John Bowlby, *Attachment and loss, vol 2; separation: anxiety and anger*, Basic Books, USA, 1973.

John Bowlby, *Attachment and loss, vol 3; loss: sadness and depression*, Penguin Books, New York, 1981.

Robert Karen, *Becoming attached: first relationships and how they shape our capacity to love*, Oxford University Press, Oxford & New York, 1994. Karen's book is a superb biography of an idea—of Bowlby and post-Bowlbyian attachment scholarship and its implications for everyday life. An essential text for anyone following these debates, since he pulls together not only the writing within the paradigm of attachment theory but also his own interviews with the main players in developmental psychology and the protagonists in the daycare debates.

Karr-Morse, Robin, & Meredith Wiley, *Ghosts from the nursery: tracing the roots of violence*, Atlantic Monthly Press, New York, 1997.

Hon. Margaret Norrie McCain & J. Fraser Mustard (co-chairs), *The early years study: reversing the real brain drain*, Canadian Institute for Advanced Research, Toronto, April 1999.

Allan Schore, *Affect regulation and the origin of the self: the neurobiology of emotional development*, Lawrence Erlbaum Associates, Hillsdale New Jersey, 1994.

Allan Schore, *Affect regulation and the repair of the self*, W. W. Norton & Co, New York & London, 2003.

Allan Schore, *Affect dysregulation and disorders of the self*, W. W. Norton & Co, New York & London, 2003. Schore is sometimes described as the New American Bowlby; superbly wide-ranging, he pulls together a vast array of cross-disciplinary work from neuroscience, psychiatry, and attachment research.

Sue Gerhardt, *Why love matters*, Brunner & Routledge, Hove & New York, 2004, is a clear account from a psychotherapist of the most recent developments in attachment scholarship and neuroscience in relation to the way that children develop. She points out the clash between what we now know about child development and the drift of modern society. She argues for a combination of parental leave and part-time work to best integrate women's and children's wellbeing in infancy.

| The daycare controversy

Stanley Greenspan, *The four-thirds solution: solving the childcare crisis in America today*, Perseus Books, Cambridge Massachusetts, 2001. Stanley Greenspan advocates a new model of shared parenting—the 'four-thirds model' of altering fathers' work times as well as those of mothers to minimise the use of childcare and protect women's careers. Based on growing evidence of daycare risk, and the crisis in quality of care. Also elaborated in:

T. Berry Brazelton and Stanley Greenspan, *The irreducible needs of children*, Harper Collins, New York, 2000.

Brian C. Robertson, *The daycare deception: what the child care establishment isn't telling us*, Encounter Books, San Francisco, 2003. An up-to-date critique and assessment of risks associated with early childcare, and the pattern of concealment by academics and journalists who have used it. Links his case to a defence of the traditional family—although there is no reason why the evidence presented could not be a part of a progressive program of shared parenting, parental leave and flexible work, as in Greenspan's 'four-thirds solution'.

Patricia Morgan, *Who needs parents? The effects of childcare and early education on children in Britain and the USA*, London IEA Health and Welfare Unit, 1996. Mid-1990s work that presents a wealth of evidence from international academic literature, showing the risks of early childcare. Like Robertson, Morgan links her argument to a defence of the traditional family.

Sally Loane, *Who cares? Guilt, hope and the childcare debate*, Mandarin Books, Melbourne, 1997. Very useful and at times moving account of Australian childcare by a Australian journalist who used childcare herself. The book was begun in anger at Michael Leunig's famous cartoon, but was finished more in sorrow at the state of Australian childcare.

P. Cook, *Early childcare: infants and nations at risk*, News Weekly Books, Melbourne, 1996. Presents the case against early infant childcare with data up until the mid-1990s.

The new capitalism

Clive Hamilton, *Growth fetish*, Allen & Unwin, Sydney, 2003. Most important and humane Australian critique of affluenza and its distorting effects on human flourishing.

Richard Sennett, *The corrosion of character: the personal consequences of work in the new capitalism*, W. W. Norton & Company, New York, 1998. The standout book on social relations and workplace conditions in the new economy.

Ulrich Beck, *The brave new world of work*, Polity Press, Frankfurt & New York, 2000.

Ulrich Beck, *Risk society*, Sage Publications, London, 1992.

Arlie Hochschild, 'The commercial spirit of intimate life and the abduction of feminism', in her book, *The commercialisation of intimate life: notes from home and work*, University of California Press, Berkeley, Los Angeles, London, 2003, pp. 13–29. A brilliant essay, showing the remodelling of women's 'feeling rules' to approximate those of the 1950s corporate man.

Arlie Hochschild, *The time bind: when work becomes home and home becomes work*, Metropolitan Books, New York, 1997. Hochschild, like Sennett, is a gifted sociologist. This is by far the best account of the dual career family, work and the new economy: subtle, nuanced, with real analytic flair. Retains a sensitivity to the world of the child—unusual when so many accounts are given from the point of view of the parents.

Barbara Ehrenreich, *Nickel and dimed: on (not) getting by in America*, Metropolitan Books, New York, 2001. A really important account of the new class system from the viewpoint of the working poor, showing how the professional overclass depends on such people.

Juliet Schor, *The overworked American: the unexpected decline of leisure*, Basic Books, New York, 1992.

Zygmunt Bauman's work has a great moral depth as he explores our predicament in the new fluid world of 'permanent temporariness' under consumer capitalism. His wide-ranging critiques of post-modern society and the new consumer ethic may be found in:

Zygmunt Bauman, *Post-modernity and its discontents*, Polity Press, Cambridge, 1997.

Zygmunt Bauman, *Life in fragments*, Polity Press, Cambridge, 1995.

Zygmunt Bauman, *Liquid modernity*, Polity Press, Cambridge, 2000.

Zygmunt Bauman, *The individualised society*, Polity Press, Cambridge, 2001. See especially the essay 'Does love need reason?'.

George Ritzer, *The McDonaldisation of society*, Pine Forge Press, California, 2000. A brilliantly inventive and indispensable sociology of postmodern capitalism, adaptable to many different domains.

| On children in the new capitalism

George Halasz (ed.), Peter Ellingsen, F. Salo Thompson & Anne Manne, *Cries unheard: a new look at attention deficit hyperactivity disorder*, Common Ground, Melbourne, 2002. Halasz, a child psychiatrist, a courageous advocate of the rights of the child, has been influential in presenting a humane, wide-ranging critique of the explosion in medicating youngsters for ADHD.

Valerie Polakow, *The erosion of childhood*, University of Chicago Press, Chicago & London, 1992. An early account from a left-wing child-centred feminist who (despite her illusions of the superiority of childhood under socialism) gives some of the most superbly observed portraits of children in childcare and the most incisive critique of the prevailing ideology of childhood in a market society.

Penelope Leach, *Children first: what our society must do—and is not doing—for our children today*, Michael Joseph London, 1994. Widely misinterpreted as a traditionalist attack on working motherhood, this is in fact a powerful cultural critique of the treatment of children in contemporary capitalism. Leach was one of the first to see the importance of parental leave programs.

Acknowledgements

Doris Lessing once said in an interview with Studs Terkel there came a time with an issue when one had to 'put the questions differently'. I discovered in the course of writing this book so many people who wanted an articulation of a position that went beyond the two exhausted positions of a 1950s traditionalist kind but also an unreflective 1970s feminism. I was often moved by the openness and honesty with which parents spoke about, and the passionate intensity by which they struggled with and lived out, those bland, mechanical words 'balancing work and family'. Although they are too many to mention, they formed the inspiration for this book. They helped sometimes in formal interviews, sometimes in long and intense conversations. And sometimes they became friends, supporting with belief, encouragement and shared passion the matters contained within these pages. They all contributed, sometimes more than is evident within the text, in shaping my thinking.

Others played a more direct role. I am grateful to my agent Margaret Connolly not only for her able advocacy and care of my interests but also her friendship. It was her insight into the character of the remarkable Sue Hines that suggested her as the best possible publisher for this book. Sue proved every bit as brave, calm and attentive as Margaret suggested. Passionate both about women's rights to take their place in the world but also about the wellbeing of children, Sue has that large spirited quality that can embrace the thought that we can not just put questions differently but do things as a society so much better. That decision for Sue Hines to publish the book also meant I was fortunate enough to be in the hands of an exceptionally professional and dedicated editorial team at Allen & Unwin. In times when publishers are sometimes criticised for lack of care, no one could say that of Allen & Unwin. Andrea McNamara proved a brilliant organiser as managing editor, overseeing the huge task of seeing a substantial manuscript through every stage to publication, keeping us all on a tight schedule with good humour, as well as unfailing care and attentiveness to detail. I was very lucky to have Caroline Williamson, as the copy editor; she proved to be a rigorous, intelligent, but also delicate reader whose skills undoubtedly improved the book. Julia Imogen and Jenni Walker also provided invaluable editorial help at various stages of the process.

Lorraine Rose, from the Australian Institute of Infant Mental Health, was generous in her support and also offered her irreplaceable insights into the world of the infant from her psychotherapy practice. With Kerreen Reiger, I have had a valuable ongoing conversation about feminism and motherhood, and benefited from observing her maternal feminism both in writing and in life. Friends like John Spooner and Susan Moore also generously supported me, often believing in this project when my own belief was faltering. Raimond Gaita has offered cherished encouragement for my writing from the very first. I am also indebted to Tamas Pataki who shared his exceptionally deep understanding of psychoanalysis and all matters of the psyche in many long conversations. None of the above, of course, are responsible for the views within these pages

My greatest debts are, however, to my family. Heartfelt thanks to my mother Beryl, who first taught me what it might mean to be a mother. To my own daughters, Kate and Lucy, goes the deepest thanks for so much they have given me; for what they have taught me about what is truly important in life, for their wit and wisdom, for so much love, talk and laughter. Without my husband Rob, my truest friend and soulmate, this book—or much else—would not have been possible. From the very first moment I began writing, he has believed in and given unstinting, unfailing support to my work. To him goes the deepest gratitude for his love and for the extraordinary life-long conversation about what matters, which has been our life together. It is to Rob and our beloved daughters, Kate and Lucy, that this book is dedicated.

Index

physical contact with baby 169–70, 171–2
Ping Tseng 274
playgroups 13
Pocock, Barbara 98, 259–60, 267
Polakow, Valerie 282, 294
The Politics of Australian Childcare: From Philanthropy to Feminism 123
Popenoe, David 38–9
postmodern cowgirl 32, 49–51, 57, 261
postmodern feminism 92
Potter, Dennis 118
Poulton, Richie 218–19
Pound, Andrea 180
poverty and depression 180
powerlessness of children 111–13, 115–16
Prague Mothers 104
premature returnism 269–71
preoccupied adults 173, 174
preservative love 59
The Price of Motherhood 70
The Progress Paradox 246
Provence, Sally 195–6

quality of care 189, 190, 191–4, 196–7, 289–90
Quality Childcare Association 288
quality time 265–6, 279

radical individualism 44–51
Raised in Captivity 299
Rapson, Virginia 46–7
Reiger, Kerreen 35, 63, 81–2
relationships
    commodification of 293–6
    in early childhood 135–8
    with loved ones (adult working models) 172–3
reparation 151–3
The Reproduction of Motherhood 39
'repudiation of motherhood' 34–41
resilience of children 118, 164–9, 210
responsibility to child 52–4
RIGs (Repeated Interactions which are Generalised) 147

risk society 249–52
Ritzer, George 282–4, 298–9
Riviere, Joan 125
Roberts, Elizabeth 63
Roberts, Ian 194
Roberts, Yvonne 268
Robertson, Brian 185, 211
Robertson, James 128–32, 135, 138, 165–6, 188
Robertson, Joyce 188
Roiphe, Anne 91, 315
Rolfe, Sharne 200, 311
Rose, Lorraine 23
Rossi, Alice 57
Rubenstein, Judith 217
Ruddick, Sara 3, 58, 59, 60–1, 64, 66, 68
Rutgers Study 45–6

Scarr, Sandra 211–12, 218
Schor, Juliet 113–14, 246, 266
Schore, Allan 137, 153–4, 182, 232–3
'secure autonomous' women 172–3, 174
The Second Sex 31–2, 34
secure base 138, 139–40
A Secure Base 139–40
self as a solo enterprise 50–1
self-fulfilment ideal 45
self-hatred 169–71
selfish working mother stereotype 79–80
Sennett, Richard 249, 251, 253, 259, 293, 295
separation 8–12
    becomes 'transient distress period' 208
    experience of 124–7
    hospitalisation 127–30
    intensity of anxiety 132–3
    long-term effects 118–24
    universal terror of 118, 121
sex
    obligation-free 46
    transformation of roles 26–7
Sex and Destiny 41–2
sexual caste 20, 24